Ch'i

The MIT Press

Cambridge,
Massachusetts,
and London,
England

Ch'i

A Neo-Taoist
Approach to
Life

R. G. H. Siu

This book was set in Alpha Gothic
by University Graphics, Inc.,
printed on Finch Title 93,
and bound in G.S.B. S/535/16 "Nugget"
by Halliday Lithograph Corp
in the United States of America.

Library of Congress Cataloging in Publication Data

Siu, Ralph Gun Hoy, 1917-
  Ch'i: a neo-Taoist approach to life.

  1. Taoism.   I. Title.
BL1923.S58 181'.09'514 74-1139
ISBN 0-262-19123-7

To George W. Beadle

Preface   xi

Acknowledgments   xiii

**Synoptic
Text**
1

Commentaries
23

Musing
25

Luminiferous Kin
29

Time
49

1. Subsuming and resonating the neo-Taoist way   25

2. Oak   29

3. Slime mold   32

4. Earthworm   34

5. Dragonfly   38

6. Man   41

7. The primitive conception of cyclic regeneration   49

8. Time's depreciation by the Hindus   50

9. The Chinese conception of time as an undifferentiated pool   52

10. The cosmic liturgy of the Persians   54

11. The Christian conception of linear time   56

12. Abstractions of the Greeks   57

13. Early disputations among metaphysicians   61

14. Continuing disputations   68

15. Whitehead's conception of incomplete occasions   88

16. Bergson's conception of creative duration   92

17. The encompassing ecstasies of the existentialists   95

18. Unending disputations   101

19. Theoretical considerations in time measure-
    ment   106

20. Empirical time-reckoning   109

21. Time-shaped geometry   112

22. The absolute concepts of the early scientists   112

23. The relational concepts of Leibnitz and Lorentz   114

24. The Relativity of Einstein   118

25. The cosmic elephant   122

Light
129

26. Properties   129

27. Corpuscular theory   132

28. Wave theory   134

29. Attempts at theoretical reconciliation   136

Life
142

30. Definition   142

31. Characteristics   142

32. Rhythm   146

33. Animals' sense of clock time   150

34. Man's sense of clock time   151

35. Heard time   161

36. Seen time   164

37. Cultural time perspectives   166

38. Western literature's treatment of time   169

39. Time and the conscious-unconscious polarity   184

40. Memory   187

41. Effects of light   199

42. Symbolisms of light   204

43. Parabiological speculations   207

44. The origin of life   210

45. Evolution of the body   211

46. Evolution of the mind   214

47. Extrasensory perception   216

48. Mankind's anastomosis   219

49. Longevity   222

50. Aging   224

51. Death   228

Continuum
233

52. Zeno's paradox   233

53. The logic of infinity   235

54. Order, direction, and irreversibility   242

55. Varieties of nothingness   249

Speculations on the Time-Light-Life Continuum
251

56. Time-binding   251

57. *Ch'i*   256

58. A neo-Taoist view   259

59. The *ch'i*-energy duplexity of light   265

60. Harmonious complementarity   266

61. Evolutionary sequence   267

62. Transmission of *ch'i*   268

63. Eternal actuations   270

64. Creativity   272

65. Well-being   273

66. Image-makers   275

67. Virtual crises   275

Living
277

68. Chains of circumstance   277

69. Our brother's keeper   280

70. Social equity   281

71. The critical packing density   282

72. Repression   282

73. Privacy   283

74. Needless anguish   283

75. Synchronicity   284

76. Uncertainty   285

77. Occam's razor   287

78. A *yin-yang* model   289

79. *Kairos*   290

80. The artist   290

81. A vignette   291

References   295

Index   327

Preface

Time . . . What is it? What meanings can it impart to our lives?

Scholars have been fascinated with these questions throughout the centuries. Some of our greatest minds have identified them as *the* unanswered questions of philosophy.

Practical men of stature have also given much more than passing thought to their earthly ramifications. Success in society, so they have experienced, rests to a considerable degree upon an intuitive feel for timing, rhythm, and other manifestations, somehow related to the nebulous entity called time. Musing on its nature might well extend and enrich the sense of fitness of things. It might even evoke the harmony that transcends the graspings of power itself.

I too have done my share of mulling and musing. Every occasion of mine, however, always seemed to fuse time with light and life as well. Excluding one or the other inevitably left an uncomfortable incompleteness. Yet the key for integrating all three kept eluding me until several years ago. It suddenly showed up one day in the form of an old nebulous Taoist concept, called *ch'i*, which had been brought into prominence by Lao Tzu himself in the sixth century B.C.

This book presents the outcome of the ensuing neo-Taoist deliberations. *Ch'i* is proposed as a time-related X. It is pictured as mating with energy in light, as constituting the essential substance of change in living processes, and as providing a natural basis for man's dealing with his fellow creatures.

The brief Synoptic Text follows the epigrammatic, cryptic, and somewhat assertive style of the ancient Taoist writings, so as to preserve some flavor of the ultimately ineffable essence of the mysteriously unifying *ch'i*.

The lengthier Commentaries provide more explicit explanations of the more significant facets.

This volume, following *The Tao of Science* (1958) and *The Man of Many Qualities* (1968), both published by The MIT Press, completes what I have come to think of as the *Tao-Time Trilogy*. The set constitutes a modest adaptation of old Chinese philosophy to modern Western living. Having experienced both a traditional Chinese family upbringing in Honolulu and a subsequent professional life as a scientist and executive on the American scene, I was led to feel that much of the classical Eastern way of looking at the world might be of value to the Occidental man of affairs trying to come to terms with his surroundings in the twentieth century. I hope my honorable Reader will find it not too unworthy of his perusal.

R. G. H. Siu

Washington, D.C.
June 1973

Acknowledgments

The author wishes to express his appreciation to the following publishers for permission to quote from their respective copyrighted books:

Basic Books, Inc., New York: Sigmund Freud, *The Interpretation of Dreams,* translated by James Strachey, 1930.

George Allen and Unwin, Ltd., London: George E. Moore, *Some Main Problems in Philosophy,* 1953.

Harcourt Brace Jovanovich, Inc., New York: T. S. Eliot, "Burnt Norton" and "The Dry Salvages" in *Complete Poems and Plays,* 1952; and Virginia Woolf, *The Moment and Other Essays,* 1948, and *To the Lighthouse,* 1949.

Macmillan, London and Basingstoke, London: Samuel Alexander, *Space, Time and Deity,* 1920.

Philosophical Library Inc., New York: Jean-Paul Sartre, *Being and Nothingness,* translated by Hazel E. Barnes, 1956.

Princeton University Press, Princeton, N.J.: *Papers from the Eranos Yearbooks,* translated by Ralph Manheim and R. F. C. Hull, copyrighted by Bollingen Foundation, 1957.

The Johns Hopkins University Press, Baltimore: Georges Poulet, *Studies in Human Time,* translated by Elliott Coleman, 1958.

Synoptic Text

Musing

I

Musing is delightful freedom. No one claims the juris-
diction, sets the rules, or challenges the outcome. You
may muse at any time, in any place, and under any circumstance.

Never does it dip into the pits of evil.

It ennobles and enlightens and suffuses as with a quiet
joy.

II

Free of logic.

Carefree of consensus.

Free and carefree in essence.

III

What could be a better place to start than that of the
not-knowing of what we are, of the not-knowing of what
it is in which we are immersed, of the not-knowing of
what it is that makes us kin to what we not-know—of the
realm of the not-knowing?

What could be a better theme than that of which the
greatest scholars, scientists, and philosophers have,
after observations and deliberations, long confessed that
they know not—for instance, *Time and Light and Life?*

This is where I will begin. May I invite your pleasant
company?

IV

Why is it, I wonder, that while there is more than ample
food available for all the feeding,

Men still have to pray, beg, sweat, and kill for it,

And so many of their brethren die for lack of it?

V

How is it, I wonder, that while creatures must consume
once-throbbing tissues of the living for surviving—

Man is no exception—

The green plants themselves can thrive on air, earth,
and sky?

VI

Reaching shoots of green search out the photons swirl-
ing.

Pulsing life reechoes God's command in banishing the
rhythmless void:

"Let there be Light!"

VII

Would it not have made more sense if that creative utterance of God had been:

"Let there be Time!"?

But the Holy Bible does not falsify. A deeper verity must lie within the Word.

VIII

Can it be that Light and Time are intertwined in meaning?

If so, then God *did* state the equivalent of:

"Let there be Time!"

IX

Would it also not seem right that God, in all His omniscience, would have already laid the basis for the living essences of His beloved creatures in that first creative act?

If so, then the unity of Time and Light and Life was ordained in *Genesis*.

It remains our pleasure now to speculate on their harmonious relationships—a most engaging leitmotiv indeed for musing.

Luminiferous Kin

X

We see Light shining forth with uniform warmth on everything and everyone. But we note that there seems to be a special kind of luminiferous exchange among the living.

It begins with photosynthesis. The animations from this source feed into the metabolic transformations of the giant oak of the forest, the lowly slime mold swarming in a decaying matrix on the ground, the earthworm burrowing below, the voracious dragonfly above, and the learned man ubiquitously lording.

Each, while sharing, still uniquely carries on with his own mode of life.

XI

Oak as tiny acorn knows already what's worth knowing. As it grows into a shady host for divers guests, a flawless synchrony persists among innumerable processes, exploring wide for minerals and water in the soil, absorbing carbon dioxide and red rays from the skies, constructing new wood, hardening against the wintry blasts, and readying the coming generations.

There is neither command post nor coodination center. Everything goes smoothly nonetheless.

XII

None surpasses the half-beast, half-plant slime mold in its social timing.

At the proper stage of its maturity, the nuclei within the delicate mycelium agglomerate to form a base for further changes. Those close to the top give up their lives to shape a stalk, which holds the future spores aloft. Additional spontaneous responses on the part of others then give rise to a protective shield surrounding the anointed few. The chosen ripen in the womb so carefully made by their sacrificial brethren and eventually ride the winds to link the generations in the continuity of life in new and distant territories.

Never is there issued a call for patriotism. And still, the species prospers.

XIII

From the evidence, it would appear the earthworm does some thinking.

When in contact with a willing mate, it first assures itself of the approximate equality of their lengths in order to ensure compatibility in the anticipated sex act. When confronted with a wanted piece of usable debris, it first tries out selected points of seizure to ensure greatest ease of dragging. When exposed to strange conditions in the laboratory, it learns adapting patterns of behavior with relative facility.

Yet the earthworm brain seems ancillary. An entirely new head can be generated, if required, by the decapitated body.

XIV

Utterly insatiable is the dragonfly skimming a body of water.

Living for the underwater nymph is a long uninterrupted search for food—stalking and devouring larvae, protozoa, bugs, worms, minnows, tadpoles. It is driven by the same mad gluttony without the slightest diminution after its metamorphosis into the winged acrobat of bright skies—scooping up bees, butterflies, and moths within its net of bunched legs; sucking them; and dumping their dry carcasses in mid-air in its full-tilt wing-beating pursuit for more.

And when crazed by hunger, it may even chew chunks from its own abdominal tail.

XV

Only man among the beasts emerged as the creator of a host of virtual presences and slave thereto. Although they are unreal in substance, they are real in impact. Wholesome living has become the art of optimizing the balance between the virtual and the real.

When the virtual presences begin to overwhelm the real, man's primal nature withers. Human beings then must step aside for new breeds of neurotic demons.

Fortunately, man has Light to Time his Way.

XVI

But oak, slime mold, earthworm, dragonfly, and man— are as they are.

They would not here be, were there not Light—the luminiferous Time of God's first command.

Life, it seems, is Light's awakening.

XVII

It might be refreshing to postpone our ruminations at this point and listen to the views of others—much more learned than the two of us lay musers. Their more relevant opinions and important data have been summarized in the next forty sections. *Time* is first in sequence. Then comes *Light*. Next *Life*. And finally, the common feature of *Continuum*.

While we may agree or disagree with part or all of their interpretations in our rationality, the fact remains that the not-knowing of the what behind their cerebrations and experimental findings is good grist for further musing.

But for this to hold, we must not lose our selves in disputations and clarifications. We need only let the *ch'i*— anticipating the resumption of our musing—come upon us as it will.

Time

XVIII

Primitives welcomed Time as an intrinsic partner in a cyclic sequence.

Their activities were brought into consonance with Time's immediacy and reversions.

Persevering equanimity became a natural reaction to the myth of the eternal inescapable return.

XIX

Ancient Indians felt insignificant, seeing their lives arrayed beside the awesome cycles of the universe.

A continuing bare time is meaningless. It is to be escaped or, better still, annihilated through its union with the cosmic Time.

It is the *moment* of enlightenment, deliverance, and living that conveys the ultimate quintessence.

XX

The traditional Chinese envisioned Time to be a deep and placid pool.

The concrete manifestations of the single life were felt to emerge from its undifferentiated depths and in due course return into the same continuum.

Ups and downs of daily happenings dissolve in calm acceptance.

XXI

Early Persians related Time to Light, as one of its dimensions in the plenum of their cosmogenesis.

The Celestial Person had projected Time as earthly image to be ultimately reunited with Himself. It was the instrument of victory of Ōhrmazd, the God of Wisdom over Ahriman, the God of Evil.

Time reveals itself throughout the cosmic liturgy.

XXII

For the Christians, Jesus constituted the historical Divide.

Time was felt to be linear and irreversible, proceeding from Nativity straight to the Last and Final Judgment. There will be no reincarnations of Christ on earth.

The tormented martyr is encouraged by the pointing finger of his Church's Time.

XXIII

Greek philosophers regarded Time to be an independent entity.

Pythagoras was the first. He saw it as the Sphere itself. But Plato thought of it more as the movement of the whole and Aristotle as the numerable aspect of motion.

Their abstraction of an emptiness gave rise to intellectual bewilderments without end.

XXIV

Disagreements deepened as metaphysicians multiplied.

Plotinus, the Roman, traced Time's substance to the Soul. Augustine, the Christian savant, rested his belief upon the temporal priority of God. ibn-Hazm, the Spanish muslim, claimed that instants in galaxies are created each in turn anew by Allah. But the Jewish-Dutch philosopher, Spinoza, stressed the order in the realm of nature as a logical necessity.

As the arguments became increasingly intense, the scholars grew more interested in the challenge of deciphering the nature of the thing called Time.

XXV

Consensus is no closer today than two millenia ago.

Kant considered Time as intuition. James dwelled on the elasticity of present stretches. Bradley treated Time as mere appearance. Royce related it to the eternal Absolute, while Alexander fixed it as the stuff common to all events. Dunne postulated an observer's moving field perceiving coexistent lay-outs of innumerable times. Ouspensky altered consciousness into a higher space; and Whitehead founded Time's source on the interplay of superseding incomplete occasions.

After cogitating much upon the situation, Moore appealed to common sense.

XXVI

Bergson spoke of the fluent, fugitive realities of Time.

Prior incarnations of the ego are united in the present and immediate duration. Each transpiring moment remakes one anew, as Time-Life interactions bring on their perpetual parade of fresh creations.

Life's creative Time is not the passive time of physics.

XXVII

Existentialists associated Time with man's attempt to liberate himself from the degenerate forms of prevailing anguish.

Heidegger envisioned the projection of one's own potential from the matters of the Care. As the potential is made present, Time is generated. Man is not comprised of the events occurring *in* Time, but encompasses the ecstasies of future, past, and present. Finitude lies not in death, but at the center of his being, which is also permeated by nonbeing. Consciousness of death reminds us of the trite banalities of mundane living and encourages us to ascend above the petty issues. Sartre saw man not as the himself of momentary nows, but rather as the being toward which he is constantly projecting. Temporality becomes thus integrated with one's possibility and value.

Life's Time scintillates within their existential light of Being.

XXVIII

Thousands of respected thinkers have had their say with all kinds and shades of hypotheses.

Among them: patterned qualities, an operational criterion, a class of shining presents, a conceptualized cognition, unities of consciousness, a purity of sensibility, a negative ingredient within the senses, an internal epoch, a purveyor of the values, and anxieties of death.

As the erudition grew progressively sophisticated, the accounts became more tenuous and nebulous.

XXIX

While the men of metaphysics contemplated, men of practical affairs worked out effective schemes to regulate routines of daily living. Seasons were established and eclipses were predicted over four thousand years ago. The subdivisions of the measures were refined with greater reproducibility as man progressed from sundials to the clepsydras, then mechanical and electronic clocks, and now, atomic and the latest nuclear devices. Accuracies on the order of a part in ten billion can be realized at present.

With increased precision, quantitative measurements of change demanded fixed frames for assessment. Greek geometry appeared in Time-shaped format with Cartesian mathematics. Galileo sought to clarify Time's measurable aspects. Barrow felt that Time flows in an even manner. Newton emphasized its independence from external things and motion.

Yet, it seems that physics, for whose purpose theories of absolute Time were proposed, can be interpreted without it.

XXX

The relational view gradually gained increasing precedence among the scientists.

Leibnitz excluded the possibility of Time consisting of identical divisions; God would not create things that could not be differentiated by Him from one another. But Lorentz began from a new starting point in trying to explain the lack of impact of the earth's velocity upon the speed of Light, as measured by the scientist; it was, so he said, due to contraction of the moving bodies and the dilatation of the Time within the ether. Einstein then fused Time with Space in his now famous four-dimensional equation, while discarding the old ether.

Time is no longer to be considered immutable and pure.

XXXI

The origin of the illimitable universe itself became the subject of scientific inquiry.

Einstein conjured up a vision of space with curvature and a cosmologic constant, but this did not give a stable universe. de Sitter's mathematical attempts, which postulated a repelling cosmic force, were also unsuccessful. Friedman offered cyclical expansions and contractions. The possibility of the explosion of a very dense primeval atom to originate the cosmos was suggested by Lemaître. Milne put forward a choice between two scales of Time, one with an origin and one without.

Such were the blind men's descriptions of the cosmic elephant.

Light

XXXII

The properties of Light have been investigated in detail, including its composition, speed in different materials, absorption, intra-interferences, behavior with respect to electricity and magnetism, and reactions with varieties of compounds.

Half of the empirical results can be explained by the old theory of Light as corpuscles, invisible in size and traveling in a straight line. The others can be comprehended only through the theory of Light as emanating waves with crests and troughs.

The opposing theories are yet to be harmoniously reconciled.

Life

XXXIII

Living organisms are alike in many ways.

Chemically, more or less the same twelve elements make up their bulk. The compounds formed within living cells are optically active, as contrasted to the ones produced in test tubes. All physiological reactions are accompanied by some electrical exchange with radioactivity invariably present. Also common to living organisms are the capacities for biological stability, metabolism, cellular division, metamorphosis, and reproduction. A dependency on solar radiation is observed, as well as complex temporal relationships.

The extensive technical investigations and experiential knowledge notwithstanding, Life remains the undefined obverse of undefined Death.

XXXIV

Life—it swings and sways.

The periodicities are apparent in the thicknesses of tree rings, the beating of the heart, the appearance of micro-filaria in the peripheral blood, the burrowing of flat-worms on the beach, the activity of periwinkles, the opening of oyster valves, the migration of the sooty tern, the abundance of the salmon and the lynx, and in a human panorama ranging from involuntary brain waves to competitive industrial transactions, and so on in an involved queue.

Living creatures generate a special kind of sinusoidal emanation.

XXXV

Many animals possess a very keen sense of clock Time. Dogs, birds, bees, and kin show up quite regularly dur-ing feeding hours. Monkeys can discriminate one-second intervals, snails .25, and the fighting fish .02.

Thus, the elemental sense of timing does not differenti-ate man from the other species.

XXXVI

Time leaves its effects on all our activities, often in very subtle ways.

Each sense has a threshold of its own. Our temporal perceptions are affected by temperature, light, space, length of interval, exposure order, and content of the interval, as well as by our age, sex, physiological state, personality and attitude, profession, and state of hyp-nosis.

There is nothing that a man does that is Time-invariant, as in the case of physics.

XXXVII

Animals can both respond and give rise to vibrations. Man alone composes poetry and music with expression, mood, dynamics, rhythm, melody. For him, Time serves as an ingredient for synthesis of something immaterial.

Life's Time is now being heard.

XXXVIII

Syncopation is inaudible in painting and in sculpture. Yet its silent rhythms are transmuted in their beauty.

Life's Time is now being seen.

XXXIX

Since the days of the ancients, man's rapport with Time has changed dramatically.

While the stone-age man was patient with the Time of Nature, his ambitious technological descendants sought to gain Time in their urge to conquer her.

Modern man has now become so Time-concerned that he is Time-impaled.

XL

Western authors seem to be obsessed with Time.

Dante yearned for the eternally Changeless and Serene One. But Montaigne depicted passage. While Pascal invoked the Time of grace, Blake fused Time and imagination. Proust explored the mysteries of memory and Woolf explored the mind's Time. Joyce repeated the dark beginnings of the soul. Lewis offered a view of art as the future's history. The intersection of the timeless and Time was Eliot's great vision. Faulkner peered at the primeval. Others wrote of spots of Time, the Time of wild goats, the abode of evil, the rejection of tomorrow, the invitation to die, the immortality of the *faena,* and the Fable.

There is no escape. Time is the Occidental's domineering trustee.

XLI

As the person falls asleep, with a few twistings of the body, a fluttering of the eyelids, and a muffled murmur, he forsakes the Conscious and the wearisome agenda of the waking hours.

And with freedom from the clock time of the office, the Unconscious takes hold with a dream or two, a fusion of a temporal gestalt, a summation of the conscious states, a memory.

Time appears to be the resonance between the Conscious and Unconscious.

XLII

Memory is tied, in many ways, to consciousness, intelligence, age, imagery. It is also influenced by emotions, drugs, diseases, and injuries.

Swedenborg assigned distinctive memories to their respective levels in the Conscious. Reid asserted memory to be an original God-given faculty, which is concerned with an immediate act. Mill entwined Time, memory, and personal identity together. Freud postulated the retention of forgotten origins in the subconscious. Others pictured traces in the neural network. Theories are many, but none is free from numerous deficiencies.

Somehow, memory is capable of coalescing Time.

XLIII

Light is as pervasive as Time in its impact on the living.

It affects the elementary responses of the protoplasm, dominates the vital processes in plants and animals, and alters their genetic composition. It reveals the paths for those with eyes to see and guides the actions of the ones without.

Photons can do what no calorie can.

XLIV

Light imbeds itself within the farthest recess of the psyche.

It exists in man's deep inner self as a symbol of consciousness, libido, God.

Our ancestors were only being true to their own natures in their worship of the Sun.

XLV

Parabiological disputes have persisted over the significance behind these observations.

Is Life shaped by the existence of a predetermined goal? Are mind and matter one? What governs the intrinsicalness of organisms?

There is no *experimentum crucis* to decide.

XLVI

In the meantime, chemists merrily pursue the origin of Life.

They begin by conjuring various schemes for the synthesis of the complex molecules that are observed in living organisms. Simple compounds are produced from inorganic ones. These then combine and thus more complicated ones are spun.

And *voilà!* they say. That is how Life began!

XLVII

Evolution seems to take place toward increasingly more complicated forms at an uneven rate and in an irreversible series.

Most biologists assert that it is brought about by numerous mutations, acting cumulatively. Some speak about an organism's active adaptations to a changed environment. A few write of the direction given to evolution by the force of reason.

But mutation, adaptation, and the force of reason notwithstanding, when enveloping conditions change, the species either accommodates or goes out of existence.

XLVIII

Psyche too might well evolve.

Laboratory results have indicated the inheritance of defects. There are also clues pointing to the biological transmission of acquired remembrances.

Scientists view this with a bit of skepticism.

XLIX

Folklore and attested studies have recorded many incidents of extrasensory perception.

An old mother's life was saved through a spontaneously apprehended vision of her heart attack. A brother's death was forecast. Shielded cards in carefully controlled investigations were identified against odds of 10^{35} to 1. Drawings were transmitted telepathically with considerable accuracy.

Scientists view this with a lot of skepticism.

L

There are many hints of some far-reaching anastomosis, which joins men into a natural fraternity.

Some allude to it as a Collective Unconscious, which constitutes the phylogenetic experience from which the individual may tap. The Indians awaken latent energies in the Goddess Shakti through an introverted concentration. Other Easterners refer to no-knowledge and Zen.

It appears that loneliness is only self-imposed.

LI

The longevity of animals is modified by many factors. Rotifers from younger parents usually live much longer than their relatives from older parents. Women outlive men. So do unmated fruit flies outlive mated.

Yet each life within a given species is predestined for a limited span. Maximum longevity for trees ranges from a few years for the cotoneaster to three thousand for sequoias, for fish from one year for the winter flounder to near fifty for the sturgeon, for reptiles from a couple for the long-tailed lizard to a hundred seventy for the Tetsudo tortoise, for birds from less than one year for the swallow to exceeding seventy for the venerable raven, and for the mammals—two years for the hampster to a hundred fifty for the human.

Of the lot, man is the only one who yearns for more Time than that allotted.

LII

At the age of ten, man first associates his death with dissolution of the body.

As the years roll on, he sees his skin dehydrating, his wounds healing at a slower rate, his mind less nimble, his will more wobbling. He pursues his studies on senescence to elucidate the process, hoping for a modern fount of youth. Aging might be the result of the wear and tear of tissues, chemical reactions in the body proteins, variation in sex endocrine capacities, or toxins. Some rejuvenating nostrum might be worked up. But all around him death strikes suddenly and without explanation. He is drenched with fear of losing consciousness, of facing the unknown, of suffering the final retribution.

In the dread of death, he postulates continuance.

Continuum

LIII

Time and Light and Life.

When and where is their beginning? And their ending?

Never, it seems. Nowhere, it seems. All is one continuum—so it appears.

LIV

Zeno once proved that fleet-footed Achilles was forever doomed to chase the tired tortoise. Modern mathematicians have lifted that old sentence by forever banishing the infinitesimal and fashioning a logic for infinity peculiarly its own.

This domain of thinking stipulates that individual elements in something like a straight line, which possesses continuity, are infinitely more abundant than those in something like the realm of rational numbers, which does not; that the number of odd integers is the same as the number of odd plus even integers; that there are just as many points in lines of various lengths; that an infinite set stays the same despite much thinning; and that there are correspondences among continua.

And the mind-boggling goes infinitely on.

LV

The equations of science can reverse themselves with undiminished rigor.

But man never retrogrades to womb.

And reality does not seem to reveal the mathematical discontinuities at zero wherein absolutely nothing happens.

Speculations on the Time-Light-Life Continuum

LVI

Now that we have listened patiently to divers counsels in the Tower of the Intellect, perhaps we should resume our musing. Your good-natured subconscious must be well titillated and quite eager to respond.

Mine has been especially attracted by the fleeting imprints of a Time-related X of some kind. It seems to appear as a ghostly accompaniment to Life. Its ineffable reality seems to persist through the stomatal regulation of exchanges in the oak, the germination of the slime mold from its spore, the locomotion of the earthworm, the learning of new preying methods by the dragonfly nymph, the creation of the virtual presences by man, and all other animate phenomena. For many years, its doings conjured up, for me, kaleidoscopes of the most fascinating bits of patterns, which I was unable to observe in the inanimate world.

Suddenly, it happened one day. X revealed itself as the *ch'i* of the old Taoist masters. And with that, the pieces fell into place and a grand design unfolded.

LVII

Wouldn't it be interesting, if the world were structured according to the diagram in Figure 1.

Then we might surmise a few diversions, which might please the erudite researcher, and some sort of practical perspective by which we might guide ourselves in daily living. It is in such a spirit, then, that we respectfully submit to our learned friend the next eleven modest sections.

LVIII

Light itself consists of energy and *ch'i*.

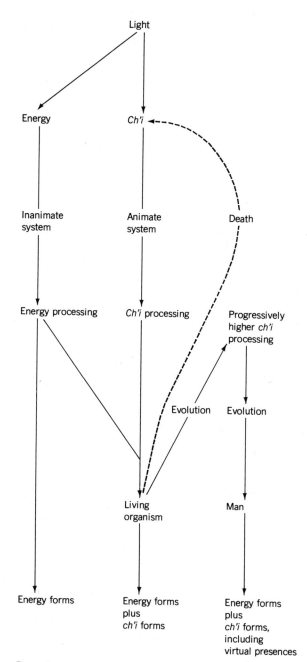

Figure 1

Quantum properties of Light are the refractions of its mass-energy component. Continua are the refractions of its massless *ch'i*.

It's no wonder that a Sanskrit root for Time is Light.

LIX

Energy and mass, inanimate—we call it visible, existent, actual.

Ch'i, our animate—we call invisible and nonexistent, useful.

Organism is the active unity. Serenity reflects the active harmony.

LX

Life is an ongoing metabolism modifying *ch'i.*

Evolution trends toward ever greater elegance of function.

Mental illness follows the uncoupling, shunting, or deranging of selected pathways. Death ensues upon the loss of such a metabolic capability, as remnants then revert to inanimate dust.

LXI

The origin of Life does not lie in the synthesis of a specific molecule, which has been arbitrarily defined to be organic.

Such a change remains inanimate.

Life arose with the first separation of the *ch'i* from Light in an assimilable form.

LXII

Every species possesses a characteristic range of capacities for transforming *ch'i.*

Normal offspring are endowed at birth with the lower threshold values; the ability to absorb and transform *ch'i* then increases with experience and with maturity. There is a steady change in the amount and variety of *ch'i* available from outside sources; and this, in turn, transmutes the former baseline for metabolism, giving rise to yet another series of resulting *ch'i.* The new *ch'i* then serves as the raw material for the succeeding process. Each exposure to a novel form of *ch'i* increases the proficiency of the inherited metabolizing apparatus.

The metabolizing apparatus thereby constitutes one's personality; its metabolic scope prescribes the fullness of one's livingness; the extension of its scope accounts for creativity.

LXIII

There is a wide assortment of means by which the *ch'i* may enter into the being of the living.

Primitive forms are continually incarnated in the tissues of green plants in photosynthesis, and these subsequently enter through the mouth as food.

More sophisticated forms come through the ear, eye, mind, and a multitude of diverse and simultaneous communication channels, as compatibility allows.

LXIV

There is no past *ch'i* or future *ch'i*.

Just as former states of energy exist in energy, so former states of *ch'i* exist in *ch'i*. And just as later states of energy exist in energy, so later states of *ch'i* exist in *ch'i*.

There is only *ch'i* with hysteresis and potentiality.

LXV

Men speak of the id, the ego, and the superego.

Id reminds us of the transporting of *ch'i* through multimedia among the organisms. Ego, of the processing of *ch'i* internally in organisms. Superego, of the forming of the virtual presences as higher forms of *ch'i* by man.

Wholesomeness of living seems dependent on continuing adjustments of a multitude of delicate coherences within the Whole.

LXVI

When the animals evolved the talent to produce a virtual presence, they acquired a soul.

Then there was a God to be adored.

And an Adam was created.

LXVII

As production of the virtual presences increases, man's tie to the Real decreases.

Soon, he praises innovation and inhuman courage. He invents thrills and excitements. He relies on myths and mysteries. He downgrades Nature with a reckless chisel.

Life becomes the Grand Illusion.

LXVIII

With facility in the manipulation of the virtual presences, the primal Superman was born.

With perfection in the art, a second Lucifer took charge.

It was then that man came to defy the Lord.

LXIX

The interminable conflict thrusting the virtual presences against the real intensifies.

As the power of the virtual grows, human values ineluctably turn phony. As the rate of change accelerates they turn ephemeral. And doubt in self and gods both virtual and real then takes its toll.

The twilight of a great civilization is at hand.

Living

LXX

We must now, as needs be in the scheme of things, return to our day-to-day preoccupations.

Musing, pleasing though it is, eventually must give way to doing.

Let us, therefore, still with some light seriousness, draw some inferences from our exercise, which may affect our own behavior toward our fellow men.

LXXI

Means and ends are but successive transformations.

The injected *ch'i* gives rise to novel forms of *ch'i,* which enters the unbounded metabolic pathways of society and generates an endless chain of ever newer possibilities of means and ends.

Recognize, therefore, this truth: intrinsic to your every action is responsibility.

LXXII

A complementarity of the externally provided *ch'i* with the internal actively metabolizing apparatus leads to action.

Given the capacity to bring forth evil, then the furnishing of *ch'i* conformable for evil will result in evil. Given the capacity to bring forth good, the furnishing of *ch'i* conformable for good, analogously will result in good. But given the capacity to bring forth evil, furnishing of *ch'i* conformable for nothing but good will result in nothing evil; the metabolizing apparatus may be bent in the direction of producing good. Yet given the capacity to bring forth good, the furnishing of *ch'i* conformable for only evil will result in nothing good and the metabolizing apparatus may be bent in the direction of producing evil.

So say not that you are not your brother's keeper.

LXXIII

Equitable ethics must entail both *ch'i* and calories in

reasonable distribution. For without *ch'i,* only death; without variety of forms, no human being; and without enriched forms, meager satisfaction.

When your employee has worked so hard and long that he sees not the Light of day, you have embezzled of his *ch'i.* When his behavior is so suppressed that his artistic, intellectual, and spiritual sources are severely shattered, you have then unbalanced his nutritious sustenance for harmony of living. When his healing myths are dogmatized, his gods decreed, his subtle links to Nature torn asunder, you have mummified his soul's dimension.

Give unto your fellow man his fair share of *ch'i.*

LXXIV

Millions of human beings live today stacked one upon another in our urban heaps. The packing densities approach explosive criticality.

If the windows for refreshing ventilations are not opened wide, the ever present primers will ignite the catastrophic inhumanity.

Do not permit the blasting calorie to primitivize the *ch'i.*

LXXV

Man's proclivity leans toward the virtual presences.

Yet the virtual one of the President is much more knowing than the real; there is naiveté in him. The virtual one of the laborer is much more stupid than the real; there is subtlety in him. The virtual one of the friend is much more loyal than the real; there is cowardice in him. The virtual one of the enemy is much more vicious than the real; there is nobility in him. The virtual one of the saint is much more holy than the real; there is sin in him. The virtual one of the criminal is much more wicked than the real; there is good in him.

Love your neighbor in the real Light and let not the real self of your own be inadvertently confused with the virtual self of the public.

LXXVI

If your personality is integrated, why need there be apprehensions? Because of real presences? No, for they are what they are. Because of virtual presences? Again no, for they are what you conjured up yourself.

Once internalized, the virtual uncertainties become anxieties.

Let the facts of common instabilities remain in their original inanimate exteriority and minimize the needless anguish.

LXXVII

The scientific modeling techniques are strictly bounded by the need for virtual fixities and linearities.

Yet in practice, fortuitous coincidences often prove decisive. Physicists cannot discern position and momentum of the simplest particle; mathematicians are forced to limit the extent of proofs.

Shun scientific proffers of exactitude on human issues and believe that you may not be right. Then reasonableness will never put you in the wrong.

LXXVIII

When the *ch'i* at hand is suitable, your metabolic readiness appropriate, and the potential consequence beneficent, then act.

Otherwise, do nothing.

Let the *yin-yang* cycle gradually ripen and reveal the more propitious opportunity.

LXXIX

Cultivate a looseness natural to *ch'i*.

Feel the tension tensing every fiber in ambitious men pursuing their apotheoses. Slacken tautly fitted collars round your neck and breathe the freedom now with greater ease.

Float as a mobile cloud; abide as the serene sea.

LXXX

Live the self that truly is.
Transient transactor of *ch'i*.
Nature's wholly, Nature's only.

LXXXI

Ever Adam is, you were.
Let your one rejoin The One.
Ledgers squared, *ch'i* adorned.

Commentaries The Commentaries are keyed to the respective sections of the Synoptic Text, as indicated below the subheadings.

Musing

A neo-Taoist would be inclined to paraphrase the well-known maxim:

Not to laugh is to cry

into:

Not to muse is to think.

For some reason I cannot help feeling that thinking is conducive more to crying than to laughing and musing more to laughing than to crying. It is a pity that our competitive Age of Institutions has placed such a premium on the technique of thinking that, as a cultural group, we are rapidly losing the art of musing. When was the last time that you sat before the fireplace on a crisp winter night or lay on the grass on a balmy spring day and enjoyed some delightful and thoroughly permeating musing?

May I suggest an occasional sabbatical leave from thinking—from squinting at evidence, choking at flaws, wincing at terminological imprecisions, and arguing at the drop of a syllogism—into the resilient passivity and relaxed receptivity of musing? The wise man does not speak, the talented man talks, the stupid argues—so said the old proverb. Once you learn to uncramp yourself and let the ineffable essences beyond words soak in you as they will, you are well on the way to becoming a neo-Taoist yourself.

To become intuitively proficient at musing, however, you must first master the game of Chinese baseball. The two go hand in glove.

Chinese baseball is played almost exactly like American baseball—the same field, players, bats and balls, method of scoring, and so on. The batter stands in the batter's box, as usual. The pitcher stands on the pitcher's mound, as usual. He winds up, as usual, and zips the ball down the alley. There is one and only one difference. And that is: After the ball leaves the pitcher's hand, and as long as the ball is in the air, *anyone* can move *any* of the bases *anywhere.*

To the neo-Taoist, Chinese baseball, rather than American baseball, is the real name of the game of living and it behooves us to learn it well. American baseball with its fixed bases of reference, is to be played only under certain special and well-controlled conditions. We may illustrate the applications of the principle with a case study of one of those multidisciplinary programs which are so popular today. As a concrete example, I shall refer to a seminar, at which I recently spoke, entitled "Philosophy and Science."

One of the main drives behind multidisciplinary programs is the expectation that such an approach to knowledge will provide us with a "real" understanding of an event in its totality. In a very approximate way, we may regard science as knowledge in the realm of the dimensional and philosophy as knowledge in the realm of the dimensionless. Thus, knowledge of the realm of the dimensional *plus* knowledge of the realm of the dimensionless, i.e., science *and* philosophy, would enable us to arrive at a "true" and "complete" understanding of events.

The neo-Taoist would suggest that this may not be so. To him, the multidisciplinary approach, as presently practiced, is only a first step to enlightenment. He would encourage us to go beyond this stage. After several years of experience with philosophy and science seminars and comparable multidisciplinary efforts, we may wish to consider using the principle of Chinese baseball to advance from knowledge into enlightenment.

It has been my experience in working with many multidisciplinary teams that the members, as a rule, continue to conceptualize segmented totalities in terms of their own respective specialties. The outcomes of such multidisciplinary efforts, more often than not, remain force-fitted composites instead of viable organisms.

The feeling of a student riot, for example, can never be acquired from listening to a theologian on the action of God's grace in men's lives, then to a physicist on the equation of force, an economist on the pressures of inflation, a psychologist on the nuances of the gestalt, a lawyer on the constitutionality of violence, and so on. A thousand and one, out of the infinite facets of man, may be analyzed in the thousand and one academic specialties. But man cannot be appreciated as man through an endless accretion of modules.

Instead of multidisciplinary adding and interacting as the approach to appreciating man in his extended reality, the neo-Taoist would suggest subsuming and resonating. Instead of expecting that knowledge of the event in its wholeness will come from knowledge of the realm of the dimensionless *plus* knowledge of the realm of the dimensional, together with the *interactions* between the two, he would seek it in the knowledge of the realm that *subsumes* them both, together with the *resonances* between the subsuming and the subsumed.

Toward this end, he begins by eliminating the coordinate conjunction *and* from "philosophy and science," for this implies a separableness and an additiveness of the two realms. The title of the seminar is recast in a form more compatible with the Taoist *yin-yang* principle.[1,†] As you probably know, the *yin* and the *yang* represent polarities, e.g., white and black, female and male, and so on. It is to be noted that the principle is entitled the *yin-yang,* not the *yin* and the *yang.* The two polarities are not separable and are not additive as discrete entities. They are intrinsically integrated. Where there is a *yin,* there is a *yang,* and where there is a *yang,* there is a *yin.* Everything is *yin-yang.* Accordingly, the title of our seminar would be changed to: philosophy-science seminar. Where there is a dimensionless, there is a dimensional, and where there is dimensional, there is dimensionless. Everything is dimensionless-dimensional.

We are now ready to subsume. In order to understand the realm of the dimensionless-dimensional, we may invoke a subsuming realm, such as that of distinction. Again invoking the *yin-yang* principle, where there is a distinction, there is a nondistinction.

The realm of the distinction-nondistinction may in turn be subsumed into that of the ineffable-effable, and so on, passing through the realm of the no-knowledge-knowledge,[2] until we end up with the unmentionable Tao.

Such a subsuming sequence may be interpreted as an array of different sets of rules by which we can play the intellectual game of life. According to American baseball rules, we should stick to fixed bases, within a set of boundaries. One set of rules is not to intrude into others. Religious dogmas, for example, are quarantined from political practices. Basic research is immune to human consequences. Logic is immiscible with hunches.

In Chinese baseball, however, all bases are in motion at the instant of enlightenment. Our sensitivity is not only subsuming all the realms but resonating among them at the same instant, like the whole subsuming its

†References will be found, collected together by Commentary number, beginning on page 295.

parts and resonating with them all. It is not bound by the rationale of the dimensional alone, or by the sense of the ineffable alone, and so on. It is responsive to all, yet dominated by none. The totality, with all of its subsumings, moves us, as we attune ourselves to its resonances. Contradictions are acknowledged yet resolved; individuals respected yet transcended; Nature encompassed yet focused.

A pervasive sharing prevails.

It all began with the tiny acorn that fell from mother oak one windy autumn day. How did she teach the young one so much about being true to the self? What did she say in her own way as she bid it adieu? An abundance of starch, proteins, fats, and vitamins had been stored in the two plump seed leaves surrounding the tiny embryo. Everything was ready for its decision to burst out of its protective shell. But the embryo was in no hurry. It slept through the first winter under a blanket of twigs and leaves. Perhaps mother oak had cautioned it against peeping out too soon, lest angry winter nip its fragile shoot. Perhaps she related the tragic experience of the wayward acorns, which did not heed this wise advice during the Cretaceous period a hundred million years ago.

The embryo awakens with the coming of spring. The chemical reactivity of the enzymes and hormones is accelerated by the warm temperatures. The reserve foodstuff is solubilized and transported to the tips of the shoot and root, where the most feverish activity is occurring. The dextrose sugar, twenty or so amino acids, and other compounds are rearranged and joined in new configurations. These are incorporated into the enlarging tissues, as the growing points burgeon through the softened wall of the acorn. The tap root sinks into the soil with firm commitment. There, at that precise spot, the oak will make its life for several hundred years. The seed leaves spread apart and the main shoot pierces the soil and reaches toward the sun. The seedling has just about used up the half-ounce of food reserve. It is now on its own.

Soon, a third region of intense activity begins to assert itself. This is the thin layer of cambrium cells between what is to be the wood and the bark. The cells undergo continuous division, forming wood on the inside and bark on the outside. The growth follows an adaptive engineering design of functionality and beauty. Every stress is accommodated. The newly formed cells on the outer arc of a limb bent by the wind are stretched, while those on the inner arc are compressed. The most rapid expansion in girth takes place during the spring, when many light-colored, thin-walled cells are formed. Less growth occurs during the summer, when the dark-colored, heavy-walled wood is laid down. In this way, a series of concentric rings is built up in the heartwood, as the bark sloughs away. The rings vary in thickness in response to the environmental conditions. When the seasons are favorable, providing abundant moisture, a rich supply of mineral nutrients, warm temperatures, and adequate sunshine, the annual rings are wide. When drought sets in, they are narrow.

Interspersed throughout the wood are numerous microscopic canals for the movement of minerals and water from the roots to the tree tops. Comparable sieve tubes are formed within the bark to transport the sugars and other compounds produced in the leaves to places of storage and use in the stem and roots.

After several decades, the oak comes of age. By then, it is anchored fast by a hundred miles of innumerable bracing roots near the surface of the ground and long tap roots sunk deep. This subterranean system accounts for a tenth of the total weight of the tree.

A large amount of water must be acquired by the roots. The young leaves and root tips must be maintained at a water content of 90 percent and the rest of the tree at about 50 percent. Nine ounces of water are required for the making of each pound of wood, during which process an additional thousand pounds of water is given up to the atmosphere through the leaves.

This transpiration constitutes an efficient mechanism for insuring the temperature equilibrium of the tree. Water is evaporated through minute pores, called stomata, on the underside of the leaves. The stomata ordinarily open early in the morning, begin to close about noon, and shut tightly after dark. When the air is excessively hot and dry, however, they remain closed for the day except for only a very short time in the early morning.

The stomata also regulate the amount of carbon dioxide to be absorbed by the leaf for photosynthesis. About a tenth of the gas dissolves in the water and penetrates into nearby cells containing small particles called chloroplasts. In the presence of sunlight, the green chlorophyll within the chloroplast catalyzes the combination of the oxygen and hydrogen atoms from water with the carbon dioxide to form dextrose sugar. The dextrose is converted into other sugars or combined with nitrogen salts to produce the essential amino acids. The latter constitute the building blocks for the vital proteins of life, while the sugars are transformed into reserve carbohydrates, structural cellulose, and other complex substances.

Meanwhile, respiration is taking place in all of the cells to furnish the energy required for growth. Dextrose is combined with oxygen to give carbon dioxide and water in the process, which may be looked upon as a reversal of photosynthesis.

The three processes of water and mineral uptake in the roots, photosynthesis in the leaves, and respiration and synthesis throughout the tree reinforce each other in a gradual crescendo until the annual shoot completes its early growth toward the end of June. The oak is now draped with a foliage of sappy green. By this time, all of the cell divisions that will account for the next year's growth have already been laid down. The microscopic leaf and floral buds have been determined a year in advance. The oak has anticipated next year's beauty; there is a vision of an enlarged canopy. All that remains to be accomplished the following spring is the unfolding of the lengthwise dimension, while the cambial activity provides the coordinated increase in girth.

Then follows the slow preparation for winter. The nutrients in the leaves are drawn back into the branches, as layers of cork cells begin to form at the base of the stems. The once soft spring leaves are now thick and scarlet. As the chilly autumn winds blow through the branches, the dry leaves fall one by one. Finally, the brawny oak stands bare, knotted with excrescences, powerful with massive trunk and limbs, confidently awaiting another siege of freezing blasts.

After twenty-odd cycles of growth, slow-down, deep-rest, and resurgence, the oak is now ready to pass its breath of life to the next generation. The reproductive stage usually follows the period of maximum growth in height. A delicate balance is effected between vegetative growth and reproduction. Flowering is favored by a high concentration of carbohydrates, whereas leaf development is favored by an abundance of nitrogen and other minerals. When the light is bright and the physiological state appropriate, the flower buds are set. The male flowers consist of several tassels of beads, hanging as a fringe from a common point on a twig. Their pollens are carried by the breeze onto the receiving stigma of the inconspicuous female flowers at the axils of the leaves on the same branch. After the fertilization is completed, the seed is nurtured to maturity in place over several years, until it plops to the ground one fall day.

The tree grows older, often attaining an age of three hundred years. It has been a rich and beneficent life. Thousands of birds have found shelter under its green umbrella. Millions of organisms have gained sustenance from its juicy leaves and rich sap. Myriad mosses and epiphytes have waxed luxuriantly under its stabilizing influence upon their environment. But now the young shoots no longer reach into the sky so vigorously. Photosynthesis becomes progressively less productive as the leaves become smaller. Respiration is inefficient. Cambial divisions slow down and the annual rings become narrower. The wood is less resilient and the moisture content lowered.

Life begins to sneak away inch by inch. Beginning at the very tips, desiccation spreads backward leaf by leaf, twig by twig, branch by branch. The heartwood is no longer tough and strong. The limbs break off with every moderate wind and litter the forest floor with a rotting matrix. As the protective bark is torn open, various organisms of decay invade the underlying tissues. The long, cottony filaments of fungal destruction search out the unused sieve tubes of the whitish sapwood just beneath the bark. As the sap interface recedes lower and lower, the hyphae follow remorselessly, growing profusely off the dead debris of a partially living and partially dying giant.

The pathos of death surrounds the oak. Once it stood defiantly before the wildest fury of the elements. Now it throws itself upon the mercy of the invading bark beetles and woodpeckers, the minute bacteria and mildew, and the little puffs and gusts. Finally, the tired and decrepit tree can endure it no longer. The oak is no more.

3.
Slime mold
XII

Scavenging under the bark of fallen logs in the moist woods, the slime mold acts like an animal during certain phases of its life and like a plant during others.

Life for the individual begins as a microscopic spore. Blown about by the wind, it eventually lands upon a suitably wet surface. The spore emerges from its dormancy as water permeates through the wall. The wall ruptures; the nucleus divides; two or more sperm cells come forth. At times a miniscule amoeboid is first formed, but this subsequently breaks up into the mononucleated swarm cells. These cells assume two principal shapes. One is comma-like, with a flagellum projecting from the tapered end—a long whip which comes in handy as the little blob swims about in the soil water. The other is amoeba-like, without any swimming appendage, and oozes along the damp ground.

The swarm cells are the sexual cells, upon which the survival of the species depends. They are very sensitive to the stresses of the environment and react in an ingenious way to insure self-preservation. When the substrate dries up or food becomes scarce, they transform themselves into cysts. Life then marks time within the secure spheres.

When moisture and food are adequate again, the swarm cells leave their fortresses and begin to pair off. Their nuclei fuse in sexual union; the flagella recede; the new amoeboid cells multiply. They divide repeatedly, giving rise to a colony of many individuals. Eventually many of them clump together. The individual membranes dissolve. A multinucleated protoplasmic aggregate is formed.

If a siege of dry weather or food shortage takes place at this point, the mass divides into coated sclerotia, each enclosing one to twenty cells. These are capable of withstanding desiccation for twenty years. When rain falls, the walls rupture and the slime mold resumes its active life.

Before long, successive nuclear divisions give rise to a bright yellow, jelly-like plasmodium with hundreds of nuclei, covering an area of about an inch in diameter. The plasmodium moves over the ground like a giant amoeba, engulfing microscopic cells and organic debris along the way. It moves by extending a viscous finger out of the forward edge, which is then filled by a stream of protoplasm. The rest of the slime mold flows in rhythmic response. Undigested fungal spores, woody particles, and other inert foreign bodies can be seen within the mass. Although plant material can serve as food, it does not suffice for a complete diet. Living or dead microorganisms are an essential supplement. On the other hand, an excessive number of live bacteria may well overwhelm the attacking slime mold, which may end up as victim instead.

A streaming pulsation is maintained to and from the

edge of the fan. As a rule, the flow forward takes longer than the reverse. The direction of movement of the plasmodium as a whole is determined by the protoplasmic flow, which in turn continually changes the outlines of the plasmodium. On occasions, smaller fans separate from the parent and go wandering off on their own.

Physical injury elicits an immediate response. When a strand is damaged, the plasmodium reacts as if shrinking from pain. A swelling occurs at the site, with gelation of the surface continuing toward the interior. If the strand is severed, gelling sets in for some distance on both sides of the divide, thereby preventing the loss of protoplasm through the cut. Within a few minutes the tissues become soft but relatively firm in texture. If no further disturbance is experienced, the stiffness is resorbed within a few hours.

Finally, the time for fruit formation arrives. For the first time the mass moves toward the light onto an elevated place with a sense of purpose. Within a short time, slow concentric waves sweep over the protoplasm toward various centers. A series of complex changes then takes place around these points. A number of nuclei become transfigured into foundation cells and the stalk, which rises half an inch above the surface. A bulbous expansion forms at the tip. More nuclei die to provide the protective coating for the precious seeds of the next generation. The nuclei within the bulb undergo a series of sexual changes to become microscopic spores. The spores gradually mature until they are scattered by the winds to begin life anew. The resourceful half-plant, half-animal has arranged for its perpetuity.

4.
Earthworm
XIII

The earthworm is a good example of structural harmony of form and function. Two layers of muscles at right angles to each other are located immediately below the skin. The upper consists of a thin circular arrangement of fibers running around the body. The lower is much thicker with similar fibers running longitudinally along the body axis. Locomotion involves their graceful and rhythmic interplay.

The worm begins its movement with a contraction of the circular muscles of the first segment, resulting in its narrowing, elongating, and stretching ahead. The wave itself moves rearward. When it reaches about a third of the way down the body, another wave begins at the tip. The circular muscles relax, while the longitudinal muscles contract. This produces a thickening and shortening of the segment at the same time. The waves of peristaltic contractions follow one after the other from tip to tail. They are supplemented by several additional mechanisms for efficient travel.

As the worm elongates, the bristles on the lower surface of the body are extended and tilted backward. Those toward the rear dig into the ground, while those at the front slide along. When the front end is shortened, the forward bristles take hold, while the rear ones slip accordingly. To move backward, the worm reverses the peristaltic rhythm of contraction and elongation of the segments and the angle of tilt of the bristles.

An even greater contribution to the locomotion is the differential friction of different parts of the body against the surface. When the worm wishes to move forward, the anterior end is lifted off the surface by the aft end. The head is thrust forward and elongated to initiate the peristaltic wave. As the wave of elongation dies down halfway along the body, the forward end drops to make contact with the surface, thickens, lifts the aft end off the surface, and pulls it toward the front.

When the going gets difficult, the worm resorts to its ultimate device. The mouth is pressed against the surface and anchored in place like a suction cup. The hind portion is then pulled forward through contraction of the body. The forward end is shot ahead a second time, the tip anchored, and the procedure repeated. In this way, a worm is able to crawl up a glass incline at a relatively steep angle.

The same long-thin and short-thick process of muscular action along the body is used in burrowing. As the tip finds a small crevice in the earth, the worm begins to press in. The body is arched off the ground just behind the pressure point to provide maximum power. After the thin tip penetrates to a sufficient depth, the front segments expand radially. By thus crowding the hole, a firm grip is provided. The thinner posterior portion is then pulled forward by means of the contraction wave. The segments slightly aft of the tip are expanded, pushing against the wall at that point. The front tip relinquishes its hold, elongates, and pushes deeper, as the cycle repeats itself. Using this technique the worm can bury itself in loose soil within a few minutes.

The opening of the burrow is usually surrounded by earth castings. Using its tail as a trowel, the worm moves the earth first on one side, then on the other, until the mouth is lipped by an elevated ring. This guides the drainage of water away from the hole during a light rain.

In general, the burrow begins by pointing straight down and the walls are lined with a thin layer of fine, dark-colored, voided earth. For insulation against the elements, the upper several inches are plugged with bits of leaves and other organic matter. The burrow then follows an irregular path. It eventually winds up in an enlarged terminal. The chamber is sufficiently roomy for a worm or two to turn around. There they lie, cozily waiting out the winter.

The main source of food is the small amount of organic substances in the large quantities of earth it swallows and passes through the digestive tract. At times the worm searches for edible material on the ground surface. One species has developed the habit of hooking its tail in the burrow opening, while stretching itself to forage over a circular area. It acts as if afraid of getting lost by letting go of home base.

The worm is nocturnal. It rarely appears during the day unless forced out of its burrow by flooding rain. During the day it normally stretches out within the hole, head uppermost near the ground level. Every now and then an unfortunate worm is seen by some keen-eyed bird. A quick jab of the beak and a tug-of-war is started. The worm contracts its length, expands its body, and holds fast against the burrow wall with its bristles dug in. Either the worm is pulled out and swallowed *in toto,* or a piece of it is torn off. For some species, the latter is by far the lesser of two evils; these worms are perfectly capable of regenerating half of their front body if necessary, head and all.

If an earthworm is placed headfirst in the straight arm of a T-tube, it will crawl to the junction, at which it will normally turn right or left at random. If the right side of the cross-arm is plugged with sandpaper or cotton soaked in dilute acid, and the left side with rich soil, the worm will recoil from the right side upon contact with the disagreeable obstruction and proceed avidly into the soil plug. After fifty trials, the worm will automatically make a left turn at the junction without experimental inducements. It has learned something, which indicates an intelligence of some kind.

Rudimentary mental activity is also exhibited in its everyday actions. For instance, the point at which a piece of leaf is seized is not a matter of pure chance. There seems to be a deliberation of some kind that goes on, in which the worm tries out one point, then another, a third, and so on until it grasps just the optimal spot, which makes for the greatest ease of dragging the piece along the ground back to the burrow. A triangular piece is gripped at the apex.

Sexual maturity is reached in about six months. Mating occurs during the warm and damp seasons, with peak romancing during the hot summer days. The worm is hermaphroditic, but it cannot fertilize its own eggs. Instead there is a reciprocal exchange between two partners. In their search for suitable mates, worms leave their burrows and move about in random directions. Upon contact two worms will feel each other out; if they find each other to be approximately equal in size, they will lie together, belly to belly, pointing in opposite directions and overlapping the first several dozen segments. A slimy girdle is secreted by the whitish ring in both worms. Their bodies are held together closely by these two elastic bands and by the bristles, which stick into each other's body. The longitudinal ventral grooves are aligned to form a channel. The seminal fluid with its sperm cells is passed into this channel by the male pores in the fifteenth segments. The fluid flows into the seminal receptacles in the ninth and tenth segments of the mate. There is a transfer of sperms but no discharge of eggs as yet.

After copulation, which lasts for about two hours, the worms pull away from each other. The wide mucous bands are then slid forward over the anterior end of the respective worms. While these cylindrical sheaths are still attached to the whitish rings of the worms, eggs are passed into them from the sacs of the fourteenth segments back along the temporary grooves. As the sheaths containing nutrient fluid and eggs pass over the spermathecal openings, the semen stored therein by the mating partner is squeezed into them. Fertilization occurs immediately in the band outside the body. As the bands slip over the anterior tips the elastic ends close, producing two oval-shaped cocoons.

Each cocoon contains about eight to sixteen eggs. Depending upon the species, one or more completes its embryonic development within a few weeks. The young worm breaks out and stretches. The earth is his.

5.
Dragonfly
XIV

As the squadrons of dragonflies dart over the rivers and ponds, the females carefully attend to their special mission. In some species, they skim along the surface, dipping their abdomens at intervals and leaving clumps of tiny eggs behind. In others, they scatter the eggs at random. In still others, they take special pains: they encase themselves in a sustaining film of air, creep along the submerged stem of an appropriate plant, find a suitable slit, and deposit a mass of eggs in it. A single mass may contain over a hundred and twenty thousand eggs.

No sooner are the eggs laid when Nature's drama of survival unfolds itself. Nearby is a tiny fairy fly, paddling along with its wings. Supported by a bubble of air, she goes in search of hidden clusters of dragonfly eggs. She then lays her own upon them. When the mixture of eggs hatches, only fairy fly nymphs emerge, healthy on a diet of dragonfly embryos that were to have been nymphs.

Those dragonfly eggs fortunate enough to escape the notice of the parasite give rise to a horde of nymphs with jet propulsion. The same mechanism is used for breathing and swimming. The hind end of the alimentary tract is enlarged and the thin walls are equipped with breathing tubes extending in all directions to form efficient gills. Water is taken into the intestinal tract. After the oxygen–carbon dioxide exchange has been completed, the water is forcibly ejected from the lower end. The resulting jet reaction propels the nymph forward.

The wings are as yet undeveloped at this stage and their rudiments are folded in four little wing pads extending down the back. The six spindly legs provide for a sluggish crawl among the rubbish of the silty vegetation. The nymph moves about stealthily and its off-gray-green coloration coincides with that of the decaying debris of the pond bottom so closely that detection by the unsuspecting prey is extremely difficult. When the nymph closes in, a unique offensive weapon is brought into action. A front arm shoots forth, grasps the quarry, flicks it backward into the mouth—zip, zip—and all is over. One life is ended so another can go on.

The appendage is actually a jointed lower lip. When not in use it is retracted between the front legs, covering part of the face like a mask. Mosquito larvae are caught by the hinged pincers and gobbled at the rate of one every three seconds during the active periods. Although the nymphs consume only live animals, they are not choosy with respect to the kind and size. Protozoa, mayfly and mosquito larvae, caddis worms, water bugs, tadpoles, and minnows—all are equally appetizing. They even eat their own kind and attack adult dragonflies emerging from their nymphal cases during metamorphosis.

The nymph is assisted in its own survival by several practices, quite apart from the natural blending of its form and color into the background. It digs into the mud, hangs inconspicuously from the lower surfaces of leaves, and lives under the protective riffles of flowing streams. It also plays possum when captured and escapes by shedding the seized appendage at will. The muscles are suddenly contracted and the leg can be severed at the lower joint without the loss of blood.

A demonstration of its creative adaptability has been recorded by an entomologist, who snipped off the prey-grappling underlip. At first, the handicapped nymph relied upon getting sufficiently close to the prey to catch it with its jaws. This mode of hunting proved inadequate to supply the requisite amounts of food. A second offensive tactic was evolved. At a distance slightly farther away from the victim than before, the nymph suddenly turned on its jet propulsion. The rocket reaction shot it forward to seize the victim in its jaws.

After ten to fifteen molts of the chitinous skin over a period of three years, the nymph begins the transition to aerial life. Finishing touches to bodily changes take place: the hair is shed from the legs; the number of lenses is multiplied in the compound eye; the number of joints is increased in the antennae; the wings are matured in their pads. One bright day, it creeps out of the water upon the river bank, a stone, a stick, or a stem protruding out of the water. The adolescent locks itself in place by two hooks on each leg and rests motionless for some time while Nature readies it for its new life. The chitin splits along the back. The dragonfly arches its midsection as the slit widens. Next out of the case comes the head and thorax. Then the legs. As if taking a breather from the ordeal, the dragonfly remains quiet for about fifteen minutes. In the meantime the limbs harden. Finally the tip of the abdomen is drawn free. The dragonfly has molted for the last time.

The liberated wings expand. As the blood is pumped from the body, they become turgid and glistening. After an hour or so in the vertical position, they are lowered in preparation for the maiden flight. The brilliance and irisdescence intensify. After several more hours the dragonfly takes off—a denizen of the air. Only a clinging ghost remains to mark the miracle of metamorphosis.

The dragonfly embarks upon its first reconnaissance of the river banks. Unless it belongs to the small percentage of loafers, who sleep through the day and night, it seldom alights from dawn to dusk. It skims along, hovers, soars, glides, devours, fights, and mates—all in the air. Its entire body has been designed for just such a life.

Over half of the head surface is occupied by the prominent compound eyes. Although the main organ of smell has been reduced to mere bristles of antennae, the amazing eyes more than make up for its ineffectiveness in the search for food. With its fifteen thousand optical units, the eyes can see to the front, sides, up, down, and a quarter of the way to the rear without moving the head. The head itself, attached in a ball-and-socket joint to the thorax, can be rotated almost completely around to offer an omnidirectional vision.

The compound eye is especially efficient in the detection of movement. A flying mosquito is detected by one optical unit after another as it moves. The messages from the successive optical units are accordingly interpreted by the brain. Objects closer at hand will appear in a greater number of optical units simultaneously than those farther away. Distance can be gauged in this fashion with a fine degree of accuracy.

The thorax consists of three segments. To each of these a pair of legs is attached. The legs are weak and skinny and do not afford a fast or graceful walk. But they are very effective for catching prey. During flight they are bunched together forward to form a spiny trap. As the dragonfly wings its way through the air, the improvised net scoops up the hapless gnats, bees, butterflies, mosquitoes, and small moths. Insects as large as a lunar moth have been snared. Their bodies are transferred by the forelegs from the net into the mouth, sucked dry, and let fall—all without slowing down in the least.

No creature surpasses the dragonfly in its insatiable gluttony. As many as a hundred mosquitoes are stuffed into its mouth at one time. Often there are so many that the mouth can not even close. A dragonfly can eat its own weight in an hour and still clamor for more food. It will even consume parts of its own body to satisfy the pangs of hunger.

The abdomen contains ten segments without attachments. The smooth structure adds to the aerodynamic streamlining. The shape of the rounded eyes, leading over the thorax to the first three bulbous segments of the abdomen, and the slender tail spoil the eddies which might otherwise form. The tip of the abdomen in the male contains two or four claspers, which hold the head or thorax of the female during mating maneuvers. The male organ itself is found on the second and third segments. While flying tandem, the female loops her abdomen forward and places its tip, containing the female sex organ, at the male's. In this way the flying sensation is consummated.

With the chill of fall and the concomitant scarcity of food, the lively child of the sun gradually becomes the stupefied adult grown mortally old. It clings spiritless to the underside of branches near the pond from which it had emerged. Then comes the freezing scythe of the first frost. The lifeless effigy drops to the ground. The baton of life has been passed to the unseen nymphs beneath the still waters.

6.
Man
XV

Man—the self-professed pinnacle of God's creation—is an ever-diverging and diversifying amplifier. Therein lies his uniqueness among the living.

Other animals are asking no more of Nature today than they did a hundred million years ago. Sun and living food were all they yearned for then, and sun and living food are all they yearn for now. They are contented with their legacy. Man, however, is ever insatiable for change.

As far as bodily structure is concerned, he is constrained to the slow trudgings of evolution. Man's outlet for self-actuated change began with the making of things.

His products were directed initially toward meeting the needs of survival, like the beavers constructing dams, the spiders weaving webs, and the woodpeckers drilling nesting holes.

Unlike animals which exercised their inventiveness only within the bounds of immediate requirements, man surged far beyond. Ideas and things were often designed and schemes devised for their own sake, and uses were chanced upon only later. The telescope extended his eyes, the radio his voice, the airplane his legs, and the missile his fist. His sphere of influence enlarged accordingly.

Man's primary impact today is no longer based only upon his personal and real presence but extends also to the virtual presences which he can create. In so doing, he has left his animal kin far and forever behind.

The manifestations of virtual presences can be illustrated by the Saturday afternoon broadcasts from the Metropolitan Opera House. While only some three thousand individuals present at the New York auditorium were able to enjoy in person the memorable performances of Renata Tebaldi, Richard Tucker, and Leonard Warren in Verdi's *Tosca,* with Dmitri Mitropoulos conducting, in the nineteen fifties, hundreds of thousands of others listened over the radio. The real performers appeared at only one place at the time, while the virtual performers were heard simultaneously thousands of miles apart in hundreds of thousands of places. The radio audience, however, was not privileged to see the singers, as well as their interactions with the rest of the cast, in their wholeness. Only those at the Opera House viewing the real presences were accorded the opportunity of sensing their total beings.

During the intermission between the acts in one of the broadcasts, several records of the great soprano Nellie Melba were played. It sounded as if one were listening to Miss Melba herself, although she had long since passed away. During interviews with the other singers present, their recordings were often played to recall highlights of their past. The real singer would listen to the virtual singer of himself twenty years earlier. It seemed as if clock-time flowed backward and he met himself along the way.

Although the effects of the efficient virtual presence are as real as those of the real for the specific purpose at hand, there are fundamental differences between the two. Real presence is single and whole; virtual presence is multiple and partial. Real presence is bound by clock-time; virtual is not.

Once created, the virtual presence is usually beyond the control of its creator. It is endowed with an independent status. It is, as it were, no longer a fetus. It has a life of its own, following its own laws of nutrition, growth, change, and death. Virtual clock-time and real clock-time are not synchronous; they bear no relationship to each other. Through such means as recordings, man has trapped, controlled, and processed virtual clock-time; but the net effect for restricted purposes is the same as if he had trapped, controlled, and processed real clock-time.

Despite its individualism, however, the virtual presence is an obligate parasite. It must be attached to a substrate of some kind. The creation of a virtual presence, then, involves the fixing of an imaginary existence onto a suitable substrate in such a fashion that the virtual presence can be remanifested. As long as there is no recall, the virtual presence lies dormant in the substrate. If the substrate disappears, so does the virtual presence. Since virtual presences have no spatial, temporal, or mass dimensions they can exist in a vast number of modes, material or nonmaterial. The carrier of a virtual presence may be a movie film, a book, or a mind.

The production of and response to virtual presences is as natural with man as breathing. Nearly everything he does leaves a virtual presence of some sort. Most of them are unintentional, trivial, and short-lived. Their social significance is determined primarily by their longevity, frequency of recall, intensity of impact, and enhancement and amplification upon each recall. Man Friday's virtual presence in the footprints on the sandy beach disappeared with the tide. A series of Duke Ellington's virtual presences dies when a tape recording is burned. A cohesive assemblage of virtual presences, which comprises a culture, continues to exert its influence for generations. The virtual presence of certain gods has lived for centuries and will continue for many more.

As civilization has advanced, man's ability to produce virtual presences has increased greatly. Thousands of years ago man relied primarily upon virtual presences formed and sustained by the minds and lips of man. The invention of writing, tablets, tracts, letters, and books offered a diversity of additional substrates. Today there is a vast armamentarium, climaxed with an awesome array of electronic devices. These have given rise to infinite alternatives for multifaceted versions of virtual presences, which can be contrived, modified, amplified, and multiplied by innumerable coarchitects. A major part of the present economic world caters to the manufacture, alteration, and emulation of virtual presences. Amusements and arts, newspapers and publications, and so on are engaged in their manufacture. Advertising firms, electronic systems, and so on are involved in their alteration. Churches, schools, and so on are concerned with their emulation.

Many of our typical "success stories" center around the creation and enhancement of virtual presences, as well as their exploitation. Reputations are built; celebrities are glamorized; social figures are manicured; political aspirants are groomed. It is the virtual image that moves the people to vote for the real candidate.

There have been thousands of religious sects, the leaders of each of which have claimed to have received the word of God. Each in turn begins by acknowledging the inherited state of affairs to be true and holy. Each in turn adds modifications and interpretations to the received virtual presence. But now *his* is the true church — the virtual God has said so. The virtual God's virtual mantle has as much impact upon him and his followers as would the real God's real mantle. Millions of people swear on it, fight for it, kill with it, and die of it.

Wars have been precipitated when the virtual presences of two parties overlap. While the real presences of the responsible perpetrators are safely far away, their virtual presences are locked in mortal combat. While their virtual presences are locked in mortal combat, the real presences of real soldiers and refugees are bombed to real smithers.

Since virtual presences have as real an effect as real presences for many purposes, those nations with the greatest capacities for the virtual also possess the greatest potential for power and influence. Conversely, those nations which emphasize real presences do not fare so well materially; their drive for progress is greatly attenuated. Technological modernization of the so-called underdeveloped countries nearly always seems to be accompanied by a diminution of their native innocence. But nostalgia notwithstanding, the world is rapidly shedding its orientation toward real presences and going over to the virtual side of the ledger. "Better that all our ancient culture disappear," said Professor Ch'en Tu-hsiu in China in 1915, "than our race perish by its inability to live in the modern world."

The same effect is observed in personal status. An individual has two main paths he might use in improving his own lot. He may rely on his real presence. This is the slow way. He must do the work himself. There is no amplification of his virtues or multiplication of his strengths. He earns only what he himself attends to personally. On the other hand, he may concentrate on his virtual presences, enlarge his virtual efforts, then heap the real rewards thus engendered upon his real person. He does not need to work as hard himself for the same return. He need only make sure that the number of augmented virtual presences is continually on the rise.

It is interesting to watch such a new executive on the scene. In typical fashion he labors diligently at projecting the virtual presence of a great leader—incisive, decisive, efficient, fair. The experienced leader recognizes that it is not essential that he himself generate the image. As a matter of fact, it can be composed much more effectively by an encircling tier of junior executives. The most productive promoters of causes often turn out to be unbelievers at heart, who undertake the task for economic advantage. If the top executive is not exhibited too frequently in the flesh to the workers and if the virtual presences are recalled to the minds of the lower echelons with appropriate reinforcing litanies, their influence can spread with considerable impression. If in his rare appearances, the chief lives up to the virtual presence for a few brief moments and adds touches of human warmth, the results are most satisfying. A pleasant surprise crosses everyone's mind—not only is the chief everything that has been said about him, but he is also so human to boot! And another round of virtual augmentation is underway. The charismatic leader synchronizes his real presence with the enlarging virtual presences in a reinforcing rhythm.

The level-headed executive realizes, however, that the instrument of virtual presences cannot be permitted to run wild. A prudent balance must be maintained between the impersonal productivity of an organization and the personal welfare of the living workers. To achieve this optimal goal, he adjusts the gap between the virtual person of himself being molded by his sycophants and the real person. Since the organization is driven as much by the virtual as by the real presences, the chief should be able to bridge this gap at all times. The moment he is unable to do so, he has lost control of the organization. On the other hand, if the span is too narrow, much less than the attainable productivity is being realized out of the organization. Again, he will fail in his role as chief executive, although for quite another reason. The continuing concern over these delicate adjustments represents one of the main sources of executive neuroses and ulcers.

Modern technological society has reached the point where the majority has, as in the story of Pygmalion and Galatea, fallen in love with its creations. It is not surprising that contemporary man is having psychiatric difficulties in coping with his virtual presences. The problem is most trying in cases involving a self-created virtual presence that is at great variance with the real self, and yet is attached to that self as the substrate. If this virtual presence is not dissipated in some fashion, any decision facing the real person will have to be debated between the real and the virtual, since both exert a real effect upon the real person. The outcome remains uncertain, because of the difference in personalities and power. While the real person is a man of limited stamina, the virtual is tireless, timeless, and unweakened by repetitive recall.

Such a situation can give rise to interminable frustrations. For example, if the virtual presence is ascribed a much higher level of competence than that of the real, the latter would continually be forced to agree to do things which are beyond his talents and resources to satisfy. If the virtual presence is overly virtuous, the real would be forced to mouth sanctimonious hypocrisies. If the virtual presence is overly ambitious, the real would be forced to amplify the power of the virtual over the real, until the real becomes as a man possessed. The situation becomes infinitely complicated if the real person is the substrate for many virtual presences at the same time, each of which claims the right and power to make every decision. What a life of endless committee meetings of vociferous, indefatigable, self-appointed experts!

Psychiatrists are concerned, of course, with the therapeutic resolution of this kind of conflict of multipersonalities. Some of them believe that bringing the dominating virtual presence to the surface will lead to a cure. Yet somehow, it would appear that the surfacing of the virtual presence is merely a recalling, like the playing of a phonograph record. The playing of the record *per se* does not erase the virtual presence. It is the nature of a virtual presence to be recalled over and over again without diminution in power. The domination of the real person by the virtual can only be eliminated when the real presence is no longer the substrate. At the least the virtual presence must be transferred to another substrate.

Among the less scientific practitioners of folk psychiatry, a typical ritual involves the transfer of the demon from the real person as a substrate onto a paper charm, placed on his head with appropriate incantations. Presumably, if the real person had the wherewithal to conjure up the virtual presence to begin with, he and the therapist should be able to transfer its abode to the paper charm. The charm, possessed, is then burnt, thereby destroying both virtual presence and substrate. The virtual presence is now irretrievably dead and cannot be recalled. The psychiatric patient is cured.

In order for psychotherapy to be constructively effective, there needs to be a modification of experience within the patient, in contrast to the modification of knowledge. The difference I take to be this: Experience is more of a living transplant and knowledge an inventoried item. A transplant continues to grow; an inventoried item is merely there to be extracted when needed by the growth process but has no independent behavioral impact. The transplant is part of the organism like the cion is part of the tree. It is the growth of this transplant, as experience, which evolves into fear, doubt, anguish, joy, and so on. The art of human influence rests largely on the art of transplantation, not necessarily that of education. We are quite proficient in the imbedding of knowledge, but seem rather awkward in the transplanting of experience.

Herein may lie some of the difficulties involved in

psychotherapy. For the therapist to transplant a viable experience, he himself must have a living cion of the desirable kind, psychically compatible to the stock, which will develop into the envisioned form within the milieu of the other person. This would imply that the therapist has the ability of identifying the troubling growth and somehow grabbing hold if it, grafting something else to it in order to mold it, and then either jerking it out or forcing the new graft to dominate it.

In other words, a repressed problem is a viable experience and not a dead knowledge. Virtual presence is one of the products of such living transplants. Incidentally, the living organism or the healthy cion can be suffocated or immobilized not only by excessive virtual presences but also by excessive dead knowledge. Perhaps educators should take note.

At the same time, the propensity of the individual to fabricate virtual presences needs be brought within healthy bounds. This is difficult. Many of the current advances of civilization rest on the multiplication of virtual presences, which in turn leads to an intensification of conflicts between the virtual and the real in the self. The payment for each unit of modern progress, it seems, is a titrated dose of neuroses.

The ancient books of the Hindu, Buddhist, and Taoist masters have been very conservative on this score. The Hindu *Tathata* and the Buddhist *Sono-mama* both suggest leaving the real presences be. "Reveal your simple self," said Lao Tzu. "Embrace your original nature."

Time

7.
The primitive
conception of
cyclic regenera-
tion
XVIII

Early man's concept of time was based upon the rhythm of Nature. The successive phases of his life—childhood, adolescence, manhood, and old age—were characterized by different qualities. Each transition was a crisis, and to resolve these crises the individual was assisted by the community in an appropriate ritual.[1]

Communal crises of transition were merely an extension of these personal crises. In many primitive societies, the New Year ritual, for instance, involved the lifting of the taboo on the new harvest, which could then be eaten.[2] Since the varieties of grains and fruits ripened at different seasons, a number of New Year festivals were celebrated.

Each transition from night to day symbolized the sun's defeat of chaos on the day of creation, an event which was also repeated every New Year's Day. For the mythopoeic mind each repetition coalesced with the original event. This was depicted by the Egyptian verse about the enemies of the Pharaoh: "They shall be like the snake Apophis on New Year's morning." As Apophis, the spirit of hostile darkness, the snake is defeated every night by the sun as he journeys in the nether world from the sunset West to the sunrise East. In the Egyptian mind the daily sunrise, the notion of creation, and the beginning of the new annual cycle all fused together in the rites of the New Year. By harmonizing his social life to the changes of Nature by means of appropriate rituals, man contributed to the victory of the good gods over the chaotic powers. Hopefully, conditions would be established "as they were in the time of Rē, in the beginning."

The same mythoceremonial beliefs were present throughout the Semitic world.[3] A prevalent theme was the annual return to chaos followed by new creation. As sung by Ephraem Syrus in his *Hymns on Epiphany:* "He has created the heavens anew because sinners have worshipped all the heavenly bodies; has created the world anew, which had been withered by Adam. A new creation arose from His spittle."

The concept of rebirth was also common in the Orphic mysteries of the cult of Dionysius around the sixth century B.C.[4] In the beginning, the silver egg of the cosmos was created by time. Out of the silver egg burst Phanes-Dionysius. Phanes was the first god. He contained all the seeds of gods and men, bisexual, bearing in himself

infinite time, and the all-creating Eros. He first created
his daughter Nyx, Night. With Nyx aeons later, he begot
Gaea, Uranus, and Cronus. Zeus was the grandchild of
Phanes, the primal god. Thus, Zeus embodied the entire
past and his world was a reborn world.

The cyclic regeneration of time raises the question
of the abolition of history. The corresponding myths
and observances may constitute a repetition of an archetypal act in an attempt to abolish concrete time.
The intent is antihistorical. There is a refusal to preserve
the memory of the past in these behavioral patterns.
In effect, time is annulled by not paying attention to
it. Events are reversed and nothing is final. Thus, as
noted by Mircea Eliade,[5] "the desire felt by the man
of traditional societies to refuse history and to confine
himself to an indefinite repetition of archetypes, testifies
to his thirst for the real and his terror of 'losing' himself
by letting himself be overwhelmed by the meaningless-
ness of profane existence. . . . in fact, this behavior
corresponds to a desperate effort not to lose contact
with being."

Nevertheless, the belief that the primordial time can
be regained in a prototype of repetition proved comforting. Through simulation of the original events, the
Egyptians could possess the immortality of Osiris.[6,7]
By recalling the myth of Odin, an old Norse poet could
acquire "the scaldic mead." He could be inspired again
by the hidden magical power, which could give him the
strength to reenact the primary divine action.[8]

**8.
Time's deprecia-
tion by the
Hindus
XIX**

Hindu cosmology divides the world into four ages or
yugas. The first or Golden Age, the Krita Yuga, was
1,728,000 years long. The second, the Treta Yuga, was
less righteous, and one-fourth darker and briefer, lasting
1,296,000 years. The third, the Dvāpara Yuga, still one-
fourth darker and briefer, was 864,000 years long. The
last is the present age, the Kali Yuga, darkest and brief-
est, which began in 3102 B.C. and is to endure for a total
of 432,000 years.

One version regards the total period of 4,320,000 years
as constituting a Mahā Yuga. The complete cycle ends
in a pralaya or an apparent destruction of the world,
which begins a night of Brahma. A thousand such ma-
hāyugas form a kalpa, which is the duration of a night
of Brahma. Another kalpa constitutes a day. A hundred

of these years of Brahma make up his "life." Then the gigantic cycle of 311,040,000,000,000 years starts all over.

Beside such figures, the four-score years of man's life pales into insignificance. Yet this metaphysical depreciation of time is not meant to suggest that man should live outside of it, which he cannot do physically. Rather he should always remember the reality of eternity. He should not fall into believing that there is nothing outside time. Yet time and eternity are really one.

The end of time does not occur in time; it is a term beyond. S. Radhakrishnan[1] advanced the view that

So long as there is the struggle, the process of becoming, the overcoming of nonbeing by being, we have the time process. But when all individuals have escaped from the alienation, from their slavery to the world, when all externality is overcome, there is awakening of the Spirit in them all. When the Kingdom of Spirit is established on earth as it is in heaven above, God the antecedent becomes the consequent. There is a coincidence of the beginning and the end. If it is held that the end will never be accomplished, that there will be perpetual singing and no completion in a song, that it is always a journeying without any journey's end, then the cosmic process will have no meaning. The truth about the earth is *brahmaloka,* the transfiguration of the cosmos, the revolutionary change in man's consciousness, a new relationship among them, an assimilation to God. It is the attainment of wholeness, the overcoming of disruption, the surmounting of all false antinomies, the transcending of time in eternity, which we objectify as *brahmaloka.*

The concept of *sakti* in the Tantric sacred texts is the projection of the "energy" of the male as the female. Male and God are the passive polar manifestations of a single transient principle, while the female and the Goddess are the active. In this manner, said Heinrich Zimmer,[2] "the male is identified with eternity, the female with time, and their embrace with the mystery of creation." Time and eternity are two aspects of the same. By abolishing opposites, the static and the fluid are viewed as a single entity. This can be imagined through the use of symbols and their opposites, such as a door through which a person cannot pass.[3]

The yogi attempts to resolve the problem of escape from time and of its union with cosmic Time through the exercise of *prānāyāma,* the rhythmization of breathing. By progressively decelerating the rhythm, he seeks to experience a time different from the ordinary. He attempts a direct apprehension of the *lived time.*[4]

Mircea Eliade[5] has written of the yogi's attempt to seek entrance into the cosmic Time by "unifying the two currents of psychic energy that circulate through . . . the two mystical veins *ida* and *pingala*." The two polar currents are concentrated and channeled into the *susumnā,* which is the third vein situated at the "center." The procedure "is equivalent to the unification of the sun and the moon—that is, the abolition of the cosmos, the reunion of contraries, which amounts to saying that the yogi transcends both the created universe and the time that governs it." In the words of the *Hathayoga-pradipikā, "Susumnā* devours 'Time.'"

The present moment, then, is all-important.[6] Mahāyāna writers point out that the semblance of unreality in the present is due to its receding into the past. But existence and nonexistence are not features of a thing but are the thing itself. The venerable Indian texts have said: "The nature of anything is its own momentary stasis and destruction." For the Buddha, who "transcends the eons," "there exists neither past nor future." Buddha himself expressed sorrow for those who fail to grasp the moment and allow it to slip by. He taught his disciples "not to lose the moment." In particular, one should respond to the illumination of the "favorable moment," which projects man into the eternal. This may be any moment —now.

9.
The Chinese conception of time as an undifferentiated pool
XX

Neither the circle nor the arrow fits the traditional Chinese model of time. Instead, it may be likened, in F.S.C. Northrop's words,[1] to a

placid, silent pool within which ripples come and go. . . . Out of it the differentiations come and back into it they go. Now it is precisely this coming into existence of the differentiations and their passage away again, to be replaced by new transitory qualities, that gives rise to the sequence of associated differentiations which is the sensed arrow of time. But the undifferentiated, all-embracing, indeterminate aesthetic continuum is not in this arrow-like temporal sequence; instead it embraces within itself this sequence and the coming and going of its associated sense data. Thus the undifferentiated aesthetic continuum is timeless. This is the reason why this component in the self, although a particular and not a logical universal with postulated immortal subsistence, is nonetheless immortal.

The mutuality between the undifferentiated aesthetic continuum and its concrete manifestations is illustrated by the Chinese attitude toward the family and its relations to time. An existent patriarchal family is regarded as the transponder between the past and the future generations. The eldest son is the reembodiment of the great grandfather. Time is transcended by this continuous reabsorption of past and future in the present. The meaning and cohesion of the family is intensified by the continual rebirth of the ancestral family through the ages.

William Haas[2] has described the place of the ancestral family thus:

Different as are the social family sphere and the metaphysical one of the Tao, the Chinese relation to time manifests itself equally in both. Just as the successive generations are revealed to the discerning mind of the sage as the recurring ancestral family, so the endless drama of the world with its pairs of opposites disappears before him and he perceives behind it the immovable reality of the Tao. This then is the way that the Chinese mind with infinite subtlety neutralizes the ghastly power of time. And it achieves it by the category of identity.

Time is always taken into account by being subsumed in everyday activities. The pervasiveness is exemplified by its consideration in the 3300-year-old book of prophecy, statecraft, and human behavior—the *I Ching*.[3,4] This venerable *Book of Changes* divides the life of man into sixty-four prototype situations. Time is implicit throughout, exerting varying influences upon the events.

In the situation entitled Youthful Folly, success is predicted for the young man because he is more in harmony with time than are the conservative policies and practices of those older and more experienced. His spontaneity and lack of premeditation keep him within the main stream of time. Even his own folly cannot obstruct the favorable outcome. Helmut Wilhelm[5] explains:

Here time is immediately experienced and perceived. It does not represent merely a principle of abstract progression but is fulfilled in each of its segments; an effective agent not only in which reality is enacted, but which in turn acts on reality and brings it to completion.

Just as space appears to the concrete mind not merely as a scheme of extension but as something filled with hills, lakes, and plains—in each of its parts open to different possibilities—so time is here taken as something filled, pregnant with possibilities, which vary with its different moments, and which, magically as it were, induce and confirm events. Time here is provided with attributes to which events stand in a relation of right or wrong, favorable or unfavorable.

Although concrete and formative time induces certain situations, it still "retains its inner cohesion amid unremitting change." From the situation entitled Grace: "This is the form of heaven. Having form, clear and still: this is the form of men. If the form of heaven is contemplated, the changes of time can be discovered. If the forms of men are contemplated, one can shape the world." From the situation entitled The Creative: "When he (the great man) acts in advance (in the *a priori,* theoretical sense) of heaven, heaven does not contradict him. When he follows heaven (in the *a posteriori* sense), he adapts himself to the time of heaven."

To be in tune with time is, therefore, all important. Yet there are certain conditions in which this can be most discouraging. In the situation entitled The Well, it is stated that "One does not drink the mud of the well. No one comes to an old well. . . . Time has rejected it." The individual is ignored by society. His services are unwanted.

But there is always hope. In the situation entitled Duration, it is stated: "The four seasons change and transform, and thus can forever bring to completion." Such is the cosmic time in the cycle of the *yin-yang.*

10. The cosmic liturgy of the Persians XXI

One of the most abstruse concepts of time is found in Mazdean cosmogony.[1] Here, Time is envisioned as a heavenly person, who projects time into the life of each earthly person in an image of itself with which it is to be reunited ultimately.[2]

A central feature of the Mazdean scheme is the dimension of light as an aspect of time, being inextricably interwoven with the personality of the primordial being. Terms such as "elevation of light" or "depth of darkness" are pervasive and important. These descriptions do not connote spatial extensions in the conventional sense; instead, the doctrine states that the space occupied by primordial Light is unique unto itself, measured in terms of light, and is not defined *a priori*. In Henry Corbin's words,[2] "The height or depth of light may be designated as eternal Time, and the space of light, in which awaken the creatures of light, who fulfill the thoughts of this light, is eternally born from this eternal Time."

The birth of time in the life of individuals on this earth, then, is not an absolute beginning but a derivation from the eternal Time. The earthly person, who "belongs to Ōhrmazd," is given a personified role with personal moments of initiation and conclusion, which are not, however, of the eternal Time of the depth of light. Personal existence is thus only a projected image which returns to its origin at death.

Since the person's time on earth is an image of the eternal Time, it possesses a dimension other than sheer chronology. The relative absence of this dimension of light indicates the degree of darkness of the individual. "Forming a bond between this being and an eternal Time to which the limited time of his actual form of existence carries him back, this archetypal dimension commands a very specific experience of eternity, or rather the anticipation which makes possible—or which translates— the conception of a cyclical time that is not the Time of an eternal return, but the time of return to an eternal origin."

In Mazdean ontology, there is a twofold state of being. *Menōk* is "a celestial, invisible, spiritual, but perfectly concrete state." *Gētīk* is "an earthly, visible, material state, but of a matter which is in itself wholly luminous, a matter immaterial in relation to the matter that we actually know." The change from the *menōk* to the present *gētīk* world *per se* does not mean a downfall, but a fulfillment. The darkness of the *gētīk* is due to the presence of the demons of evil in the material world. Ultimate redemption restores the *gētīk* to its archetypal dimensions.

The planes of being in the embodiment of time as a person are regarded in the context of an archetypal Person. In other words, "this time configures and pre-figures the form that a luminous being must take or regain—and because, as time of trial and of combat, it is the mediator of this metamorphosis. Thus is estab-lished a homology between the time of action of each personal being and the Time of the total cycle; between fulfilled personal being and the 'Person' of eternal Time."

The characteristics of this person of Time vary among the different schools. Zoroastrian Mazdaism subscribed to the dualistic description of the precosmic drama. Ōhrmazd, the God of Light, is attacked by Ahriman, the God of Evil. They are separate individuals. Zervanism, on the other hand, adopted the monistic belief. The struggle takes place within the same person of Zervān. He is the supreme godhead, eternal Time, out of whom arise both the principle of light and the antagonist.

In Mazdean mythohistory Ōhrmazd invokes the cycle of time as the decisive weapon in defeating Ahriman. The view of the future destruction of the demons is inflicted upon Ahriman, together with the coming of the Resurrection and the "Future Body." Whereupon "Ōhrmazd sings the *Ahuvar* stanza, the resounding incantation shatters the space intervening between them, and Ahriman falls prostrate to the bottom of Darkness, where he remains for three millennia. But . . . the celestial archetype of the sacred *Ahuvar* stanza is a personification of Ōhrmazd's Time and eternal Wisdom. Thus time is the mediator of Ahriman's defeat."

Time is thereby related to the cosmic liturgy of Ōhrmazd. The subdivisions of this liturgical time are in turn liturgical moments, created first in the *menōk* state. Each moment has its own celestial archetype. Each has a "height or depth in Light," the dimension of eternal Time.

11.
The Christian
conception of
linear time
XXII

Christian teachings stress the notion of a linear progression toward a final time. Predictions of the end of the world were a common pastime among the early believers. In the second century, a Syrian bishop led his entire congregation into the desert to meet the Lord.[1]

The epistle of Barnabas contains the passage: "The present sabbaths are not acceptable [saith the Lord] but that which I have made, in which I will give rest to all things and make the beginning of an eighth day, that is the beginning of another world." A greater significance may be ascribed to this pronouncement than mere distinction between the Jewish and the Christian sabbaths. The life of Jesus Christ had revealed a time scheme in which there exists a final time which is not open to us. Only God is there. There is no dimension in this final time. It begins, however, in the midst of historical time and is usually considered to involve a time of decline and despair before its advent. As G. van der Leeuw[2] has described the situation, "The final time was about to begin; the great despair was ready to set in. . . . the time had grown full; a new creative act of God was about to be fulfilled through Him. When nothing seemed to happen, He drew the consequences by seeking a sacrificial death and giving himself over to extreme despair. Then with His death and resurrection the new beginning is at hand, which He calls the kingdom of God." In so doing, Christ released the world from the clutches of Satan, just as Satan was overthrown in heaven.[3]

The time of primitive Christianity is thus the result of the continuous action of God.[4] It has a definite beginning at the creation of the world. It is directed toward a definite future unfolding in a progressive manner. Time is not reversible and its decisive feature is the life of Jesus Christ in the midpoint of this historical flow. The course of time continues from this event toward an end. "For in that [Christ] died, he died into sin once."[5] "The time is fulfilled and the Kingdom of God is at hand."[6] "There is a divine *ephapax,* a 'Once and for all,'" explains Gilles Quispel.[7] "In this historical unfolding the religious vision discovers the workings of an *oikonomia,* a divine plan of Salvation . . . And when man is placed in this *oikonomia,* he experiences his *kairos*—that is to say, a tension and a meaning enter into his inherently profane and aimless life 'time,' because it becomes related to the plan of Salvation and is thus in direct relation to God."

The expectations of Iranian and Jewish eschatology are fulfilled. The Kingdom of God is close at hand. "The blind receive their sight, and the lame walk, the lepers are cleansed, and the deaf hear, the dead are raised up, and the poor have the gospel preached to them."[8]

12.
Abstractions of
the Greeks
XXIII

Plato (427–347 B.C.) attempted to bridge the realms of becoming and being through the concept of time. He first distinguished "that which always is" from "that which has no beginning."[1] "That which is apprehended by intelligence and reason is always in the same state; but that which is conceived by opinion with the help of sensation and reason, is always in a process of becoming and perishing and never really is." To be created requires a cause of the creation. There was a choice of patterns for the artificer: "the pattern of the unchangeable, or of that which is created? If the world is indeed fair and the artificer good, it is manifest that he must have looked for that which is eternal." Because the creator was good, free from jealousy, and wanted everything to be as much like himself as it could be, he made this world in the likeness of the eternal gods.

When he saw the results, "he rejoiced and in his joy determined to make the copy still more like the original." This required rendering the universe as eternal as it could be. "Wherefore he resolved to have a moving image of eternity, and when he set in order the heaven, he made this image eternal but moving according to number, while eternity itself rests in unity; and this image we call time."

The creator first made the soul, followed by matter, and then something in-between. He then compounded all these together, divided the mass into parts in different ratios and derived series. By manipulating the system, he organized various spheres and orbits and assigned the sun, the moon, and the five planets to their proper motions. The previously random and chaotic movements became ordered and intelligible. With this, time was created. "For there were no days and nights and months and years before the heaven was created, but when he constructed the heaven he created them also." As the heavenly motions follow each other, numbers are generated and the sets of their relations constitute time. When the circle is completed and they return to the starting position, the state of greatest harmony and unity is attained.

Nature, however, is in the realm of becoming rather than being. It is erroneous to regard it as eternal, "for we say that it 'was,' or 'is,' or 'will be,' but the truth is that 'is' alone is properly attributed to it, and that 'was' and 'will be' are only to be spoken of becoming in time, for they are motions, but that which is immovably the same for ever cannot become older or younger by time."

Time and the heavens will also dissolve together, should there be a reason for it. The eternal pattern, however, will remain. "Such was the mind and thought of God in the creation of time. The sun and moon and five other stars, which are called the planets, were created by him in order to distinguish and preserve the numbers of time."

Plato thus differentiated the World of Ideas from the

World of Sense. The World of Ideas or Forms is unchanging, immovable, indivisible, without beginning. The World of Sense is subject to change, motion, division, and acts of creation.

The Forms are also eternal in the sense of being perfect and everlasting. A thing is beautiful because "the Form of beauty is present to it."[2] The human soul remembers the Forms even before birth. Frank Brabant[3] felt that

It is this recollection which proves it immortal, for in the *Phaedo* it is rather the nonbeginning than the nonending of the soul which is demonstrated. It is not that the soul *will* be immortal, but rather it *is* already immortal and cannot really be affected by what happens in this life. This is the true meaning of the doctrine that Vice is Ignorance: the inner principle of knowledge may be clouded but cannot really be contaminated by the tumult of bodily passions; if, therefore, a man really lives an evil life, it must be because the reasonable element is wanting or dormant.

Aristotle (384–322 B.C.) took cognizance of Plato's account of time as "the movement of the whole" and the Pythagorean description as "the sphere itself." He began his own analysis of time with a recitation of the difficulties which needed to be surmounted.[4] Since neither the past nor the future exists and "now" is just the knife-edge boundary of past and future, time could not logically exist. But Aristotle rejected the view that time belongs to things that do not exist. The "now" is not considered as a part of Time and "Time is not held to be made up of 'nows.'"

He was not as certain regarding the constancy of the "now":

If it is always different and different, and if none of the *parts* in time which are other and other are simultaneous . . . and if the "now" which is not, but formerly was, must have ceased-to-be at some time, the "nows" too cannot be simultaneous with one another, but the prior "now" must always have ceased-to-be in itself (since it then existed); yet it cannot have ceased-to-be in another "now," for we may lay it down that one "now" cannot be next to another any more than point to point. If then it did not cease-to-be in the next "now" but in another it would exist simultaneously with the innumerable "nows" between the two—which is impossible.

Yet he could not see how the "now" can always remain the same.

No determinate divisible thing has a single termination, whether it is continuously extended in one or in more than one dimension: but the "now" is a termination, and it is possible to cut off a determinate time. Further, if coincidence in time (i.e., being neither prior nor posterior) means to be "in one and the same 'now,'" then, if both what is before and what is after are in this same "now," things which happened ten thousand years ago would be simultaneous with what has happened today, and nothing would be before or after anything else.

Aristotle associated time with motion. In some of his writings he gave the impression that he viewed time as a prerequisite of motion. There were also suggestions of time as a consequence of motion,[5] but, in any case, time was not regarded as synonymous with motion.

Two arguments were presented in support. "Now the change or movement of each thing is only *in* the thing which changes or *where* the thing itself which moves or changes may chance to be. But time is present equally everywhere and with all things." Furthermore, "change is always faster or slower, whereas time is not: for 'fast' and 'slow' are defined by time—'fast' is what moves much in a short time, 'slow' what moves little in a long time." But since time is not movement, it must then belong to movement.[4]

Both time and movement were considered by Aristotle as being continuous. "What is moved is moved from something to something, and all magnitude is continuous. Therefore the movement goes with the magnitude. Because the magnitude is continuous, the movement too must be continuous, and if the movement, then the time; for the time that has passed is always thought to be in proportion to the movement."

Time is grasped only when motion is marked with a before and an after. Motion too occurs over different parts of the spatial magnitude it traverses in succession; one part of the path is the before and another the after. "Time is the numerable aspect of movement in respect to the before and after."

The question then arises as to whether there are many times because of the many motions or only one universal time for all motions. Aristotle believed that "there is the same time everywhere at once, but not the same time before and after, for while the present change is one, the change which has happened and that which will happen are different." His rationale follows somewhat along these lines: If a given moment in one motion would correspond to a certain moment in another motion, then all moments before the former would also occur before the latter. Similarly, all moments coming after one of the corresponding pair of moments would also come after the other. In this way there is only one universal order of before and after.

He was impressed with the uniformity, periodicity, and endlessness of motion of the celestial bodies. He, therefore, adopted the motions of the celestial bodies as the natural as well as the practical standard for the measure of motion. Their circular movement, without beginning or end, was considered the perfect movement. "If, then, what is first is the measure of everything homogeneous with it, regular motion is above all else the measure, because the number of this is the best known. Now neither alteration nor increase nor coming into being can be regular, but locomotion can be. This is always why time is thought to be the movement of the sphere, viz. because the other movements are measured by this, and time by this movement."

Could time exist were there no soul to count it? Aristotle thought not, "for if there cannot be someone to count there cannot be anything that can be counted, so that evidently there cannot be number; for number is either what has been, or what can be, counted. But if nothing but soul, or soul reason, is qualified to count, there would not be time unless there were soul, but only that of which time is an attribute, i.e., if *movement* can exist without soul, and the before and the after are attributes of movement, and time is these *qua* numerable."

Motion is ultimately generated by an unmoved Mover, which is the final cause of all motion and therefore the primal source of time. Time is thus traced back to the first heaven. Beyond this, there is no time.

13.
Early disputations among meta-physicians
XXIV

Plotinus (204–269) attempted to find something substantial for his definition of time. Looking for a vital activity, he derived time from the Soul.[1] Time was envisioned as originating in the differentiation of life. It is generated as the Soul moves from one experience to another. It disappears when the Soul withdraws "into its primal unity. . . . the activity is Time, the universe is a content of Time."[2]

He related his three hypostases of soul, intellect, and the One to each other and derived time in the process. As John F. Callahan[3] noted,

"Life" also offers a convenient means of relating soul to the prior hypostasis, intellect. Since motion is in time, time is prior, because for Plotinus everything "exists in" something that is prior to itself, and ultimately all things exist in the One. Since the universe proceeds from the soul, it seems reasonable to him to make time the life of the soul insofar as soul is productive of the universe, an effect lower than itself. "Life" therefore, is an effective term from Plotinus' point of view, since it explains how soul is an intermediary between the motion of the universe and the intellect, which is the life of thought. The latter is on the same level as eternity and time.

The concept of the Soul was also invoked to describe the measure of rest, the unit of time, and the unity of time. The measurement of rest is based on the thesis that the Soul has made both time and the universe and that the universe, which was placed by the Soul into time, moves only in that time and belongs to the Soul. Therefore, should the sensible universe ever stop in its movement, the length of the rest can be measured because the Soul can continue to act. Otherwise there would be no world.

The Soul produced day and night, which gave the number two. From one and two come all the numbers which make measurements possible. Hence the diurnal motion of the sun is taken as the unit of time.

With respect to unifying the many separate ideas of time in the minds of individuals, Plotinus dispersed the unity of time as the life of the Soul into the individual minds. "Is time then in us also? It is in every such soul and is similarly in all, and all souls are one. Therefore time cannot be broken apart, anymore than eternity can, though contained in all the eternal beings."[4]

Plotinus' position, however, is not free from difficulties. Gordon Clark[5] mentioned that "in particular the life of the Soul and the unchanging life of eternity can both be called life only homonymously. Aristotle's illustration of homonyms, a man and his portrait, allowed for imitation. . . . but Plotinus points out no such similarities between eternity and time—it is all difference. . . . for if time is in no clear sense an image of eternity, then the more basic similarity of this world to the higher world also is devoid of meaning."

To understand Plotinus completely, we need to appreciate his thesis of the world as a series of emanations from the One. The first of these is the timeless and spaceless Intelligence. Out of it comes the Soul, which in turn produces the material world. Conversely, there is an ascent to union with the One. He asserted[1] that

since in the vision there were not two things, but seer and seen were one, if a man could preserve the memory of what he was when he was mingled with the Divine, he would have in himself an image of Him. For he was then one with Him, and retained no difference, either in relation to himself or to others. Nothing stirred within him, neither anger nor concupiscence nor even reason or spiritual perception or his own personality, if we may say so. Caught up in an ecstasy, tranquil and God possessed, he enjoyed an imperturbable calm; shut up in his proper essence he inclined not to either side, he turned not even to himself; he was in a state of perfect stability; he had become stability itself. The soul then occupies itself no more even with beautiful things; it is exalted above the Beautiful, it passes the choir of the virtues.

Augustine (354–430) formulated one of the most fully argued of the early theories on time.[6] *Genesis* was his explicit guide, and faith his point of departure.

As to what God was doing *before* the heavens and the world, Augustine stated that God was doing nothing. Had He done anything the resulting thing would have been created. Obviously He could not have made anything before He created anything. Time did not exist before God created the universe. It came into existence when the world was created *ex nihilo* by God. But God Himself is timeless. He is exempt from any relation to time.

Actually, Augustine's thesis that God made time when He made the world should not be taken in a chronological sense. It is more appropriate to think of it in the logical sense of God being temporally prior to the world as a consequence of His power. Furthermore God does not create in increments as time progresses. Augustine[7] contended that "He does not will, now this, now that. But in one all-embracing, consistent act, He wills all the things which He wills. He does not will bit by bit, again and again, now these things now those. He does not will later on what before He did not will and He does not refrain from willing what He formerly willed. For a will of that sort is a changing one and no changing thing is eternal. But our God is eternal."

It was not chance that determined the particular time and place of creation. "And as it does not follow that God set the world in this very spot it occupies and no other by accident rather than by divine reason, although no human reason can comprehend why it was so set, though there was not merit in the spot chosen to give it the precedence of infinite others, so neither does it follow that we should suppose that God was guided by chance when He created the world in that and no earlier time."[8]

As to the difference between time and eternity, Augustine stated that, since

time does not exist without some movement and transition, while in eternity there is no change, who does not now see that there could have been no time had some creature been made which by some motion could give birth to change . . . Since then, God, in whose eternity is no change at all, is the Creator and Ordainer of time, I do not see how He can be said to have created the world after spaces of time had elapsed, unless it be said that prior to the world there was some creature by whose movement time could pass. And if the sacred and infallible Scriptures say that in the beginning God created the heavens and the earth, in order that He may be understood that He had made nothing previously,—for if He had made anything before the rest, this thing would rather be said to have been made "in the beginning"— then assuredly the world was made, not in time, but simultaneously with time.

The reality of the present, past, and future posed special problems. Neither the past nor the future exists; yet we talk about past periods being long or short—a quality which can hardly be applied to a nonexistent thing. Does this mean that the past is long after it has become past or when it was present? Yet the present is only a split moment which cannot be long; it has no duration. "Let us not, therefore, say 'Time past hath been long,' for we shall not find what may have been long, seeing that since it was past it is not; but let us say 'that present time was long, because when it was present it was long,' for it has not as yet passed away so as not to be, and therefore there was that which could be long. But after it passed, that ceased also to be long which ceased to be."[7] But "the present hath no space. Where, therefore, is the time which we may call long? Is it future? Indeed we do not say, 'It is long,' because it is not yet, so as to be long; but we say, 'It will be long.'"

Yet we do compare intervals of time, as well as the past with the future. How can this be done if they are nonexistent? The only way out of this dilemma is to say that the past and the future must exist somehow. Past and future can be thought of as present in the soul as memory and expectation. There is a present of things past as memory, a present of things present as sight, and a present of things future as expectation. These are not three times but one time in three modes in the mind.

With the past and future nonexistent in reality but present as memory and expectation, respectively, and with the present without duration, how can we measure time? Augustine's solution to the measurement riddle is not comparison of the events themselves but of their images in memory. "In thee, my soul, I measure my times." By distending my memory toward what I have said and my attention toward what I am going to say, my consciousness will be able to compare the lengths of two syllables.

The definition of time in terms of memory and expectation itself involves terms with temporal connotations. Augustine attempted to avoid the circularity by resorting to a metaphorical distention of the soul. The soul uses time because it is placed in a context of change. It distends itself by means of memory into the past and expectation into the future. "I am divided up in time, whose order I do not know, and my thoughts are torn with every kind of tumult."

The soul should strive to rise above this dispersion in temporal existence into a higher status of contemplation of God through divine grace. In this way, according to Augustine, man participates in the creative time of God through an *intentio* toward eternity.[3]

ibn-Hazm (994–1064) divided time into portions with different names, such as 'awaat, 'ahyan, and 'azman. Whether or not these are further divisible is not clear. In any case, they are central to his idea of creation.[9]

His interpretation was in line with the muslim view that time is not a continuous duration but a galaxy of instants, which depicts the order of Allah. Each instant is given existence perpetually at every appearance by Allah. This concept permeates the life of the devout muslim in profound ways. In following the Koran, in the words of Louis Massignon,[10] he "apprehends the divine causality only in its actual 'efficacy.' There exists only the instant, *hīn, an,* the 'twinkling of an eye,' the laconic announcement of a judicial decision of God, conferring on our nascent act His decree, which will be claimed on the day when the cry of Justice is heard." The temporal reference for important legal as well as religious observances is the instant of appearance of the new moon, *ghurrat al-hilāl.* The determination of this instant must be made by two "witnesses of the instant."

After many imperfect instants of delay, including catastrophic days of forewarning, the devout followers await with sacred awe the advent of the perfect instant. This is the hour of the Last Judgment and the "witness of the instant" is the Divine Judge.

Benedict Spinoza (1632–1677) looked upon time as unreal, and its division into past, present, and future as illusory. The conventional tenses and predicates are merely aids to imagination. They are nonexistent in the language of the highest levels of knowledge.

The wise man senses things from this highest level of knowledge in so far as this is possible within human bounds. Nature is witnessed *sub specie aeternitatis.* It is not a temporal sequence. The order of Nature is a timeless logical necessity. All things are in God and His modifications and there is only one self-dependent being, called Nature or Substance. The parts, or modes as designated by Spinoza, are assigned independence only by our imagination. The finite and with it the notion of quantity results from negating the infinite.[11]

To the extent that one's mind reflects the timeless sequence of modifications, it becomes part of the infinite God. It sees the world as God sees it. It is eternal. Disasters in our own time are regarded with no greater concern than disasters of the distant past. All events are equally parts of the same timeless eternity of God, where chronology is but logic. Hope is a misapprehension of the future—an illusion, which characterizes the lack of wisdom.

To understand, even approximately, Spinoza's concept of time, one needs to appreciate his idea of the mind. To him, the mind is not the conventionally understood entity. As amplified by Stuart Hampshire,[12] it is

a particular set of modifications of Nature conceived as extension, these latter constituting what is called my body; there is no persisting thing or quasi-substance, "the mind," which is distinguishable from the ideas of the modifications of my body. The possible eternity of the human mind cannot therefore be intended by Spinoza to mean that I literally survive, as a distinguishable individual, in so far as I attain genuine knowledge; for in so far as I do attain genuine knowledge, my individuality disappears, and my mind becomes so far united with God or Nature conceived under the attribute of thought.

Spinoza defined duration as "the attribute under which we conceive the existence of created things, in so far as they persevere in their own actuality."[13] An important connotation is associated with the word "actuality." By this usage he intended to emphasize existence and not motion. It conveys a linkage of duration with existence. Fictitious things have no duration. "Duration is an affection of existence, not of the essence of things."

The word "created" does not mean being brought into existence ex *nihilo*. Rather things of duration possess existence by virtue of a cause, regardless of the presence of a beginning. The crucial point is that their existence is not intrinsic to their nature but is caused by some other influence. The term "attribute of existence" is a subjective aspect of the thing in a technical sense. "Duration is distinguished from the whole existence of a thing only by reason. For, however much you take away from anything, so much of its existence you detract from it."

Two features were thereby ascribed to duration. The first is the possibility of its existence, which depends upon God's creative act. The second is its indefiniteness, unlimitedness, and undeterminedness. The former differentiates duration from eternity and the latter from time.[14]

Time itself was assumed to be partly real and partly ideal. It "is not an affection of things but only a mode of thought or . . . a being of reason; it is a mode of thought serving to explain duration."[13] It can be determined by comparison "with the duration of those things which have a fixed and determinate motion, and this comparison is called time."[15] Time is related to motion. "No one doubts, too, that we imagine time because we imagine some bodies to move with a velocity less, or greater than, or equal to that of others."

Neither is an unequivocal concept of survival-after-physical-death associated with immortality nor is a temporal implication of any kind applied to infinity or eternity. It is as inappropriate to say that there was a time when the three angles of a triangle became equal to two right angles as it is to say that God began at a certain time. To raise questions about the duration of God or Nature requires the existence of something external to God or Nature. But this would be meaningless since God or Nature really is "the sum and substance of all that is." External causes can be assumed only for created things, for which time-determinations can be related.

Spinoza's time is an expression of his mysticism.

14.
Continuing
disputations
XXV

During the last three centuries, the metaphysical theories of time have become far more diversified and imaginative. Consensus, however, is still absent.

Immanuel Kant (1724–1804) suggested that what appears to us in perception is a result of two inputs. One is the sensations, which are caused by things-in-themselves, and which belong to the external things. The other is called the *form* of the phenomenon, which is due to our own perceptive apparatus. One of the pure forms of sensibility, or pure intuition, is time. These are *a priori* and not determined by experience.

In Kant's own expression,[1] "Time is not an empirical concept deduced from any experience, for neither coexistence nor succession would enter into our perception, if the representation of time were not given *a priori*. Only when the representation *a priori* is given, can we imagine that certain things happen at the same time (simultaneously) or at different times (successively)." Our intuition rests on this representation.

Although phenomena can be taken out of time, time cannot be taken away from phenomena in general. "In time alone is reality out of phenomena possible. All phenomena may vanish, but time itself (as the general condition of their possibility) cannot be done away with." This *a priori* necessity was also taken as the basis for "the possibility of apodictic principles of the relations of time, or of axioms of time in general. Time has one dimension only; different times are not simultaneous, but successive, while different spaces are never successive, but simultaneous. Such principles cannot be derived from experience because experience could not impart to them absolute universality nor apodictic certainty."

There is only one time, as a pure form of sensuous intuition.

To say that time is infinite means no more than that every definite quantity of time is possible only by limitations of one time which forms the foundations of all times. The original representation of time must therefore be given as unlimited. But when the parts themselves and every quantity of an object can be represented as determined by limitation only, the whole representation cannot be given by concepts (for in that case the partial representation comes first), but must be founded on immediate intuition.

Kant's accounts have not been the easiest to follow.[2] He said that time is empirically real but transcendentally ideal. Yet he also maintained that material objects are ideal, as apprehended, and different from what they are in themselves. He had hoped that the concept of the "transcendental reality" of time would reconcile the fact that we experience time ordered in a real sense yet not as real a sense as material objects.[3]

As far as succession is concerned, Kant insisted that we make the necessary inference because of the existence of an objective series of time-order. Without this there can be no consciousness of time-series. Objectivity is attributed by Kant to that which is unaffected by what we do. But John Gunn[4] objected to this line of reasoning: "Kant's criterion of objective sequence is inadequate. It needs to be checked by other considerations, for, if an observer stood near a gun, then whatever he did the flash would invariably precede the roar, but if he acted on Kant's criterion he would assume that the flash objectively preceded the roar, and this would be incorrect."

Kant was also equivocal in his treatment of simultaneity as a mode of time. He implied that the three modes of time, which are duration, succession, and coexistence, can be separately intuited. The transition from his starting point of succession of sensations to objective simultaneity was rather difficult. At times, circularity of reasoning surreptitiously crept into the text. The principle of causality was invoked to determine time-order, when the sequence of events had actually been used to establish the principle of causality.

The inconsistency of Kant's overall thrust was accented by A. C. Ewing[5] as follows:

It is one thing to say that statements about physical things relate only to appearances, and another to say that all temporal statements do so. For what is meant by saying that something is merely an appearance? It is not to deny its existence altogether—otherwise we could not make any true affirmative statements about experiences—but to say that it exists only for our experience. Therefore to say that the self we perceive in time in introspection is an appearance is to say that we experience it in time, though it does not really exist in time, but if we can even experience it in time, something temporal is real, namely our experience. We cannot rid ourselves of anything by calling it an appearance; if it is anything at all, even only an experience, it as such still falls within the real. Experience is as real as the physical objects of the realist, if a different kind of real thing. I therefore think Kant's position an untenable compromise.

William James (1842–1910) focused on the psychological aspects of time.

As far as the relationship between consciousness and time is concerned, James[6] noted that our consciousness always seems interrupted in everyday experiences. This raises the question: "*Are we ever wholly unconscious?* . . . Sleep, fainting, coma, epilepsy and other unconscious conditions are apt to break in upon and occupy large durations of what we nevertheless consider the mental history of a single man. And the fact of interruption being freely admitted, is it not possible that it may exist where we do not suspect it, and even perhaps in an incessant and fine-grained form?" We awake from the unconsciousness of an operation under ether without remembering there has been a gap in consciousness. Although we have lived through a stretch of time, we have not *felt* it. "The question is how often does this happen? Is consciousness really discontinuous, incessantly interrupted and recommencing (from a psychologist's point of view)? And does it only seem continuous to itself by an illusion analogous to that of the Zoetrope? Or is it at most times as continuous outwardly as it inwardly seems?"

No satisfying answers seem to be forthcoming. James believed in "the existence of a highly developed consciousness in places where it has hitherto not been suspected at all." He supported his hypothesis by drawing on classical sources, as well as observations on hysterical and hypnotized subjects.

Many observations on the display of intellectual activity during somnambulism have been recorded. The actions are usually forgotten upon awakening. Nevertheless, James felt that the mental activity is real, as indicated by the fact that hypnotized somnambulists who are instructed to remember the interim events upon awakening will do so. People who are roused from the middle of a dream often recall the contents for a short while, although they may be lost thereafter. Furthermore, we frequently entertain thoughts while awake, only to forget them forever after that. Asleep or awake, we remain insensitive to habitual noises around us. "The mere *sense impressions* are the same when the sleep is deep as when it is light; the difference must lie in a *judgment* on the part of the apparently slumbering mind that they are worth noticing."

If our consciousness is made up of separate sensations and images, we would be hard put to acquire experience. James therefore insisted that "our consciousness never shrinks to the dimensions of a glow-worm spark. *The knowledge of some other part of the stream, past or future, is always mixed with our knowledge of the present thing.*" Attention on *A, B, C, D, E, F,* is succeeded by *B, C, D, E, F, G,* then by *C, D, E, F, G, H,* and other sliding arrays, *ad infinitum.* In this way new objects enter the scene as old ones linger on and finally go off the stage of the "specious present."

The span of the specious present was regarded to vary from a few seconds to usually not more than a minute, depending upon the activities and conditions under experience. This duration, containing an earlier perceived part as well as a later, is regarded as the original intuition of time. The feeling of past time is thus a feeling in the present. "What is past, to be known as past, must be known with what is present, and *during* the 'present' spot of time."

This intuition of duration in the specious present is not to be confused with memory. "Please observe that the reproduction of an event *after* it has once completely dropped out of the rearward end of the specious present, is an entirely different psychic fact from its direct perception in the specious present as a thing immediately past. A creature might be entirely devoid of *reproductive* memory, and yet have the time sense; but the latter would be limited, in his case, to the few seconds immediately passing by."

James' theory was challenged by Herbert Nichols,[7] who particularly disliked the idea of time-sense as a separate feeling.

But do we have any such extra feelings? How could any such feeling be other than just another feeling as separate as all the rest? How could it join these overlapped feelings any more than they could join themselves—or than merely successive feelings could join themselves? Who is it that sits in the saddle-back and look both ways? How does this Jack-in-the-saddle *know* which way to look; *which way* the overlapping feelings are overlapped? *which way they are moving? How does this feeling know or constitute anything regarding time direction, more or other than the passing sequence constitutes of itself?*

F. H. Bradley (1846–1924) argued that time is unreal.[8] He was pessimistic particularly over the possibility of finding any solution to the problem of "the qualitative content—which is not merely temporal, and apart from which the terms related in time would have no character . . . How to combine this in unity with the time which it fills, and again how to establish each aspect apart, are both beyond our resources. And time, so far, like space, has turned out to be appearance."

Yet time is not to be considered under a spatial form. If it is regarded as a durationless relation between units then there is no time. But if the entire time is accorded duration, then the units themselves would have duration and there would be no units. He felt that

Time in fact is "before" and "after" in one; and without this diversity it is not time. But these differences cannot be asserted of the unity; and on the other hand and failing that, time is helplessly dissolved. Hence they are asserted under a relation. "Before in relation to after" is the character of time; and here the old difficulties about relation and quality recommence. The relation is not a unity, and yet the terms are nonentities, if left apart. Again, to impart an independent character into the terms is to make each somehow in itself both before and after. But this brings on a process which dissipates the terms into relations, which, in the end, ends in nothing. And to make the relation of time an unit is, first of all, to make it stationary, by destroying within it the diversity of before and after. And, in the second place, this solid unit, existing only by virtue of external relations, is forced to expand. It perishes in ceaseless oscillations, between an empty solidity and a transition beyond itself toward illusory completeness.

He contended that time must be presented as time present, as "now." To account for the temporal continuum of nows necessitates a character of diversity. Time cannot be simple and indivisible, since there must be before and after, as well as diverse aspects. Instead of the aspects being past, present, and future, he preferred to regard the future as a construct which is not presented. Time is the present turning into past. Some process is taking place within the now.

But complications arise at this point:

For any process admitted destroys the "now" from with-. in. Before and after are diverse and their incompatibility compels us to use a relation between them. Then at once the old wearisome game is played again. The aspects become parts, the "now" consists of "nows," and in the end these "nows" prove undiscoverable. For as a solid part of time, the "now" does not exist. Pieces of duration may to us appear not to be composite; but a very little reflection lays bare their inherent fraudulence. If they are not duration, they do not contain an after and before, and they have, by themselves, no beginning or end, and are themselves outside of time. But, if so, time becomes merely the relation between them; and duration is a number of relations of the timeless, themselves also, I suppose, related somehow so as to make one duration. But how a relation is to be a unity, of which these differences are predictable, we have seen is incomprehensible. And if it fails to be a unity, time is herewith dissolved. But why should I weary the reader by developing in detail the impossible consequences of either alternative?

The real, which is perceived, is not to be identified with momentary appearance. The assumption that the real is that which is confined to the here and now would banish synthetic judgments extending beyond the instant. The now is bare position and reality is not present in the sense of an atomic unit. The real is something one encounters directly and the perception is here and now only if he comes in immediate contact with it.[9] The here and now, in which the real appears,

are not simply discrete and resting moments. They are any portion of that continuous content with which we come into direct relation. Examination shows that not only at their edges they dissolve themselves over into there and then, but then, even within their limits as first given, they know no repose. Within the here is both here and there; and in the ceaseless process of change in time you may narrow your scrutiny to the smallest focus, but you will find no rest. The appearance is always a process of disappearing, and the duration of the process which we call our present has no fixed length.

Space and time are not regarded as "principles of individuation." The so-called events are not considered to be real particulars. Getting down to particulars, "the question arises, what space and time do we really mean, and how can we express it so as not to express what is as much, something else?" Even if uniqueness is established within a given series of events, this does not mean that there may not be other series which may be internally indistinguishable from the former.

It is idle to say "this," for "this" does not exclude except in *this* sphere, and it is idle to say "my," for it is only in *my* element that yours and mine collide. Outside it they are indifferent, and the expression "my" will not distinguish one world from the other. If we simply attend to the series itself (as we have it before us), and, declining to look outside, confine ourselves to the consideration of its character, then all that it contains might be the common property of innumerable subjects, existing and enjoyed in the world of each, a general possession appropriated by none. The mere quality of appearance in space or time can not give singularity.

Bradley therefore concluded that time is mere appearance. But time does exist and he goes to some length to show that the appearance of time is not incompatible with the concept of the Absolute, and that "by its inconsistency time directs us beyond itself. It points to something higher in which it is included and transcended."[8]

Yet Bradley's mere appearances are not those of Kant. *Josiah Royce* (1855–1916) was of the opinion that facts as such are not the fruitful elements of knowledge.[10] To be useful, facts must be augmented by some relation so that an interpretation is possible. The given must point beyond itself. His concept of time was based on this foundation.

Several features were ascribed to time.[11] First, there is a variation, whether it be of sensations, emotions, or ideas. Second, the variation is presented in a definite order, so that succession and irreversibility are corollaries. Third, the entire succession is presented at the same time to our consciousness. Except for such a capacity for "mastering a succession, and of considering at once its constituent events, which are serially given and exclusive of one another we could know nothing of the existence of succession and there would be no problem of time." All of our experience is colored by no-longer and not-yet.

There is a practical value involved in temporal determinations. "Time to every mind is an essentially practical aspect of reality which derives its whole meaning from the nature and from the life of the will."[12]

An implied relationship links time and eternity. Goals are attained in time. The objective is not only that toward which the finite is striving, but also a totality. One's internal meanings are fulfilled through union with this totality. A degree of communication must occur within this totality, however, before the full truth can be ascertained. "Our finite life has its inner aspect in so far as it is just individual, the truth of our moments as such, the breaking of just our waves of consciousness on the beach. But our finite consciousness relates to outer and physical truth in so far as it *means* something that may be present for any and all intelligent moments and individuals."[13]

The generation of an idea through time is not a simple process. This is amplified by Gabriel Marcel[14] with an example from music:

The realization of a desired goal involves more than any future moment taken in itself, could ever provide. In the same way that a musical composition *exists* in every bar, not only in its final chord, ideas win their final expression of their concrete being, through their process of actualization. In other words, an idea cannot be conceived as a mere result, all by itself, if not in fact, then at least in respect to the development which produces it. For this development is an integral part of the idea. To distinguish between the idea and its development would be to mislead ourselves by the most vicious of abstractions.

The fact that the total melody is present as an indivisible unity does not prevent the awareness of the notes in succession. Becoming is felt both as a totality and a successive order. Distinction of past, present, and future is maintained in an eternal knowledge, which is not above time.

Marcel identified serious difficulties in Royce's relation of time and eternity. The latter had admitted an infinity of possible kinds of consciousness with different spans of apperception. Each of these grasps situations successively. Yet he also postulated a timeless consciousness which transcends all of our successive moments of awareness and understands them as a *totum simul*. It is difficult to see how such an omniscient consciousness can become involved in the experience of the limited consciousness without controlling it, yet remain completely aware of the future as well.

Bernard Bosanquet[15] expanded the argument against Royce's doctrine of the Absolute as a complete experience within which finite experience is contained and transformed. He cited the case of a man saddened because he thought he had insulted and hurt a good friend only to find out several days later, with great relief, that he had not done so. The higher consciousness, which senses everything at once, would have the early feelings tempered by knowledge of the subsequent outcome. Hence the higher consciousness can never actually share the same experience of the lower. Can the higher consciousness actually be an Absolute if its participation is limited?

Samuel Alexander (1859–1938) looked upon the issue of the nature of space and time and their relationship as fundamental to all of the vital problems of philosophy.[16] At the outset, he was faced with two alternatives: Either spatial and temporal characteristics are properties of sensible things or they delineate relations of coexistence and succession, respectively, among them. He staked out three principal premises.[17] The first is that space and time are not relations but the very stuff of events and things. The second is that we are dealing with one and the same space and time whether in physics, psychology, or mathematics. The third is that time and space are inextricably bound together but not in the four-dimensional manner envisioned by Minkowski, which is touched upon in Commentary 24 on Einstein's relativity.

Alexander considered succession from the past to the future as not physical but psychical time. But the present is regarded as "a moment of physical Time fixed by relation to an observing mind in the boundary or section or cut between earlier and later, which may be called past and future." In this manner physical time can be considered a succession from earlier to later. Yet successiveness alone does not provide for continuity. Space was invoked as the form of being to sustain the togetherness of earlier and later. Furthermore, a nonsuccessive continuum is essential to provide continuity to the successive. "There must be some form of existence, some entity not itself spatial which distinguishes and separates the parts of Space. This other form of existence is Time. . . . Thus Space and Time depend on each other but for different reasons."

What is ordinarily known as motion is "the occupation by that body of points which successively become present, so that at each stage the points traversed have different time values when the line of motion is taken as a whole. Thus Space-Time is a system of motions." The components of space-time are point-instants. "Space itself has no movement. The corresponding proposition is that Time as it moves from past through present to future (from earlier to later) is the occupation of a stretch of Space." Space-time is thus a combination of the static and the dynamic. If we consider that the advance in time results in "an infinite spatial present sweeping forward in Time," then space would be defined "as the assemblage of events at one moment."

A perspective of the heavens at any given moment involves the different stars appearing at the present of the observer as they were at different times earlier, inasmuch as it takes light varying times to travel the many distances concerned. Hence it is "filled with times of various dates." Also "having regard to the differing dates of its points with reference to the centre, which is the present of that perspective, we may say that Space at any moment is full of memory and expectation." Accordingly, the perspectives of space-time differ depending upon the point-instant. "Points which were simultaneous in the one may be successive in the other; the interval of time or space and even two points may reverse their dates in the different perspective."

The synthesis of all perspectives provides space-time. Each perspective constitutes a historical phase which is seen from one center of reference. However, in considering total space-time, "any point of Space is occupied, not as in the single time-perspective by some one moment of Time but by the whole of Time. The whole of Time in the totality of such perspective streams through each point of Space . . . in total Space-Time each point is in fact repeated through the whole of Time and each instant over the whole of Space." But Alexander's space-time is a vision of neither eternity nor an eternal present. His time retains both the successive order and infinity. It is not the *totum simul* of theology but an infinite historical series. "The physical universe is thus, through and through historical, the scene of motion."

All empirical point-instants and objects are made up of the "one-stuff of Space-Time." The stuff for space-time, however, should not be confused with the common-sense meaning of the term material. The former is anterior to materiality. Material existence is but one of its outgrowths, although continuous with it. There is no independent substance occupying the point-instant conceived as a vacuum.

The question arises as to whether or not mental acts belong together in space and time and whether or not the mind is together with its objects. Alexander attempted to clarify the distinctions.

By mental or psychological time I mean the time in which the mind experiences itself as living, the time it enjoys; by mental space I mean, assuming it to exist, the space in which the mind experiences itself as living or which it enjoys. They are contrasted provisionally with the space and time of the objects of mind which the mind contemplates. I hope to show on the strength of experience that mental space and time possess the same characters and are related in the same intimacy of relation as physical Space and Time; that the time of mental events is spatial and their space temporal precisely as with physical Space and Time, and further that mental time . . . is a piece of the Time in which physical events occur.

Alexander invited the agreement of his readers to his view that the mind is "the experienced continuum of mental acts." Events occurring to the normal mind are not disconnected from each other. They constitute a time-series and

in that sense [are] in time or [have] Time in [their] very constitution. . . . It is only when philosophy steps in with its hasty interpretations that we can say that Time belongs, as Kant believed, to external events because they have a mental or internal side in an experiencing of them. . . . to be aware of the date or duration of physical events is the most glaring instance, derived from direct experience of how an enjoyed existent, and a contemplated existent can be compresent with one another. In that case the compresence is a time-relation which unites both terms within the one Time.

The proposition that the mind is in space is more difficult to demonstrate. Granting that the mind is in space and time, then the place of a mental process may be taken as identical to that of its brain process. An exceedingly difficult related question is whether or not their times are identical. Suppose we are enjoying the sight of a color and remembering a friend's conversation. Is the latter a present enjoyment?

We are forced, therefore, to ask ourselves whether the time of a mental enjoyment is always that of its underlying neural process, or in other words whether a remembered enjoyment is not itself a past enjoyment, not a present one. We shall find, strange as the statement may seem, that this is the truth. But the inquiry cannot be an easy nor a short one.

His analysis begins with the memory of objects.

The pastness of the object is a datum of experience, directly apprehended. The object is compresent with me *as past.* The act of remembering is the process whereby this object becomes attached to or appropriated by myself. . . . The past object is earlier than my present act of mind in remembering, or my equivalent bodily state, whichever may happen to be more predominant in my mind. When the past object is thus appropriated by myself, I am aware of it as belonging to me. . . . as occuring in *my* past. . . . The object is then not only past life but belongs to a past in which I contemplate myself (that is my body) as having been existent also and related to the object.

A single memory by itself, is not complete. The particulars are only parts, which need to be made coherent and continuous with other memories or expectations. Remembering and expecting

do occur at the present moment; but we are not entitled, therefore, to declare their objects simultaneous with the present. To be apprehended as a memory in the act of remembering simultaneously with an act of present perception is not to be apprehended as simultaneous with the "present" object. The simple deliverance of experience is that it is apprehended as past. The notion that it must be simultaneous with the present in order to be referred to the past is thus the intrusion of a theory into actual experience.

Not only are all empirical existents configurations of Space-Time, they are also emergents according to a hierarchical scheme. New qualities arise at certain point-instants and are added to the previous existent. Beginning with the fundamental level of Space-Time, successively higher echelons are exemplified by atoms, complex molecules, life, mind, and deity. For each new level, a specific quality is added. Within the hierarchy of qualities, each

quality performs to its equivalent lower existence the office which mind performs to its neural basis. Mind and body do but exemplify, therefore, a relation which holds universally. . . . In the hierarchy of qualities the next higher quality to the highest attained is deity. God is the whole universe engaged in process toward the emergence of this new quality, and religion is the sentiment in us that is drawn towards him, and caught in the movement of world to a higher level of existence.

The creativity of Time, of Space-Time, is continually bringing some higher level of existence into the empirical view. "That the universe is pregnant with such a quality (of deity) we are speculatively assured. What the quality is we cannot know: still less can we contemplate it. Our human altars still are raised to the unknown God."

There are many criticisms that have been raised against Alexander's comprehensive scheme. The hierarchical all-inclusive picture is meagerly supported with facts. The transition from Space to Time to Space-Time seems forced. Like other emergent theories, Alexander's has not solved the dilemma of retaining self-identity yet undergoing changes at the same time. His statement that "Time is in truth the abiding principle of impermanence which is the real creator" remains a vague assertion.

J. W. Dunne (1875–1949) proposed a theory of time as a basis of precognition. He was especially interested in how time gets confounded in psychical phenomena, how images of past and future experiences are blended together in present dreams.

In some respects, his approach was an extension of C. H. Hinton's suggestion on the fourth dimension.[18] A creature with a vision limited to one dimension would only see an assemblage of moving particles when it is actually crossing several irregular lines at various angles to its path. Another creature with a multidimensional view would not see moving points at all but the reality of a group of stationary lines. Hinton considered the latter as seeing Time's extension of the former creature.

Out of Hinton's line of reasoning one can envision a Time behind time, a *Time* behind Time, a **Time** behind *Time*, and so on. There would be no movement except of time in Time, Time in *Time*, *Time* in **Time**, and so on. As far as the subjective observer is concerned, there is a corresponding infinite regress in consciousness. He is conscious in **Time** that he is conscious in *Time*, that he is conscious in Time, that he is conscious in time. There is something special about the first term, however. It must be started by an external power. From this Dunne deduced the unendingness of both observers and time series in all times except time-one and that is considered to be "the first scientific argument for human immortality."[19]

It is not suggested that a person actually sees an event ahead of time. If this were the case, there would be nothing he could do to change the event. On the contrary, Dunne's hypothesis states that what is precognized is the event as it appeared at an earlier state of cognition. It is entirely possible that, given this advanced notice, appropriate measures can be taken during the intervening period to frustrate the event from occurring.

Essential to his explanation of time is acceptance of the infinite regress.[20] Dunne embraced it as the very nature of time itself and as the key to certain ultimate questions of psychology, physics, and philosophy of religion. The nature of the series stems from repetition of everything in a higher dimensional form.

On the one hand, he seemed to infer that time is the last term of the regress with the others being only reflections of the real. On the other hand, he also seemed to say that time is continually turning into space.

The difficulty involved in the use of spatial language in the interpretation of time had been set forth by L. J. Lafleur.[21] "If time is one of four equivalent dimensions, any general statement applying to space must apply to time: any statement true of two or three dimensions taken together must be true of any other set of two or three dimensions; and in any equation expressing the behavior of objects, for each appearance of a term involving one dimension or set of dimensions, there must appear identical expressions of each of the other dimensions or sets of dimensions." He maintained that all of these statements are fallacious. A simple case in point is the reversibility of space but not of time.

C. D. Broad[22] raised the question whether or not Dunne's theory is anything more than "an ingenious formal curiosity." Broad was unable to see how Dunne was able to connect the field of observation with the observer's brain, for example, or the other stationary higher dimensions of the manifold with any empirical object. Out of Dunne's four postulates, Broad agreed with only one. This was the one that states that if it is necessary to start on the infinite series, then it would be impossible to stop anywhere in it. Broad did not subscribe to the harmlessness of the regress; he considered it to be delusive and vicious, involving such self-contradictory concepts as an observer at infinity. He also rejected the first assumption that even in the absence of any evidence for precognition, the facts about time necessitate the beginning of the infinite series. No conclusive reason nor logical necessity could be found for taking this first step. Finally, the fourth assertion that precognition emerges as a collateral consequence can be permitted only on the empirical ground that the facts about time can be explained thusly and not otherwise. This, Broad was not willing to concede. In any case, Dunne left unanswered the central issue of just how a regress does explain time.

P. D. Ouspensky (1878–1947) tried to correlate the different grades of consciousness as found in vegetable, animal, and man with the sense of space.[23] As consciousness develops, so does the sense of space. He considered space as the multidimensional mirror of consciousness, with time and motion as the movement of consciousness upon a higher space. He searched the literature of mysticism for support to his concept of superior states of consciousness, where time shall be no longer.

He began by accepting Kant's concepts of space and time as categories of the intellect. He was not quite certain, however, that our divisions of space and time match those of things-in-themselves, which are presented through our senses. It is possible that another kind of animal may react in a different manner.

Ouspensky used the analogy of the blind man to depict the absurdity of our concept that the present is the only existent part of time and that the past and future are nonexistent.

We are going forward like a blind man, who feels paving stones and lanterns and walls of houses with his stick and *believes* in the real existence of only that which he touches *now*, which he feels *now*. That which has passed has disappeared and will never return. That which has not as yet been does not exist. The blind man remembers the route which he has traversed; he expects that ahead the way will continue, but he sees neither forward nor backward *because he does not see anything;* because his instrument of knowledge—the stick—has a definite and not very great length, and beyond the reach of his stick nonexistence begins.

Accordingly, it is "consciousness bounded by the conditions of sensuous receptivity" that gives us the feeling that past and future don't exist. Actually this cannot be. If they do not exist, neither can the present. All three must exist *somewhere* together as "*one present*—the Eternal Now of Hindu philosophy." Furthermore, the past is as undetermined as the future. It contains not only what has actually happened but also what could have happened. The future, likewise, includes not only what will be but also what may be. In his view, time is

the distance separating events in the order of their succession and binding them in different wholes. This distance lies in a direction not contained in *three-dimensional space,* therefore it will be the *new dimension of space.* . . . Usually, we see in *time* the idea of motion, but cannot say from whence, where, whither, nor upon what space. Attempts have been made heretofore to unite the idea of the fourth dimension with the idea of time. But in those theories . . . appeared always the idea of some spatial element as existing in time, and along with it was admitted *motion upon that space.*

Actually they are demanding a *new* time, since motion occurs only in time. As a result, time keeps eluding us. To view the situation correctly we need to recognize that two ideas are associated in the term *time,* viz., "a certain space" and "motion upon that space." The motion is not real but results from incomplete sensation on our part. If our psychic life can rise above the usual plane of consciousness, we would be able to perceive a greater number of events simultaneously and as one view, including some which are separated in time in the plane of mundane consciousness. To the higher consciousness, man would be able to see as simultaneous "events which ordinary consciousness *never* sees together, as: cause and effect; the work and the payment; the crime and punishment . . . the birth and the death of a man. The angle of vision will enlarge during such an ascent, the *moment* will expand."

In order to realize this higher level of receptivity, we need "to liberate ourselves from matter, because matter is nothing more than the condition of space and time." Ouspensky felt that "the finer the state of matter the more energetic it is considered to be, that is to say, containing as it were less substance and more motion. If matter is opposed to time, it will be possible to say that each finer state contains more time and less matter than a coarser state."[24] Thus a gas has more time than a liquid, which in turn has more time than a solid. The "fine states of matter," such as "disincarnated spirits" or "astral beings" should not be considered in the same time condition as physical bodies. Their time existence is of a different kind.

The fourth coordinate is therefore not considered as an adequate picture of time. Instead, three dimensions are postulated for time, which may be represented as a spiral line. "The three dimensions of time can be regarded as the continuation of the dimensions of space, i.e., as the 'fourth,' the 'fifth' and the 'sixth' dimensions of space. A 'six-dimensional' space is undoubtedly a 'Euclidean continuum' but of properties and forms totally incomprehensible to us. . . . Every six-dimensional body becomes for us a three-dimensional body *existing in time* and the properties of the fifth and the sixth dimensions remain for us imperceptible."

The fourth dimension is that determining the Before-Now-After. The perpendicular lines represent the perpetual nows belonging to the respective moments and these constitute the fifth dimension of the ares and nows. Each of these moments, however, contains a number of possibilities and an infinite number of impossibilities. The line of the direction of time is determined by the actualization of these possibilities, which provides the line of the fourth dimension. A particular actualization of one of the possibilities of a given moment will determine the following now, and so on. The lines of the fifth dimensions form a surface, which may be looked upon as an infinity of times or eternity. At every point, however, there are unactualized possibilities in the fifth dimension. They are actualized in the sixth dimension, which constitutes the summation of all times, in the pictorial form of a solid. Beyond this solid there is nothing. "This is the point at which we can understand the limitedness of the infinite universe," asserted Ouspensky. *George E. Moore* (1873–1958), after studying such sophisticated treatises on the nature of time, returned to common sense. Common sense holds the following as true: Everything is, was, or will be in time; it exists at the time I say it does; I know these things to be so.[25]

Moore's attack upon Kant's thesis on existence in time illustrates his approach. Kant had claimed to have proven rigorously that the world had a beginning in time and also that the world had no beginning in time. As an outcome of this contradiction, Kant had concluded that both must be false. He also rejected the other logical possibility that both must be true. Moore pointed out that Kant had overlooked a third alternative: If,

> instead of supposing Kant to have proved both of two contradictory propositions: the world had a beginning in time; and: The world has no beginning in time; we merely suppose him to have proved both of the two hypotheticals: *If* the world is in time at all, it had a beginning; and: *If* the world is in time at all, it had no beginning, we then get a perfectly clear and straightforward argument . . . [yielding] with absolute certainty the definite conclusion that the world does not exist in time at all. It yields this conclusion, that is to say, provided Kant really *has* proved the two hypotheticals in question.

Moore then went on with how Kant's arguments, if they *do* prove anything, prove the two hypotheticals. Kant's first argument concludes that the world began to exist at a definite moment in the past; otherwise it would have had to exist at each of an infinite number of previous moments, which Kant asserted to be impossible.

Kant's second argument states that if the world had a beginning there must have been a time before its appearance when nothing existed. Since no part of this time differed from any other, no explanation can be advanced why something should have begun to exist at a particular time.

The results were extended further. "Kant's two arguments, if they prove anything at all, prove this: namely, that *if* anything whatever exists at any time at all, then *both* contradictory propositions would be true. And since

it is impossible that *both* of two contradictory propositions should be true, they prove, absolutely conclusively
(if they prove anything) that nothing whatever really
exists at any time at all." Although Kant's argument

does really prove (if it proves anything) that nothing
whatever can really exist in Time, [it] does not prove
that nothing can *appear* to be in Time: it only proves
that, if anything does appear to us to be in Time, this
fact itself—namely, the fact that something *does* appear
to us to be in Time—cannot itself really be in Time—
cannot occur at any time at all: it leaves open the abstract possibility that such a fact *may* really exist, provided that it does not occur *at* any time at all.

One key proviso in Kant's line of reasoning is a proof
that an infinite number of hours elapsing before the
present moment is impossible. He could not envision
how the world could have gotten to the present moment
if it had to pass through an infinite number of hours
to get here, which recalls the puzzle of Achilles and
the tortoise, which is discussed in further detail in Commentary 52.

But are we to conclude from this apparent difficulty that
the thing is really impossible? especially, when there will
follow, if we do so conclude, a further conclusion, which
seems so obviously false, as that nothing can exist in
time at all? that there is no such thing as time? It seems
to me we are certainly not—especially as it is so difficult to put the difficulty quite precisely; and Kant at
least certainly does not succeed in putting it more precisely . . . we cannot agree to Kant's claim that he has
proved rigorously that an infinite series of hours cannot
have elapsed before now.

The next notion dissected was that of infinity. We normally feel absolutely confident that we *know* about the
hours and days of ordinary life and many propositions
about them. But when we analyze this obvious truth
philosophically, the situation becomes murky. If we consider the time elapsed before the battle of Waterloo and
now, for example, there are four plausible arguments
which we may consider.

It may be argued (1) . . . that if [it] exists or did exist
at all, there must exist also or have existed an infinite
number of other quantities, of precisely the same length
—or in other words that Time . . . must be infinite in
extent; and it may be argued (2) that [it] may be infinitely divisible. But it may be argued also with some plau-

sibility, that there *cannot* be an infinite number of quantities like [it] and that [it] *cannot* be infinitely divisible. And, *if both* arguments are sound, then it follows . . . that no time can have elapsed since the battle of Waterloo.

Another issue carefully examined by Moore on the basis of common sense was: Is time real? "The difference between what the Universe must be like, if *nothing* ever exists at any time at all, and what it must be like, if, as we commonly suppose, ever so many different things *do* have and *have* had temporal relations to one another, is surely immensely greater than the mere difference between supposing that everything that exists at all exists in Time, and supposing that though many things do, there are *some* which don't." He regarded the question whether or not the huge numbers of various things in the Universe do have temporal relations to one another as one of the most significant that can be raised about the Universe.

It is apparent that considerable improvement is needed in the precision of philosophical usage of words, such as "real," "exists," "is," "is-a-fact," and "is-true." In ordinary parlance the word "real" is the opposite of the word "imaginary." Lions are real and centaurs are imaginary. Yet imagining an imaginary centaur is not the same as imagining nothing. Even though there is no such thing in reality as a centaur, it is still something. Imagining an imaginary centaur is different from imagining an imaginary griffin.

Moore therefore rhetorically asked how we can be certain that there is *no* such a thing as a centaur.

So that in one respect, we should be maintaining about a centaur, exactly what Bradley seemed to maintain about Time: just as he seemed to say Time indubitably *is* and yet is not real; so we seem driven to say: Centaurs indubitably *are* but yet they are certainly not real. It is true we are not necessarily driven to agree also with Bradley's other distinctions. We should hesitate to say that a centaur exists and is a fact, because it *is.* We should be rather inclined to keep these expressions "exists" and "is a fact" as equivalents of "real" in the sense in which we now distinguish "reality" from mere "being." We should be inclined to say: though centaurs *are,* they nevertheless don't exist, are not facts and are not real; instead of saying as Bradley says: Though Time is and exists and is a fact, it is nevertheless *not* real.

Morris Lazerowitz[26] summarized Moore's thrust using the word "now" as an example. The "now" in the statement: "Now is the time for the equinoctial storms." is used in a way resembling the "month" in the statement: "During this month we may expect equinoctial storms." This "now" is not used in the sense of "zero time." "This would make us tend to exaggerate the similarity and to speak of 'now' as if it were the name of a unit of time," explained Lazerowitz.

But noticing that it is *not* leads to the opposite extreme; it tends to make us exaggerate the difference to the point where we wish to deprive "now" of a use having any such resemblance. This produces a feeling of uneasiness about the word which is based on a desire to make irregular words behave in strict ways. And what the philosopher wants is *to get rid of the word* and so rid himself of his uneasiness. By his argument he shows us what a queer irregular word it is, and tempts us to acquiesce in his recommendation, which he misleadingly expresses in the word, "The 'now' is self-contradictory," "Time is unreal." What he really means is this: "'Now' is not the name of a unit of time, nor does it mean no time; let us stop using it." Moore of course knows these facts and apparently they produce in him no desire to give up the word. . . . his defence of Common Sense is a defence against *changing* the language of Common Sense; and his refutations are simply counter proposals, to be understood as recommendations not to follow academic wishes to alter it.

15.
Whitehead's
conception of
incomplete
occasions
XXV

Alfred North Whitehead (1861–1947) formulated the most thoroughly thought-through metaphysical theory on the nature of time. He allowed for flux transcending fixed structures in his concept.[1] Flux is intrinsic to reality. His vision of the whole is embodied in a philosophy of process, in which time is the essence of materiality, the world is related to every actuality, and conformal inheritance accounts for endurance. It includes the concepts of creativity, actual occasion, and nexus.[2]

The ultimate metaphysical problem is to determine the nature of the "complete existent," "the things that are actual," which are fully existent in the complete sense of "existence." This is termed the ontological principle. All actual entities are generically of one kind. Although "there are gradations of importance and diversities of function," the same set of universal principles apply to all actual entities, God included. Otherwise, coherence could not be achieved.[3] These happenings are the final real things. Matter and mind are not the ultimate stuff; they are merely derivative of the actual occasions, in which creativity itself is intimately merged with the creature.

Temporality thus remains essential to materiality; the universe is interlaced with all of its innumerable actualities; endurance is ensured through the conformal passing on of patterns. Creativity serves as the motive force of the totality and the transition, and external ties of time are brought about through its transitivity. Yet temporality, in itself, is not a fact, but an abstraction.

The actual entities, or actual occasions, never move. They build up the world and "by the ontological principle whatever things there are in any sense of 'existence,' are derived by abstraction from occasions. [Whitehead uses] the term 'event' in the more general sense of a nexus of actual occasions, interrelated in some determinate fashion in one extensive quantum. An actual occasion is the limiting type of an event with only one member."[2] A nexus, therefore, is simply an assemblage of actual occasions which are related to one another in some influential way. No particular order or relationship is necessarily involved.

This is the basis for Whitehead's philosophy of organisms.[3] Properties qualify something actual. In addition something extra is involved—a relational property, an "immanence of one thing in another," within certain limitations.

The source of time is located in the interplay of three fundamental categories: supersession, prehension, and incompleteness.[4]

Supersession is part of the real essence of a concrete entity. It is regarded as a three-way process. "Each occasion superseded other occasions, it is superseded by other occasions and it is internally a process of supersession, in part potential and in part actual." The mental occasion internally supersedes the physical occasion. As a result, "the physical pole must be explained before the mental pole, since the mental pole can only be explained as a particular instance of supersession disclosed in the analysis of the fully concrete occasion." Since time is concerned primarily with the physical poles

of occasions and only derivatively with the mental, supersession transcends time.

It is important, however, not to combine the notions of
supersession and continuity. Otherwise we will become
embroiled in an infinite regress.

If *B* supersedes *A*, then the continuity of *B* requires that
some earlier portion of *B* has superseded *A* antecedently
to the latter portion of *B*. This argument can be repeated
on that earlier portion of *B*, however you choose that
portion. Thus we are involved in an infinite regress. Also
the supersession of *A* has to commence at what should
be the infinite end of the regress. But there is no infinite
end. Hence supersession cannot be regarded as the
continuous unfolding of a continuum.

Supersession is not becoming. Time is considered as
"*epochal.* The occasion *B* which acquires a concretion
so as to supersede *A*, embodies a definite quantum of
time which [Whitehead calls] the *epochal character* of
the concrescence." The time quanta in supersession are
not all equal, but there is always some time quantum
involved.

Prehension is the way in which an occasion includes
other occasions in its concretion. It prescribes how an
actuality is related to other actualities of the past and to
potentialities for future actualization. It shows the world
as a system of organisms, each of which in turn is a concretion of different elements. These elements may be
other occasions or the eternal objects or universals.

The eternal objects are the intuitive but not conceptual
defining elements of the physical world.

The conceptual introduction of eternal objects is effected by the mental occasions, which achieve knowledge by
their conceptual analysis of their associate physical
occasions. But pure perception is the fundamental relationship of physical occasions in the physical world.
It has wrongly been assigned to mentality, which is merely analytic; though this analysis, being partial and also
having regard to the exclusions as well as the including
can exhibit a contingent originality, in the forms of "attention" and "imagination."

By reason of the limitations from the exclusions, each
occasion achieves only a certain depth of actuality.
"Occasion *A* does not prehend occasion *B* *simpliciter,*
but *B* under a limitation which is its objectification.
This objectification is provided by the eternal objects

whereby *B* is prehended into *A* as an example of those objects. Thus *B* is objectified for *A,* and the eternal objects are the relational elements which effect this objectification."

There are different modes of ingression of the eternal objects into the actual occasions. "These modes define the objectivity of the prehended occasions in any one physical occasion, and they define the concepts whereby the associate mental occasion analyzes the physical occasion, thereby effecting a new synthesis which is the unity of consciousness. Thus eternal objects define— both for physical and mental poles—the functional process of concretion, and are thus always relational in their operation."

Prehensions, however, are not capable of independent reality. They cannot be complete apart from their related occasions. We can understand the data of an occasion, such as the purpose, valuations, and emotions of the mental pole, only in the context of the total aim.[5]

Incompleteness characterizes the actualities. "The category of incompleteness means that every occasion holds in itself its own future; so that anticipation is primarily a blind physical fact, and is only a mental fact by reason of the partial analysis effected by conceptual mentality."[4] An example of incompleteness is physical memory. A given occasion, such as *B,* contains a physical memory of the antecedent occasions, such as *A.* The latter is prehended into the former, providing a relational functioning "with an individual character expressible in terms of eternal objects. These eternal objects, thus functioning, determine the objectification of *A* whereby it becomes a constitutive element in the concrescence of *B.* This transaction exhibits *A* as relatively determinate, except for its indetermination arising from the indetermination of *B* in the converse anticipatory objectification of *B* in *A.*"

Whitehead then suggested that "each occasion *A* is immortal throughout its future, since *B* enshrines the memory of *A* in its own concrescence, and its essence has to conform to its memories." In this way, he identified physical memory as causation and causation as objective immortality. The image of the present results from "the outcome of the gathering up of the true memory into the creativity of the present." Furthermore, the "irreversibility of time follows from this doctrine of objective immortality. For the later occasion is the completion of the earlier occasion, and therefore different from it."

Since the passage of something cannot be measured unless it is spatially extended, and since Whitehead's time is not so extended, then time itself is not directly measurable. To him, absolute time is a "metaphysical monstrosity," a "half-something and half-nothing." Instead, becoming is explained by combining temporal extension and atomic unity.[6] He incorporated change-lessness and change in his actual entities. The actual entity is changeless but it perishes. Yet it changes in the sense of becoming but does not move. Laws are quantitatively definite but not eternally fixed.

Time then is not a self-subsistent reality. It is placed *in* Nature and not, as by other metaphysicians, vice-versa.

16.
Bergson's
conception of
creative duration
XXVI

Henri Bergson (1859–1941) believed not only in Darwin's evolution of the visible body, but also in the evolution of the deeper creative self as well. He considered culture itself to be a consequence of this process in which time, a creative time, plays a central role.

A sharp distinction is drawn between the time of physics and the time of the self.[1] Science regards time as an independent variable. By definition, a certain mobile t moves in a uniform trajectory. Dividing this trajectory into equal parts $t_1, t_2, t_3, \ldots$ gives units of time 1, 2, 3, . . . when a mobile t traverses the corresponding imaginary stops. Corresponding stops are made for all other mobiles at $t_1, t_2, t_3, \ldots$ upon the passage of t. If the rapidity of the flux were increased to infinity, the trajectory of t would be given all at once and the entire history of the physical universe would be spread out in space instantaneously; the scientific equations describing the universe would, however, remain unaffected.

Because it thus spreads time out in space and regards succession as juxtaposition, Bergson claimed that[2] science "takes account neither of *succession* in what of it is specific nor of *time* in what there is in it that is fluent. It has no sign to express what strikes our consciousness in succession and duration. It no more applies to becoming, so far as what is moving is concerned, than the bridges thrown here and there across the stream follow the water that flows under their arches." The physicist is concerned with the *number* of units of duration rather than the nature of the units themselves in the process. This is "why the successive states of the world might be spread out all at once in space without his having to change anything in his science or to cease talking about time. But for us, conscious beings, it is the units that matter, for we do not count the extremities of intervals, we feel and live the intervals themselves."

It is the inner psychical life which furnishes the nonspatial, nonquantitative reality needed for that understanding of time of which intelligence is incapable. This particular source is not the psychological personality which is studied by the empirical psychologist through retrospective introspection. It is, rather, the suprapersonal and metaphysical basis of conscious living. What Bergson sought was the driving power operating during rare moments deep in the region of the diffused boundaries of mental states, the region of the qualitative multiplicities of feelings, images, and volitions. What is perceived of an external cause is "a certain estimate of the magnitude of the cause by means of a certain quality in the effect—it is, as the Scottish philosophers say, an acquired perception." The interpenetration of the multiplicities becomes complete at the occasions of free decisions. There is a conative *élan* at work.

The core of Bergson's philosophy is what he called duration. It "is the form which our conscious states assume when our ego lets itself *live,* when it refrains from separating its present state from its former states." The states melt together in the duration in which we act. Duration is perpetual becoming, never something made and remaining the same thereafter. It bears a special kind of mutual dependency with the duration of the universe. "Within our ego, there is succession without externality; outside the ego, in pure space, there is mutual externality without succession."

Duration of living has its own rhythm, which is different from the rhythms found in the time of the physicist. In the latter case, as many phenomena can be stored within a given interval as we wish. There are four hundred billion vibrations occurring per second in red light. If a person wishes to witness these vibrations in some slowed-down form as distinct phenomena, he would be confronted with a dilemma involving the lower bound on his ability to distinguish discrete events. This is .05

second. More than twenty-five thousand years would be needed for him, if he were to complete the task as if in abstract space. Obviously he would not be able to do this. Yet he is conscious of the content of this impossible experience. This points to one of the principal differences between our own living duration and physical time in general.

As long as we are concerned with space, we can keep on subdividing as finely as we please. Not so with duration. It is part and parcel of the moments of our act. Divisions and terminations are determined by the elementary acts of life. There are no further subdivisions.

In reality, there is no one rhythm of duration; it is possible to imagine many different rhythms which, slower or faster, measure the degree of tension or relaxation of different kinds of consciousness, and thereby fix their places in the scale of being. . . . Do we not sometimes perceive in ourselves, in sleep, two contemporaneous and distinct persons of whom one sleeps a few minutes, while the other's dream fills days and weeks? And would not the whole of history be contained in a very short time for a consciousness at a higher degree of tension than our own, which should watch the development of humanity while contracting it, so to speak, into the great phases of its evolution? In short, then, to perceive consists in condensing enormous periods of an infinitely diluted existence into a few more differentiated moments of an intensive life, and in the summing up a very long history. To perceive means to immobilize.[3]

Without the individual's consciousness to perceive, the material universe proceeds on its own merry way. It is in memory that the unity of the self is found. There, mind intersects with matter. The past is preserved for the present through memory.

In holding to the proposition that duration is creative and that time passed is distinct from time passing, Bergson was saying that duration is irreversible.

From this survival of the past it follows that consciousness cannot go through the same state twice. The circumstances may still be the same, but they will act no longer on the same person, since they find him at a new moment of his history. Our personality, which is being built up each instant with its accumulated experience, changes without ceasing. By changing, it prevents any state, although superficially identical with another, from ever repeating itself in its very depth. That is why our duration is irreversible. We could not live over again a single moment, for we should have to begin by effacing the memory from all that followed. Even if we erase this memory from our intellect, we could not from our will.[2]

His concepts have encountered some resistance. The identification of time with the free act of the self has been regarded as beyond intellectual conceptualization.[4] E. B. McGilvary[5] felt that Bergson had been mistaken in not recognizing the mutual externality of instants:

But there is a partial mutual externality in that the part of a preceding moment is not part of a succeeding moment and is external to the latter. Such externality however is compatible with continuity. While the temporal stretches in question lie on different sides of the same instant and are thus mutually external, the instant interposes no gap between them. Mutual externality does not mean necessarily an *externality between* mutual externals. Again there is order in succession, else there were no dates. . . . In short Bergson's attempt to differentiate time and space as one a nonexternalizing continuum and the other a noncontinuous externality fails."

J. C. Smuts[6] voiced his reservations about the reality of Bergson's duration. He could not see how concrete reality can be produced from pure duration. "From bare, undifferentiated, homogeneous unity you cannot reach out to multiplicity. You may call Duration creative, but it will create nothing until it is mixed with something very different from itself. And indeed Bergson has had to summon to his rescue another principle, which he had so carefully deprived Duration. This is the intellect." It is this practical, analytical, selective, and purposive intellect, which "is at once the principle and the instrument of action." Duration itself is incapable of analyzing the available material and choosing what is useful in it for the purpose at hand.

17.
The encompassing ecstasies of the existentialists
XXVII

Martin Heidegger (born 1889) called for a new approach in the search for the Being of the concrete things-that-are, not in the spheres beyond but in those within the human existent.[1] It is within the temporal horizon of existence that things acquire meaning and therefore can only in this sense be said to be in time.

One commonly thinks of psychic events as originating in the past, moving into the present, and then into the future. We consider only some of these events to be active in nature: those which we refer to as wishing or willing. Heidegger, however, felt that *all* of one's existence is active or conative. This active structure of existence is called "Care." The Care is always ahead of itself and the individual, therefore, is always oriented to the future. As discussed by John Wild,[2] "It is this envisaged future which directs my care. But I myself and that which I care for, already exist in the world. As I exist with this being and care for it, I am thus both ahead of myself in some possibility and already in the factual world. This three-fold order of human existing is the structure of care: ahead of itself . . . as already in the world . . . as being with."

At the root of human Care lies time. Man's being is stretched out from the very beginning into the possibilities ahead of himself, as well as into the past as part of the *de facto* present. Time is not confined to the present moment, but encompasses the three "ecstasies"— future, past, and present. A span of time cannot be said to belong to the past, the present, the future, nor to all three added together. It is something unique to itself, giving rise to the ecstasies. The latter are not intermingled in some contradictory fashion. Each of the modes has its own nature and cannot be indiscriminately transformed into another.

The future tense is the most important. It is the future that pulls the past along, the "resolve running forward (in thought) to" as the "Being toward its own eminent potentiality of Being." This "*Dasein* [Man's "being-there"] can move forward toward itself in its own potentiality and endures the potentiality as potentiality in this itself-moving-toward-itself."

Just as the future is never separated from present responsibility, similarly my past is not a now that once was and is gone. The importance of both future and past is felt now, in the present continuity of existence. Past responsibilities are repeatedly assumed by choice and thereby personal integrity is achieved.

The conventional concept of the present fails to distinguish the vulgar from the authentic. The former takes the present for granted, ignores the creative possibilities, and forgets the ecstatic character of temporality. The instants are fragmented. The authentic present occurs in the full *Augenblick* (Moment) of Kierkegaard.[3] It is unveiled from the interaction among the toward-itself of the future, the back-to of the past, and the encountering of the present.

To repeat Werner Brock's remarks:[4]

All planning, taking of precautions, preventing or calculating of *Dasein* in its Care says, audibly or inaudibly: "then" this is to be done; "before" that work has to be finished; "now" this has to be tried once more, after I failed in it "at this time." In the "then" the Care speaks in the "anticipation," relating to the future; in the "now" in the mode of "rendering present;" in the "at that time" in the mode of "bearing in mind," relating to the past. The horizon of these three modes of everyday Care is the "later," "today" and the "earlier." This common structure of the "now," "then" and "at that time" is termed the "datableness" . . . It is this "rendering present" which interprets itself that we call "Time" and the "datableness" of the "now," "then" and "at that time" is considered to be the reflection of the ecstatic constitution of Temporality.

As *Dasein* projects itself either in its authentic temporality as horizon-opener or in its unauthentic temporality in the world of things, changes occur in various facets of living. The understanding which one has of a situation is a function of his perspective. If he views events in their full range of temporal contexts of the past and future, his understanding is considered to be authentic. Otherwise he is trapped in the petty vanities of a narrow horizon without the proper relation to the real Being. This concern with happenings of the mundane now inhibits him from taking advantage of all of the possibilities of the past. Heidegger used the curiosity of people to illustrate one of the unauthentic modes of temporality. People seek neither origins nor ultimate meanings, they are satisfied with "They say that . . ." in their superficiality.

As a result of the progressive unfolding of authentic existence, speech is manifested. The origin of conversation itself is wrapped up in the history of man's experience. The first conversation originated at the realization of something "that remains and is constant," which provided a background for current changes. Time then became experienced as present, past, and future. From one point of view we may regard one's entire life as one long conversation involving himself, and all the lives of all men as a much longer conversation lasting thousands of years.

The drama of history is born of the interplay of the authentic and unauthentic existence of *Dasein.* History is not just a record of the past. Its deeper significance emerges only with man's decision in view of the future. History "as event is the acting through and suffering through of the present, determined by the future and taking over the past."[5] Nor do inanimate objects have histories.[6] Only man makes decisions. These are existential choices in the historicity of *Dasein.* Mountains, stones, and trees are passive objects of succession.

In particular, man's attitude toward death requires proper orientation. The fact that every man dies is usually regarded as outside oneself. The shattering experience of death is the transforming of the proposition "One dies" to the proposition "I am to die."

Consciousness of death is the key factor in shaping our personality. One can die at any moment; the possibility is always present. And one must die alone. Because of this, man should take death into himself. In this way he frees himself from the shackles of the petty cares of daily life and conserves his resources for the significant projects. Heidegger terms this condition as freedom-toward-death or resoluteness. We remain aware of the finitude of our existence yet we are resolute in our decision to assume it. By taking death into our living, we attain a totality of being. Through death as its end, *Dasein* becomes whole.

Jean-Paul Sartre (born 1905) suggested that consciousness is a Nothingness, which is a revelation of Being at the same time.[7] "Man is the being through whom nothingness comes to the world."

He made the point that "temporality is evidently an organized structure. The three so-called 'elements' of time, past, present and future, should not be considered as a collection of 'givens' for us to sum up—for example, as an infinite series of 'nows' in which some are not yet and others are no longer—but rather as the structured moments of an original synthesis." Otherwise we are faced with the paradox of a practically nonexistent instantaneous present, a nonexistent past, and a not-yet existent future. Temporality then is to be approached "as a totality which dominates its secondary structures and which confers on them their meaning."

The term "was" is a mode of being. I *am* my past and cannot dissociate myself from it. At death the For-itself becomes an In-itself forever. Yet I *am* not my past. The very moment I make a pronouncement about myself, I am no longer that which I was. This is not because a change has occurred but rather "a becoming is possible there only because on principle my being and my modes of being are heterogeneous. . . . It is within being qua being that non-being must arise, and within non-being that being must spring up; and this relation cannot be a fact, a natural law, but an upsurge of the being which is its own nothingness of being."

To be present means to be present to something. The In-itself merely is and only the For-itself can be present to something. The relation between the present being and the beings to which it is present is an internal affair. It is not external contiguity. Nor is it reciprocal in character.

Beings are revealed as co-present in a world where the For-itself unites them with its own blood by that total ekstatic sacrifice of the self which is called presence. "Before" the sacrifice of the For-itself it would have been impossible to say that beings existed either together or separated. But the For-itself is the being by which the present enters the world; the beings of the world are co-present, in fact, just in so far as one and the same For-itself is at the same time present to all of them. Thus for the In-itselfs what we ordinarily call Present is sharply distinguished from their being although it is *nothing more* than their being. For their Present means only their co-presence in so far as a For-itself is present to them.

We are attracted by the future to unite ourselves with the "lacking" being. But the lacking as such is never attained. A For-itself seeks a future co-presence with some In-itself. "The Future is revealed to the For-itself as that which the For-itself is not yet, inasmuch as the For-itself constitutes itself synthetically for itself as a not-yet in the perspective of this revelation, and inas-much as it makes itself be a project of itself outside the Present toward that which it is not yet. . . . Thus every-thing which the For-itself is beyond being is the Future." But this is not all there is in the Future. There is also

something which waits for the For-itself which I am. This something is myself. When I say that *I* will be happy we understand that it is the present "I" dragging its Past after it, who will be happy. Thus the Future is "I" in as much as I await myself as presence to a being beyond being. I project myself toward the Future in order to merge there with that which I lack; that is, with that which if synthetically added to my Present would make me be what I am. Thus what the For-itself has to be as presence to being beyond being is its own possibility.

Yet there exists the constant perspective of the possibility of my not being this Future.

Hence that anguish . . . which springs from the fact that I am not sufficiently that Future which I have to be and which gives its meaning to my present: it is because I am a being whose meaning is always problematic. In vain would the For-itself long to be enchained to its Possibility, as to the being which it is outside itself but which it is *surely* outside itself. The For-itself can never be its Future except problematically, for it is separated from it by a Nothingness which it is. In short, the For-itself is free, and its Freedom is to itself its own limit. To be free is to be condemned to be free. Thus the Future qua Future does not have to be. It is not *in itself,* and neither is it in the mode of being of the For-itself since it is the *meaning* of the For-itself. The Future is not, it is *possibilized.*

Having provided a phenomenological description of the three temporal ecstasies, Sartre then proceeded to present time as an organic unity. This was approached from two points of views. From the static temporality the constitution and requirements of before and after are considered. From the dynamic temporality the becoming is dissected — how an after becomes a before and a present becomes a past. The former treats of the formal structure, the latter of the course of time. In this way we "approach temporality as a total structure organizing within it secondary ekstatic structures."

The main problem connected with the before-after aspects of the concept of time as a "dust of instants" is the mechanism of their joining together into time. Time is regarded "not so much a real multiplicity as a quasi-multiplicity in the heart of a unifying act." It is the For-itself which brings unity into the succession of time through a process of nihilation. The before and after are understood as an internal relation. "It is there in the after that the before causes itself to be determined as before and conversely. In short the before is intelligible only if it is the being which is *before* itself. This means that temporality can only indicate the mode of being of a being which is itself outside itself."

Emphasis is placed not on the future, but on the present, in Sartre's philosophy. The present

> is as a revelation to itself that the For-itself *is* its Past, as that which it has-to-be-for-itself in a nihilating surpassing; and it is as a revelation to itself that it is a lack and that it is haunted by its future—that is, by that which it is for itself down there at a distance. The Present is not ontologically "prior" to the Past and to the Future; it is conditioned by them as much as it conditions them, but is the mould of indispensible non-being for the total synthetic form of Temporality.

Sartre did not permit life to be dominated by death. Death is absurd. We cannot forsee it. A person prepares twenty years to be an author and dies before he completes his first page. Death puts an end to the For-itself, an end to expectation. It lies outside For-itself, which disappears when the individual dies. He then becomes a sort of solidified being, to be passed over to the Other. Whatever happens to himself thereafter depends upon the memory and actions of the living. Where life is freedom and choice, death is the external limit. As a mortal a person is free, but he is not free to die. Sartre repeated Epicurus' views on this score: Death "is the moment of life which I never have to live."

As long as a person is alive, he has a chance to negate his past. A coward may perform a heroic act and redeem himself. But a dead coward remains a coward forever. Unfortunately, all too frequently death does not come at a time when a rounded totality can be imparted to our lives. "One always dies too soon or too late," says Inex in Sartre's *No Exit.*

18.
Unending
disputations
XXVIII

Thousands of other thinkers have deliberated at great lengths on the subject of time. A dozen quotations are presented below to illustrate their range of conceptualizations.

Nicolai Berdyaev: [1] "The metaphysics of history therefore must be based upon the fundamental hypothesis that the 'historical' is part of, and has its roots in eternity. History is neither the sum of the world process nor the loss of all association with the roots of being; it forms a necessary part of eternity and of the drama that is fulfilled in it. History is the result of a deep interaction between eternity and time; it is the incessant eruption of eternity into time."

Percy Bridgman:[2] "From the point of view of operations the time of the mathematician is merely the time of memory. The time of memory has the property that we may imagine ourselves situated at any point of it and from that point our recollections may range in either direction backward or forward, provided only that they do not touch the present. But this is a dead time, divested of the living hazard of the present, and when the mathematician uses this time he can give an account only of the dead. Our consciousness of this vital limitation must not be dulled by the enormous effectiveness of the mathematical concept of time in dealing with the situations of past experience, nor must we, on the other hand, think that the mathematician's concept of time is capable of dealing with all the questions that we may put. I suspect that if it had been vividly realized that the time of experience is not homogeneous backward and forward, unlike the time of a mathematician, a certain very eminent speculator would not have sought in the structure of mathematical time an explanation of the fact that 'time's arrow' always points forward. Whether the question as to why it is that time moves forward can be given meaning in terms of any possible concept of time may well be open to doubt, but it certainly cannot be given meaning in terms of the dead time of the mathematician."

Martin Buber:[3] "Time in respect of actual, consciously willing man, cannot be comprehended, because the future cannot be present, since it depends to a certain extent, in my consciousness and will, on my decision. Anthropological time is real only in the part which has become cosmological time, that is, in the part called the past. . . . It is true that we do not know cosmological time as a whole either, in spite of our knowledge of the regular movements of the stars, and so on; but our thoughts may be engaged with it as with something real, even in what we do not know of this, and naturally even in what we do not know of future human actions, since in the moment of thought all their causes are present. With the anthropological future, on the other hand, our thoughts cannot be engaged as something real, since my decision, which will take place in the next moment, has not yet taken place. The same is true of the decisions of other men, since I know, on the basis of the anthropological concept of man as a consciously willing being, that he cannot be understood simply as a part of the world. Within the boundaries of the human world which is given in the problem of human being there is no certainty of the future."

Ernst Cassirer:[4] "One and the same form of relation can undergo an inner transformation if it occurs within a different *formal context.* Each particular relation belongs—regardless of its particularity—to a *totality* of meanings which itself possesses its own 'nature,' its self-contained formal law. Thus, for example, the universal relation which we call 'time' is just as much an element of theoretical scientific *cognition* as an essential factor in certain structures of the aesthetic consciousness. Time, as explained in the beginning of Newton's *Mechanics* as the stable basis of all motion and the uniform measure of all change, seems at first sight to have nothing more than the name in common with the time that governs a work of music or its rhythmic measures—and yet this unity of nomenclature involves a unity of meaning at least insofar as both posit that universal and abstract quality which we term 'succession.' But the consciousness of natural laws as laws of the temporal form of motion and the consciousness of musical measure have each their own specific mode of succession."

Henry Corbin:[5] "It is 'interpreting' the *signs,* explaining not the material facts but way of being, that reveals being. . . . Past and future thus become *signs,* because a sign is perceived precisely in the *present.* The past must be 'put in the present' to be perceived as 'showing a sign.' . . . In short, the whole contrast lies here. With *signs,* with hierophanies and theophanies, there is no making history. . . . The only 'historical causality' is the relations of will between acting subjects. 'Facts' are on each occasion a *new creation;* there is a discontinuity between them. . . . To perceive a causality in 'facts' by detaching them from persons is doubtless to make a philosophy of history possible; it is to affirm dogmatically the rational meaning of history on which our contemporaries have built up a whole mythology. But it is likewise to reduce real time to abstract physical time, to the essentially *quantitative* time which is that of the objectivity of mundane calendars from which the *signs* that gave a sacred qualification to every present have disappeared."

Aurobindo Ghose:[6] "Eternal change of form is the sole

immortality to which the finite living substance can aspire and eternal change of experience the sole infinity to which the finite mind involved in living body can attain. This change of form cannot be allowed to remain merely a constant renewal of the same form-type such as constitutes our bodily life between birth and death; for unless the form-type is changed and the experiencing mind is thrown into new forms in new circumstances of time, place and environment, the necessary variation of experience which the very nature of existence in Time and Space demands, cannot be effectuated."

Charles Hartshorne:[7] "The future contains no particulars, but only the law, that certain more or less broad or narrow generalities will be *somehow* further particularized. This law is part of the present and is the future as such, i.e., as a fact in the present. . . . all such specific characters as robin's egg blue are emergents at a certain date, *created* rather than 'selected' out of the primordial potentiality."

John MacMurray:[8] "[Purely on a hypothetical basis I am permitted to] select any point in time I please as the present, and call what came before it the past and what came after it the future. But as Agent the present is determined for me. It is the 'here-and-now,' my only point of action, for I can neither act in the past nor in the future. And even in reflection, I can only *think* here and now; and my ability to place myself in thought at any point in time I please depends on the fact that all points in time are represented here and now, for my reflection, simultaneously. Now an order of simultaneity is spatial. In so far as time is a given order within which the events can be assigned to determine positions, the time is past time, and the determination is a theoretical determination. A determinate future is not a real future. The real future is the indeterminate which is determined in action, and in being determined becomes the past. The physicist's time is not real time; it is time represented as past, without a future."

Misha Maisels:[9] "If we may designate natural space as *present time,* we may designate personality as *living time.* The personality of man not only lives its life *within* time, as in an inert vacuity, but *it lives time* and time lives within it. A moment of personality bears within it all the past and all the future of personality and these come into being only within it, within that moment. A moment of personal time, then, is possessed of creative power: it brings into being all that is not within it. . . . each of its moments is unique in its personality. . . . glimmers once, never to return. It flashes out of non-being and fades into non-being. . . . Each moment of personality is the whole of personality, a creation of the moment and a creation of the past and future. . . . And yet, the miracle of the identity of the personal whole lives in it, shines through it."

George Mead:[10] "The animal in which the act originates is not yet the material organism which in its own conduct exists over against other material things. It is a stimulus to other animals to seize and devour it, or to avoid it, or to woo it, or to suckle it. These stimuli are spatiotemporally separated from the animal they excite. They have as yet no existence present as objects for the animal. To assume such present existence, they must assume the 'now' that belongs to the manipulatory area of the animal. If the act of the animal with reference to the second animal calls out a response in the second animal, such as flight or an answering cry, these responses become important stimuli in the continuation of the act. . . . [Thus, the unity of the act] is not given in a permanent space, abstracted from passage, until the 'now' of the ongoing process in the animal becomes identified with the spatiotemporally distant stimulus through acts of identifying itself with the stimulus, thus enabling the stimulus to share in the resistance which is the reality of the percept in the manipulatory area."

Adolf Portman:[11] "And time, too, is a medium of this manifestation of inner life. In song the temporal sequence is utilized to display the characteristics of the bird—in flowering a change in the plant's inner state is manifested in time; in their changes of garb from childhood to old age the higher animals disclose their innermost transformations; the scarcely perceptible flow of life is punctuated, articulated, enriched. The higher we go in the scale of life, the more *form* becomes an expression of innermost being. The succession of manifestations in time increases the expressiveness of an organism undergoing inner changes. Thus the dimension of time serves to enhance and enrich life; empty clock time helps to configure hidden transformations. And thus the solar year with the changes it creates on earth is integrated with all life. An extreme fulness of life is

realized in the migratory bird which travels nearly to
the ends of the earth in pursuit of longer days. Here time
becomes an essential trait in the life picture."
William Sheldon:[12] "Not to man the knower but to man
the striver does time show its deepest significance. And
its significance hereby is, to be the opportunity for good
or evil. As said, time is a value, the basis for all values
to come for us unhappy human creatures. Time is the
incarnation of hope. If all nature were good, there would
be no need of time; if evil were presented in a timeless
world, there would be a good excuse for introducing
time."

19.
Theoretical
considerations
in time
measurement
XXIX

A number of considerations should be taken into account
in the measurement of clock time. At the outset, we
should be clear as to the definition of the term "objective" in physical measurements. The word does not
necessarily mean accurate. It only refers to a common-
ness to all investigators. Everybody obtains the same
results using the same procedure. After all is said and
done, however, our measurements fall back on our primitive perception of the passing of time. Unlike distance,
time intervals cannot be compared side by side. They
do not exist together. As a result, the question arises
as to whether or not our primitive perceptions are capable of deciding the equality of two successive intervals
of time in the same fashion as the equality of two adja-
cent lengths of lines. The task is rendered more difficult
by practical imperfections and statistical fluctuations[1]
and a fixed point of reference seems impossible to
attain.[2]

By dissecting the epistemological aspects of the scientific measurement of time, Hermann Weyl[3] clarified how
it is that a theory of relativity is inherent in the process.

Before we are able to make temporal measurements,
we must postulate a point of time in the present as a
starting point. Furthermore, we must be able to say of
any two points in time which is the earlier. If *A* is earlier
than *B* and *B* is earlier than *C*, then *A* is also earlier
than *C*. A length of time is marked off between two
points, one of which is earlier than the other. This length
will include all points later than one and earlier than the
other.

The empirical content of a length of time *AB* can be put

into any other time without change. The length of time occupied by the content would be equal to *AB*. Together with the principle of causality, this concept of time equality provides the basis for clocks. It is operable under the assumption that all points in time are like all others, and that the two basic relations of earlier-and-later and equal-times apply to all point-pairs. A new relation comes into play, however, in the case of three point-pairs.

Given time-point *O*, which is earlier than another time-point *E*, a time-point *P* can be fixed conceptually relative to *OE*, by the equation:

$$OP = t \times OE.$$

There can be only one time-point for *P* which satisfies the equation. For example, when

$$OE = EP,$$

the equation would read:

$$OP = 2 \times OE.$$

"Numbers are merely concise symbols for such relations as *t*, defined logically from the primary relations," Weyl pointed out.

> *P* is the "time-point with the *abscissa t in the coordinate system* (taking *OE* as unit length)." . . . Numbers enable us to single out separate time-points relatively to a unit-distance *OE* out of the time-continuum by a conceptual, and hence objective and precise, process. But the objectivity of things conferred by the exclusion of the ego and its data derived directly from intuition, is not entirely satisfactory; the coordinate system, which can only be specified by an individual act (and then only approximately) remains as an inevitable residuum of this elimination of the percipient. . . . [By] formulating the principle of measurement in the above terms we see clearly how mathematics has come to play its role in exact natural science. *An essential feature of measurement is the difference between the "determination" of an object by individual specification and the determination of the same object by some conceptual means.* The latter is only possible relatively to objects which must be defined directly.

In agreeing upon the Mean Sun traversing the ecliptic as the average, we are actually depending upon motion through space as the index of time. Ordinarily, we determine motion through space by reference to a fixed point. Such a fixed point in space or an astronomical body with known exact speed of revolution is not available. Even the conventional clock star used as a reference is moving.

In referring to the standard of the beat of a pendulum of a given length, we are again adopting an arbitrary reference. Since the beat is dependent upon the gravitational force, it would be affected by the movements of the center of gravity of the earth. Similarly, the movements of the tides and the attractive power of the sun and the moon also contribute to the variability of the beat.

In this connection, clocks should be distinguished from calendars.[4] The former determine duration; they answer the question: "How long?" The latter determine time placement in the sequential ordering of events; they answer the question: "When?"

To designate the sequential position of an event, a temporal coordinate is required. Such a coordinate must be capable of expressing the before-and-after relation of events. At the same time, some particular event, such as the birth of Christ, the beginning of a dynasty, 12 M. Greenwich time, or the present event, can be adopted as the origin of the coordinates. By means of the before-and-after relations, events can then be arranged in temporal sequence.

As ordinarily used, clocks serve as calendars to a certain extent. They perform functions of measuring durations as well as dating. Five o'clock is a date with respect to noon or midnight, the two conventional origins of coordinates for the day. The date of five o'clock is obtained by the adding of five successive durations of one hour each to the origin of coordinates. This implies that the clock is capable of specifying equal durations of time.

Instead of perfecting the determination of time-intervals by operational procedures, physicists have attempted to clarify the character of an ideal clock. The intervals of the ideal clock are said to be equal according to some formula, which is part of a broader physical concept. Whether or not the time-interval congruence of the ideal clock is correct is contingent on the effectiveness of the concept as a whole. The question as to whether the ideal clock of relativity or the ideal clock of Newton is more accurate does not rest upon what is usually considered as the procedure of time measurement. Rather it is a test of the validity of the two theories as overall physical principles. This, in itself, dooms the hope of ever achieving a perfect clock, for there are no perfect theories.

This holds particularly in the submicroscopic realm of physics, in which considerable theoretical difficulties are being experienced. It has been shown[5] that quantum mechanics imposes certain limitations on the possibilities of measuring distances between events in space-time. Using clocks to measure space-time, analysis shows that the mass of the clock and the uncertainty or spread of this mass exceed certain values. They are dependent on the accuracy of the intended measurement, the running time of the clock, as well as the size. A minimum mass uncertainty is contributed by the size of the clock.

Furthermore, there is considerable agreement that no real meaning can be attached to subdivisions of the geometrical continuum beyond a certain limit. An indivisible unit of time has even been suggested.[6] This is assumed to be equal to $h/m_0 c^2$, where h is Planck's constant, m_0 is the rest mass of the particle, and c is the velocity of light.

For everyday purposes, the useful clock is simply a convenient device for the observation of some time-dependent phenomena. In its design we may embody Newton's equation of the Second Law of Motion, describing the position of a body; Maxwell's equation, relating electromagnetic force to the rate of change of magnetic flux; Schrödinger's equation, depicting the time-dependent wave function; or Poisson's equation, describing the probability of observing radioactive disintegrations. The surprising practical fact is that all these clocks seem to agree within experimental error.

20.
Empirical
time-reckoning
XXIX

Primitive peoples were not guided by a fixed unit of time. Recurring tasks, such as milking cows, were used to mark off intervals of shorter divisions of time, while natural phenomena, such as the seasons, were used to mark off the longer divisions. Traces of the most primitive images still persist in the Indo-Germanic languages.[1]

The Adaman Islanders separate the year into seasons by the odoriferous flowers that bloom successively throughout the period. Life follows a calendar of scents.[2] The Bigamul follow the flowering of trees.[3] September, for example, is described as *yerrabinda* (yerra blossoming), Christmas as *nigabinda* (apple tree blossoming), and midsummer as *tinnakogealba* (when the ground burns the soles of the feet).

The Aranda of Western Australia divide the day into twenty-five parts.[4] Typical reference points are *lentara* (when the first streaks of light are seen in the east), and *ingrintingunta* (when the birds begin to twitter). The Greenland Eskimos follow the ebb and flow of the tide, without reference to the moon and sun.[5]

As civilization advanced, the reckoning of time became a guarded and respected art. Record-keeping of the passage of time and seasons was entrusted to selected individuals. In many clans these were the oldest or the wisest members of the tribe. The custodians of the calendars frequently belonged to a single family or a single familial line, as was the practice during the early city periods of Egypt, Sumeria, and Yucatan. They accumulated a wealth of knowledge concerning the heavens. The Chaldean priests of five thousand years ago predicted eclipses with considerable accuracy.

More dependable schemes were gradually evolved for marking off the day and the year.[6] Shadows were among the most popular during the earlier days. One of the simplest adaptations of the principle of the sundial was the method of the people of Borneo. It merely consists of the movement of the sun through the portals of their houses, which were built facing the West. Times were designated by such indices as "the sun at the rice-pounding place" and "the sun at the place of tying the calf."

The hours of daylight were identified beginning about 160 B.C. About the time of Christ, the day was divided into five periods or "hours." In the year 605 Pope Sabianus added two more divisions, forming the seven canonical hours. This determined European time-keeping for centuries. The present system of twenty-four hours began to gain acceptance after 1600.

In the evolution of the calendar, the Egyptians used the lengthening and shortening of the shadows as early as 3100 B.C.[7] They discovered the summer and winter solstices by observing the shortest and the longest shadows cast at high noon, respectively. Between these two points, they established the vernal and the autumnal equinoxes. The oldest fixed date appears to be 4236 B.C.[8] This was the year in which the Egyptians supposedly adopted the sun as the standard for time measurements.

There are indications that Stonehenge, a stone circle

about four thousand years old in England, was used as a time-telling device.[9] The seasons could have been noted by keeping track of the shadows cast by the huge reference stones in relation to one another; proper calibration could have been made against the solstices for this purpose.

The Sumerians used a calendar with seven days a week, twelve periods a day, and thirty parts a period. The Egyptians had a far more accurate calendar. Their year was divided into twelve months of thirty days each. The five days left over were devoted to celebrating the birthdays of the gods. The calendar employed in most of the world today resulted from a series of adjustments dating back to the original Roman calendar beginning around 738 B.C. This "Romulus calendar" consisted of ten lunar months of thirty days each. The year began in March and ended in December. The winter months were disregarded, since "nothing happened" during those cold days.

Improvements were also being made in the devices for measuring the day's subdivisions. The water clock was already in official use during the days of the Roman Empire. More recent centuries saw the rapid rise of mechanical and electronic clocks, which are carefully calibrated against some natural process such as the rotation of the earth. To obtain maximum accuracy in these devices, various corrections must be applied. Even after all the known adjustments are made, however, an unpredictable fluctuation still remains. In contrast, the atomic clock appears to be independent of other natural processes and to follow regularities on its own.[10] Because of this, it makes a far more accurate time-keeping instrument,[11] although not completely free from the possibilities of secular variations.[12]

A typical atomic clock is one based on the cesium atom with its characteristic vibration of 9192 megacycles per second. The ticking of the cesium atom is due to the wobble of the single electron in its outermost shell. The electron acts like an electromagnet. As energy is absorbed or emitted to an applied electromagnetic field, the electron changes its orientation of spin.

Gaseous cesium atoms generated in an electric furnace are fed through a nonuniform magnetic field. After the atoms have been exposed to a magnetic sorting process which selects those with a certain chosen velocity, they are permitted to drift into a low field space exposed to radio waves vibrating at 9192 megacycles. The stimulated atoms are then discharged past a second identical magnetic field toward a detector hot wire. A current is produced by the ionization of the atoms. The current is used to regulate the frequency output of an external crystal oscillator. The output is then amplified and injected into the cesium beam through a waveguide.

Through a properly coupled circuit, accuracies up to at least one part in ten billion are within reach.

21.
Time-shaped geometry
XXIX

During the time of Euclid in Greece, geometry involved static positions and forms. Since change was not a factor in the depiction of permanent buildings and land by lines, angles, and curves, time was not incorporated into the calculations. The fundamental thing was the point of beginning, which was a point of position, pure and simple. Beginning with this point, the line, which can be regarded as size, could be drawn, perhaps at a predetermined angle. With the basic concepts of point, line, and angle, the Greek geometer could meet all of his needs.

René Descartes (1596–1650) put time into geometry, thereby extending its conceptual usefulness. He noted that a line is described not only by the properties of position and magnitude but also by that of direction. An area consists not only of a certain number of square units, but also of the difference between the units of an area in one situation and in another. The advantage of the Cartesian method of description over the classical Greek method can be illustrated by the swinging pendulum. The former records the horizontal displacement to the right and left of the center positions with time, thereby revealing the kind of to-and-fro swinging motion. The latter does not do this; it merely records the total horizontal distance traveled by the pendulum at the end of various times.

22.
The absolute concepts of the early scientists
XXIX

There were three scientific advancements which greatly influenced Isaac Newton (1642–1727). The first was Galileo's (1564–1642) definition of matter as mass, and his analysis of motion which implied space and time in a fixed frame of reference. The second was Descartes' identification of matter with extension. The third was the quantitative description of space and time, with matter treated as mass, by Henry More (1614–1687) and Isaac Barrow (1630–1677).

The most immediate impact was that of Barrow, Newton's teacher at Cambridge. In developing his conception of geometrical magnitudes as being generated by motion, Barrow considered whether time existed before the creation of the world or beyond the world limits in the realm of nothing. His conclusion was that "before the world and together with the world time was and is; since before the world arose, certain beings were able continually to remain in existence, so now things may exist beyond the world capable of such permanence. . . . Time, therefore, does not denote an actual existence, but simply a capacity or possibility of permanent existence."[1]

Time does not depend on motion. It "flows in its even tenor" whether all the stars move or remain fixed. Motion may be invoked as an aid in the measurement of time. As something measurable, then, time implies motion, "since if all things had remained unmoved, in no way would we be able to distinguish how much time had flowed past; the age of things would have been indistinguishable to us and its growth would have been undiscoverable." The motion of the stars, sun, and moon are considered acceptable for the purpose. Since there is no way of comparing the cycles of the heavenly bodies of today with those of millenia ago, it is similarly impossible to compare the two times involved.

There is a mutual aid of motion and time in the measurement of each other. Thus,

we first reckon time from some motion and afterwards judge other motions by it; which is plainly nothing else than to compare some motions with others by the mediation of time. . . . Furthermore, since time . . . is a quantity uniformly extended, all of whose parts correspond to the respective parts of an equable motion, or proportionately to the parts of space traversed by an equable motion, it can be represented, that is, proposed to our mind or fantasy, in a most successful manner by any homogeneous magnitude; especially by the simplest, such as a straight line or circular line; between which and time there are also not a few similarities and analogies. . . . And just as the quantity of a line depends on length alone, the result of motion, so the quantity of time follows from a single succession spread out, as it were, in length; which the length of traversed space proves and determines. So we shall always represent time by a straight line.

Much of Barrow's thoughts formed the basis of Newton's absolute theory of time in the *Principia*.[2]

Newton did not link time with motion, as did Aristotle. Nor did he regard time as dependent upon the existence of external material, as did Descartes. Despite his experimental reliance upon sense measurements, however, Newton adopted the antiempirical premise that "we ought to abstract from our senses, and consider things themselves, distinct from what are only sensible measures of them." He did this to preclude empirical prejudices.

Hitherto I have laid down the definitions of such words as are less known, and explained the sense in which I would have them to be understood in the following discourse. I do not define time, space, place and motion, as being well known to all. Only I must observe that the vulgar conceive those quantities under no other notions but from the relation they bear to sensible objects. And thence arises certain prejudices, for the removing of which it will be convenient to distinguish them into absolute and relational, true and apparent, mathematical and apparent.

Relative time is considered a segment of absolute time. Such a given segment may be calibrated against a given arbitrary segment such as an hour. By means of the standard, a number can be obtained and referred to as a measure. These are some of the characteristics of the time of physics in contrast to the all-embracing temporal matrix of absolute time, holding all events in coherent order. The term "measure" therefore applies to space and time and not to motion. The latter acquires meaning only from space and time and not vice-versa.

23. The relational concepts of Leibnitz and Lorentz XXX

Gottfried Wilhelm Leibnitz (1646–1716) adopted a relational theory of time. He based his arguments upon the principles of sufficient reason and of the identity of indiscernibles.

The former principle asserts that there is a sufficient reason for things being as they are and not otherwise. God always has a sufficient reason for doing anything He does. "When two things which cannot both be together, are equally good; and neither in themselves, nor by their combination with other things, has the one only advantage over the other; God will produce neither of them."[1] The latter principle asserts that two indistinguishable entities cannot exist in nature. There seems to be no sufficient reason for God to create two identical entities. A concept of absolute time would imply the existence of homogeneous time, with portions thereof identical to one another. This would be contrary to the principle of indiscernibles.

Only individual substances are considered to possess ultimate reality, and time is not such a substance. Furthermore, there is no vacuum in nature, since this would infer the presence of a homogeneous empty space, one point in which is exactly like any other. Occupying any point in this vacuum would be like occupying any other and no particular reason would exist for a choice between them. This state of affairs would be contrary to both principles of sufficient reason and the identity of indiscernibles.

Moving a stone from one place to another does not leave the stone unchanged. There is now a completely new set of interrelationships among the active forces exerted by the different bodies in the universe. Time is not real; it only represents the order of real existences. C. R. Morris elaborated:[2]

If we wish to understand the true nature of reality we must banish from our minds all notions of space and time. Instead we must conceive of an order of relations between entities whose essence is active force. In conceiving of these entities as exercising their forces in an ordered system we must not think of them as operating at points in space or of the system as a mechanical system, excellently as such a fancy may seem to satisfy the imagination. We must think of real entities as acting intensively, rather, in the manner a soul acts, though without the consciousness which attends upon some of the activities of souls. If we think of the universe as a system, or ordered unity, of the activities of monads, we shall be in no danger of thinking of space and time as real existences. Such a mistaken notion would be entirely due to imagination.

Space and time are thus dependent on things and events. "*Space* is nothing but the order of existence of things possible at the same time, while *time* is the order of things possible successively."[3] When his correspondent objected that "space does not depend upon the situation of bodies," Leibnitz replied:[1] "'tis true, it does not depend upon such or such a situation of bodies; but it is that order, which renders bodies capable of being situated and by which they have a situation among themselves when they exist together, as time is that order, with respect to their successive position. But if there were no creatures, space and time would be only in the ideas of God." Eternity itself is not a matter of duration but of things. Everlasting things endure eternally.

The eternity of God, however, does not depend upon things. He exists without them. "The immensity of God is independent of space, as the eternity of God is independent of time. They only signify with regard to these two orders of things that God would be present and co-existent with everything which existed. Thus I do not admit what is here advanced, that if God alone existed time and space would exist as at present. On the contrary, on my view, they would exist in ideas only, like mere possibilities."

Keith Ballard[4] claimed that Leibnitz's theory of space and time was not consistent with his overall outlook. In the former, the reality of extended substances was implicitly admitted; in the latter, it was implicitly denied. Furthermore, since the monads are essentially window-less, space and time constitute real relations among them, even taken as real. Ballard therefore suggested the following modifications of Leibnitz's theory of space and time to bring it in line with his metaphysical doctrines:

Just as we regard our notions of *material* substances as resulting from a confused state of perception of *mental* substances, so likewise we may regard the relations of space and time between these material bodies as resulting from a confused awareness of the "point of view" of mental substances. In other words, the "point of view" is a determinable quality of monads—each monad having its own particular determinate value of this quality. But in the state of *confused* perception, in which mental substances are misperceived as material bodies, the "point of view" (which normally represents a relation among mental substances) is also confusedly interpreted as the relation of space and time among material bodies.

Hendrik Antoon Lorentz (1853–1928) made the first major contribution to the solution of an apparently paradoxical experimental finding, which was puzzling scientists. A. A. Michelson and E. W. Morley[5] had observed the same velocity of light when measurements were made in the direction of the rotation of the earth and at right angles to it. The motion of the earth seemed to add nothing to the speed of light.

Lorentz[6] proposed that a rigid body moving relative to

the ether undergoes a contraction in the direction of the motion in the following ratio:

$$\frac{1}{\sqrt{1 - \frac{v^2}{c^2}}},$$

where v is the velocity of the body through the ether and c is the (constant) velocity of light.

He then advanced the following equations of transformation between the space coordinates (x, y, z) and time coordinate (t) of a system stationary relative to the ether; and the space coordinates (x', y', z') and time coordinate (t') of a system moving uniformly with velocity v relative to the ether along the x-axis:

$$x' = \frac{x - vt}{\sqrt{1 - \frac{v^2}{c^2}}},$$

$$y' = y,$$
$$z' = z,$$
$$t' = \frac{t - (v/c^2)x}{\sqrt{1 - \frac{v^2}{c^2}}}.$$

This set of transformation equations would account for the null results of Michelson and Morley. When the velocity v is low relative to c, as obtains under normal conditions, the ratios v/c^2 and v^2/c^2 are practically zero, considering that c is 186,000 miles per second. Consequently, t would be the same as t'.

Two events at the same time at the same place would be observed as occurring simultaneously by observers in both coordinate systems; only the time of observation would be different. When two events occur in one system at the same time but at *different* places, however, different times would be observed for the two events in the other system. When two events happen at different times and places in one system, observers in the other system might see the events in an order reverse to that seen by observers in the first system.

There is a difference therefore between a body at rest and one in motion. But this difference cannot be detected because of compensatory changes, which give rise to identical results in both cases. The simple Galilean transformation,

$$x' = (x - vt),$$
$$y' = y,$$
$$z' = z,$$
$$t' = t,$$

is still considered true. But it *appears* to be violated.

24.
The Relativity
of Einstein
XXX

Albert Einstein (1879–1955) announced a transcending principle to subsume the *real* Galilean transformation and the *observed* Lorentz transformation.

To achieve his purpose, it was necessary to analyze the precise meaning of the concepts of spatial coordinates and of the temporal duration of events in physics. The former entails a fixed frame of reference in a definite state of motion (an "inertial system"). Coordinates within that inertial system are determined from measurements with rigid rods. Analogously, a clock at rest within the inertial system defines a local time. The time of a particular inertial system would then be made up from the local times of all the space-points collectively, provided means are available to set the local clocks relative to one another. It is not essential that the time of one inertial system agree with that of any other.

Einstein noted that the classical rules for the transformation of space and time from one inertial system to another do not insure compatibility between the assumption of the constancy of the velocity of light and that of the universality of the laws of physics. The two assumptions were made compatible by accepting the Lorentz transformation for the conversion of spatial coordinates and time from one inertial system to another. The same practical ramifications of Lorentz's theory follow, such as the electromagnetic field equations, contractions of rigid rods, and dilatation of time.

Einstein's underlying explanation, however, was diametrically opposed to Lorentz's. He did not ascribe the results to motion through the ether; in fact, in his theory, the very existence of the ether was denied. Instead, his postulate was a direct consequence of the verifiable behavior of measuring rods and clocks in motion. The lengths and the time intervals are the observations we make after the performance of certain operations. They are not objective properties of bodies or events. When two bodies are in relative motion, each observes the other to be contracted. Neither has shrunken in actuality, but only appear so to each other because of their relative motion. The Special Theory of Relativity postulates that the laws of physics are invariant with respect to the Lorentz transformations.

A number of new insights have been introduced by the Special Theory; among the most interesting are those concerning the four-dimensional continuum, the notion of the simultaneity of distant events, and the measurement of time.

A physical event is addressed by four numbers in both Newtonian and relativity physics. For this reason we say that the totality of all possible events forms a four-dimensional continuum. This continuum is called space-time. Each point in space-time is identified by its coordinates. There are important conceptual differences, however, between the two four-dimensional space-time continua.

In classical physics the three-dimensional space is distinctly separable from the one-dimensional time. There is no necessity of union into a single four-dimensional continuum. The Special Theory, on the other hand, establishes a formal description for the way in which spatial and temporal coordinates are necessarily fused together in natural laws. The absolute independence of Newtonian space from time gives way to a necessary relation among them.

In Euclidean geometry the distance, *ds,* between two neighboring points is given by the formula:

$$ds^2 = dx^2 + dy^2 + dz^2.$$

This was extended by Minkowski to a generalized Pythagorean theorem as follows:

$$ds^2 = (dx_1)^2 + (dx_2)^2 + (dx_3)^2 + (dx_4)^2.$$

In this equation, it is assumed that no gravitational field exists. Usually x_1, x_2, and x_3 denote space coordinates and x_4 relates to time. Specifically, x_4 is *ict,* where i is the square root of minus one. The equation is commonly seen in the form:

$$ds^2 = dx^2 + dy^2 + dz^2 - c^2 dt^2.$$

The minus sign before the fourth term on the right side leads to two types of distances. When the sum of the first three terms is larger than the fourth, *ds* is positive, and the four-dimensional separation is real. When the reverse holds, the result is the square root of a negative number, and the four-dimensional separation is imaginary. The so-called spatial distance between events is no longer an interesting physical fact; a space-time interval has taken its place.

Einstein went on to show logically that simultaneity cannot be determined by experimentation. It cannot be verified; it can only be defined. As long as the measurements are consistent with the assumed definition, the results would also appear consistent within the context.

Two events which are simultaneous in one coordinate system may not necessarily be simultaneous in another. A moving clock ticks more slowly than an identical one at rest.[1] A clock ticking at one-second intervals when permanently situated at the origin, would show

$t = 0$ and $t = 1$

as two successive ticks. The Lorentz transformation for two successive ticks in a moving clock would be

$$t' = 0 \text{ and } t' = \frac{1}{\sqrt{1 - \frac{v^2}{c^2}}}.$$

A further analysis of the space-time continuum resulted in the General Theory of Relativity. It took Einstein seven years to formulate the General Theory because he found it difficult to dissociate himself from the idea that coordinates must have immediate metrical meaning,[2] and to accept the condition that differences in coordinates do not necessarily mean measurable lengths.

There are innumerable frames of reference which can be used for dating events in nature. The Special Theory restricts itself to Galilean frames. It would be simpler, however, if natural laws could be described in a manner totally independent of particular frames of reference. The General Theory addresses itself to this objective for the case of the structural laws for the gravitational field. It proposes to reduce rotational and accelerated motions, as well as the uniform motions in the Special Theory, to a relativistic basis.

Fundamental to the General Theory is the principle of equivalence. This is illustrated by a person living in a large closed box away from other bodies in space, so that the system is free from gravitational forces.[3] Suppose the box is moving at a velocity which is changing at the rate of thirty-two feet per second per second. The person inside the box would go about his rounds and make his calculations on the basis of a force of gravity exerting a pull of thirty-two feet per second per second. A person outside of the system would observe that the box was accelerating at the rate of thirty-two feet per second per second. The principle of equivalence acknowledges both views to be equivalent and equally valid.

From the viewpoint of a third observer, the outside person holds the correct interpretation. The latter would see the floor rise and hit the objects released by the inside occupant of the accelerating box. This is the natural thing to expect and can be predicted *a priori*. Nevertheless, it is contrary to the Newtonian answer, which rests upon long and careful experimentation showing that the gravitational and inertial masses are proportional. But in such times, it is preferable to follow the usual scientific practice and select the simplest of the alternatives which would explain the facts at hand. Of the two, the outside person's description is the simpler. The real world is to be modelled after a four-dimensional geometric continuum subject to certain intrinsic laws.

When Einstein generalized his relativity theory from uniform motion to all kinds of motion, matter had to be taken into account, since there is always an interaction between motion and matter. Gravitational fields can be detected by the way in which objects move, and two consequences were drawn by Einstein from this relation.

The first can be deduced from the Special Theory's stipulation of the equivalence of energy and mass. Since light is energy, it therefore carries mass. Consequently it would be expected that a light ray would be deflected in a gravitational field. The effect of gravity upon a moving mass is a function of its velocity in a formula advanced for light by Einstein. A star near the edge of the sun would be observed as displaced from its normal position.

The second consequence is the effect of gravity on time scales. A clock coming close to the strong attracting gravitational potential of a large star would appear to slow down. This can be demonstrated through observations on the spectral lines of atoms, resulting from the vibrations of the electrons. Einstein predicted a shift in the spectrum of light from the sun toward the red end, as compared to that of light from an earth source, due to the retardation of the motions of atoms by the gravitational field of the sun. A sun-second was calculated to be equal to 1.000002 earth-seconds.

In the absence of gravitation, the structure or physical properties of space can be described by an Euclidean expression of space-time. In the presence of gravitation, however, the Riemannian geometry of curved surfaces is more appropriate. The structure of space-time is affected by the disposition of its matter, and gravitation is described as the curvature of space-time, which depends in turn upon the masses distributed throughout space-time. Speaking to reporters upon his first arrival in the United States in the nineteen twenties, Einstein commented: "If you will not take my answer too seriously, but regard it only as a kind of joke, I can explain it as follows: It was formerly believed that if all material things disappeared from the universe, time and space would still remain. According to the theory of relativity, however, time and space would disappear along with the things."

25.
The cosmic
elephant
XXXI

The origin of the universe. Man has always been awed with the immensity of the heavens.

Our little earth belongs to the Milky Way galaxy of stars, which is but one of the billion galaxies within sight of the Hale 200-inch telescope which has a radial range of 3×10^{22} miles. Beyond the range of our telescope, the galaxies may continue without limit. Our galaxy alone contains several billion stars, distributed over a vast space with an average density of about 10^{-30} gram per cubic centimeter.

There has been endless speculation about the origin and age of this impressive cosmos. Such considerations are but a reflection of our own mortality. Because we are born, we speak of origin. Because we die, we speak of age. We look at everything through these lenses. Were we immortal, such concepts would never have crossed our mind.

In 1954 the *British Journal for the Philosophy of Science* sponsored an essay competition on the question: What is the logical scientific status of the concept of the temporal origin and age of the universe? Four typical comments are excerpted below.

M. Scriven concluded that "no verifiable claim can be made either that the universe has a finite age or that it has not. We may still believe that there is a difference between these claims: but the difference is one that is not within the power of science to determine, nor will it ever be." The universe was very different at various stages of its evolution and extrapolation from present state to point zero in time is unwarranted. He further emphasized that estimates of the temporal origin of various processes within the universe are not sufficient for that of the universe itself.

R. Schlegel suggested that it may be that "only for limited subprocesses of the universe that time order, or past and future, may be defined." There is no such thing as absolute time for the universe as a whole. "Time is then only a 'local' property, as for example, in the domain of our observation of galactic expansion and evolution, and questions about the extent in time of the local universe may not properly be asked."

G. J. Whitrow insisted that the term "cosmical time" may be used only if time had a beginning. But time cannot be discussed without assuming time. The implication is that the concept of time is either invalid or ultimate.

R. Abramenko brought out the difficulties of pinning down the meaning of the term "absolute age of the universe." It is impossible to find an *a priori* basis for selection among the "Newtonian uniform time flowing from $-\infty$ to $+\infty$. . . . time represented by a hyperbola . . . [and] mathematically possible time of positive curvature analogous to Riemannian closed space." The latter time-dimension "curves upon itself:" a point T_0, the temporal origin of the universe, does not exist in such a circle of finite time. Any point on this circle may serve as an origin for a local event or phase, but not for the universe.

From a practical standpoint observations cannot be made at the actual beginning of the universe. The question arises as to observations which can be made today, from which a calculated determination can be made at least in principle. Investigators who adopt empirical approaches to support evolutionary theories attempt to find some readily observable natural processes which can act as clocks. By extrapolating backward the temporal behaviors of several such clocks, their point of convergence is obtained. This is then taken by the scientists as the origin of the universe. Typical time-pieces are radioactive decay rates to produce radiogenic lead in rock ores on the earth's surface, thermonuclear conversion of hydrogen into helium, and the Hubble-Humason red shift in the spectra of the nebulae. The various attempts seem to converge at the finite age of about four billion years, with no apparent chronological progression, such as from the earth, star, galaxy, to universe.

Einstein attempted to apply his relativity concepts to the universe as a whole.[1] The universe was regarded as homogeneous with a mean density of about one hydrogen atom per cubic meter. This led to the picture of a constant curvature of space like that of a ball instead of an egg. In analyzing the properties of the four-dimensional space-time continuum, he concluded that the curvature of space is independent of time. The universe is generally static. No matter how hard he tried, however, he was not able to find solutions to the mathematical equations.

  He then attempted to surmount the dilemma by introducing a new arbitrary universal constant. This cosmologic constant was supposed to indicate a new kind of force between galaxies. Unlike the Newtonian force of attraction, which varies as the mass of the bodies involved and is inversely proportional to the square of the distance, the new force is supposed to be a cosmic repulsion independent of mass and varies directly with the distance between the bodies involved. This unique force was superimposed on Newtonian attraction. At equilibrium conditions the cosmic repulsion balances off the Newtonian attraction. This effort also failed.

Willem de Sitter formulated another mathematical approach to Einstein's spherical universe involving the postulated cosmic repulsion force. The law of gravitation permits the universe in equilibrium to be either full of matter in the sense that attraction and repulsion balance each other, or empty. These two fictitious extremes may be regarded as the limiting cases, the asymptotes of cosmology. Einstein's equation described the former alternative; de Sitter's the latter. As in the case of Einstein's model, de Sitter's was not confirmed by astronomical data. Both were replaced by models based on a continuous expansion of the universe.

E. P. Hubble observed that the spectra of light coming from the galaxies shift toward the red. Furthermore, the amount of shift seems to vary directly with the distance. The only explanation that could be given was that the galaxies are receding from each other and that the universe is in a state of uniform expansion.[2]

Observations covering areas out to 2.5×10^8 light-years indicate that the universe expands at the rate of about 100 miles per second per million light-years distance. In addition to this uniform overall recession, there are random motions of the galaxies of about 100 to 200 miles per second. Every point is moving away from every other, since the universe has no center. As a result of such observations all modern cosmological theories conform to the Cosmological Principle, which states that every observer in the universe is equivalent to every other.

Alexander Friedman attempted to answer the question whether or not the expansion of the universe will ever stop. His analysis of Einstein's cosmological equations and astronomical observations permitted two types of expansion: a periodic and an aperiodic type. In the former case the universe alternately contracts to a maximum density, such as that of a nuclear fluid of 10^{14} times the density of water, and expands. In the latter case, it is assumed that the universe underwent a contraction beginning an infinite time ago to a state of maximum density, following which it began its present phase of unlimited expansion. Observations on the rate of the present expansion imply that the velocities with which the galaxies are moving from each other are seven times that necessary for their mutual escape. This favors the nonpulsating one-swing representation, which places the universe on its present ever-expanding course.[1]

Georges Lemaître[3] rejected de Sitter's theory because it implied an Euclidean metric. He began with the closed space of Riemann and other geometric conceptions, giving rise to a space with a variable radius. Also considered essential were certain aspects of relativity which led to the cosmologic constant and cosmic repulsion. This line of thinking gave birth to the expansion theory. According to his concept, the universe started a definite time ago from the explosion of a highly compressed, extremely hot, homogeneous state, which he called the primeval atom. The universe expanded rapidly after the initial explosion, with the state of high density lasting for only a few minutes. Clusters of galaxies formed after about a billion years and continued to move away from each other over the course of the aeons.

Although Lemaître's hypothesis has many attractive features, it has not achieved general acceptance. Typical reservations were presented by W. H. McCrea.[4]

[Our] present knowledge of the properties of nuclear species seems to show conclusively that the supposed initial nuclear processes would not produce the observed abundance of the elements. But at the same time, it has been found that the observed abundance can almost certainly be accounted for by processes that are going on all the time in the interior of certain stars. Finally, in spite of interesting attempts, it has not been possible to ascribe the main characteristics of the universe, such as the formation of galaxies, to an evolutionary history of the whole universe.

E. A. Milne developed one of the more controversial general theories of the universe.[5] He gave the following account of how he became interested in the mathematics of time, which was the cornerstone of his cosmology.[6]

In applying Lorentz's formulae to the gravitational field of the entire universe, Milne felt that

the crux of the matter was Einstein's empirical assumption of the constancy of the speed of light to all observers. One could not have taken this over as it stood, as its validity might be affected by the pressure of a gravitational field; on the other hand one could not with effect replace it by any other convincing empirical assumption. It was therefore necessary to dispense with the assumption. The assumption came in expressing the relation of the metre-scale to the standard clock. If one dispensed with Einstein's assumption, one would have to rely solely on measures with the standard clock, and derive space-measures from time-measures. The problem resolved itself therefore into whether the Lorentz formulae could be established on the basis of time-observations only, without employing Einstein's assumption about the velocity of light.

By expressing all measures as time measurements or light-time, the traditional relativity space-time was not employed to describe the motion of a body or its kinematics. Both space and space-time were considered as artificial constructs. The assumption of the curvature of space was regarded as unnecessary. No physical properties at all were ascribed to space.[7] The observer may use an arbitrary private space with arbitrarily calibrated clocks to describe phenomena presented to him in nature.

Milne emphasized three principal points of difference between his theory of gravitation without general relativity and Einstein's theory with general relativity as follows: First, all observers are not regarded as equivalent. Only those observers standing in the same relation to the distribution of matter can be considered to be equivalent, such as the limited group associated with the nuclei of galaxies. Second, the choice of a space is arbitrary for an observer. He may even choose a private Euclidean space to describe and locate the events within his cognizance. Third, there is no so-called natural or proper time. The time-scale is a matter of choice. The observer need only find the conditions required for congruence among the clocks.

A consistent system of time-keeping throughout the universe is maintained by construction of an equivalence. In view of the fact that there is only one universe, there can essentially be only one equivalence. It is not necessary that only a single uniform time-scale be adopted. Any number may be chosen, each with a different dynamics. Two were chosen by Milne because of the particular significance of two species of dynamics.

He began with the definition of a substratum, which is identical with the universe. It is represented by a uniform collection of particles carrying ideal observers, none of whom has a preferential position. Hubble's law is assumed, as well as the Cosmological Principle. The time scale involved in this expansion is called kinematic time. It is the time of Maxwell and Lorentz, which suits the interpretation of electromagnetic phenomena. It is the time kept by disintegrating atoms and fundamental particles all in uniform relative motion.

The second time scale is called dynamic time. This is the time of Newtonian mechanics, which is applicable to real macroscopic observers and massive bodies, relatively stationary in a nonexpanding universe.

The two time-scales can be regraduated in terms of each other by a suitable equation. On the dynamic scale, a pendulum has a constant period and would take an infinite number of swings to go back to creation in dynamic measure. On the kinematic scale, however, the period gets progressively shorter and the number of vibrations approaches infinity as the figure approaches zero.

As we go backward in time, the form of dynamics is increasingly unlike that of the present. We may continue to use the same everyday dynamics if we insist, of course. But the mathematical results would not be phenomenologically true.

Theoretical disarray. Many other scientific cosmological theories have been advanced, such as J. B. S. Haldane's quantum transactions,[8] A. S. Eddington's expanding universe,[9] Bondi-Gold-Hoyle's steady-state universe,[10] F. L. Arnot's static universe,[11] and W. H. McCrea's "interaction in existing matter in which matter is not strictly conserved."[12]

There seems to be an inordinate temptation to substitute logic for observation.[13] Beneath much of the disarray, however, is the lack of a clear conception of what is meant by the beginning of the universe. The essential problem, as A. C. B. Lowell[14] maintained,

is the transfer from the state of indeterminacy to the condition of determinacy, after the beginning of space and time when the macroscopic laws of physics apply. When viewed in this way we see that the problem bears a remarkable similarity to one with which we are familiar. This is the indeterminacy which the quantum theory of physics introduces into the behavior of individual atoms compared with the determinacy which exists in events where large numbers are involved.

Light

As far as effects upon the earth is concerned, the most powerful source of light is the sun. This dazzling white disc appears to us as the largest and the brightest of the stars. Actually it is among the faintest. The reason for the illusion is its proximity to the earth. The next nearest is three hundred thousand times farther away. Nevertheless it is huge by earthly comparisons. It has a diameter of 865,000 miles. The surface at 6000°K radiates 3.79×10^{33} ergs of energy into the void every second, ninety-three million miles away from the earth. Of this massive output only about one part in 120 million is absorbed by the planets and their satellites. Even so, 1.94 calories impinge perpendicularly upon each square centimeter of the surface of the earth's outer atmosphere per minute. A total of 13×10^{23} calories is received by the earth per year from the sun. Geological studies and astronomical calculations suggest that the sun has been radiating at about its present rate for the greater part of the four billion years or so of its estimated life.

The transmutation of hydrogen is presently accepted as probably the principal source of the sun's energy. Assuming that each square inch of the sun's surface is equivalent to a searchlight of fifty horsepowers, and such a source loses about .05 ounce of matter per century, the total loss in weight so far would be about 4×10^{23} tons, or about .0002 of its total mass.

Light itself consists of radiations spanning a spectral range of more than sixty octaves in wavelength from a few hundredths of an Ångstrom (Å) unit to some miles. Only one octave from 4000 to 8000 Å in wavelength is visible to the human eye. About half of the incoming rays from the sun lie in this visible range. The ultraviolet portion is greatly increased during certain solar disturbances. As the radiation penetrates the earth's atmosphere, the spectrum is changed considerably by a series of interactions. The oxygen in the stratosphere is converted into ozone through the absorption of ultraviolet light. Ozone itself is even a stronger absorber of ultraviolet light, so that the biologically harmful ultraviolet light below 3000 Å never reaches the earth's surface. The three-mile layer of water vapor in the earth's atmosphere is an additional filter.

The velocity of light in a vacuum is 186,000 miles per second. In reflection off any fixed or rotating mirror, the frequency of vibration remains the same. When the light source and an observer are moving relative to each other, or when light is reflected off a moving mirror, however, there is a change in frequency. This is known as the Doppler Effect. The wavelength is decreased as the source of light approaches and increased as it recedes from the observer.

Light travels in an essentially straight line. It can traverse a vacuum and matter is not necessary for its transmission. It is regularly reflected at a smooth surface. In the process, the angle of incidence is equal to the angle of reflection. It is also refracted at the interface between two transparent media of unequal density. Snell's Law holds for a plane surface: The sine of the angle of incidence bears a constant ratio to the sine of the angle of refraction. The refractive index, which gives this constant ratio, is equal to the ratio of the velocities of light in the two media.

When certain crystals, such as Iceland spar, quartz, mica, and topaz, are involved, a single beam of light is refracted into two different directions. This phenomenon is known as double refraction.

Alternate light and dark zones are observed in the phenomena of diffraction and interference. The former results from the passage of light through a slit, forming shadows and light patterns. The latter results from the interaction of two or more sources of light, again forming fringes of darkness and light.

Actually, interference patterns are observable only when the two light beams bear a definite and constant phase relationship to each other. Such coherent beams are not produced directly by the more common light sources. They are usually produced for interference demonstrations by splitting the light beam from a single source. Since 1960, intense beams of coherent light have been obtained in a single ray by special devices called lasers. The atoms in a gas mixture, such as helium-neon, or a solid, such as ruby, are first excited to emit radiation at their characteristic wavelengths by electrical or radiant energy. Some of the emitted radiation stimulates other atoms to emit in time with the original wave passing down the laser tube. In bouncing back and forth between the silvered ends, ever-increasing numbers of atoms are stimulated to emit in the same tightly organized coherence. The effect cascades until the laser beam bursts from the transparent end of the tube. These pulses are characterized by a high power concentrated over a small area, a low dispersion, a sharply defined wavelength, and a high coherence.

When light is viewed through a single Nicol prism, nothing unusual is observed. When it is viewed through two Nicol prisms, one of which is rotated while the one nearest the light is held stationary, however, a continuous change of intensity is observed. A maximum is reached at a certain point of rotation and a minimum at right angles to it. This is due to the phenomenon of polarization. The light vector is resolved into two component rays as it goes through the first Nicol crystal. The planes of polarization of these rays are perpendicular to each other and both are perpendicular to the line of travel of the light itself. One of the rays, called the "ordinary ray," is prevented from passing. Only the other, called the "extraordinary ray," goes through the first crystal to impinge upon the second. As the second crystal is rotated the extraordinary ray acts as an ordinary one, or an extraordinary one, or partly both, depending upon its direction relative to the crystal face.

Light bounces off electrons in the same way one billiard ball bounces off another in what is known as the Compton Effect. It also exerts pressure, the magnitude of which is equal to the density of energy in the radiation. This is quite small in everyday events, so that it is not noticed. Under special circumstances, such as the hot interior of the stars, however, it amounts to enormous values.

A single spectral line is broken up into components by a magnetic field. This is known as the Zeeman Effect. It is also broken up into components by a strong electric field. This is known as the Stark Effect.

The spectral components of light differ considerably in their absorption and interaction with various substances. Water, for example, is strongly absorptive in the infrared region of the spectrum. A centimeter path will filter out nearly all of the infrared rays beyond 14,-000 Å. All proteins absorb below 2000 Å, while most amino acids do not. Chemical compounds can thus be identified by their respective absorption spectra.

Many chemical reactions are stimulated by light. The photochemical changes are induced only when the light is actually absorbed.

All this and a lot more about the behavior of light has been known for some time. These observations have continued to challenge the most brilliant of scientists to produce some comprehensive theory that will bring to them all an intellectual unity.

27. Corpuscular theory XXXII

The Pythagoreans long ago subscribed to the belief that light is a manifestation of particles emitted by the luminous object into the eyes. This view was adopted by Newton two thousand years later.

A corpuscle is the localization of energy or momentum in an extremely small volume, which is invisible and moves through space with a definite velocity. The history and identity of the corpuscle can be followed continuously. Over a lighted area the energy from the source is distributed discontinuously and concentrated at these corpuscular points.

In order to have something available in which these corpuscles can move, Newton postulated an ether. This ether was supposed to be of a composition not unlike that of air but "far rarer, subtiler, and more elastic." It is presumably denser in free space than in solids. The speed of light corpuscles is accelerated going from a more dense ether, as occurring in air, to a less dense ether, as occurring in glass. Reflection is accounted for by the peculiar surface effect that ether "in the confines of two mediums is less pliant and yielding than in other places." According to Newton's ideas the light beam reverses itself under these conditions because of the resulting difficulty in penetrating the surface. On the other hand, "if the differing densities of the medium be not so great, nor the incidence of the ray so oblique as to make it parallel to that superficies [surfaces] before it gets through, then it goes through and is refracted."

To explain simultaneous reflection and refraction, Newton resorted to "fits of easy reflection and easy transmission." As the rays "impinge on the rigid resisting ethereal superficies," they "cause vibrations in it, as stones thrown in water do in its surface; and these vibrations . . . alternately contract and dilate the ether in that physical superficies." Rectilinear propagation of light was readily explained by the corpuscular theory although it was subsequently observed that actually there is a slight deviation around the edges of an obstacle.

Subsequent to Newton, a series of optical phenomena was discovered which could not be explained by means of the corpuscular theory. The principal ones that led to the abandonment of Newton's corpuscular theory in favor of a wave theory (described in more detail in the next Commentary), were interference, diffraction, polarization, double refraction, and electromagnetic phenomena.

Just about the time when physicists had become used to the idea of the wave theory as the basis for explaining the behavior of light and were ready to bury the corpuscular fits of Newton, however, additional observations were made in the laboratory, which compelled a reconsideration of the corpuscular concept. This modern development began about 1900 with Max Planck's (1858–1947) theory of black-body radiation, which introduced a new fundamental unit of action.

The stage was set by observations on the so-called ultraviolet catastrophe. According to the classical Rayleigh-Jeans Law, the density of radiant energy of a heated body is proportional to the square of the frequency. It should increase without limit as the wavelength is made progressively shorter. All energy should, therefore, have escaped from matter long ago in a burst of ultraviolet light. But this has not happened. Actually the formula did serve to explain the behavior of the lower frequencies reasonably well; and another empirical formula was contrived which turned out to be suitable for the higher frequencies but not the lower. At this point Planck entered the scene.

He considered a model of the heated body as an array of innumerable minute oscillators, operating at various frequencies. In this model, heat is absorbed by an increase in frequency and released by a decrease. He found that if the calculations permitted the change of frequencies to take place in a continuous fashion, the end result would be the ultraviolet catastrophe. The higher frequencies would take up all the energy. To avoid this situation, Planck introduced two restraints: (1) energy must be exchanged in discrete packages, and (2) these packages, called "quanta," are equal to a constant, h, times the frequency. This means that the higher frequencies require a greater amount of energy to build up their units of exchange than do the lower frequencies. Hence the lower frequencies are able to undergo energy exchanges much more readily. This resolved the problem of the ultraviolet catastrophe.

By means of the constant h, Planck was able to provide mathematical form to the concept of energy corpuscles. However, he was not sufficiently confident to give it universal status. While he specified that energy is absorbed from matter only in discrete quanta, he acquiesced to the continuous wave demands of Maxwell's theory for light radiation outside of matter. This split personality of the quantum was overcome in the explanation of the photoelectric effect given by Einstein in 1905.

Einstein postulated that light is propagated as individual "photons." Each photon is a distinct quantum of energy, which maintains identity throughout its path. Certain observations were only explainable by Planck's unit of energy and not by the wave theory. For instance, it is observed that an insulated negatively charged metallic plate loses its charge when illuminated by light below a critical wavelength. The total number of electrons emitted per second depends on the incident light intensity. The maximum velocity of the emerging electrons for a given wavelength of light, however, is independent of the intensity but *is* a function of the frequency.

The electron also emerges with the same energy regardless of the distance between the light source and the metallic plate. According to the wave theory, energy is distributed evenly over the entire wave front. As the wave front spreads, the amount of energy per unit area decreases as the light source is moved away from the metallic plate. It would be difficult to see how such a hypothesis would lead to the same maximum kinetic energy of the ejected electron when the light is one foot away, as compared to a hundred. The observation can be accounted for readily by the corpuscular theory, whereby one photon ejects one electron.

Despite the regaining of much status of late, however, the corpuscular theory of light still has a long way to go to afford complete intellectual satisfaction.

28.
Wave theory
XXXII

The long-standing rival to the corpuscular theory of light is that of the wave.

A wave moves through something, which does not itself move. The energy is continuously and uniformly distributed. Newton's objection to the wave theory was based on its alleged inability to explain the rectilinear propagation of light. "If it consisted in pression or motion . . . it would bend into the shadow. For pression or motion cannot be propagated in a fluid in straight lines, beyond an obstacle which stops part of the motion, but will bend and spread every way into the quiescent medium which lies beyond the obstacle."

Actually, rectilinear propagation and reflection can be explained by the wave theory. Christian Huygens (1629–1695), the formulator of the wave theory, was able to advance a satisfactory answer by detailed consideration of the nature of wavelets at the wave front. Interference was also explained. The series of alternately light and dark bands is the result of the interaction between the two light waves. When two troughs or two crests of the respective waves meet together, they reinforce each other and produce a bright region. When a trough and a crest meet, they neutralize each other and produce a dark region.

The electromagnetic version of the wave theory originated in an attempt by James Clerk Maxwell (1831–1879) to describe the properties of a medium that transmits electric action. Michael Faraday had observed that the plane of polarization of light in a refractive medium is rotated under the influence of a magnetic field. Maxwell developed equations which expressed the laws of induction and creation of electric fields by charges and of magnetic fields by currents and which showed the nonexistence of "true" magnetism. This approach ran into some difficulties with respect to the conservation of electricity and the comparative behavior of open and closed circuits. This was met by introducing the idea of a "displacement current" which could exist even in empty space.

A series of mathematical considerations led to the conclusion that electromagnetic disturbances travel as transverse waves, involving an oscillating magnetic vector. The two vectors are equal to each other and perpendicular to the direction of propagation of the electromagnetic disturbance. The velocity of the latter is a function of the ratio of the units of charge in the electromagnetic and electrostatic systems. Laboratory observations showed the electromagnetic constant of Maxwell's equation to be the same as the speed of light. His conclusion that light is an electromagnetic phenomenon was thus confirmed experimentally.

It was further supported by the results of Ludwig Boltzmann and Heinrich Hertz. The latter had generated electromagnetic waves by purely electrical means, and showed that these waves possess many of the properties of light.

Generally speaking, the wave concept, particularly in its modern formulation, explains the behavior of light in its common aspects, involving light propagating in space, light interacting with light, and light interacting with electricity. However, it remains wanting in phenomena involving the interaction of light with matter. Many properties of electrical waves differ from those of light waves. For instance, some electrical waves go through a brick wall, whereas light does not. This particular difference may be due to the differences in the wavelengths. As the wavelength becomes shorter, the wave properties give way to corpuscular properties. It is difficult to detect wave properties with x rays or gamma rays, although interference properties have been detected with x rays. In addition, Maxwell's findings have been challenged with new experimental results which lay completely beyond the possibilities of the electromagnetic wave, such as the photoelectric effect.

29.
Attempts at theoretical reconciliation
XXXII

Diligent attempts have been made toward reconciling the two conflicting theories of light. We may begin this part of the story with Hero of Greece in the third century.

Hero stated that the rays of light reflected from a mirror always take the shortest path between two points. Actually, this is not always the case. With the concave mirror, the path taken may be the longest among the neighboring alternatives. His assertion has been accordingly modified to: The paths of rays of light are relative extrema.

Descartes' laws of reflection and refraction may be reduced to a single all-embracing minimal law of the optical path: When a ray of light is emitted from a point A, reaching a point B after any number of reflections and refractions, the optical path will be a relative extremum—usually a minimum. The law of the optical path, as stated, applies to the transmission of light, regardless of the theory under consideration. It may assume different forms, however, depending upon whether the corpuscular or the wave theory is accepted.

If we assume that light is a wave, then the law of the optical path can take the form of Pierre de Fermat's (1601–1665) Principle of Least Time: When a ray of light is emitted from a point A, reaching a point B after any number of reflections and refractions, it will follow that path for which the time of transit will be a relative extremum—usually a minimum. If ds represents an element of length, μ the refractive index of the medium, $\mu\,ds$ becomes the optical path over the distance ds. The Fermat Principle may be expressed in another manner: Along the ray of light transmitted between A and B, the optical path,

$$\int_A^B \mu\,ds,$$

will be an extremum—usually a minimum.

If light is treated as corpuscular in nature, then the law of optical path assumes the form of Pierre de Maupertuis's (1698–1759) Principle of Least Action: A particle m, thrown from a point A with a total energy E in a conservative field of force and reaching a point B, will follow that path for which the Maupertuis action,

$$\int_A^B mv\,ds,$$

is an extremum—usually a minimum. Here v is the velocity of the particle and the momentum mv takes the place of the refractive index μ.

William Hamilton (1805–1865) was the first to notice the close resemblance between the two principles. By analyzing a particle's momentum along the path of a ray of light, he concluded that the paths of the rays of light in a refractive medium and the paths of energy E of the particles in a field of force, where $\mu = mv$, will be the same. This theoretical discovery that the orbit of a mass point moving in a force field follows the same principle as a ray of light proceeding between the same points of origin and ending became the forerunner of the third phase in the development of the quantum theory. This new start was made about 1926.

Louis de Broglie initiated the new phase by introducing the concept of wavelength into the classical Hamiltonian analogy between optics and dynamics. He was struck with two difficulties in the then-prevailing theories on the nature of light. On the one hand, the energy of a light corpuscle according to the quantum theory is equal to Planck's constant times the frequency. But the purely quantum theory of light has no provisions for the definition of frequency, and it would thus appear that the ideas of a light corpuscle and of periodicity must be introduced at the same time.

On the other hand, stable electronic motions in the atom are governed by integers. The only known phenomena in physics involving integers were those of interference and of the normal modes of vibration. It appears therefore that the idea of an electron corpuscle and of periodicity must also be introduced at the same time.

In this connection, it is necessary to remember that the waves in wave mechanics are not physical ones. They do not describe the behavior of individual photons. They indicate the probability of the distribution of energy involving a large number of photons. They only give a statistical distribution or probability that an electron or a photon will be found in a given region of space. The complete path of a single photon cannot be traced.

Accepting the relativity idea of the equivalence of mass and energy, de Broglie postulated that in a mechanical system mass particles also show wave characteristics. Rectilinear propagation of light beams is used to explain optical behavior involving large openings, and the spreading out of waves is needed to explain behavior involving small openings. Similarly, wave mechanics, instead of ordinary mechanics, are required for masses of atomic dimensions. He predicted in 1923 that a particle of mass m and velocity v would behave as a wave with a wavelength equal to h/mv. This was experimentally confirmed by others two years later by reflecting electrons and x rays against a crystal face.

Erwin Schrödinger believed that de Broglie had oversimplified the problem of quantization of the associated wave motion of the electron in the atom. de Broglie had assumed the applicability of ray-optics to waves of atomic dimension. Schrödinger referred to the analogy between the interrelationship of true quantum mechanics and classical mechanics and that of physical optics and geometrical optics. In the latter case, the ray-tracking characteristics could not be used to explain diffraction and interference. Analogously, classical mechanics cannot explain phenomena of atomic dimensions. He sought to develop a more rigorous treatment of the wave motion. His efforts gave rise to a fundamental differential wave equation, in which the symbol Ψ represented the amplitude of the waves associated with a particle. Since the equation involves partial differential terms, the question arises as to how quantized phenomena can be extracted from it. Schrödinger accomplished this by imposing restrictions to insure "physically admissible" solutions, which meet certain requirements of continuity, single valuedness, and finiteness everywhere. The solutions are called "characteristic functions," "proper functions," or "eigenfunctions." The values corresponding to these functions are called "eigenvalues."

Schrödinger's theory of radiation encountered many difficulties because of the assumption that the space occupied by the de Broglie wave is filled with a continuously distributed negative charge, the density of which is proportional to the wave intensity at any given point. This charge cloud replaced Niels Bohr's corpuscular electron. Werner Heisenberg later showed that most of these wave packets spread very rapidly. The wave packet then is not a satisfactory representation of a corpuscular electron even over a relatively short period. The packet also makes it difficult to place the potential energy of an electron at a particular point in space as called for in Schrödinger's wave equation. Similarly, the mass, energy, and other characteristics must be diffused throughout space.

Further modifications were made by Paul Dirac by assuming that the wave associated with the electron is represented by a function of four components. This replaced the original single scalar function. In this respect it is to be noted that a wave associated with an electron does not follow the classical wave picture in several respects. The associated wave is restricted to regions, the dimensions of which are of the same order of magnitude as the wavelength. Furthermore, when the associated wave meets an obstacle, the classical wave picture cannot be invoked to explain interference. We can only say that in some fashion the electrons congregate in the area of greatest intensity of the associated wave, as assumed in wave mechanics.

Dirac's advances led to equations involving mass, charge, magnetic moment, and angular momentum in electron particles. These are capable of predicting the Zeeman Effect, the fine structure of the spectrum, and the existence of the positron. They also explain electron diffraction by crystals and their undulatory behavior in an atomic system where spin results in a certain anisotropy of the associated wave. When applied to photons, however, his concepts did not give a completely satisfactory interpretation. The photons would only possess half of the symmetry necessary for an adequate description of light.

In order to account for the existence of photons, another quantum version of the electromagnetic field was formulated by Werner Heisenberg and Wolfgang Pauli. Their proposal invokes a limit to the accuracy with which one can simultaneously determine the electric and magnetic fields. However, the theory works for only weak electromagnetic fields in empty space, and for the interaction of light with elementary particles in the first approximation. Under these conditions it can explain the photoelectric and Compton effects, which are normally considered corpuscular properties, and interference, Doppler phenomena, and polarization, which are normally considered wave properties. Dispersion, the Raman Effect, and the conversion of radiation into matter as in the creation and annihilation of positrons are also within its scope. Planck's Law is explained, provided it is assumed that one photon is the same as another.

Despite all of this impressive progress, neither quantum mechanics nor electrodynamics is completely satisfactory. Electrodynamics definitely fails for very short wavelengths and strong electromagnetic fields, and for dealing with the question of the finite size of the electron. A fundamentally new approach to explain phenomena occurring in spaces comparable to the size of electrons is required if the theories of light and matter are to be unified. Reconciliation between optics and mechanics can be made if: (1) the photon can be regarded as exactly a corpuscular particle with extremely minute rest mass, so that its velocity is always close to that of light, and (2) the classical light wave can be made identical with its associated wave, the propagation speed of which is always greater than that of light.

Given these two premises, one would only need to determine the order of magnitude of the difference between the masses of photons and those of material corpuscles. But this cannot be done. To do this requires that the two mathematical entities should possess the same elements of symmetry and other properties so that they can reduce to each other. The Ψ-wave of primitive wave mechanics is scalar, while the electromagnetic wave is described with two-vectors. The Ψ-wave of Dirac's magnetic electron has four components, which, moreover, are not the components of a vector. Some success has been achieved in connecting the light field of classical theory and the associated wave despite the difference in elements of symmetry. But the electromagnetic light wave and the associated wave with photons as corpuscles are not identical.

While much of the experimental results appear to bear out similarities in behavior between electrons and electromagnetic rays, the two are not identical. Electron waves are deflected by magnetic fields although light waves are not. The penetrating power of electron waves is very limited when compared to x rays of equal wavelength. And finally, what is meant in a physical sense by the rest mass of a photon?

And so the effort toward the synthesis of the corpuscle and the wave goes on . . .

Life

30.
Definition
XXXIII

Attempts at a precise definition of life usually wind up as tautologies. The definiendum is introduced, albeit in different words, into the definition itself. In some cases, life is defined by its manifestations. Even in these instances it is difficult to arrive at a list of necessary and sufficient properties. Many individuals have been content to accept the thesis that life involves some happy combination of capabilities, including some not yet detected involving laws of physics not yet known.[1]

One of the most poetic definitions of the nature of life was written by V. M. Garshin[2] in 1881:

A young disciple asked of that saintly sage, Jiaffir: "Master, what is life?"
In silence, the Master turned back the soiled sleeve of his sackcloth burnoose and showed the disciple a revolting sore that was eating into his arm.
And, at that very time, the nightingales were trilling in full song, and all Seville was fragrant with the sweet odor of roses.

31.
Characteristics
XXXIII

Composition. The bulk of the tissues are composed of the following elements: carbon, hydrogen, nitrogen, oxygen, phosphorus, sulfur, chlorine, sodium, magnesium, aluminum, silicon, potassium, iron, and calcium. Elements present in trace quantities include manganese, copper, zinc, arsenic, cesium, and boron. At least thirty five of the hundred or so elements have been found in eggs, including strontium, lead, uranium, and selenium.

Most of the chemical compounds consist of highly polymerized substances colloidally dispersed in a dilute solution of electrolytes. Among these protoplasmic constituents, the proteins are especially conspicuous in animal cells. Their functional forms include the enzymes, which account for a major fraction of the total proteins in the protoplasm.

In the case of plants, most of the dry weight is made up of carbohydrates. Cellulose forms the structural components of the trunks and branches and starches and sugars constitute the main energy sources and food reserves.

Size. Galileo calculated that a tree about a hundred meters tall would bend under its own weight when subjected to the slightest force. Such a mechanical problem does not confront the whale, which is buoyed up by the enveloping water; but other limiting factors do come into play. While the volume of the tissues to be nourished increases as the cube of the length, the absorptive surface of the gut increases only as the square. This factor alone tends to set an upper limit to the size of an organism of a given form.[1]

At the opposite extreme of size, the smaller bacteria measure around a tenth of a micron in diameter. A cell of such dimensions can still contain the full complement of chemicals required for the living processes that go on in the larger cells of plants and animals. This would represent the order of magnitude for the lower limit in size for a living organism.

Individuality. Within these boundaries, the organism undergoes continuing chemical changes and yet maintains a characteristic form among the million and a half species of plants and animals. It exhibits both irritability and adaptability. The former represents the capacity to respond to changes in the environment, peculiar to various groups of organisms. The latter provides the added ability of directing the response in such a way as to increase its survival level under the new conditions.

Within the same organism, the different cells react differently. In the case of the preembryo of the sea urchin, for example, the equatorial group is capable of maturing into a complete sea urchin without the north and south polar cells. Neither of the polar groups can do so alone, although they are able to do so together.

Metabolism. There are physical systems, such as a flame, which meet most of the conventional criteria of metabolism. There is an interchange of materials..The flame has a definite boundary. It remains steady and continuous over a long period of time. It produces new chemical products out of the original raw materials. Yet a flame is not metabolizing in the living sense.

An essential criterion which is not met in physical systems is the incorporation of the products into the very structure of the system, thereby bringing about a renovation of the system in the very process itself.

Reproduction. Living organisms can be altered in such a way that reproduction would be an impossibility. Yet they remain as alive as ever. It is the reproduction of constituents of the living cells, therefore, rather than that of individuals which constitutes the fundamental property of life. In this regard, an offspring can be considered to be the reproduction and metamorphosis of a particular kind of cell, namely the fertilized egg.[2]

Of the various constituents of the cell only those which contain nucleic acid have been observed so far to reproduce directly by a self-duplicating process. The gene itself has been considered to be a string of nucleotides, each position in the string marked by one of four nucleotide units—adenine, thymine, cytosine, and guanine.[3] The complete nucleic acid molecule is a rigid helix involving two strands. Adenine occupies a position on one strand just complementary to that of thymine on the other, and cytosine is likewise complementary to guanine. The gene self-replicates itself by suitable polymerization and fitting addition of the four nucleotide units from the metabolic mix onto a preexisting template. The process has been duplicated in the laboratory by means of extracts from bacteria.[4]

The life of an individual may be said to begin the moment the fertilizing sperm triggers a series of reactions in the egg. Supernumerary sperms are excluded and the cytoplasm of the egg is activated.[5] The block previously preventing the development of the egg cell is removed.[6] The interchange is restored between the egg nucleus and the egg cytoplasm.

Energy sources. There are two main sources of energy immediately available to the living organisms. One is the energy stored in chemical compounds. The other is the energy of impinging radiation. In general, green plants and some colored bacteria are capable of direct utilization of solar radiation, which is then transferred to their chemical constituents. Other organisms depend primarily upon the resulting stored energy.

Quite apart from the energy aspects, living organisms are profoundly dependent upon solar radiation. Their most important responses are treated in Commentary 41 below.

Electricity. Electrical manifestations are observed in all living organisms. The total power dissipation by a plant root, grown in a weakly conducting salt solution, is about 10^{-9} watt, with a potential of a few millivolts and a current of about one ampere per square centimeter.[7] Mormyd fish emit several weak electrical pulses per second which cease for a second or two when the fish are stimulated. This rate of electrical discharge can be changed through avoidance conditioning.[8]

Identifiable electronegative voltage patterns have been detected in 118 out of 123 female patients with malignant changes. In the group without malignancy, 611 showed electropositive fornix readings and 126 electronegative.[9] Special intensities in voltage gradients have been noted in the process of wound healing. Recovery from nerve injuries in rabbits and man has been observed to be preceded by electrometric shifts to optimal levels.[10]

Radioactivity. Albert Nodon,[11] for example, believed that living plants and animals exhibit radioactivity as a function of their vitality. He reported radioactivity to be higher in the reproductive organs than in the vegetative, and higher in freshly cut plants than in faded. Dried plants showed a very low level. Healthy insects contained as much radioactivity as plants, but sick insects contained less. Dead insects had none.

Temporal relations. As a rule, physical events reflect the momentary demands of the immediate situation. The trajectory of a falling body is not affected by the manner of its arrival at the point of origin. The equilibrium constant of a chemical reaction is not influenced by the history of the reactants.

Living organisms, however, exhibit a complicated temporal relationship. The historical past involves a series of qualitatively different experiences which is continually changing. There seems to be a responsiveness not only to the past but also to the future. Reference to the past is summed up in the laws of heredity and recapitulation. Reference to the future is expressed in morphogenesis, regeneration, goal-seeking, and, in some respects, reproduction. The gill clefts displayed in the human embryo are the vestiges of our fish-like ancestors in geological times. The human embryo repeats its phylogenetic heritage by proceeding from the protozoon through the fish, amphibian, and reptile to the mammal. At the same time an ontogenetic transformation occurs in which the process is compressed to nine months and the history of the immediate parents is impressed upon the system.

Past experience is also reflected in the reaction of an organism to stimuli. As E. S. Russell[12] puts it:

When we see in the development of the frog the reproduction of stages passed through by its ancestors near
and remote, the formation and destruction of organs
which had significance in some distant past and now
have none, when we see the mature eel setting forth on
its dangerous journey to spawn thousands of miles away
in the depths of the Atlantic, we must in accounting for
these facts bear in mind their essential relation to the
past history of the race; they can be understood only
on the hypothesis that in some way or other the past of
the organism and of its ancestors still influences its present activities.

The formation of an eye in the embryo long before it
can see, the early segregation of germ cells, the building of nests by the mother bird when the eggs are not
yet ready to be laid—all appear anticipatory of the future. Certain types of cell cleavage cannot be understood
except with reference to the end-result of the formative
process.[13]

32.
Rhythm
XXXIV

Rhythm is all-pervasive.[1] It exhibits itself in such elementary physiological processes as cell division, electrical firings in sense organs, and contraction of vac-
uoles,[2] and such behavioral patterns as the gobbling
and strutting of turkeys.[3] Some of the responses, such as
shivering movements, are simple wave forms; others,
such as heart actions, are complex.
Plant growth. An approximately 24-hour rhythm occurs
in the opening and closing of flowers, leaf movements,
rates of respiration, photosynthesis, and other processes
in plants. Many of the patterns retain the circadian
period as long as the external conditions remain the
same.[4] Tree rings follow cyclic variations.[5] The single-
crested 11-year cycle of the North American pine is
characteristic of a relatively damp climate. The double-
crested 11-year cycle of the Arizona pine tends to occur
when the summers are relatively dry.
Animal metabolism. The rate of metabolism in animals
is peculiar to the species. The heart rate varies from 6
per minute for the leech, 8 for the hibernating hedgehog,
16 for the whale, 20 for the bass, 30 for the camel, 40
for the crocodile, 72 for man, 75 for the cockroach, 150
for the dolphin, 260 for the shrimp, 300 for the buzzard,
600 for the mouse, to 920 for the finch.[6] The metabolic
rate within a group of animals is roughly dependent on
the size. The smaller the animal and the more food and

oxygen it consumes per unit weight, the more energy it produces and the higher its rate of metabolism.[7] The hummingbird weighing no more than a dime has a metabolic rate fifteen times as fast per gram of tissue as that of the pigeon and a hundred times that of the elephant.

Parasite population. The microfilarial parasite in man migrates in a periodic fashion.[8] Peak population in the blood occurs at midnight and the minimum near noon for *Wuchereria bancrofti.* The cycle is related to the 24-hour habits of the host rather than to the alternation of day and night. Men on the night shift show a reverse periodicity in microfilariae. The transition occurs in about a week, so that the sleeping-waking rhythm does not exert the decisive influence, but rather the entire 24-hour rhythm as a whole. The microfilariae are most abundant in the peripheral blood during the time when the arthropod vector bites to suck blood. During the rest of the period they move into the small vessels of the lung.

Seashore activities. There is no more fascinating place to observe periodicity at play than the seashore.[9] Among the well-known examples is the behavior exhibited by the flatworm, *Convoluta roscoffensis.* It contains green algal cells, with which it lives symbiotically. The flatworms exist in large numbers on the sandy beaches of Normandy and Brittany. As the tide covers the habitat, the animals burrow into the sand and reside in darkness twice a day. This protects them from the shock of the waves. As the tide recedes, the animals again come to the surface, enabling the algae to photosynthesize. Egg-laying also follows the rhythm of the tides. It begins with the spring tide and continues for a week.[10] Some eighteen hours are available to the worm for the surfacing and laying of its eggs.

The common periwinkle alternates between an active life in the water and moist air at high tide and suspended animation within its shell. This constant tidal rhythm seems to leave a lasting effect on the shore animal. Inactive periwinkles can be activated by shaking. More rapid shaking is required at certain times than at others. Even after having been kept for some time in the laboratory, periwinkles behave in consonance with the tidal rhythm. At periods corresponding to low tide, they have to be shaken much longer than when the tide is high.[11]

A striking case of adaptation to local tidal rhythm was

reported by F. A. Brown.[12] He transported oysters in sea water in light-proof containers from New Haven Harbor, Connecticut to Evanston, Illinois. The oysters gradually rephased their cycles of shell opening in the dark from the precise lunar-day of high tide at New Haven to the theoretical time of high tide in Evanston, were there a coast line at that location.

Bird migration. The annual migration of many species of birds is familiar.[13] The golden plover travels its entire 2400 miles nonstop. The champion traveller of them all, however, is the arctic tern, whose summer and winter homes are some 11,000 miles apart. Unlike other birds, the sooty tern follows a 9.7-month cycle.[14] After breeding, the birds fly all over the seas to unknown points and reassemble at Ascension Island to breed in a season adjusted to the tenth full moon.

Game cycle. The small game cycle of North America is most definitive in Alaska, Canada, and northern United States.[15] It becomes less distinct as one proceeds farther south. It is evident in hares and rabbits; meadow mice, lemmings, and squirrels; lynx, wildcats, pine martens, fishers, foxes, wolves, coyotes, mink, and other predators; owls, goshawks, and marsh hawks; ring-neck pheasants, northern grouse, Hungarian partridge, and bobwhite quail.

There are suggestions of two major types of cycles for the European lemming, the snowshoe rabbit of North America, and its predators.[16] A short period of four to five years corresponds roughly to the half cycle. The arctic lynx, marten, skunk, and mink follow a cycle of 9.5 years. The arctic fox exhibits a four-year cycle. The wolf's population curve is a discordant one, while the bear, badger, and wolverine fluctuate relatively little. Variations in the densities of foxes, martens, rabbits, and lynx show a correlation with the frequency of sunspots.

Many of the biological cycles are parallel over a 9⅔ year period. These include the number of tent caterpillars in New Jersey,[17] of salmon in the Restigouche River,[18] and of lynx in Canada.[19]

Human manifestations. Human rhythms are matters of common knowledge and experience. The heart beats faster at night; blood pressure is lower; electrical resistance of the skin is higher; sight, taste, smell, and touch cease.

One of the basic expressions is the alpha rhythm of the brain. This oscillation is characterized by an electrical potential at the scalp of about fifty millivolts with a frequency of nine to ten cycles per second. Such a potential would suggest that a large number of brain cells must be working in unison at the same rate. The alpha rhythm disappears when the eyes are opened or the brain is otherwise occupied with a problem. The pattern appears to be one of inattention.[20]

E. M. Dewan[21] noted that the rhythm can be switched on and off by various means. It can be blocked when the eyes are closed by looking as if through the lid at a nearby object and can be restored by flipping the eyes upward in a relaxed way. Whether the brain waves can be entrained by external frequencies or not has been much discussed. It has been shown experimentally that light flickering in the range of brain waves can cause sensitive individuals to go into a state of seizure or disorientation under certain conditions.

Based on an analysis of such electrical manifestations in various parts of the brain, H. Gastaut[22] proposed a theory of transmission in the central system. Particular significance was given to the means by which the organism insures the necessary continuity and amplitude. "In fact, any slowing down or speeding up in transmission would lead to a lack or excess of information, whilst any diminution or increase in the amplitude of the transmitted signals would lead to an insufficiency or an excess of the transformation of these signals into sensations, ideas, or actions." He cited this as the reason "why the alpha rhythm is so strictly regulated at 10 cycles per second. A subject with more rapid rhythms, having more functional groups at his disposal, must have more information transmitted; conversely, a subject with slower rhythms must have a lower rate of transmission. The former will not be *better* informed, for an excess of information is itself a fault; the subject will indeed be quickly disturbed by the excess of information. As for the latter, the undesirability of being insufficiently informed needs no comment."

Periodicities also exist in the facility of performing tasks and it appears that information-processing in human beings is quantized rather than continuous.[23] Preliminary experiments suggest that the distribution of response time is lumpy. Observations on a human subject doing two laboratory tasks indicate that at least two associated periods of 50 and 100 milliseconds are present plus a third period of 265 connected only with the scanning task.

There is a seasonal change in the reaction times to optical and acoustic signals.[24] Human births show a cyclical maximum after midnight and a minimum around midday.[25] About 2000 periodic pathological disorders are now on record.[26] The frequency of manic-depressive attacks[27] and eclampsia[28] fluctuates as a semiannual cycle with maxima at the solstices and equinoxes. Even food allergy seems to occur according to a rhythmical distribution.[29]

Social activities also feature alternating upward and downward sweeps.[30] A 41-month cycle in prices, production, and sales has been noted.[31] Other economic cycles include an 8-year cycle for the average yields of the chief crops in central United States from 1881 to 1921,[32] an 18-year cycle for real estate transactions,[33] and a 54-year cycle for wholesale prices in England.[34]

33.
Animals' sense
of clock time
XXXV

People with a very low IQ appear to have an animal-like sense of time.[1] Idiots are unable to distinguish morning from afternoon. But, like fish and bees, they are aware of the hour when lunch is due. There is some indication of a relationship between the position in the phylogenetic ladder and the acceptable interval of delay in reaction experiments. The rat is capable of four minutes or less, the cat seventeen hours, the monkey twenty, and the chimpanzee forty-eight.[2]

A few examples of time sense in animals are presented below.

Snails. The moment for *Helix pomatia* is about .25 second.[3] In the case of the Japanese sea snail, *ishida-tami,* the time threshold turned out to be about .05 second. This snail shows a conspicuous shadow reflex, which disappears when a ray of light is interrupted at a higher frequency, as can be seen by increasing the speed of rotation of a slotted disc in its path.[4]

Fish. The fighting fish, *Betta splendens,* has been trained to react negatively to a revolving two-colored disc and positively to a uniformly gray disc. When the bicolored disc was rotated at a rate of 130 successive impressions per second, the fish reacted as it would to the gray disc. The fusion threshold was determined to be about 110 and the moment of discreteness calculated to be about .018 second.[5]

Insects. Bees can be trained to come for food at a definite time.[6] After regularly being fed at 24-hour intervals or greater frequencies, the bees begin to arrive ahead of schedule, as if anticipating food. The conditioning is apparently unaffected by light, humidity, temperature, or atmospheric electricity.[7] The behavior is tied in some way to the 24-hour rhythm. Attempts to condition the bees to a 19-hour cycle failed. The temporal memory persists for six to thirteen days.[8]

Birds. The sense of pitch and time of canaries was determined by means of photographic comparison of the rendition of simple songs by the birds and those by the trainer, as well as comparison of repeated patterns of the same bird.[9] The average deviation of eighty notes in pitch from the average of equivalent fractional points in repeated patterns ranged from .06 to .29 step. The average deviation in time of 128 notes was .01 second.

Rats. Rats are able to select the temporally shorter of two routes to food.[10] When spatial and other factors are ruled out in laboratory tests, they show no difficulty in differentiating between one-minute and five-minute choices. In some cases one-minute and four-minute alternatives are distinguished.

Dogs. T. J. Hudson[11] reported on his mastiff which would awaken the family at a certain hour, lead them to feed the horses at another time, and come to the kitchen for his own meal at yet another time. Variations were said to seldom exceed one minute from the appointed time.

Monkeys. H. Woodrow[12] trained two monkeys to reach for food upon raising of a screen after a longer interval but not after a shorter interval. After 2640 and 3600 trials, respectively, the monkeys responded accurately on the last day in 92.5 and 90.0 percent of the cases. A discrimination between 1.5 and 3.0 seconds was readily achieved.

34.
Man's sense
of clock time
XXXVI

Perception. No sense receptor has been identified for time. Consequently it is not reasonable in the light of available evidence to say that the passage of physical time is the stimulus for perceived time. It may be one of the contributing factors in shaping the configuration of perceived time. But as questioned by E. G. Boring,[1]

"How can a duration that takes time be immediately known, since the duration, not being instantaneous, is itself not all immediate? At what time in a time does one perceive that time?"

G. Iacono[2] reserved the term "temporal perception" to time as an explicit object of perception. He distinguished it from time as a mere immanent dimension of perception. Likewise, A. C. Moulyn[3] suggested that the specious present differs from physical time in being discontinuous. The process of learning consists in integrating the specious present of the mind with continuous physical time. Actually, the continuity of a time series is not necessarily that of an arithmetic continuum. The rapid succession of separate picture frames in the cinema can provide the sensation of continuity.

Experienced time itself is exhibited in various forms. J. Cohen[4] identified five, namely: the apparent duration of an interval of time which seems to last; the experience of the pastness of an event in a sequential fashion; the localizing of an event in time; sinceness; and futureness.

A. S. Eddington[5] noted that the time of our consciousness emphasizes intervals. Physics is concerned with descriptions in terms of coordinates. It is not the external events but their sense impressions, which provide our conscious time-succession. This is not clearly sorted out by us and "hence events throughout the universe are crudely located in our private time-sequence. Through this confusion the idea has arisen that the instants of which we are conscious extend so as to include external events, and are world-wide; and the enduring universe is supposed to consist of a succession of instantaneous states." We now know that it takes time for light to travel from an external event to our eyes and we have given up the idea of the instant of the external event being coincident with the instant of our sense impression.

But the theory was patched up although its original *raison d'être* had vanished. Obsessed with the idea that the external events had to be put somehow into the instants of our consciousness, the physicist succeeded in removing the pressing difficulties by placing them not in the instant of visual perception but in a suitable preceding instant. Physics borrowed the idea of world-wide instants from the rejected theory and constructed mathe-

matical continuations of the instants in the consciousness of the observer, making in this way time-partitions
through the four-dimensional world.

We should recognize the arbitrary nature of this construction, as well as the fact "that the original demand
for a world-wide time arose through a mistake. We
should probably have had to invent universal time-par-
tition in any case in order to obtain a complete mesh-
system; but it might have saved confusion if we had
arrived at it as a deliberate invention instead of an inherited misconception." We should not be surprised
therefore to find that many of the properties of the
physicist's time do not make common sense.

Perceived time is thus not a matter of mere intervals.
It is also a structuring mechanism, somewhat in the
fashion of mental coordinates.[6] Time is perceived as
background and as figure. This can be illustrated by
tapping pairs of sounds with a pencil. When the interval
is relatively short, we become aware of a pair of taps,
acting together like a pair of dots on a line. The sounds
are structured. But if the interval is greatly lengthened,
we no longer associate the taps as pairs. Instead we find
our mind drawn to the time flow itself. We begin to perceive the properties of fastness or slowness of passage.
In addition to these two aspects of background and
figure, other time perspectives come into play as our
minds wander over vast backward and forward extensions.[7]

Sense thresholds. Our impression of instantaneity ceases
at a critical duration for each sense. A. Charpentier[8]
found that a seven to fourteen millisecond flash of light
would not be distinguishable from a longer flash until
about seventy milliseconds. The point of time has an
extension of about .1 second for vision and .01 for
hearing and touch.[9] In the latter case, the threshold of
distinction, as well as the errors of estimations and
fluctuations, increase when the points of stimulation are
separated progressively farther apart on the body.[10]

An interval of .11 second is the shortest to provide a
perception of permanence. In the case of touch a minimum of about .002 second is required to separate two
stimuli; for sight, .043 second.[11]

Temporal acuity is highest for auditory perception. The
succession of two identical sounds, each reaching a dif-

ferent ear, can be recognized when only .002 second apart. When the sound reaches both ears from a source within a few degrees of the longitudinal plane perpendicular to the midpoint between the ears, a difference of arrival time of as low as .000025 second can be detected. There is a quick instinctive turning of the head toward the sound.[12]

Age variations. An infant less than a year old does not show a significant sense of time. He lives in the present and has no idea as to the duration needed to perform a given task. At two years of age, the average baby begins to become aware of temporal designations, which are marked by the character of action. By means of motor activities, the child implicitly makes reference to time.

The use of the term "today" appears at two years of age, "tomorrow" at two and a half, and "yesterday" at three years. Divisions into morning and afternoon occur at four years and into days by five. A gradual emergence of an objective socialized time concept takes place as the child grows older.[13] In answer to the question, "How long do you stay in school?" Louise Ames[14] received the following kinds of replies: Four-year olds usually said: "We will take a nap and then our mother comes." Five-year olds said: "Until lunch time." Six-year olds: "Until twelve." Seven-year olds: "Four and a half hours." A major improvement in understanding of temporal words is made between the fifth and the sixth grades. Maturity in this comprehension is reached by the tenth grade, at the age of sixteen.

The apparent duration of a given interval varies considerably with age.[15] Experiments have shown that a given period may appear to pass as much as five times less rapidly for a child of ten as for a person of sixty. A. J. Carlson[16] and others are of the opinion that the gauging of lapsed time is purely dependent on the particular concern of the individual and that age has little to do with the illusion. They do not accept Paul Janet's Law, which states that the length as which a given interval appears to an individual is inversely proportional to the length of his past life.

Sex variations. Women exhibit a stronger tendency toward overestimation of duration than men.[17] The appraisals of women are also more variable. They are less accurate in general and lean more toward figures ending in 0 and 5.

Personality variations. A person's concept of time is closely related to his character. It changes with his behavior during various periods of his life.[18]

Individuals who are considered highly integrated according to E. Jaensch's psychology of types are more susceptible to temporal distortions.[19] They are less capable of conceiving time as an abstract entity which is devoid of content. Experimenting on ninety-five high school girls, Y. Usizima[20] noted that time consciousness in the extroverted undergoes a certain modification, depending upon the content of the time interval. This was not the case with the introverted.

Parental dominance is reflected in an overestimation of time.[21] Middle-class children reveal a more extended time sense than those from other social classes.[22] Individuals with a high achievement motivation tend to be more occupied with anticipating future goals, scheduling, and other activities related to the management and the measurement of time.[23] A three-way correlation seems to exist involving acute time awareness, ascetic aesthetic taste, and high achievement motivation.[24]

Orientation to the future exerts considerable tension with a strong emotional gradient. Kurt Lewin[25] noticed that inmates of reformatories tend to become more recalcitrant as the day of their discharge draws near. One individual serving a three-year sentence tried to escape within a few days of his release.

Under experimental conditions 87 percent of the satiated subjects underestimated the time required to become satiated.[26] Of those not yet satiated, 52 percent overestimated the time involved up to the point of questioning. The underestimation was greater than the overestimation.

Perception of time and apparent duration is strongly affected by the presence of purpose and a person's feelings toward the task with which he is engaged.[27] R. J. Filer[28] asked three groups of individuals to estimate the duration of four minutes and thirty-seven seconds. The first group, writing words on pieces of paper, was told they could leave at the end of the session. The second worked for a prize against time. The control group just began at the beginning of the session. Both experimental groups estimated the time to be longer than the control.

Temperature effects. When subjects are requested to

tap out what appears to them as one-second intervals, the unit of time for each ten-degree rise in temperature becomes 2.8-fold shorter.[29]

Illumination effects. Decreased illumination increases the apparent frequency of a flickering light.[30] This occurs both for abrupt as well as for continuous variations.

When the subject attempts to compare two flickering light fields with cadences equalling a fixed ratio, the critical cadences appear to be the same as they approach the critical fusion frequency, regardless of the frequencies involved. Similar results were obtained on the relation between brightness and apparent frequency in comparisons between flickering lights and clicking sounds.[31] When the brightness was increased from 1 to 10, 100, and 1000 successively, the rhythm of sound clicks at 20 per second was judged to be approximately 40, 30, 20, and 15 per second. It is to be noted, however, that the sound rhythms above ten per second are difficult to judge on their own.

Spatial effects. The judgment of duration is affected by the spatial component in what is known as the "kappa effect."[32] This is demonstrated by the following experiment. A person is exposed to three flashes of light situated at various unequal distances from him. He is given control of the middle light in order to equalize the two time intervals being adjusted. In general, if d_1 and d_2 represent the successive distances corresponding to the intervals t_1 and t_2, respectively, then t_2/t_1 decreases as d_2/d_1 increases. When d_2/d_1 equals 1/10, the subject underestimates by 12 percent; when d_2/d_1 equals 10/1, he overestimates by 13 percent. Furthermore, time intervals presented in succession over greater space intervals seem longer than in other cases.[33]

The same response was seen in auditory measurements.[32] The flashes of light described were replaced by tones and the spatial distances replaced by tonal intervals. In this way the influence of tonal intervals on temporal judgments could be determined. When the temporal interval was indicated by a continuous tone of a different pitch, there was a tendency toward ascribing a shorter time interval to the higher tones.

Interval-length effects. Variations in the experience of sinceness show up when a subject is asked to mark off on a line the length corresponding to the time since various events in the past. If the lengths of the line are plotted against the logarithm of the corresponding time interval, a straight line is obtained. This holds for periods up to six months from now. The results follow the Fechner-Weber Law that perception is proportional to the logarithm of the stimulus. The results for intervals greater than a year from now do not follow such a pattern; they show a generally linear relationship.

In these and other estimates of time lengths, there are certain intervals which are more accurately sensed than others.[4] Men in general do better in estimating up to about six seconds than in estimating hours. Certain individuals, however, show remarkable ability in judging the length of time since a given event. R. B. MacLeod and M. F. Roff[34] reported an experiment in which two persons were placed for forty-eight and eighty-six hours, respectively, in a sound-proof room without time cues of any kind. The errors in judging lapsed time were twenty-six and forty minutes, respectively.

Interval-content effects. The structure of the filled interval exerts a considerable effect on the estimation of time.[35] A minute was judged by individuals reading from an editorial page as 1 minute 23 seconds, from a poem as 44.3 seconds, and doing nothing as 37.9 seconds.[36] Ten seconds on the witness stand was thought to be forty-five.[37]

As far as sounds are concerned, an increase in intensity results in overestimation of durations.[38] When two stimuli are presented at the same time, the weaker one appears to occur later. Such variations impose important nuances in the field of artistic rhythms. E. Meumann[39] found that a loud sound tended to shorten the apparent interval preceding it and increase the one following it. The overall effect is a completion of the rhythmic foot. He concluded that a series of sounds at equal actual intervals would be heard as an iambic rhythm and not a trochaic. Other workers, however, came to an opposite conclusion. H. Woodrow,[40] for example, observed the trochee to be more natural a rhythm than the iambus and felt that the accented member tends to begin the foot.

In the performance of a musical piece, A. Guttman[41] noted that the influence of the written material is stronger than that of the individual's tempo. Some conductors are extremely constant. But others exhibit considerable variation. Generally speaking, conductors may be divided into fast and slow types. The individual differences are more marked at the beginnings of symphonies than at the conclusions.

Exposure-order effects. The comparative judgment of the phenomenal lengths of two intervals of time is affected by the order of presentation.[33]

Activity effects. Awareness of time is reduced under Yoga discipline in which attention is fixed on momentary experience.[42]

The kinaesthetic perception of intervals is also radically altered by their activity content.[43] A time-interval with much activity seems greater than one with less. In war-prison camps, time appears to have no meaning because there is nothing to do.[44]

H. Gulliksen[45] found that subjects engaged in the following occupations overestimated a duration of two hundred seconds: relaxing, holding arms extended in order to produce fatigue, listening to a slow metronome, to a fast metronome, and holding the palm on a thumb tack. Subjects engaged in the following underestimated: reading from the reflection in a mirror, taking dictation, and doing problems in division.

Wish-fulfilling may homogenize the past and the future. Some moments may be prolonged; others transposed. As P. M. Symonds[46] explained, "Fantasy [may be] stimulated by present desire and its frustration. . . . [It may go] back to the past when a similar wish was fulfilled; and it is only through past experience that imagination can conjure up fulfillment. Then fantasy imagines how this wish must be fulfilled in the future."

The apparent duration is greatly increased over the actual in narrow escapes. Sensory experience appears slow, although the real speeds are high. The volume of nonsensory activities, such as imagination and thinking, is greatly increased per unit time, although the rate appears normal to the individual.

Illness effects. The perception of time is one of the first mental functions to be adversely affected in psychopathology.[47]

J. Coheen[48] compared fifty noninstitutionalized subjects with sixty-nine patients with brain disease. The latter group exhibited varying degrees of time agnosia, roughly proportional to the degree of deterioration. Seven cases of traumatic, alcoholic, and circulatory distur-

bances of the brain were pictured by G. M. Davidson[49]
as follows:

Common to all cases was a confusional state of short
duration. Following [this state] the patients would regain
orientation in space but remain disoriented in time for
the immediate present, as well as the element of time of
past events to a varying degree. While they recognized
and used, when questioned, verbal terms of time, it was
apparently meaningless to them. Otherwise their sen-
sorium was essentially unclouded. If impairment of
memory was at all present, it was insignificant. Other
traits common to all cases were apathy and unconcern
about their condition (the present) and indifference to
the past and future. They were unable to estimate short
and long intervals of time. The appreciation of rhythm
and chronology was intact. Aphasic status was negative
in all cases.

One of W. van Woerkom's aphasiacs[50] could not ordinarily follow the simplest rhythm tapping. Yet he could
do it very easily by clothing it with some melody.
    As mentioned by O. Fenichel,[51] some neurotics exhibit
a claustrophobia in time. The patient feels cooped up
by his duties and oppressed by the shortness of time
just as the claustrophobic feels hemmed in by the walls
of space. On the other hand, others "are afraid of 'broadness' in time; they hasten from one activity to the next
because empty time has for them the same significance
as empty space for some agarophobics."
    Difficulties in perceiving simultaneity and in reproduc-
ing short durations of empty time characterize some
psychotics.[52] Schizophrenics show temporal distortions
in various forms.[53] They tend to ignore proper time
relationships. They are plagued with disorders of association and affect. They withdraw from the world of
reality and slip over into the world of fantasy and
dreams. There seems to be some forgetfulness during an
impending schizophrenic break, over which the patients
themselves are concerned. F. Fischer[54] wrote about one
of his patients, who perceived everything as changing,
feeling more at east when he saw moving things. Another
patient said: "My head is a clock, an apparatus. I make
the time, the new time as it should be." Other patients
make such statements as: "I can't orient myself in the
world—I am not clear any more. Previously I was a
human being with body and soul and now I am not such

a being. I don't know anything any more. . . . The body is light and I am afraid it will soon fly away. I continue to live in eternity. There is no hour, no wavering between past and future." and "Is there any future? Previously I had a future, but now it shrinks more and more. The past is so obtrusive, it throws itself over me and draws me back." One of the important consequences of the schizophrenic's symptoms is the closing of the future to him. "I have a sort of routine which prevents me from considering the future. My creative power has been destroyed. I see the future as a repetition of the past," said a patient of E. Minkowski.[55] Many cases of paranoid schizophrenia reveal complaints of time shrinkage.[56]

P. Schilder[57] viewed the above expressions of schizophrenics as partially artificial as far as their real perception of time is concerned. In varying degrees, they represent a withdrawal from the real world. "These time disturbances are farther away from the immediate experience than the time disturbances observed in depressive cases and in depersonalization cases. Still it is an important fact that the patients use a time symbolism. We measure ourselves by the experience we have had, and from time to time everybody experiences the feeling that he has withdrawn from the world and that the flow of time is then changed. Everybody has some symbolism of time."

Drug effects. Certain drugs appear to decrease the subjective appraisal of clock time, such as cocaine,[58] thyroxine, and caffeine.[59] Others are said to increase such appraisal, such as amphetamine,[60] opium,[61] mescal, hashish, *Cannabis indica,*[62] marihuana,[63] and psylocybin.[64]

Hypnosis effects. Hypnotized subjects are capable of gauging short intervals during sleep with considerable accuracy, out-performing waking subjects.

The subject's time sense can be altered by the operator.[65] F. Podmore[66] recorded an interesting case. Under hypnosis, a subject was told to do something after 123 days. In the interim he was rehypnotized occasionally. While under the spell he correctly stated the number of days remaining, which completely escaped him during the waking hours. Podmore suggested the existence of a continuing stream of subconscious cerebral activity which is capable of remembering instructions during the hypnotic trance, or receiving impressions from the outside world, and of noting the passage of time. If the subject is made to promise under the hypnotic state to perform a certain act at a given hour on a given day, he will frequently do it while fully awake, yet not knowing why he is doing it, as if obeying some vital impulse. W. R. Wells[67] reported an experiment in which the subject remembered a series of nonsense syllables precisely at the appointed hour, a year after the hypnotic suggestion.

35.
Heard time
XXXVII

"Music makes time audible and its form and continuity sensible," said Susanne Langer.[1] In contrast to clock time, duration in music is an image of what may be called experienced time. Music creates a virtual time "in which its sonorous forms move in relation to each other—always and only to each other, for nothing else exists there." Thus Basil de Selincourt[2] advised that "there is no more crucial test of a composition than the test of length. The piece that seems long is the piece that has failed to suspend our consciousness of real time. The meaning of the sounds has died away from us, and we have remembered that the hands of the clock are going around."

Silence itself "bears and supports music," wrote Gisele Brelet,[3] by removing "it from the external world, by creating around it an atmosphere of calm collectedness in which it can flower." This birth of sound is contemplated by Hindus and Tibetans as a religious mystery. "A good silence, *heard* by the performer who is about to play, brings him an intense confirmation: already he is one with his audience, in proportion as they, with him, are discovering the inner principle from which he is born, and through which he will live, the sonorous force. . . . In any silence, indeed, an echo of the past meets an inkling of the future: a memory and an expectation." It is because of this silence that we are led to a whole series of expectations by the stimulus of a few sounds and chords.

Imagination, then, lies at the root of musical listening. As Aaron Copland[4] puts it,

at no point can you seize the musical experience and hold it. Unlike that moment in a film when a still shot suddenly immobilizes a complete scene, a single musical moment immobilized makes audible only one chord, which in itself is comparatively meaningless. This never-

ending flow of music *forces* us to use our imaginations,
for music is in a continual state of becoming. . . . This
elusive quality of music, its imagined existence in time,
is made the climax of Jean-Paul Sartre's treatise on
L'Imaginaire. Sartre in a well-known passage on Beethoven's Seventh Symphony, very nearly succeeds in
convincing us that the Seventh isn't really there at all.
It's not on the page, for no music can be said to exist
on the silent page, and it's not in any one performance,
for they are all different and not one can be said to be
the definitive version. The Seventh, Sartre says, can
only be said to live, if it does live, in the unreal world
of our imagination.

Music itself is inseparable from the other activities of
men. Their doings and the spirit of the age are embodied
in the popular music of the day.[5] The merry lilt of English madrigals of the sixteenth century is contrasted to
the twanging dissonance of American acid rock of the
twentieth century. When the patrons are the nobility, as
was the case with eighteenth-century concert music, the
style is formalized to suit the aristocratic salons. When
the prime customers are the adolescents, as is the case
with twentieth-century phonograph records, the rock
form floods the radio waves.

As the milieu surrounding the lives of composers change,
the compositions change. Dutch and Flemish musicians
reflected the temper of the Middle Ages, and Mozart
the elegance of Louis XIV. Caught up with the age of
revolutions, Beethoven's symphonies were a drastic departure from the tradition of Haydn. Wagner's *Ring of
the Nibelungs* was, in some respects, a protest against
the thinking of the day. In the modern world, the most
impressive outcropping of the personality of a people
into a body of music has been the transformation of
the African slave into an American citizen, as reflected
in his blues changing into jazz.[6]

This is why a musical experience can never be duplicated. Each rendition carries with it a *de novo* quality.
The relationship between composer, performer, and
listener is forever changing, not only in their impact
upon each other but also in their individual predisposi-
tions as effected by the environment. Bach, for example,
had composed his *St. Matthew Passion* for religous observances in a Catholic Church in the eighteenth century,
only on that special day to which the liturgical year had
been pointed. That experience of the devout is a far cry

from the response of a Madison Avenue atheist listening to the *St. Matthew Passion* as background music over a hi-fi in his sumptuous living room.

In the case of poetry, the metric form conveys a subconsciously audible time in its "patterned expectancy." To quote I. A. Richards:[7]

Rhythm and its specialized form, metre, depend upon repetition and expectancy. Equally where what is expected recurs and where it falls, all rhythmical and metrical effects spring from anticipation. As a rule this anticipation is unconscious. . . . The mind, after reading a line or two of verse . . . prepares itself for any one of a number of possible sequences, at the same time negatively incapacitating itself for others. The effect produced by what actually follows depends very closely upon this unconscious preparation and consists largely of the further twist which gives it expectancy. It is in terms of the variations in these twists that rhythm is to be described. . . . This texture of expectations, satisfactions, disappointments, surprisals, which the sequence of syllables brings about, is rhythm. . . . Evidently there can be no surprise and no disappointment unless there is expectation. . . . Hence the rapidity with which too simple rhythms, those which are too easily "seen through," grow cloying or insipid.

Patterned expectation requires the reinforcement of a binding resemblance of some kind. It may be in the realm of the audible, such as the succession of accents. Or it may be in the realm of the inaudible, such as metaphor.[8] Wallace Stevens[9] suggested that this "creation of resemblance by the imagination" in poetry may be "first, between two or more parts of reality; second, between something real and something imagined or, what is the same thing, between something imagined and something real as, for example, between music and whatever may be evoked by it; and third, between two imagined things as when we say that God is good, since the statement involves a resemblance between two concepts, a concept of God and a concept of goodness." There is a natural pleasure that arises spontaneously in us upon noticing a resemblance, a feeling of increased harmony, an intuitive resonance, as it were—an inaudible time.

To quote Stevens further:

We say that the sea, when it expands in a calm and immense reflection of the sky, resembles the sky, and this statement gives us pleasure. . . . when we think of

arpeggios, we think of opening wings and the effect of
the resemblance is pleasurable. When we read Ecclesiastes the effect of the symbols is pleasurable because
as symbols they are resemblances and as resemblances
they are pleasurable and they are pleasurable because
it is a principle of our nature that they should be . . .

36.
Seen time
XXXVIII

Rhythm in art is not the recurrence of material units but
of relationships. John Dewey[1] reminded us that

recurring relationships serve to define and delimit parts,
giving them individuality of their own. But they also
connect the individual entities they mark off, *because*
of the relations, association and interaction with other
individuals. Thus the parts vitally serve in the construction of an expanded whole. . . . The objective measure
of greatness is precisely the variety and scope of factors
which, in being rhythmic each to each, still cumulatively
conserve and promote one another in building up actual
experience.

Raymond Bayer[2] offered the following law of aesthetics:
"Phenomena of the aesthetic order are all characterized,
on every level, by a certain constancy: and this constancy is revealed to us by the study of rhythm." He
discusses a book by Petrovitch, who gave examples of
this underlying mechanism in different phenomena and
showed that, even though the major arts appear quite
different in form, they share common rhythms.

The dynamic rhythm of grace is affected by speed in
effort, languor in repose; tonal rhythm is marked by
a transient excitement and a surrender; pictorial rhythm
is built up on sporadic tension together with nonchalant
relaxation, so that these pulses of alternate storm and
calm are based on a balanced dispersal of the stress,
whatever graceful object we may be considering. It happens that, in working with this idea, one may reach a
more abstract invariance, which would hint at the existence of an archetype of rhythms: a patient inventory of
the denumerable riches in the realm of the Graceful
reshapes it into images of a rare coherence for the mind.
Its realm exhibits a system—as your eyes finally discover—of an invariable mode of being of the psychic Self:
I mean all the distinct gestures and appropriate rhythms
of *alacrity*.

According to Bayer, rhythm penetrates the subject at
different levels. The first level of rhythm is called the
mimetic stage. Here the actual feeling is directly represented in the work. For example, the ambiguous expression of the Mona Lisa provides the direct psychic rhyth-

mic translation of a complex personality. It is a play on moods. The second level of rhythmic penetration is called the symbolic stage. Here the rhythmic composition of the pattern reaches us. Looking at the Gioconda, at the cadence in her countenance, the rhythm of her crossed hands, and the turning of her torso, we acquire a feeling of its rhythmical intention. The third level is called the cryptogrammatic stage. Here the rhythm is imparted by virtue of its strangeness. This is regarded by Bayer as "the height of art and at the same time attains the abstract perfection of its calligraphy." It is rhythmic order in the abstract. Art is regarded as the precise interplay of these three phases.

Another analysis of the various levels at which temporality exhibits itself in art was made by Micheline Sauvage.[3] The first and general level concerns the changes in a piece of art with time, such as the dulling of the colors with age. At the second level, time itself is a working element, such as the time required in a sonata, a play, and a novel. At the third level, a temporal mode is evoked by encounters such as the presence of a sarcophagus in a museum or the age of the subjects in a painting. He kept searching, however, for yet another level of time over and above these times.

In studying Poussin's *Shepherds in Arcadia,* he found in it a

sort of insistence by the artist which unmistakably goes beyond the purely temporal description of an episode . . . above the tomb, the dead man in the tomb, above the shadows cast by the lateness of the day, above the prolonged perspective of future and past which opens at the heart of this so-called Arcadia instant. . . . Have we not here a *time intention,* or somehow an exhibited as opposed to an *implied* time . . . Or, perhaps even better, a time *represented* over and above the time of what is *represented?*

This time is not temporal in the sense that it "is not the work in time but time in the work." Instead of being referred to, as in the former case, as temporal, it is designated as chronian, after the French word *chronien.*

The artistic essence was captured in the following passage by Étienne Souriau:[4]

But the painter, the architect, and the sculptor are masters, by a more subtle magic, of an immaterial time which they establish when they create a universe whose temporal dimension can extend or contract in a moving or curious way. Now a brief and and fragile moment is brought to life brilliantly, perfectly; again the extent of the universe can reach to the equivalent of eternity. On this temporal frame is molded a content that can be as rich in rhythm, in impetus, in variation of speed or slowness (and hence in human and transcendental significance) as all musical or literary temporality. But this time is never suggested except by means that are indirect, oblique, and subtle. However fragile, delicate, unsubstantial may be these means of suggesting time, they are the key to the greatest success in these arts.

Thus it was that Paul Klee[5] reiterated that in a great painting the moment "must penetrate the soul. The formal element must blend with one's philosophy of the universe." He felt that the polyphony of painting brings the reality of simultaneity much more forcefully to the fore than music, for yesterday and tomorrow coincide. "Only the dead point as such is timeless," he said in his *Credo.*[6]

37.
Cultural time perspectives
XXXIX

The time perspectives of individuals are conditioned by their cultural contexts.[1,2] The rhythm of collective life often fixes the practical units of time.[3] The relation between the unconscious libido and the superego as it expresses itself in various cultures is an important factor.[4]

The origin of speech itself seems to be closely tied with man's appreciation of the future. Available evidence indicates that human speech began during the Upper Paleolithic.[5] At that time man started to show interest in the future. Unlike the Neanderthal, the Paleolithic man fashioned tools, which were used to make other tools for future use. A large variety of flint, bone, and wooden implements began to supplement the handaxe of the previous half a million years.

The subsequent evolution of the various languages led to a wide variety of ways in which time was expressed in the words of the different races and cultures. The Hopis, for example, lack words that refer directly to what we mean by time.[6] Their verbs have no tenses. There is an implicit feeling that everything that has happened still exists, although perhaps in a different form. The present is a sort of preparing for a continuous transition. The time reflects the individual. There is no simultaneity and time cannot have a number greater than one. Instead of saying, "I will leave in five days," the Hopi says, "I will leave on the fifth day." Yet even without any explicit or implicit reference to time in their language the Hopis are still able to be operationally effective.

Benjamin Whorf[7] showed that their model of the universe differs from both our commonsense and relativity concepts. The separation of space and time and the division of the latter into past, present, and future are not their classification. Instead, the cosmic forms are divided into two categories. The first is what Whorf called the objective or manifested. These forms are accessible to the senses, excluding everything belonging to the future, but are not divided into present and past. The second is the subjective or manifesting. This

comprises all that we call future, but *not merely this;* it includes equally and indistinguishably all that we call mental—everything that appears or exists in the mind, or as the Hopi would prefer to say, in the *heart* of man, but also in the heart of animals, plants, and things, and behind and within all the forms and appearances in the heart of nature, and by an implication and extension which has been felt by more than one anthropologist, yet would hardly ever be spoken by a Hopi himself, so charged is the idea with religious and magical awesomeness, in the very heart of the cosmos itself.

The Algonquins' concept of causality is one of fate. The portent need not precede the event, so that the Algonquin can do something about it. Instead, every single event is connected to everything else not in a cause-and-effect relationship but concretely in a fateful quality-of-the-whole relationship.[8] When the Indians saw the eclipse of 1642, they were no longer surprised over the Iroquois massacre of a group of them the previous winter.

From her study of the temporal descriptions of the Trobrianders, Dorothy Lee[9] concluded that they are not concerned with change so much as with what is, not with becoming so much as with being. "And each event or being is grasped timelessly; in our terms, it contains its past, present, and future, but these distinctions are nonexistent for the Trobriander. There is, however, one sense in which being is not self-contained. To be it must be part of an ordained pattern." A thing has no attribute outside of itself. As a result, there is no word *to be* or *to become.* The fully ripened yam, for example, is *taytu.* But there is no term for an unripened *taytu.* The tuber is not a *taytu* but a *bwanawa*. If overripe, it is a *yowana;* if blighted, a *nukunokuna*. In the mind of the Trobriander,

being or event remains discrete, sufficient unto itself, true and of value as itself, judged and motivated and understood in terms of itself alone. In the face of this apprehension of being, concepts such as causation and purpose appear irrelevant. . . . In the language of the Trobrianders there are no terms such as *because, so as to, cause, reason, effect, purpose, to the end, so that, why*. This does not mean that the Trobrianders are incapable of explaining a sequence in terms of cause and effect, but rather that this relationship is of no significance.

According to A. H. Gardiner,[10] the Middle Egyptian (2010–1788 B.C.)

had not yet developed, as Coptic later did, a precise set of tenses relating the time of verbal action to the time-standpoint of the speaker. The tenses which we discover in the earlier period are concerned, like the Semitic tenses, rather with the singleness or repetition, the momentariness or continuity, of the notion expressed by the verb; though particular forms have become already specialized for use in connection with past and future time, and so approximate our English tenses.

Before that period, the pictures did not even distinguish between a simultaneous spatial status and a temporal sequence.[11]

As culture advanced, language made progressively greater use of temporal ideas and less of spatial.[12] More objective factors were gradually supplemented with more subjective ones. These changes are reflected in language and can be detected from an analysis of the units of grammatic arrangement and the ideas of classifying and clarifying thought. As individuals begin to enlarge and organize knowledge, they move from the percept of time to the concept of time.[13] Formerly, their perceived time was always limited in span, involving a succession of concrete events. It was sensibly continuous. The perceptions of now and then, earlier and later were bounded by limits, such as this week and today. Now they develop an implied temporal perspective. Time is conceived as an immediately sensed passing-on continuum, unlimited and infinitely divisible, unified and coherent. They begin to grapple with related ideas, which will continue to plague them, such as change, past, and eternity.

Today's technological man has come a long way from his stone-age ancestor's lack of concern for the future and the Mesopotamian's resignation to the effects of time.

The American tends to view Nature as something to be mastered.[14] He refuses to lose himself in time's unfolding of Nature's way. Instead he tries to "gain" time. Efficiency is an economy of time.[15] Time is the scarcest resource and technology is designed to save time. His tradition is an ever faster movement toward somewhere. It provides the mechanism of cramming more and more objective experience per unit of time that gives rise to rapid cultural change.[16] The rapidity of change becomes accelerated by skillfully orchestrated competition. There is concern even in reducing the time it takes to make a decision.[17] Undue reflection is not to slow down the overall rate of change. Even increasing the frequency of paydays affects the temporal horizons of the workers in the appropriate direction.

To Albert Levi,[18] "the timetable, the schedule and the clock" are the "symbols of man's alienation from an intrinsically human world." In distinguishing the abstract physical clock time from the psychological personal time, he believed that the modern technological society has imposed "the abstract time of physical nature upon men whose dignity and importance lies wholly in the domain of time lived. This is the philosophical explanation of the crisis in the modern industrial world."

In analyzing the ontological origin of this preoccupation with time, Edmund Bergler and Géza Róheim[19] represented timeliness as "the fantasy in which mother and child are endlessly united. The calendar is an ultimate materialization of separation anxiety. . . . The obsessional overevaluation of time appears in our culture in part as a striving to achieve mastery over infantile disappointments."

38.
Western literature's treatment of time
XL

The paragraphs immediately following describe the concepts and attitudes of representative men of Western letters toward time, as embodied in their works.[1,2,3,4] *Dante Alighieri* (1265–1321) connected the origin of time with the creation of the universe.[5] God had simultaneously brought the angels, the Empyrean heaven, and corporeal matter into being. The source of motion was created when the Divine Will set the *Primum Mobile* in motion. With the birth of motion, which spread to all spheres, time was also created, since time is but the measure of motion.

In Dante's scholastic philosophy, motion included intellectual as well as physical change. Everything in its activity is seeking to return to God as the Source of its being. Time is important to man because it is through time that man reaches his final goal, guided by the flow of Love and Light from God. Dante also emphasized the importance of time in the *Purgatorio*. He was trying to teach men how to live so that they would not have to spend time in Purgatory but go straight to heaven after death.

While man is subject to time and should therefore use it well, God Himself is above time and motion. He is the changeless Serene One, in the Empyrean beyond space and time where "everywhere is here and everywhen is now," and the living Light has never varied.

Michel de Montaigne (1533–1592)[4] considered duration only as a momentary consciousness of "occasions unexpected, actual and fortuitous."[6] Yet he shares the human compulsion "always to think somewhere else." We go on living as if "we are never present with, but always beyond, ourselves. Fear, desire, hope launch us forth toward the future and rob us of the sense and consideration of what is." In our overzealous anticipation of the future, we lose our grasp of the present. The ultimate reference is death, and life becomes dying.

He rejected the wisdom of the Stoic, who accepted the course of things in the cosmic order, unfolding in time to the dictates of destiny. "Transport yourself into the experience of the evils that may happen to you. . . . prove yourself there, they say: affirm yourself there." He also rejected the advice of the Scholastic, who spoke of Being which transcends the world's events. We "have no communication with Being because all human nature is always being born and dying." Following this trend of reasoning Montaigne arrived at an acceptance of the human condition as one of "flux, shadow, and perpetual variation." It is not a matter of being but of passage. "I depict passage."

To depict passage, however, is not an easy feat. It involves the simultaneous seizure of the departing self and the evolving self. The difficulty is further aggravated by irregularities in the occasions of the world in the successive selves and in the instability of the mind. Thus the self becomes "an infinite diversity of faces." I at this now am a separate person from I then. The personalities pass into their successors as they respectively disappear during the passage of the instant. "Thus diversity and imperceptibly our soul darts out her passions."

Montaigne began the resolution of the dilemma with the concept of *prise,* the taking into oneself. This notion was the heart of his admonition to the teacher: "Let him make the pupil put what he has learnt into a hundred different forms and accommodate it to as many different subjects to see if he has really taken it to himself and made it his own." Since only things within reach can be grasped and only the present is within reach, "we must learn how to grasp the present good, and rest there; we have no hold upon that which is to come." The execution must be quicker than the flight of time. "I want to stop the rapidity of its flight by the suddenness of my seizing it." Each new moment brings new riches, for which we should be ready to grasp. And the means to do this is judgment.

In contrast to memory, judgment is "born of present occasions." It is the means by which the mind takes something into itself. It is based neither on science, knowledge, nor memory. "It plays an independent part." We have "knowledge only of the present, and none of all of what is past, no more than of what is to come." One must therefore free oneself from the bondage of preconceived knowledge and at the same time engage in the spiritual exercise of seizing the present in its power of apprehension. By thus "finding oneself always in the right place" the mind no longer is forced to oscillate over the temporal hiatus between birth and death, but simply *is.*

Blaise Pascal (1623–1662)[4,7] felt that animals experience only a succession of disconnected instants; and that this recreation of the instant at the lowest level is similar to that at the highest level of grace. Between the animal and the supernatural lies the rational time of man.

Ideas and facts can be retained by means of memory. An idea is not created anew but is actually an addition to a long series, in the extension of their preservation in the present moment. The function of these present moments is to continue the past. Rational time lies in the preservation of acquired ideas. It embodies the purpose of science. In so doing, not only does the individual himself advance, "but all mankind together make continual progress in proportion as the world grows older."

But Pascal had strong reservations about reasoning. "Reason acts slowly and with so many views upon so many principles which always must be present, that at any time it may fall asleep or get lost, for want of having all its principles present." The life-giving principles are neither preserved in memory nor captured by rational augmentation of the past. "Our memory, as well as the instructions it contains is nothing but an inanimate and Judaical body without the spirit that should vivify them." Rational time is a lifeless time.

He therefore sought Time not in science but in life. He recognized that our nature is in a state of continual change and looked to the acts of the mind for the principle of duration. Continuity is based on change, not the permanence of the preserved past; on novelties, not additions. There is a spontaneity which creates its own moments of time as it goes along. Each moment is unique. "Love has no age; it is always born again." We are therefore not conscious of continuous time but rather only of different times, in which we successively find ourselves. We feel only of the moment. "Past harms do not hurt anymore, present ones smart."

The problem arises as to the bridging of the inventive and the reflective parts of the mind in passing from one moment to the next. One registers the feeling while the other the consciousness of feeling—both occurring within the moment itself. "Thought escaped: I wanted to write it down: I write, instead, that it has escaped me." By dint of effort spent acquiring "a more facile credence which bends all our powers," it is possible to bridge the fatal interval between the inventive and the reflective and seize the instant in the instant. In this moment all are united—we feel and we feel and we feel. But those "efforts of the mind, which the soul occasionally reaches, are such as it cannot sustain. It reaches them only by a bound, not as on a throne, continuously, but for an instant only."

To Pascal, then, there is no pure present, no repose for

man. Because of "his nothingness, his abandonment, his insufficiency, his dependence, his powerlessness, his emptiness," he seeks to make up his deficiencies in the future and "anticipates the future as too slow in coming." In effect, man flees from himself to seek an imaginary self—a discontinuity of being. He refuses the God-given moment. "The present is never our end, the past and the present are our means; the future alone is our end. Thus we never live, but we hope to live."

At this point in the movement from animal instants and human time to the time of the fallen soul, Pascal found nothing else to do but "offer oneself through humiliation, to the inspirations which alone have a true and salutary effect." He craved the time of grace which *is,* creating the soul continuously anew. It is the continuity of the instantaneous. "Thus the continuation of the justice of the faithful is nothing else than the continuation of the infusion of grace, and not a single grace that subsists continually."

William Blake (1757–1827) occupied himself with the problem of the fleeting and the abiding in *Jerusalem.*[8] The struggle of man, sustained by the unchanging self in the flux of the world is reflected in his myth by the giant Albion (man) and Jerusalem (his spiritual self). Complicating the picture is a third personification, which is Time itself, represented by Los.

Time is regarded as male and Space as female:

He called it Divine Analogy, for in Beulah the Feminine Emanations Create Space, the Masculine Create Time.

This constituted the first step in Blake's attempt to reduce his six principal characters to one Male and one Female to be united in the Lamb and his Bride.[9] The three Male characters became a Time-Trinity and the three Female characters became the Space-Trinity. They were respectively Past, Present, and Future; Right-left, Behind-before, and Above-below. To these rather impersonal forms, Blake imparted a more personalized character. In the case of Time, the three aspects were Time-eternal, Time-prophetic, and Time-earthbound.

Of the three, Time-prophetic, or Time-poetic, was most immediate. "Time less than a pulsation of the artery . . . the Poet's work is done." The poet need not look far afield for the eternal. It is always present to him:

To see a World in a grain of sand,

And a Heaven in a wild flower,
Hold infinity in the palm of your hand,
And Eternity in an hour.[10]

In Blake's allegory, Time is bounded by the creation or fall at the beginning and apocalypse at the end.[11] The unfallen world is eternal and the fallen temporal. Personal immortality is not the transformation of the individual into a generalized entity of some sort. Instead, man survives in the permanence of acts of imagination. The unimaginative are transitory. "Eternity is in love with the production of time."[12]

Blake described seven major historical cycles. Each cycle begins with a youthful Orc, and progresses through less energetic stages to an aged Urizen. These are visions of the world's tragedies and failures. Our imaginative efforts are subject to the squirrel-cage of nature. The cycle goes on regardless of man's will and desire. The mythical Orc is the reenactment of birth, life, and death in another member of the same form. Orc's crucifixion as Christ marked the end of the sixth cycle. Presumably it also happened five times before. Orc may also assume a form of rejuvenation. Blake's process, however, does not involve reincarnation. In any case, Orc is completely tied to the cyclical wheel. Orc and Los, then, may be roughly identified with becoming and being, respectively.

The real man exists continuously. His total form of being is a work of art, infinite or eternal, existing in the unity of time and space. His becoming evolves in time and space. Immortality for Blake is not the eternal survival of this becoming but the being, which is the total form of these creative acts and visions. These total forms, or identities, provide the eternal reality of the individual. While an oak tree reproducing itself exists as the eternal form of the oak and hence may be regarded as having consciousness of some kind, Blake distinguishes it from human consciousness. The latter is called imagination. It is the rising Orc who gives life and shape to matter. But it is Los who gives imagination to Orc. "Orc brings life into time; the shaper of Orc brings time into eternity, and as Orc is the driving power of Generation, so his shaper is the power of 'Regeneration.'"[13]

But Los, the imaginative shaper of time, is not the only offspring of the eternal Urthona. The other descendant is the Spectre of Urthona, clock time. The Spectre may be looked upon as the will, the part of the poet that works and lives in the everyday world, the provider of the tools —all necessary for the imagination of Los to express itself, but is yet linear time itself. The climax of *The Four Zoas* occurs at the union of Los and the Spectre in *Night VII* and *Jerusalem.*

With the merging of the two descendants of Urthona, Los gains a conscious will and a vision of history from the sense of passing time. Imagination and time are finally made one and art begins to flourish.

Marcel Proust (1871–1922)[4, 14, 15, 16] began with an instant without a preceding one. "And when I awoke in the middle of the night, not knowing where I was, I did not even know at first who I was; I had only in its primal simplicity a sense of existing, such as may flicker in the depths of an animal's consciousness; I was more destitute than the cave dweller."[17] The world of Proust is "flickering and momentary," a matter of transitoriness and mutability. "How perishable is the love of earthly grandeur and even human pride itself," Proust mused to himself after seeing the almost blind Charlus bow to a lady he had snubbed for many years.[18]

In the midst of this state of disconnected sequences without fixity, the anguish of solitude expresses itself. "Having no world, no room, no body now that was not menaced by the enemies thronging round, invaded to the very bones by fever, I was alone, I wanted to die."[17]

One must find oneself in the midst of these uncertain substitutions, which are independent of the considerations of time. It is by memory that the self is regained. "That explained why my apprehensiveness of death vanished the moment I instinctively recognized the savour of the little madeleine because at that moment the person within me was a timeless person, consequently unconcerned with the vicissitudes of the future. That person had never come to me, never manifested himself except independently of all immediate activity, all immediate enjoyment, whenever the miracle of a resemblance with things past enabled me to escape out of the present."[18] The real past is not recovered by the intellect. "What the intellect restores to us under the names of the past, is not the past. In reality, as soon as each hour of one's life has died, it embodies itself in some material object as do the souls of the dead in certain folk-stories, and hides there. There it remains captive, captive for ever, unless we should happen on the object, recognize what lies within, call it by its name and so set it free."[19]

The real past is buried deep within the being. To regain it is difficult. On many occasions Marcel came close to giving up, such as when he rediscovered the vanished Combray of his childhood, after losing Albertine. One requires the "intuitivism of the unconscious," so natural to the believing child but edged out by the intellect in the maturing man. It is only infrequently that we "penetrate to the very depth where truth lies, the real universe, our authentic impression." The sentient being attempts to reproduce within himself the processes in the object. He tries to identify himself with the object. "Higher up their corollas were opening, keeping around them so negligently, like a lost vaporous garment, the nosegay of stamens which so entirely enveloped them with the mist, that when I tried to mime in the depths of my mind the gesture of their efflorescence, I fancied it, without being aware of the process, the flighty motions of a thoughtless and vivacious young girl."[20]

We may also lose our present existence by being overly absorbed in it as in drunkenness. In this case, the object exists without our internal equivalence. There is neither past nor future. Man again would be split from himself.

The alcohol that I had drunk, by unduly straining my nerves, gave to the minutes as they came a quality, a charm which did not have the result of leaving me more ready, or indeed more resolute to defend them; for while it made me prefer them a thousand times to anything else in my life, my exaltation made me isolate them from everything else; I was confined to the present, as heroes are, or drunkards; eclipsed for the moment, my past no longer projected before me that shadow of itself which we call our future; placing the goal of my life no longer in the realization of the dreams of that past, but in the felicity of the present moment, I could see nothing now of what lay beyond it. . . . I was glued to my immediate sensation.[17]

In a properly functioning memory, a sensation may come to us from the long past and we may become free from the flow of time that sweeps us along. The function of the mind is to recognize the identity of the actual present sensation, as in the recognition of the similarity of the starched glossiness of the towel used by Marcel to that of one used before at the Balbec hotel and the similarity in unevenness of flagstones at St. Mark's and in the Guermantes' courtyard. This re-cognition binds the present and the past to provide the foundation of the cognition of the essential self. The function of the artist is to convey the texture of the intensely lived moments.

Duration for Proust, then, is a sequence of isolated, discontinuous moments. "We live over past years not in their continuous sequence day by day but in a memory that fastens upon the coolness or sun-parched heat of some morning or afternoon, receiving the shadow of some solitary place, enclosed, immovable, arrested, lost, remote from all others." There arises a new kind of time, which is a simple collection of moments, arranged by the mind into an everchanging constellation according to the state of meaning. Proust's regret is the failure to enclose all motions within this time. "His only sorrow was not to be able to reach immediately all the sites which were disposed here and there, far from him, in the infinity of his own perspective."[21]

There is no supratemporal action, which is capable of infusing the Meseglise way and the Guermantes way in their respective "sealed vessels."[17] Their contents cannot be mingled. The action of memory is only metaphoric in nature. But if one is able to raise himself above temporal extension as the parish priest of Combray expressed himself from the top of the steeple, "one encompasses at once things he can habitually see only one by one." By thus regaining "a plenitude of music, made complete, in effect by so many various musics, each one a being," time is transcended.

Yet as Marcel caught sight of his grandmother's face, her aged features, he realized "suddenly . . . in our drawing room she belonged to a new world, the world of time." Marcel sees himself moving toward death under the domination of chronological time. He must complete his work of art within his allotted time. He will work with the "time regained," with the reality that is at once subjective and external. Yet there are objective limits. Death is not far away for Marcel as well.

Virginia Woolf (1882–1941) pursued the mind's time. "But time, unfortunately, though it makes animals and plants blossom and fade with amazing punctuality, has no such simple effect upon the mind of man. The mind of man, moreover, works with equal strangeness upon the body of time. An hour, once it lodges in the queer element of the human spirit, may be stretched to fifty or a hundred times its clock length; on the other hand, an hour may be accurately represented on the time-piece of the mind by one second."[22] She continued to seek that which endures: "there is a coherence in things, a stability; something, she meant, is immune from change, and shines out . . . in the face of the flowing, the fleeting, the spectral, like a ruby; so again tonight she had the feeling she had had once again, already, of peace, of rest. Of such moments, she thought, the thing is made that endures."[23]

But just what *is* a present moment? Woolf gave an indication.[24]

She related the sensation of sitting down after a hot day on hard roads. Now one is in his slippers, watching the sun go down and the leaves shimmer. There is "a sense that the legs of the chair are sinking through the center of the earth, passing through the rich garden earth; they sink, weighted down. Then the sky loses its colour perceptibly and a star here and there makes a point of light." One has the feeling of passive participation in the ordered succession, as he accepts and watches. "Now little sparks, which are not steady, but fitful as if somebody were doubtful, come across the field. Is it time to light the lamp, the farmers' wives are crying: can I see a little longer? The lamp sinks down; then it burns up. All doubt is over. Yes the time has come in all cottages, in all farms, to light the lamps. Thus then the moment is laced about with these weavings to and fro, these inevitable downsinkings, flights, lamp lightings." In the center of this wider circumference of the moment "is a knot of consciousness; a nucleus divided up into four heads, eight legs, eight arms, and four separate bodies. They are not subject to the law of the sun and the owl and the lamp. They assist it. For sometimes a hand rests on the table; sometimes a leg is thrown over a leg. Now the moment becomes shot with the extraordinary arrow which people let fly from their mouths—when they speak.

"'He'll do well with his hay.'"

James Joyce (1882–1941) attempted to attain an immediacy of the continuing present flux of undifferentiated experience.[25] There is no past tense. Events are recorded as they occur, ignoring the difference between the things being described and the words being used to describe them.

A dominant theme in *Ulysses* is the soul's returns and rebeginnings. There are suggestions of a determinism and pessimism of history. "What if that nightmare gives you a back kick?"[26] History repeats itself: "a theory none too rectiline of the evolution of human society and a testament of the rocks from all the dead unto some the living." When viewed against the background of eternity, mankind is "a human pest cycling (pist!) and recycling (past!)." His hero "moves in vicious cycles."

Joyce reconciled the absolute in time with eternity in art.[27] In the words of William Noon,[28]

the "transcendent" poet-maker of the *Wake* takes in with one steady, sweeping glance the temporal events real and imaginary of past, present, and future, and expresses himself most fully by a work in which all these events have their own quite special existence as interrelated parts of his poem: for example, Adam's fall from grace in the garden of Eden; the fall of the hod carrier Tim Finnegan from his ladder; Earwicker's fall from respectability in Phoenix Park, Dublin; Humpty Dumpty's fall from his perch on the wall; Everyman's daily fall from grace. Within this single atemporal dimension all the temporal consequences of fall, in guilt and in sorrow, are comprehensively included: the frustrated love of Tristram and Iseult, of Swift and Vanessa, Earwicker's nameless, unconfessed love for his own adolescent daughter. Confronted with the vision of the core of pain at the heart of things human, at the center of the created being of his poetry, the poet-maker of the *Wake* is not troubled. "O foenix culprit," he says, for having seen the end he sees the contradiction cancelled. "Remember made (thou who are *made*), thou dust art powder but Cindarella thou must return."

Wyndham Lewis (1886–1957) attacked the contemporary emphasis on change and becoming.[29] He derided subjective experience which assumes introspective modifications often engendered by trivial impulses.

It was against Bergson's influence that he directed his primary criticism.[30] Referring to the works of Proust, Joyce, and other "time philosophers," he wrote: "The method of *Ulysses* imposes a softness and vagueness everywhere in its bergsonian fluidity." Reliance on sensation in lieu of perception is typical of the American businessman.[31] "Perception, in short, smacks of contemplation, it suggests leisure: only sensation guarantees action, and a full consciousnes that 'time is money' and that leisure is made for masters, not for men, or for the old bad world of Authority, not the good new world of alleged mass-rule."[1]

The theme is repeated over and over again—the subjective approach, making everything transitory, injures the stability of common sense. Lewis proclaimed his own Vortex:[32] "With our Vortex the Present is the only active thing—Life is the Past and the Future. The Present is Art." He was uncompromising in his insistence on purity. "Any moment not weakly relaxed, or, on the other hand, bloated into an optimist Nirvana, is Art. 'Just life'—the *soi-disant* 'reality'—is a fourth quantity, made up of the Past, the Future, and of Art." Lewis disowns such an impure Present.

"For our Vortex is uncompromising: we must have the Past and the Future—straight life that is—to discharge ourselves into and to keep us undefiled for nonlife, that is for Art."

Between the past and the future, Lewis chose the latter. "The future possesses its history as well as the past indeed. All living art is history of the future. The greatest artists, men of science and political thinkers come to us from the future—from the opposite direction to the past."

T. S. Eliot (1888–1965)[4, 33, 34] saw the moments as not fixed. Now and then a sudden illumination focuses the mind on a momentary vision which appears to possess an existence by itself:

There are hours when there seems to be no past or future

Only a present moment of painted light.[35]

But the glory of the "positive hour" does not last. Instead of grasping the fleeting present, one looks to the permanence of the past to live in "the present moment of the past."[36] A lifetime burns in every moment.

The moments are not discontinuous; the past is a part of the greater pattern. The artist must grasp the historical sense of the timeless and temporal together.[37] "No poet, no artist of any art has his complete meaning alone. His significance, his appreciation is the appreciation of his relation to the dead poets and artists. . . . The necessity that he shall conform, that he shall cohere, is not one-sided; what happens when a new work of art is created is something that happens simultaneously to all the works of art which preceded it."

In contrast to the frenzy of the temporal, there is the still point of eternity. Only through the still point "where past and future are gathered" is meaning given to experience:

To be conscious is not to be in time
But only in time can the moment in the rose garden,
The moment in the arbour where the rain beat,
The moment in the draughty church at smokefall
Be remembered . . .[38]

We should follow the "occupation for the saint" and seek the "point of intersection of the timeless with time."

However, these are only hints to us. We are driven to action by our own guesses about them. We seek the freedom. But most of us fail. Yet:

Who are only undefeated
Because we have gone on trying
We, content to the last
If our temporal reversion nourish
(Not too far from the yew-tree)
The life of significant soil.[39]

William Faulkner (1897–1962)[40, 41, 42] showed primary interest in time as psychological, although he recognized the presence of an objective time. This natural time, actualized in the flow of the seasons, is an immediate affair, cyclical in movement.

Introspectively, man conceives of a linear time by logical reference to himself as observer. Clocks and calendars were invented to assist him in fixing any given point in this linear time. Actually this is not the real time as Mr. Compton remarked: "time is dead as long as it is being clicked off by little wheels; only when the clock stops does time come to life."[43] The man who lives by the clock becomes purely mechanical. He resembles Mr. Hooper, who said: "Well, well, I must run along. I run my day to schedule."[44]

The real time goes on, whether the clock tells the hour or not. Faulkner's present is controlled by an undefinable timeless fate, which bears no relation to chronological time. It is symbolized by the continued ticking of the faceless watch whose hands had been twisted off by Quentin Compton.[43] There seems to be a structureless absence of beginning, middle, and end.

There are individuals with excessive concern for the past. Gail Hightower and Rosa Coldfield were oriented "irreconcilably back toward old lost battles, the old aborted cause, the old four ruined years where very physical scars ten and twenty and twenty-five changes of season had annealed back into the earth."[45] A person should maintain proper balance between cyclical and linear times. He should submit to change and time, yet preserve identity and continuity in his interaction with nature. Like young Bayard in his planting, he should welcome "the sober rhythm of the earth in his body."[46]

Eventually, however, the interaction of natural and human time leads to doom: "All man had was time, all that stood between him and the death he feared and abhorred was time."[47] Doom exists not only at the end of life but throughout time. Various attempts are made to evade doom, such as Cowan Stevens' idea of drowning in order to "stop having to remember, stop having to be forever unable to forget."[45] Thomas Sutpen, Colonel John Sartoris, and the other Faulkner hero-founders chose to evade doom by molding the future. But finally, doom conquers all. Time becomes mere remembering for the young descendants reliving the life of their ancestors.

The individual man, family, and even society cannot hope to overcome time. The hope lies with humanity, "in more than the divinity of individual man . . . in the divinity of his continuity as man."[47] Man then begins to realize that the past and future are fictions. He abandons his search for linear time and seeks the continuity of the real time in primeval form.

Additional quotations. A dozen additional excerpts from Western writers are given below to emphasize the diversity of treatment of the subject of time.

Albert Camus:[48] " During every day of an unillustrious life, time carries us on. But a moment always comes when we have to carry it. We live on the future: 'tomorrow,' 'later on,' 'when you have made your way,' 'you will understand when you are old enough.' Such irrelevancies are wonderful, for, after all, it is a matter of dying. Yet a day comes when a man notices or says that he is thirty. Thus he asserts his youth. But simultaneously he situates himself in relation to time. He takes his place in it. He admits that he stands at a certain point on a curve that he acknowledges having to travel to its end. He belongs to time, and by the horror that seizes him, he recognizes his worst enemy. Tomorrow, he was longing for tomorrow, whereas everything in him ought to reject it. That revolt of the flesh is the absurd."

Paul Claudel:[49] " Time is the invitation to die, the means by which all things are able, on the threshold of eternity, to confess their naught in their Creator's bosom."

Jean Cocteau:[50] "My principal business is to lead an existence in the present which is my own. I do not boast that it is more rapid than another's, but more to my taste. This present life of mine abolishes time to the extent that I can talk with Delacroix and Baudelaire. When Marcel Proust was unknown, this sense of time allowed me to look upon him as famous and to treat him as if he possessed the fame he was to enjoy one day. When I discovered that this timeless state was my privilege and that it was too late to acquire a better state, I perfected it and grew into it."

Benjamin Constant:[51] " Love is only a luminous point, and nevertheless it seems to lay hold of all time."

Ralph Waldo Emerson:[52] " In stripping the time of its illusions, in seeking to find out what is the heart of the day, we come to the quality of the movement and drop the duration altogether."

André Gide:[53] " And do you not understand, that no instant would ever assume that admirable lustre unless standing, so to speak, against a dark background of death."

Nathaniel Hawthorne:[54] " Shall we never, never get rid of this Past. . . . It lies upon the Present like a giant's dead body!"

Ernest Hemingway:[55] " Now the essence of the greatest emotional appeal of bullfighting is the feeling of immortality that the bullfighter feels in the middle of a *faena* and that he gives to the spectators. He is performing a work of art and he is playing with death, bringing it closer, closer, closer to himself. . . . He gives the feeling of his immortality, and as you watch it, it becomes yours."

Aldous Huxley:[56] " Time and craving . . . craving and time—the two aspects of the same thing; and that thing is the raw material of evil."

Thomas Mann:[57] " The perception of time [is] so closely

bound up with the consciousness of life that the one may not be weakened without the other suffering a sensible impairment."

Paul Valéry:[58] " In the mythical void of a time pure and bereft of whatever element may be similar to those that border us, the mind—assured only that there had been something, constrained by an essential necessity to suppose antecedents, 'causes,' supports of what is, of what it is—gives births to epochs, states, events, beings, principles, images, or histories. . . . That is why it came to me one day to write: In the beginning was the Fable."

Alfred de Vigny:[59] " I was like the Jesus of Manzoni: remembering the future."

39.
Time and the
conscious-
unconscious
polarity
XLI

Experimental attempts have been made to clarify the relationship between consciousness and time by studying the kinetics of nervous integration. Electrophysiological measurements have shown correlations between cerebral activity and states of consciousness.[1] A relationship seems to hold between the moment initiating a voluntary movement and a certain phase of a cortical alpha rhythm.[2]

The integration experienced is not instantaneous. It involves events occurring over a span of time. However, the successive events are perceived as a unified configuration or a temporal gestalt. The conscious mind is unable to perceive components within time intervals of duration less than about .07 second. New perceptive modalities appear, which act as a time-linking mechanism to provide a single integrated experience.[3]

There is an unconscious process in which the succeeding conscious states are delivered in an orderly sequence by some as yet unknown mechanism.[4] As individuals, the instantaneously experienced integrations are relatively bare of content, but are of infinite variety. It is the coherence of their summations and interactions that determines the dynamics of our judgment.

The conscious and the unconscious are in continuous opposition in their impact upon our behavior. The conscious mind is always changing, while the unconscious is relatively steady. The former is active, the latter passive. The unconscious exerts considerable demands on man's conscious energy and resourcefulness, often to the point of retarding his forward striving. The conscious mind emphasizes the ego and the separate existences; the un-

conscious, the oneness of life.[5] The conscious
mind appears to reason problems out in consecutive
steps, whereas the unconscious grasps the solution simultaneously. The latter neither vacillates nor doubts.
The thought of the unconscious is not only timeless, but
also nontemporal. It is out of time. It seems arbitrarily
spontaneous.

The unconscious rests completely at ease with what appear to the conscious as contradictions. The simultaneous occurrence of what are ordinarily considered as
mutually exclusive events is not unusual in dreams or
in the fantasies of neurotics. There is a lack of appreciation of the boundaries of time. Events of the past as well
as of the future are experienced as taking place in the
present. Experiences long past are active in the unconscious as if they had just occurred and remain with almost undiminished intensity. One of Herman Nunberg's
patients, for example, was unconsciously still "having
a bitter struggle with his father, who actually died eight
years ago, as if the latter were still alive."[6]

Edmund Bergler and Géza Rôheim[7] showed that the
normal progression of time is disturbed by fantasies of
infantile omnipotence in neurotic adults. These individuals cling to a life of make-believe free from the progression of time. A typical behavior is that of the schizoid writer who followed an unconventional schedule,
dining at 3 A.M., working during the night, sleeping during
the day, and so on, in an exaggerated adult compulsion
to defy the routines imposed by his parents upon him as
a child. As the fantasies of the child give way to the time
progression of reality he begins to accept the association
of duty and time. The "autarchic fiction," which deexists
things contradicting the child's fantasied omnipotence,
is gradually overcome. Bergler and Rôheim argued that
"time perception is an artefact built in the unconscious
ego after partial mastering of blows against the 'autarchic fiction.'"

In this connection, there are several connotations to
the proposition that the unconscious is timeless: It may
mean that the unconscious knows nothing about the concepts of the intellect, that time does not affect the unconscious, or that the unconscious fails to perceive
time.[8]

The autonomy of dreams from the constraints of clock

time is impressive. A large amount of material can be packed into a dream within the short period between the rousing stimulus and the awakening.

The following dream by L. F. A. Maury[9] typifies the packing density. He dreamt that:

he was ill and lying in his room in bed, with his mother sitting beside him . . . during the Reign of Terror. After witnessing a number of frightful scenes of murder, he was finally himself brought before the revolutionary tribunal. There he saw Robespierre, Marat, Fouquier-Tinville and the rest of the grim heroes of those terrible days. He was questioned by them and, after a number of incidents which were not retained in his memory, was condemned, and led to the place of execution surrounded by an immense mob. He climbed on to the scaffold and was bound to the plank by the executioner. It was tipped up. The blade of the guillotine fell. He felt his head separated from his body, woke up in extreme anxiety—and found that the top of the bed had fallen down and had struck his cervical vertebrae just in the way in which the blade of the guillotine would actually have struck him.

It appears that dreams with accelerated passage are especially coherent. The recollection is usually more of a summary in character rather than detailed. Freud's version of the situation is as follows:[10]

But it seems to me unnecessary to suppose that dream-processes really maintain, up to the moment of becoming conscious, the chronological order in which I have described them: that the first thing to appear is the transferred dream-wish, that distortion by the censorship follows, then the regressive change in direction, and so on. I have been obliged to adopt this order in my description; but what happens in reality is no doubt a simultaneous exploring of one path and another, a swinging of the excitation now this way and now that, until at last it accumulates in the direction that is most opportune and one particular grouping becomes the permanent one.

The dream itself may require over a day for development, which may account for the ingenuity in many of them.

In my opinion even the demand for the dream to be made intelligible as a perceptual event may be put into effect before the dream attracts consciousness to itself. From then onwards, however, the pace is accelerated, for at that point a dream is treated in the same fashion as anything else that is perceived. It is like a firework, which takes hours to prepare but goes off in a moment.

Freud regarded it as an undisputed fact that all of the material in a dream is drawn from actual experience. Much of it had taken place in childhood. In general, however, most of the contents are concerned with impressions, which had been acquired during the immediately preceding few days. One of the interesting aspects of the material selected for reexpression in dreams is that indifferent and insignificant happenings are usually much favored over what is considered by the waking process as major and stirring. As far as potential appearance in dreams is concerned, all experiences are never lost for later expressions. The presentation of events in the dream is fragmentary and may not follow a logical sequence. Frequently, a logical connection is expressed in the dream by simultaneity, much like a single painting including all philosophers of the same school. At times, a chronological reversal of the actual chain of events may occur. This is observed, for example, in hysterical attacks, perhaps as a device to disguise their true meaning from observers.

Kinds of remembering. A distinction has been made between the forgetting of knowledge once gained and the forgetting of the intention to carry something out. The latter is often referred to as forgetfulness.

G. Birenbaum[1] requested individuals to do a number of tasks and at a predesignated point to sign and date the paper, which was handed in after the exercise. The signature was frequently forgotten when six similar activities were carried out and subsequently a seventh of another type. K. Lewin[2] believed that generally "an intention is not an isolated fact in the psyche, but *belongs,* rather, to a *definite action-whole,* to a definite *region of the personality.* Thus, for instance, the signature is usually not embedded in the 'objective work' of the task, but rather in that 'personal' region which is involved in 'handing the work over' to the experimenter." The forgetting of the intention is due to "the transition from the action-region in which the intention is *embedded* to another."

Some authors even distinguish memory as occurring in man from that in animals. F. H. Bradley,[3] for example, wrote:

The animal world . . . has neither past nor future. It has no world but the reality felt present and given, a present qualified ideally and qualified incompatibly with itself, but never transcended and itself degraded to be but another qualification. It has ideas assuredly and from the first, and, if it had not ideas, it could most assuredly have no conation or desire. But the ideas of the animal mind are but adjectives of the given ideas that enlarge the given and may indefinitely distract it, but never can set themselves up beside it as other and equal realities. Hence the animal could never say, Yesterday I was sad but I shall be happy tomorrow. Its present is clouded and is brightened by the movement of its ideas, but remain always its present; its revenges are never retributions for the past, and even its plans, where it has plans, are no forecast of the future. It has in brief, no world sundered from the world of its immediate practical interest, and to take an immediate practical interest in the past as past is surely not possible.

T. V. Moore[4] classified memory into two types, which may be designated as sensory and intellectual memory. He cited six kinds of supporting evidence: Meaningful material is more readily learned than nonsense syllables. Meaningless material is forgotten sooner than material with meaning. The curve of forgetting for meaningless material is a gradual and steady decline; that for meaningful material, however, has periods of pronounced elevations. There is poor correlation between the various kinds of memories. The child develops rote memory gradually. Logical memory in the case of morons shows a sudden development between ten to eleven years of age. Finally, during the attempt to understand, comprehension frequently appears in a sudden burst.

There is evidence to suggest a two-stage storage. Certain inbred mice, for example, can be divided into two strains, one with a short memory and the other with a long one.[5] D. A. Norman[6] advanced two modes of activation. The primary storage is a short-term affair, a temporary excitation; the secondary is long-term. As far as efficiency of short-term storage is concerned, the number of meaningful units appears to be of greater influence than the duration of the physical representation of the items.[7]

In human beings, the system handling long-term events can be separated from that concerned with recording recent events.[8] Old people are frequently able to tell a story in great detail, without realizing that they have related the same story just a little while before. In clinical studies of brain injury, the more recent experience seems to be more susceptible to environmental interference.

Brain centers. Various studies have been carried out on the areas of the brain responsible for recording events of the past. Electrical stimulation of local areas or epileptic irritation recalls past sequences of experience. Gentle electric stimulation of the temporal lobes of the interpretative cortex causes the return of past events with considerable detail, although the particular item seems to be taken at random. The recollection ceases when the electrical current is turned off. On the basis of such analyses, W. Penfield[9] came to the following conclusion: "Transient electric potentials move with (consciousness) through the circuits of the nervous system, leaving a path that can be followed again. The pattern of this pathway, from neuron to neuron along each nerve-cell body and fiber and junction, is the recorded pattern of each man's past. That complicated record is held there in temporal sequence through the principle of durable facilitation of conduction and connection." An electrical pulse applied at the proper spot in the cortex

causes a stream of excitation to flow from the cortex to the place where past experience is recorded. This stream of excitation acts as a key to the past. It can enter the pathway of recorded consciousness at any random point, from childhood on through adult life. But having entered, the experience moves forward without interference from other experiences. And when the electrode is withdrawn there is likelihood, which lasts for seconds or minutes, that the stream of excitation will enter the pathway again at the same moment of past time, even if the electrode is applied at neighboring points.

It appears that the scanning of past records by a beam of excitation from the interpretative cortex follows the same principles of transient facilitation which have been noted for the anthropoid motor cortex. It has been reported that a patient in an operating room heard the same orchestra playing the same tune each time an electrode was applied to his temporal lobe. This was repeated twenty times, and it was noted that the music stopped upon each removal of the electrode.[10]

Actually, considerable difficulties are encountered in correlating behavioral changes with changes in the nervous system. Norbert Wiener[11] warned against going too far in nervous analogies to the artificial computer, built according to information theory. Typical of the important differences is the erasing of unneeded memory data.

The artificial machine carries the special data and special numbers needed for a specific operation, say, on a tape. When the machine has done its task and settles down to rest, these data are removed and replaced by other elements or by others of the same kind, and the machine is set up for another problem. But the human machine is never completely cleared. It always retains memories, from the past, of every situation which has ever confronted it. The depth and permanence of these memories is indicated by the success of the hypnotist or psychoanalyst in summoning them up from the depths. In other words, we can regard human life only as one grand problem and its separation into particular smaller problems as relative and incomplete. This coupling of all problems to all previously undertaken problems greatly complicates the behavior of the brain and may significantly contribute to its pathology.

Effect of age. There is a general loss of memory with age.[12] A marked break seems to take place between the early and the late twenties. The decline is gradual thereafter.

Effect of emotion. Memory is significantly affected by the state of emotion.[13] Psychogenic amnesia is usually precipitated by some acute emotional incident, such as a quarrel or an assault.[14] This is followed by a memory gap until the patient decides to confide his problem to somebody else. Of sixty-three patients studied, forty-seven recovered spontaneously. They revealed normal intelligence in mental tests conducted during the amnestic period. The duration of amnesia varied between three hours and a month.

Psychogenic blocks against recall are often induced by violent emotional crises. J. M. Charcot[15] recorded a case of this kind. A woman was informed that her husband would be brought home dead. Despite the fact that her husband returned alive, she was seized with a hysterical crisis lasting about three days. Upon recovery, she found she had lost all memory of the prior six week period and was not able to acquire any new memories. Under hypnosis, however, she did remember her shock and many other things which transpired.

Even mild emotional conditions affect memory. Children take a longer time to learn a memory series when aware of a failure in a previous performance and a shorter time when aware of a success.[16]

Amnesias caused by intense emotion can sometimes be cleared by another emotional excitement. M. R. Benon[17] treated a patient who forgot the facts of his life following an emotional episode. In the midst of an emotional excitement he recalled an address, which was promptly forgotten after the excitement had passed. P. Haushalter[18] told the episode of a sixteen-year-old boy, who lost his memory after falling from a horse. The next day, a shell exploded near his house, restoring his memory. "I am cured, I can remember!" he cried.

Effect of mental illness. In severe cases of Korsakow syndrome, amnesia sets in for both the remote past and the immediate past.[19] In mild cases, only a loss of immediate memory is observed. In paretic patients, those items first acquired by memory are the first to disappear gradually, while recent events are forgotten only as the disease progresses toward its later stages.[20] In some cases the ability of looking back is lost but the storing of new memories is possible.[21] In a patient poisoned by carbon monoxide, the storage of impressions was abolished, but the recollection of information and other mental functions were left intact.[22] A nine-year-old child with an attack of diphtheria was unable to recall anything that occurred before he entered the hospital.[23] He was forever moving about, incapable of remembering for more than a minute or two.

In some cases of toxicity, loss of immediate memory as well as past recall is observed. This had been noted in patients suffering from malaria or excessive use of strong Puerto Rican tobacco.[24]

These losses of memory are often due more to differences in individual ease of utilization than loss of memory material.[25] Psychoanalytic evidence shows that memory pictures cannot be lost as such. There are residues of apparently forgotten material even in Korsakow patients.[26] Alcohol amnesia can be overcome by hypnosis. Even some skull fractures have surfaced apparently forgotten material.[27]

Relation to intelligence. As a rule, the more intelligent subjects show superior memories when young and retain information longer when old than the less intelligent.[28] The famous memory-man, Rueckle, performed so well in his number feats because he also delved deeply into the nature of numbers. Like blindfold chess-playing, this kind of memory requires continuous preoccupation, which calls for a directed interest, a drive toward an intelligent or understood goal.

Some psychotic patients show high vocabulary and information scores on intelligence tests,[29] while imbeciles often show considerable achievements in feats of memory.[30] In such cases, however, the memorizing of calendar dates and similar disconnected data cannot be used for any other purposes than sheer memory.

Relation to imagery. E. Jaensch[31] found the "eidetic image" to be a relatively normal constituent of the mind of a child. In the eidetic image, certain characteristics of both percept and image are fused. If a child is requested to reproduce pictures he has seen only once and briefly, he sometimes describes considerable detail in the eidetic image which he certainly has not seen in the original.

These images follow rules of their own. They are affected by the will and undergo considerable changes. They may even fuse with the true percept. This is illustrated by the following experiment: A child with the capability is permitted to look at a blue square on a white background. After the child's eidetic image is formed, a yellow background is substituted for the white. The eidetic image of the square on the screen will be gray. This follows from the law of spectral color resulting from the mixture of yellow and blue. Actually, the child himself is surprised by this color, inasmuch as he had previously been taught from mixing blue and yellow pigments that a green color should result. The results show that eidetic images can be used with objective colors as if they were true percepts.

About 10 to 60 percent of all children possess the eidetic faculty. There are indications that imagery among primitive people approaches the eidetic character. Heinz Werner[32] pointed out that:

aborigines are much more subject to the compulsion of visions than western man, visions which arises spontaneously or are suggested by the shape of trees, the rocks in a cliff and so on. . . . But these visions would be impossible, so far as their concrete sensuous character is concerned, were they not supported by a lack of differentiation between the objective perceptual experience and the subjective representation. Everywhere in primitive society we find that visionary appearances not only are accorded a superior significance but also invested with a superior significance in that they may even supersede the common reality of life from day to day. One is proud of seeing things that others do not.

The amazing sensuous memory of primitive men may be partially due to the close functional relation of the percept and the ideational image. The unbelievable geographical memory of some Eskimos[33] and the extraordinary memory of songs from unintelligible texts by Queensland aborigines[34] are additional examples. As man advanced in his culture the images and the percepts became more differentiated from each other.

Swedenborg's theory. Emmanuel Swedenborg (1688–1772) did not limit himself to considerations of flesh and bones. He felt that there are different memories, corresponding to the various levels of consciousness in man. The external memory is concerned with material ideas resulting from the physical stimulus of the senses. It is useful because it responds to the requirements of things of this worldly life. The external memory dies or becomes passive with death. But it is not without continuing influence. To quote Signe Toksvig:[35]

After a brief period of stupor, the recollection of physical sensation is still so strong that the recently arrived souls continue to think or to remember themselves as they were in the body, with clothes, possessions, appetites, etc. and thus in a sense they recreate themselves as they were. Out of these memories they scaffold "the phantasies which they love," which he also now and then describes as a kind of dream world. When they are in "these physical phantasies," he says, they are really asleep and dreaming.

Swedenborg[36] expanded on the theme:

Souls in the other life seem indeed to themselves to have lost the memory of particulars, or the corporeal memory in which merely material ideas were, because they are unable to excite anything from that memory, though they still have the full faculty of perceiving and speaking as in the body. . . . Still that memory remains, not however as an active but as passive, and it can be excited by others, for whatever men may have done, seen or heard in their lifetime, when these things are spoken of to them with a like idea, then they at once recognize them and know that they have said, seen or heard such things, which has been evinced to me by such abundant proofs that I could, in confirmation, fill many pages with them.

The reason the souls are not "allowed" to remember more details from the worldly life is that the Lord wanted them to follow a more "interior" life after death of the body. But unfortunately the spirits do not always appreciate the wisdom of this constraint.

Reid's theory. Thomas Reid (1710–1796) insisted that memory is an original God-given faculty.[37] "I can give no reason why I should have [it] . . . but that such is the will of my Maker. I find it in my mind a distinct conception and a firm belief of a series of past events, but how this is produced I know not."

He criticized the common theory of his day that memory involves images impressed upon the brain or mind. Even if there is a relation between the impression in the brain and the remembrance of the object, "how the impression contributes to this remembrance we should be quite ignorant. . . . To say this impression is memory is absurd if understood literally. If it is only meant that it is the cause of memory, it ought to be shown how it produces this effect, otherwise memory remains as unaccountable as before." Furthermore, there is no evidence that the impression remains after the object is removed. If we grant that the impression remains, then another assumption is required that the same cause, which originally produced sensation and perception, afterwards produced the entirely different operation of memory. This sometimes works and sometimes does not. "Thus, when philosophers have piled one supposition upon another . . . memory remains unaccountable; and we know as little how we remember things past as how we are conscious of the present."

Mill's theory. According to James Mill (1773–1836), not every mental succession will produce a perception of time-relation, memory, or identity.[38] Particular successive combinations of sensations, reproductions of sensations, and their repetitions are required. "Imagination consists of ideas. . . . Memory has in it all that imagination has, but it must also have something more. . . . In memory is not only the idea of the thing remembered, there is also the idea of my having seen it. . . . these two . . . combined, make up . . . the whole of that state of conscience we call memory. But what is it that we are to understand by what I have called 'the idea of my having seen the object'?"

Given two successive sensations, *A* and *B*, the consciousness of the present moment

calls up the idea of the consciousness of the preceding moment. The consciousness of the present moment is not absolutely simple; for whether I have a sensation or idea, the idea of what I call myself is always inseparably combined with it. The consciousness then of the second of the two moments in the case supposed, is the sensation combined with the idea of myself, which compound I call "Myself Sentient." The Self Sentient, in other words, sensation *B* combined with the idea of self, calls up the idea of sensation *A* combined with self. This we call Memory.

His memory consists of three components: "The remembering self; the remembered self; and the train which intervened. . . . The analysis . . . of self, or the account of what is included in that state of consciousness commonly called the idea of personal identity, is still wonting to complete the development of memory." *Freud's theory.* Sigmund Freud (1856–1940) felt that the past plays a determining role in a person's life. Forgetting something is not abolishing it. On the contrary, it may even exaggerate its importance in the unconscious. As recapitulated by Philip Rieff:[39]

Memory, for Freud, is not a passive receiver whose performance can be measured quantitatively; it embodies a moral choice, a sequence of acceptance and rejections. Forgetting is active; it is not the absence of an action, something dropped out of the container mind. Freud felt his way down into the container until he found its false bottom, repression; below this memory reality begins. Certain crucial events of the past may, at the behest of the ego, which does not want to remember them, be at some time repressed. Repression thus becomes an infallible index of ethical import. What is too imperative to be remembered suffers the compliment of being forgotten.

In choosing to forget the painful past, a person courts psychic illness. The partly successful repression erupts into neurotic symptoms. The psychoanalyst therefore attempts to begin with the small available window to illuminate the entire heretofore hidden story. In this way, the neurotic patient is relieved from the "abnormal attachment to the past." According to Freud,[40] "the analysis of each single hysterical amnesia is seen to be a direct continuation of the infantile amnesia which hides the earliest impressions of our mental life from all of us." The early experiences are emphasized and the later played down as far as their impact upon character is concerned. There is an attempt to discover the original emotional crisis, which inevitably led to the present manifestations. The past is determinant.

Freud's thinking was the natural outgrowth of a long series of deliberations by many people on the relation of sickness and the past. These led to an identification of the abnormal with the primitive. The dream was found to be the first locus of the primitive. By an archeological analysis of dreams, as it were, we can arrive at a "knowledge of man's archaic heritage, of what is psychically innate in him."[41] Childhood years constitute a second locus, ascribing to "the psychic life of present-day children, the same archaic moments . . . which generally prevailed at the time of primitive civilization."[42] The wishes of the later neurotics correspond to the deeds of the primitive men. With the primitive men, thinking and doing were one and the same. Now, they are separated. But we "retain an impression of the past in unconscious memory traces" both as a group and as individuals. This accounts for the development of tradition and culture. Tradition is "equivalent to repressed material in the mental life of the individual," although on the conscious level the repressed past is "vanished and overcome in the life of a people."

Engram theories. Friedrich Beneke (1798–1854) was the forerunner of many psychologists advancing the concepts of engrams, memory traces, and psychophysical dispositions.[43] An idea leaves a trace, which brings it back to consciousness upon stimulation by another idea. For Beneke, however, the trace is neither unconscious nor physiological. He felt that psychology does not need to explain itself in terms of other disciplines. It can make its own language and laws.

One of the earlier proponents of memory being biological traces transmitted through the germ plasm from one generation to the next was Ewald Hering.[44] He believed that activity leaves an imprint on the organs and nervous system. These memory habits are passed on to succeeding generations as reflexes and instincts.[45] What a person remembers is not the past event but a present state.[46] The latter is a modification of the body, which resulted from the previous excitement. The difference between the two states of bodily equilibrium before and after the excitement is called the engram.

So far, direct experimental study of the memory trace has not been possible. As a result, the only thing physiologists can do is to speculate as to the character of memory traces based on what the prevailing knowledge of the nervous system happens to be. There are suggestions, however, that nerve elements are affected by activity and inactivity. Max Verworn[47] alluded to the fact that ganglion cells of the cortical visual areas develop normally only with sensory stimulation. The same necessity of activity seems to hold for motor cells in the anterior horns of the spinal cord.[48] The various schools of thought regarding the mechanism of retention of memory traces range from those emphasizing the natural decay of the traces[49] and their transformation[50] to those emphasizing the interference by competing responses during the acquisition or retention period.[51]

George Katona[52] addressed himself to the nature of occurrences between the learning period and the recall. He regarded individual traces to be formed, usually after a long and strenuous process, in response to specific items; they are characterized by a certain degree of rigidity and fixation, requiring reinforcing for persistence. On the other hand, structural traces are formed, quickly and with relatively less effort under conditions of understanding, in response to the total process; these are more flexible and readily adaptable and persist for longer periods. The meaningfulness of learning is determined by the manner of transition from individual to structural traces.

F. C. Bartlett[53] noted the difficulties in the conventional theory of traces and proposed an alternative. In contrast to each trace retaining its essentiality while stored in the organism and each act of remembering being a simple reexcited reproduction, Bartlett theorized that "the past operates as an organized mass rather than as a group of elements each of which retains its specific character. . . . very probably the outstanding characteristics of remembering all follow from a change of attitude toward those masses of organized past experiences and reactions which function in all high-level mental processes." The reproduction of an event is not an identical replica. One does not "produce something absolutely new, and I never repeat something old. The stroke is literally manufactured out of the living visual and postural 'schemata' of the moment and their interrelations. I may say, I may think that I reproduce exactly a series of textbook movements, but demonstrably I do not; just as under other circumstances, I may say and think that I reproduce exactly some isolated event which I want to remember, and again demonstrably I do not."

Holographic theory. As a new discovery emerges in the physical sciences, an analogy of it will often be invoked to explain some aspect of memory. For example, the physicist Dennis Gabor[54] invented the optical hologram in 1947, a three-dimensional photography without lenses; and, after its impressive progress in the 1960s with the use of laser beams, the principle was adopted as a functional model for the neural storage of information.

In holography, two sets of coherent orderly light waves, such as laser beams, are used. One is shone through the object, while the other is angled in a direction such that it misses the object and collides with the first beam after its penetration. The results of the collision between the distorted and undistorted waves are collected on a film or a cathode ray tube. The picture of the original object is then regenerated by reversing the sequence, so to speak. Unlike conventional photography, each part of a hologram contains the entire message. Any piece of the hologram can be decoded to provide the same complete regenerated image. The intensity and sharpness of the image, however, lessen as the piece becomes smaller.

Paul Pietsch[55] has suggested this as a physical model for the observations of Karl Lashley on animal brains during the 1920s. He had found that amputation of the brain would dull the animal's memory in proportion to the amount removed. However, he was not able to remove memory entirely. Furthermore, one residual part of the cortex could serve as well as another.

Current state of theorizing. Paul Schilder[56] has listed the following eight factors which a general theory of memory must take into consideration:

1. Based on observations in psychoanalysis and hypnosis, any psychic experience which is acquired is never completely erased from the psychic field.

2. The primary experience is evoked when the immediate situation resembles the past, becoming less available for recall as time elapses.

3. Memory is but one of a number of psychic experiences generated by constructive processes responding to biological needs. The original psychic experience is modified in its reproduction.

4. Repetition of a psychic experience makes it more available for further use.

5. Successful learning takes place with the onset of some stability without rigidity.

6. The past is rendered useful for the present in the case of both learning and remembering.

7. Habit formation depends not only on the repetition but also on the importance of the habit for the subject.

8. Pleasure and pain are unimportant factors in learning.

None of the theories on memory published so far satisfies these eight conditions.

41.
Effects of light
XLIII

Protoplasmic responses. Exposure to light brings about changes in electrical characteristics, viscosity, permeability, and streaming in the protoplasm.

The potential of sunflower leaves, for example, reacts rapidly to illumination.[1]

The viscosity of the cortical protoplasm of *Spirogyra* decreases rapidly when exposed to light, increasing again when kept in the dark.[2]

The permeability of cells is altered either directly or indirectly. The amount of direct change in the passage of substances through the protoplasm depends upon the species, age, and type of tissue illuminated; the pretreatment; and the intensity, duration, and wavelength of the light. Indirectly, light may affect the physiological state of other than the illuminated part of the plant, and this, in turn, alters the permeability of the nonilluminated part. Exposure of the aerial portion of *Sanchezia nobilis* modifies the salt intake of the roots growing in the dark.[3]

The oat coleoptile shows a retardation of the streaming when exposed to a small amount of light in the range of two to eleven ergs per square centimeter for about four minutes and an acceleration when exposed to larger amounts of about 800 ergs.[4] Blue light produces the greatest effect, followed by violet, ultraviolet, and green in that order. Yellow and red produce no measurable change.

Genetic changes. Ultraviolet light brings about drastic changes in the basic constituents of the hereditary apparatus. The gene molecule itself is altered.[5] Unless the damage is repaired by the specific healing enzymes present in the cell, mutations may result.

One of the first observable signs is interference with

the process of cell division, especially during the early stages.[6] There is a general slowing down. Cells in the later stages of division, however, complete the process without being inhibited.

The reaction of fungi to lethal doses of ultraviolet light generally follows that of bacteria.[7] Maximum killing for yeast occurs between 2600 and 2700 Å, which corresponds to the ultraviolet absorption of nucleoproteins. In the case of *Chaetomium globosum,* a sectorial mutant is produced at about 2800 Å but not at 3300 Å.

The frequency of recessive lethals in *Drosophila* is increased by ultraviolet light.[8] The same response is elicited through the irradiation of the adult fly, larva, and egg,[9] as well as the mature spermatozoon.[10]

In the case of maize, point mutations and certain chromosomal effects have been noted. The shorter wavelengths appear to be more damaging in inducing endosperm deficiencies.[11] Wavelengths above 3100 Å are relatively ineffective.

Some of the damage brought about in organisms by ultraviolet radiation 'at 2500 Å can be reversed by exposure to radiations of longer wavelengths from 3300 to 4800 Å. The same phenomenon has been observed in enzymes,[12] bacteriophages,[13] bacteria,[14] fungi,[15] protozoa,[16] echinoderm gametes,[17] salamander larvae,[18] higher plants,[19] and others. In simple cases photoreactivation appears to be a one-quantum affair.

Hormonal activity in animals. Certain birds are brought to a partial or a complete testicular activity by exposure to additional light during November, but not in the first half of October.[20] Direct light to certain regions of the brain stimulates the gonads in ducks.

Light also enhances the pituitary-gonadal functioning in many mammals.[21] Sunlight influences the breeding behavior of sheep, dog, rabbit, and rat. When light is shone directly through implanted tubes to the hypothalmus of rats, a continuous estrous-like cycle is produced. There is a rise in ovarian and pituitary weight.

Germination in plants. A fifteen-minute exposure to strong moonlight or a .01 second exposure to direct sunlight stimulates the germination of tobacco seeds.[22] The total quantity of light is the controlling factor for many varieties of plants.

The response also varies with the wavelength. The optimum occurs around 6400 to 7000 Å for *Amaranthys*, *Phacelia*, and *Lactuca*, while inhibition sets in around 4300 to 4800 Å for all three genera and also at 7000 to 7700 Å for the first and the last.[23]

There is some similarity between the action spectra for seed germination and other light-conditioned physiological processes in plants.[24] The region between 6000 and 7000 Å promotes leaf elongation in etiolated pea seedlings, flowering of barley, cockleburr, and soybean, and germination. Radiation between 4200 and 5200 Å inhibits germination. The most effective region for phototropic responses, however, corresponds to the germination-inhibiting blue portion.[25]

Photosynthesis. Photosynthesis is distinguished from other photobiological reactions in that it increases the energy of the system. In the other photoreactions, there are usually breakdowns of compounds and losses of energy. In phototropism, the primary effect of one or a few quanta of light may ultimately lead to the involvement of large numbers of molecules; an amplification is thus realized. In photosynthesis, however, the changes are not greater than the original energy absorbed; a large number of quanta must be absorbed to give an appreciable photosynthetic result.

The green pigment, chlorophyll, is the necessary catalyst for photosynthesis. Yet the formation of chlorophyll itself requires light. The precursor is protochlorophyll.[26] Plants placed alternately in the light and the dark repeatedly form protochlorophyll, which is rapidly and completely converted into chlorophyll in the light.[27]

Specific anatomical structures are identified with photosynthetic capacity. The chlorophyll is usually contained in the chloroplasts, which are discrete disc-shaped entities in plants. The chlorophyll is contained in flat layers sandwiched between layers of proteins, within the highly organized structure. The pigments of chlorophyll and carotenoids form particles, called quantsomes. The lamellae are stacked into grana, surrounded by colorless material called stroma. The complete chloroplast is seven microns in diameter. There is evidence of specialization in chloroplasts. Unique histological features exist in the leaf cells of *Amaranthys edulis* and *Atriplex* species, which correlate with the ability to fix carbon dioxide photosynthetically through the four-carbon-dicarboxylic-acid pathway.[28] Again, light is necessary for the development of the colorless, self-duplicating proplastids into chloroplasts.

Phototropism in plants. Certain parts of the plant bend toward the light, some away. Still others, such as leaves, often place themselves at a definite angle to the incident light. The latter phenomenon is called diaphototropism.

Phototropic reaction is usually due to growth movements and occurs only when the tissues are still young. The response is a function of the total quantity of light received. It may be periodic, as in the oat coleoptile. As the amount of illumination is progressively increased, there is first an increasing curvature, a decreasing, then a negative curvature, followed by a second positive curvature, and even a third.[29]

The sporangia of the fungus *Pilobolus* are shot in the direction of light with considerable accuracy. When two sources of light are used, they are directed at the midpoint between them. With a divergence of four degrees between the sources, half of the sporangiophores face one and half the other. Complete separation occurs at eight degrees.[30]

Photoperiodism in plants and animals. Plants may be divided into three groups, according to their flowering responses to day length.[31] The long-day plants, such as barley, wheat, and other small grains, bloom when the night is short and the day long. The short-day plants, such as maize, chrysanthemum, and cockleburr, bloom under reverse conditions. The third group is more or less indifferent to day length. The positive reaction is not a phylogenetic matter. One particular variety of a given species may react but not another.

Continuity during the dark period is essential. Interruption of the nine-hour period with only one minute of light in the case of *Xanthium pennsylvanicum* changes the behavior pattern.[32] On the other hand, interrupting the light period by darkness in the case of *Soja max* does not alter the results.

The leaf appears to be the organ of perception. Exposure of a single leaf to the proper day length is sufficient to evoke a response.[33] The effectiveness of the leaf reaches its maximum when fully expanded.

As a rule, red light is the most effective, although exceptions have been noted. G. L. Funke[34] classified responsive plants into four groups. In the first group, the red and unfiltered light is effective while the blue-filtered light is ineffective. In the second, the red, unfiltered, and blue light are all effective. In the third, the unfiltered is effective but the red and blue are not. In the fourth, the unfiltered and blue are effective but the red is not.

The silkworm is a typical short-day insect.[35] It overwinters as an egg and hatches into a larva during the short days of spring. The larva passes through the pupa stage into a moth, which then lays eggs during late summer. These eggs, however, do not hatch immediately, but overwinter in diapause to repeat the cycle. As long as the egg and larva are kept under short-day conditions of about twelve hours of light per day, the moths do not undergo diapause generation after generation. But when reared under long-day conditions, the resulting eggs undergo the temporary stopping of activity in the laboratory as readily as in nature.

In contrast, the aphid is a long-day insect. Asexual reproduction occurs indefinitely when the colonies are exposed to sixteen hours of light per day. The young do not hatch from eggs but are produced asexually. When provided only twelve hours per day, egg-laying sexual generations are produced. The aphid's photoperiod response is already fixed at birth.[36]

Higher animals can also be divided in accordance with their responses to the relative length of day and night. With respect to reproduction, short-day animals include deer, goats, and sheep.[37] Long-day animals include pheasant, raccoons, and stickleback fish. Man belongs to the indeterminate category.

In some birds the eyes act as the organs of perception. Covering the eyes when these birds are otherwise exposed to favorable light periods prevents the expected reproduction.[38] In the case of ducks, however, sexual response occurs despite the severance of the optic nerve and even after extirpation of the eyes.[39]

Photoreceptors. Despite the absence of eyes, all invertebrates have the ability to distinguish light from dark. They also respond to spectral distribution.[40]

Most protozoa possess pigment spots. Amoeba and ciliates, however, lack even such an elementary photosensitive organ. Nevertheless, by means of a dermal receptor system, amoeba can detect vertical beams of light only twenty microns in diameter at a distance of 100 to 150 microns, and usually move toward it. They seek out and

ingest food laid over a beam of intense white or blue
light but frequently avoid food laid over green or dark
spots.[41]

A progressive photoreceptor series can be seen from
the annelids, through the mollusks, to the arthropods.
It begins with a simple cup lined with sensory cells.
From this initial arrangement, different modifications occur to provide lens action. Image formation and greater
resolving power are achieved by separation of the sensory layer from the lens. There is a progressive enlargement of the ocellus and infolding of the cuticular lens
into a spheroidal body, lined with sensory cells.

In *Antedon* of the *Echinodermata,* the entire upper surface of the body is photosensitive.[42] Sudden illumination
causes a contraction of the longitudinal musculature.
Compound ocelli are found at the arm tips of the star-
fish.[43]

The pedicellariae of *Toxopneustis* respond to light,
even when separated from the body.[44] It appears that the
photosensitive centers lie in the pedicellariae tissues
themselves. This is unlike the case of *Diadema,* in which
the severance of the radial nerve to the spine base prevents the photosensitive motion.[45]

The sea urchin, *Strongylocentrotus,* which normally
carries debris on its back using its tube feet and pedicellariae, reacts in an almost intelligent fashion upon exposure to strong and directed light.[46] It will pick up glass
discs from the bottom of the aquarium and hold them
over its back to provide maximum shade. Red glass is
much preferred over green. If a piece of glass has a
transparent spot on it, another one will be used to cover
the light spot. It will also reorient its body as well as the
glass disc in response to changes in the direction of
light.

42.
Symbolisms of
light
XLIV

Carl Jung (1875–1961) studied the symbols of transformation in the different mythologies in an attempt to understand the unconscious as "an objective and collective
psyche." By myth he meant "what is believed always,
everywhere, by everyone." The psyche is said to go back
millions of years, with individual consciousness only a
passing expression. He sought the archetypal context in
which specific symptoms are grounded.

The following summarizes his interpretations concern-

ing the symbols of light as God, libido, and consciousness.[1]

God. God, sun, and fire have been mythologically identified with one another. Worshipping of the sun means,
in essence, that one recognizes the power of the generative force of nature. The energy of the archetype is symbolized by God. The neophyte in the third logos of the
Dieterich papyrus prayed as follows, after stars had
floated down to him from the disc of the sun:

Give ear to me, hear me, Lord, who hast fastened the
fiery bolts of heaven with thy spirit, double-bodied, fire-
ruler, creator of light, fire-breathing, fiery-heated, shining
spirit, rejoicing in fire, beautiful light, lord of light, fiery-
bodied, giver of light, sower of fire, confounding with
fire, living light, whirling fire, mover of light, hurler of
thunderbolts, glorious light, multiplier of light, holder
of fiery light, conqueror of the stars . . .

The Egyptians incorporated all of their local gods such
as Amon of Thebes, Atum of Heliopolis, Khnum of Ele-
phantine, Horus of the East, and Horus of Edfu into the
sun-god Ra. The pharaoh Amenophis IV even designated
the "great living disc of the sun" as the "Lord of the Two
Horizons, exulting on the horizon in his name: Glittering
Splendour, which is in the sun-disc." According to Adolf
Erman,[2] the material sun itself was adored and not a
sun-god. There was a seeking of the direct eternal life,
which the sun can bestow upon man by means of its
light beams.

The vision of God as Sun or Light is also found in pas-
sages of the Mithraic liturgy:[3] "The path of the visible
gods will appear through the disc of the sun, who is God
my father." The chief god consists of Helios and Mithras.
Helios is described as "a god, young, comely with glow-
ing locks, in a white tunic and a scarlet cloak, with a
fiery crown." Mithras has similar attributes: "a god of
enormous power, with a shining countenance, young,
with golden hair, in a white tunic and a golden crown,
with wide trousers, holding in his right hand the golden
shoulder of a young bull. This is the constellation of the
Bear, which moves and turns the heavens round, wandering upward and downward according to the hour. Then
you will see lightning leap from his eyes, and from his
body, stars."

The Jewish philosopher Philo Judaeus,[4] who flourished
around the time of Christ, regarded the sun as the image

of the emanations of God, or even of God himself. Saint Ambrose worshipped Christ with the salutation, "O sol salutis." Certain Armenian Christians as late as the nineteenth century still prayed to the rising sun to "let its foot rest on the face of the worshipper."[5] The sun-symbol of the pagans survived in Christian practices for centuries. Remnants of the old practices still can be seen in ecclesiastical art in the nimbus around the head of Christ and the haloes of the saints.

Libido. The human figure as a demon or hero is the finest symbol of the libido, the energy of primitive instincts that drives man's psyche. Now, if we consider that, just as the sun rises from the East, passes through the zenith, and then plunges into the dark night only to rise again the next day, so does man go from birth to the height of manhood to the darkness of death only to have a form of resurrection in his children, the symbolic equivalence of the sun and man becomes apparent.

One of the more common suggestions in this direction is the coupling of the sun with a phallic symbol as a libido representation. On a Babylonian gem there appears a sun halo on the head of a snake on the masculine side and a sickle moon over the head of a snake on the feminine side.[6] The sexual connotation is seen in the lozenge, a favorite symbol of the female genitalia, on the masculine side, and a wheel with only spokes ending in knobs, a phallic symbol, on the feminine side. In many Roman inscriptions on coins, and other antiquities, the sun is coupled with phallus and the moon with woman or vessel.

The direct connection between libido and light can also be gathered from a consideration of the word, "$\phi\alpha\lambda os$," bright, shining. Its Indo-European root is *bhale,* meaning to bulge, to swell. It brings to mind Faust's "It glows, it shines, increases in my hand." Jung found the same analogy in sections of the Rig-Veda in which "the various aspects of the psychic life force, of the extraordinary potent, the personified mana-concept, come together in the figure of Rudra: the fiery-white sun, the gorgeous helm, the puissant bull, and the urine (*urere,* to burn)."

Consciousness. The union of consciousness and unconsciousness to produce the wholeness of the self results in the fusion of light and darkness into one symbol.

The struggle between the conscious and the uncon-

scious has been dramatized throughout literature[7]—
from the polynesian myth of Rata and the valiant Nga-
naoa to Longfellow's sun-hero, Hiawatha, and the monster fish, Mishe-Nahma. The typical tale concerns the
hero going on a sea journey. He fights the sea monster,
is swallowed, continues the fight within the monster,
finds a vital organ and destroys it or overcomes the
monster by lighting a fire inside him. Finally, the monster drifts to land and a bird guides the hero to sunlight.

The battle with the sea monster symbolizes the freeing
of the ego-consciousness from the control of the unconscious. The lighting of a fire in the belly similarly is "a
piece of apotropaic magic aimed at dispelling the darkness of unconsciousness. The rescue of the hero is at the
same time a sunrise, the triumph of consciousness."

It is in the darkness that one gains enlightenment. It
was in the belly of the whale that Jonah saw the "mighty
mysteries." Yet there are risks. If the "mighty mysteries"
can be assimilated by the conscious mind, a rejuvenation
and growth will result. Otherwise a schizophrenic situation sets in. Often, as in Friedrich Hölderlin's poem
Patmos, the hero has neither the will nor the power to
emerge from the darkness. Jung agreed with the poet
that his hero might just as well die:

For if he allows his libido to get stuck in a childish milieu, and does not free it for higher purposes, he falls
under the spell of unconscious compulsion. Wherever
he may be, the unconscious will then recreate the infantile milieu by projecting his complexes, thus reproducing
all over again, and in defiance of his vital interests, the
same dependence and lack of freedom which formerly
characterized his relations with his parents. His fortunes
no longer lie in his own hands: his fortunes and fates
fall from the stars.

43.
Parabiological
speculations
XLV

A distinction should be made between those theories
which can be empirically confirmed, at least in principle,
and those which cannot. Much of parabiological speculation falls into the latter class. An unambiguous correlation is absent between the symbols and observable facts.
This is exemplified by the statement: The positive photo-
tactic reaction of an *Euglena* is proportional to its light
requirement. This would be a useless tautology were the

"light requirement" to be experimentally determined by the organism's reaction to the stimulus of light. The underlying problem for statements of this sort has been dissected by F. Mainx.[1]

For example, there is no conclusive way to select from among the current formulations of the mechanistic and vitalistic theories. Both of them ascribe life to a principle with executive causality instead of the consecutive causality of empirical science. The fact that the mechanist locates the principle in a basic unit of matter, the bio-molecule, or the vitalist in an entelechy of Driesch, the biodynamic guiding fields of Reineke, the life-stuff of Pflüger, or the monad of Leibnitz does not alter the unexpressed tautological commonality in their arguments. Attempts at elaboration of the entelechy as being legislative rather than executive in maintaining order is merely anthropocentric flavor added to the tautological view.

One can always marshal evidence against either side.[2] There is temptation to weigh the preponderance of evidence as a basis for selection. But the methodological defects of the systems make a convincing decision unlikely.

The cliché that the whole is greater than the sum of the parts is another popular rallying theme. Investigators continue to be intrigued with such statements as: "The whole determines the parts, not the parts the whole" and "The whole is the cause of the particular course taken by the single processes." These assertions presuppose the presence of an approach toward understanding the whole other than the empirical analytical scientific approach. They become useful if testable. The concept of *gestalt* has value in behavioral investigations on the physiology of the senses, or in experimental psychology, because the organism reacts to a complex of stimulations as if this were a gestalt.

The idea of an individual life is at bottom a social concept and not a natural one. There is no such thing as an individual life with a identifiable beginning. There is only one life, from which various parts wither and die, that we can attest to as far as empirical evidence of initiation. At no point in the flow of life from one generation to the next has life actually stopped and begun again. When we say that the lifespan of man is seventy-five years, we merely mean that when a part

of the human stream eddies off by itself, it is expected
to last seventy-five years on its own. In this regard,
someone once remarked that the purpose of the hen
is to bridge the gap between one egg and the next.

The question has been repeatedly raised as to the
identity of the laws governing living organisms to those
governing inanimate systems. L. V. Bertalanffy[3] traced
a continuity in the sequence of physical appearances
from micromolecules and colloidal structural entities
through elementary biological units with the capacity for
reduplication, to the simplest cell, and thence to the
manifold forms of plants and animals. Lively debate continues on the applicability of the Second Law of Thermodynamics to living organisms. This law states that
entropy tends toward a maximum; there is an inexorable
trend in the direction of disorder. Authoritative partisans
are found on both sides of the divide. Most of the discussions are plagued with circumlocutions about the
character of life and the peculiarity of law.[4,5]

Another of the long-standing controversies concerns
the mind-matter issue.[6,7] The monist claims that mind
and matter are basically one and the same. They may
be different forms of the same substance, being inter-
convertible into each other, as proposed by the neu-
tralist. The materialist regards mind to be the product
of matter, while the idealist believes the reverse. The
dualist, on the other hand, asserts mind and matter
to be completely different substances, which may be
causally connected or synchronized with each other
like clocks.

The monist is not able to explain how mind and matter
exhibit such drastically different characteristics if they
are indeed the same substance. The dualist is equally
hard put to explain how interaction can take place between mind and matter if they are indeed distinctly
different. Some authors even called for a new realm of
dimensions, such as the psychic ether.[8] Such an ether
for images that lie between the realms of mind and
matter would account for apparitions and ghosts. This
would be the abode of images conjured up by the mind.
The idea is reminiscent of suggestions granting independent existence to memories, feelings, and fantasies
in multiple personalities. Other conjectures include
nonquantitatively describable patterns,[9] tendencies,[10]
and fifth dimensional configurations.

Sooner or later, however, all songs return to the same refrain of oneness.

It has been actually observed in the laboratory that relevant muscles make minimal contractions when a subject thinks about bending his arm or remembers lifting a cup, picking flowers, and similar activities.[11] When he performs mental exercises involving words and numbers, minimal contractions of a similar type take place in the tongue.

As recounted by J. C. Powys,[12]

Nature begins to present herself as a vast congeries of separate living entities, some visible, some invisible, but all possessed of mind-stuff, all possessed of matter-stuff, and all blending mind and matter together in the basic mystery of being. . . . The world is full of gods! From every planet and from every stone there emanates a presence that disturbs us with a sense of the multitudinous of god-like powers, strong and feeble, great and little, moving between heaven and earth upon their secret purpose.

44.
The origin of life
XLVI

In their investigations on the origin of life, scientists have concerned themselves primarily with the external sources of free energy, the energy interchange within the isothermal system, the dynamic stability of the structure, and its reproduction.[1] Attention has been focused on the formation of the first organic compounds and the first organic polymer.[2] The rationale begins with extrapolations based on the geochemistry and physical chemistry of the cooling planet and the organic decomposition chemistry of organisms. The first compounds on earth were presumably inorganic. These were then converted into simple organic compounds, then into more complex molecules, which in turn arranged themselves into structural forms.

The formation of organic compounds from such simple inorganic compounds as might have been present on prebiological earth has been confirmed in the laboratory.[3] Formaldehyde, formic acid, and simple amino acids have been obtained from exposing carbon dioxide, hydrogen, methane, ammonia, and water to such things as electrical discharges.[4] More complicated molecules of glycylglycine and glycylalanine were produced by the action of ultraviolet light upon amino acids. Synthetic polymers resembling the simpler naturally occurring proteins in their elemental composition and their reaction to a number of biochemical tests have been synthesized, although they differ in antigenicity, optical activity, and other important properties.

During recent years, scientists have expanded their horizons beyond isolated molecules. They have attempted to account for the mechanism of homeostasis in cells[5] and living organisms[6] by chemical oscillator systems. Typical of the suggestions for the molecular level is the one proposed for the catalytic oxidation of malonic acid by potassium bromate.[7] The periodic swelling and relaxation of a clay substrate has been proposed as an illustration of coupled escapement on the larger scale of around 1000 Å.[8]

45.
Evolution of the body
XLVII

Phylogenetic processes are strongly irreversible.[1] Dollo's Law[2] seems to hold: An organ once lost will never reappear; an organ once reduced in importance never regains its original importance. Occasionally, there may be suggestions of the reappearance of the original character upon return to the original environment; however, this is due to the emergence of analogous but not identical structures.[3] This is exemplified by the cotyledons in gymnosperms. The primitive cotyledons are acute and the more evolved ones are bifid. Later, the two points coalesce and the cotyledons become acute again. On first look, the last form may be considered an identical throwback to the first. Actually the two are not identical: The original acute form contains only one bundle while both of the latter two possess two bundles.

Structures and functions, once gained, may be lost, but the reverse does not occur. The uraemia of elasmobranchs and uricotelism of mollusks were acquired and lost. The glomerulus of the teleostean fishes and the water metabolism of the cleidoic egg of the sauropsida were lost and never reacquired. Many morphological examples of Dollo's Law are recorded in the biological literature.[4, 5, 6]

The rate of evolution appears to be periodic in certain groups, such as the fossil Cephalopod Mollusks.[7]

With most animals the most rapid evolutionary advances take place during fairly defined periods.[8] In the diversification of the phylum *Brachiopoda,* relatively high rates occurred from the Ordovician to the early Carboniferous with another peak in the Jurassic.

Among vertebrates, rates are very uneven.[9] Evolution has been halted for the coelacanth fish, horseshoe crab, and tuatara. While the opposum was one of the most progressive forms during the late Cretaceous, it has done little in the last seventy-five million years. The marine brachiopod *Lingula* remained static at least in outward appearance for 400 million years. On the other hand, none of the modern mammals existed in the late Cretaceous, few even in the Tertiary, and the man of a million years ago was quite different from the man of today.

There are indications that local races may actually evolve in as short a period as a century, although subspecies usually require 10,000 years. A new species of animal may take half a million.[10] There seems to be a gradually increasing tempo in the formation of new forms.[11] Primitive finless, fishlike creatures took 200 million years to evolve into the more advanced fish and amphibians. In the succeeding 150 million years, a many-fold increase in evolutionary events occurred, leading to the reptiles on land and the flying animals in the air. Within the next 100 million years, the earth became filled with deciduous trees and flowering plants with large numbers of different insects, birds, and mammals. Ten million years later, grasslands covered the warmer regions of the earth, and apes were roaming the land. Within another million, the subhuman began to give way to man.

The neo-Darwinians explain the present forms of life as the outcome of cumulative mutations during the past billion or so years and the machinery of natural selection. The theory, however, is far from complete. Although there are no significant facts which contradict the theory, nevertheless it merely explains and does not predict the emergence of forms. Looking at fossil records, one can speculate that the ancestor of the horse was much smaller, fed on leaves, and had four toes. Gradually it increased in size, which benefitted its survival capacity. At the same time, the number of toes decreased to three then to one for swifter running. The teeth were modified to take advantage of the changing grazing conditions. Possibly the horse *could* have evolved in just this way. But had Darwin lived fifty million years ago, when all this started, he would never have been able to predict the sequence of events, even if he had a precise premonition of the geological and other environmental changes.[12]

In opposition to Darwin's theory is that of Lamarck. The latter emphasizes the contributions of behavior patterns originating in the organism's attempt to adapt to the environment.

Parents, feeling the need for greater strength, set about to develop stronger muscles. Continual use brings about morphological changes with time. The offspring would then inherit these acquired tendencies toward enlarged muscles. To a certain extent, Darwin also subscribed to the behavioral influence on evolution. But this is exhibited in his theory principally in the selection process. The inherited characteristic results solely from random mutations.

Around the turn of the century, attention shifted from the adult to the fertilized egg. Evolutionary changes were held to be those which bring about an impact in the gametes, which transmit their newly acquired traits to the next generation. However, even accepting neo-Darwinian concepts, we are not able to account for the recognized rate of evolution. Man may be taken as an example. Taking the estimate of forty thousand generations to cover the million years since the "missing link," we would arrive at a number of humanlike creatures who lived up to our grandfather's generation approximately equal to the number of human beings alive today. If the random mutation theory holds completely, there ought to be sufficient mutations occurring on earth today to combine the existing traits into a superhuman species. The fact that this has not happened is taken to infer that there are nonrandom influences as well which need to be taken into account. We have not heard that last of Lamarck. There are renewed efforts toward reconciling behavior and mutations, cytoplasmic and genic inheritances.

In contrast to the more mechanistic theories, the vitalistic theories insist that the living forces play a major role. They point to the tendency of species to keep developing in the same direction, even beyond the point of diminishing returns. The size of horses kept increasing; so also did the teeth of the saber-tooth tiger and the V-shaped horns of the *Titanotheriidae*. The school of orthogenesis therefore claims that the reproductive cells carry not only the determinants of traits but also innate tendencies to develop along a certain fixed direction.

The evolution of a particular group, of course, does not take place in isolation. The entire ecological complex, with its fauna and flora, is evolving at the same time. The future form of a given species is influenced by the concurrent changes brought about on its neighbors as well as those upon its own immediate ancestors. The close association of the development of insect flight and the appearance of tall plants is a case in point.[13]

It is estimated that life first appeared in some form on this earth about a billion years ago. More than half of that time passed before the first insects came upon the scene. These had no wings. They fed on the plants then existent, which were prostrate. A hundred million years later, the plants evolved into erect forms, rising four to five feet above the ground. Most of them probably grew out of the shallow swamps. It was during this period that wings began to appear on insects. It almost seems that the posing of the food challenge of plants being isolated from crawling insects elicited the evolutionary response of wing formation.

Behavioral patterns are also inherited. Gulls may be taken as an example.[1] They communicate by calls, postures, and other signaling movements, which reflect the influence of the environment on gull evolution. When a young bird is raised away from the family, it displays the usual repertory of the species and understands all the messages involved.

There are fragmentary experimental results which indicate that the capability of an animal to solve complex problems is related to its position in the phylogenetic scale.[2] Furthermore, there seems to be no discrete break in the evolution of learning. Nor was there any abrupt increase when the animals emerged from the sea, or when the shift over to the primates took place.

In discussing the inheritance of such things as instincts, one should bear in mind that it is difficult to draw a precise line between the part of behavior which is instinct and the part which is acquired through learning. W. J. Thorpe[3] suggested that the difference is one "of degree of rigidity and plasticity." There is a hard core of fixed behavior patterns which is as reliable for classification purposes as anatomical features. Some of these may be quite complex, like those of the digger wasp described by N. Tinbergen:[4]

A female of the species, when about to lay an egg, digs a hole, kills or paralyzes a caterpillar, and carries it to the hole, where she stows it away after having deposited an egg on it (phase *a*). This done, she digs another hole, in which an egg is laid on a new caterpillar. In the meantime, the first egg has hatched and the larva has begun to consume its store of food. The mother wasp now turns her attention again to the first hole (phase *b*), to which she brings some more moth larvae; then she does the same in the second hole. She returns to the first hole for the third time to bring a final batch of five or six caterpillars (phase *c*), after which she closes the hole and leaves it forever. In this way she works in turn at two or even three holes, each in a different phase of development.

There are suggestions of quantitative variations in the interactions between learned and inherited behavior characteristics. R. C. Tryon's carefully controlled psychogenic experiments,[5] for example, showed that the progenies of highest performing rats in maze learning are much better performers than those of poorest performing rats. His results have been reproduced by others.[6,7]

The mental retardation syndrome has been placed on a chromosomal basis in the case of mongolism in which only forty-seven chromosomes instead of the normal fifty-six are present.[8] Monozygotic twins show .77 correlation in intelligence tests.[9] They also reveal the same tendency for schizophrenia.[10] About 45 percent of the children of a single schizophrenic parent are schizoid or schizophrenic, as compared to about 66 percent in cases where both parents are schizophrenic.

R. B. Cattrell[11] subjected the published experimental results on the inheritance of personality to multiple variance analysis and obtained clear evidence for heredity in the comparisons of the characteristics cyclothyme versus schizothyme, excitable versus phlegmatic, and in superego strength factors. On the other hand, the environment played the main role in the characteristics tender versus tough-minded and fatiguability versus will-responsiveness. A genotype-environment interaction theory has been proposed.[10] According to this explanation, only a neural integrative defect, called schizotaxis, is inherited. The individual is pushed over into schizo-

216–217
Life

47.
Extrasensory
perception
XLIX

phrenia after being subjected to an unfavorable environment and other constitutional weakenings.

Spontaneous apprehensions. As a rule spontaneous extrasensory perceptions occur to the individual when he is alone and relaxed.[1] Frequently the psychic experience is emotionally connected with a close friend or a relative.

Among the many reported cases was that of Mrs. Jeanie Gwyne-Bettany:[2]

I was walking in a country lane at A, the place where my parents then resided. I was reading geometry as I walked along . . . when, in a moment, I saw a bedroom known as the White Room, and upon the floor lay my mother, to all appearance dead. . . . I could not doubt that what I had seen was real, so, instead of going home, I went at once to the house of our medical man. . . . He at once set out with me for my home, on the way putting questions I could not answer, as my mother was to all appearances well when I left home. I led the doctor straight to the White Room, where we found my mother actually lying as in my vision. . . . She had been seized suddenly by an attack at the heart.

Precognition. H. F. Saltmarsh[3] examined 349 cases of ostensible precognition according to strict rules. It must have been recorded in writing, told to a witness, or acted upon in a definitive manner *before* the incident; the event must have been described in sufficient detail; the conditions must rule out telepathy, autosuggestion, hyperaesthesia, and inference from subliminally acquired knowledge. From this critical analysis, 183 cases were judged susceptible of no explanation other than precognition.

Mark Twain related a typical experience.[4] When he was a steersman on a Mississippi River steamboat, he and his brother Henry stayed overnight at their sister's home in St. Louis enroute to New Orleans on one of their trips. That night Mark Twain had a dream. He saw his brother in a metal casket, with a spray of white flowers and a red rose in the center on his chest. When he awoke the next morning, he told his sister about it.

Henry left on the *Pennsylvania* and Mark Twain left two days later on the *A. T. Lacey.* When the *A. T. Lacey* reached Memphis, the whole town was buzzing with the news of the explosion of the *Pennsylvania.* Mark Twain finally located his brother in a hospital. Four days later

Henry died. Weary and grieved, for he had remained at his brother's bedside all the time, Mark Twain dozed off for a few hours before going to the funeral parlor. All of the dead victims were laid out. But Henry was the only one in a metal casket. The ladies of Memphis were touched by Henry's youth and good looks and had donated the special casket. As Mark Twain looked on, an old lady walked slowly up to Henry's casket and laid a bouquet of white flowers, with a red rose in the center, on his chest.

Quantitative experiments. Quantitative telepathic experiments were attempted as early as 1884 by Charles Richet.[5] A popular form consists in having the subject guess at the identity of cards which are hidden from his view. At times, ordinary persons may exhibit a short-lived ability to achieve a statistically significant increase in their percentages of correct answers.[6] This is not as striking as those exceptional individuals who are able to repeatedly produce dramatically significant successes. The most impressive instance on record was compiled by Basil Shackleton,[7] a professional photographer, who ran odds up to 10^{35} to 1.

Qualitative experiments. Qualitative experiments involve the transmission of drawings, solid objects, verses, and the like. One of the more convincing exhibits was that of Mrs. E.[8] There was no contact of any kind between her and the transmitter. The six drawings shown in Figure 1 were telepathically communicated, one at a time. Mrs. E. drew the diagrams shown in Figure 2 in response. When the last figure was being transmitted, she asked: "Are you thinking of the bottom of the sea with shells and fishes?"

Theories. Many attempts have been made at an adequate theory for extrasensory perception. They include a

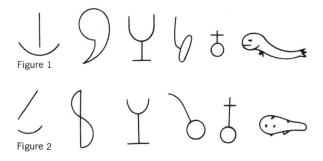

Figure 1

Figure 2

strange kind of communication, a field theory modeled after the M-fields affecting morphogenesis and the B-fields affecting behavior, the specious present of James, and the extra dimensions of Dunne.

One of the most recent, although only casually noted, is phase-locking. Suggestive observations have been made on the induction of illness or trauma in one identical twin by a similar mishap in the other, when the two are widely separated and ignorant of each other's whereabouts. It was hypothesized that photic driving might have been involved. In this connection a linkage of the alpha rhythm of the brain has been shown experimentally.[9] Two of the fifteen pairs of twins were found to exhibit the extrasensory electroencephalographic induction. When one twin closed his eye in a lighted room thereby generating an alpha rhythm, the other twin in a separate room six meters away also showed an alpha rhythm at the same time. The successful pairs were relatively unconcerned about the tests, since they were knowledgeable of the procedures involved. The thirteen unsuccessful pairs, on the other hand, were anxious and apprehensive.

Considerable skepticism continues to exist not only on the theories but also on the very reality of extrasensory perception itself. There are four principal reasons, as far as scientists are concerned. These are: the seeming irrelevance to the subject matter of the natural sciences, the lack of repeatable experiments, the disagreements over the quality of the evidence, and the unsupported claims.

Perhaps the greatest obstacles to scientific respectability is nonreproducibility. Talented subjects are hard to find and they perform well only when teamed with a few investigators. D. J. West[10] searched for twelve years before obtaining what he considered indisputable results. S. G. Soal tried vainly for five years to reproduce J. B. Rhine's card-calling results and tested hundreds of subjects before meeting with Basil Shackleton.[11] Furthermore, Shackleton gave the best results only with certain agents looking at the cards. When Soal's colleague substituted for him while the latter was away one day, Shackleton gave only random results.[12]

Another major difficulty stems from philosophical considerations.[13] It is impossible to reconcile precognition with the conventionally accepted relationship of cause and effect. There can be no precognition unless the future event is already in some sense given and the precognition and the event are somehow tied together in the proper order. It is as disagreeable scientifically to accept the premise that the effect (future event) precedes the cause (dream) as to consider that the dream causes the future event.

48.
Mankind's
anastomosis
L

The Collective Unconscious. Carl Jung[1] advanced arguments for the existence of a Collective Unconscious and its organs, the archetypes, on the premise that the psyche is fundamentally uniform in structure. If consciousness were to be eliminated, every mind would thus resemble every other. Unlike the repressed personal contents of the individual unconscious, those of the Collective Unconscious would be transpersonal and need never have been conscious before. They would emerge in each individual *de novo* from the Collective Unconscious as archetypal images.

An event is not the result only of what has gone before. Causality is not to be regarded as the sole factor in psychological manifestations: a directed aim or purpose is also required to explain our actions. There is a meaning as well as an explanation. The meaning is continually being evolved as life goes on, although we may never discover its full content.[2]

In Jung's theory, the unconscious is not regarded as an empty vessel, which becomes slowly filled with the frustrations growing out of envy, sex, and other desires. He, thus, did not feel that the unconscious can be emptied of these contents by some psychological manipulation. There are "possibilities of wisdom that are completely closed to consciousness" as well as the "wisdom of untold ages, deposited in the course of time and lying potential in the human brain." These predetermined patterns, which influence the unfolding of the unconscious, are called the archetypes.

Yet the world of the archetypes can be modified by the individual ego. According to Gerhard Adler,[3] man is born into certain *a priori* facts—the outer world of surrounding events and the inner world of the Collective Unconscious and of the archetypes. The ego-personality must absorb them and relive them. If the individual is able to change the world constructively through his own consciousness, then he will advance the state of *a priori* facts for the next infinitesimal ego yet to emerge. If he doesn't, then the individual has merely lived.

It is only consciousness which has a sense of time. Life *per se* has no conscious history.

Yoga. Many practices in Eastern cultures involve the introversion from the Conscious into the Unconscious.[4]

The object of *Kundalini Yoga,* for example, is to arouse the goddess Shakti, who is the personification of latent primordial energy, by such an introverted concentration. The introverted stream of consciousness, or *tapas,* releases her emanation, or *prana,* which rises through the successive centers, or *chakras,* and finally unites with Shiva, the Lord of Light or consciousness. The ascending *prana* is the kinetic effect of the awakened Shakti, who remains unchanged and externally unmanifest.

The realm of no-knowledge. The introverted emptying of the Conscious into the Unconscious is also a *conditio sine qua non* for psychological development in Zen Buddhism. This process is depicted by the series of classical Chinese paintings of the twelfth century, called *The Ten Bulls.*[5] The series describes the sequential steps in the realization of one's true nature. The first five frames follow the search of a child for the bull, the daemonic aspect of the libido, and his coming to terms with it. The last five show the progressive attainment of enlightenment through introversion. This is symbolized by an empty ring in the eighth frame and a blooming tree in the ninth. The former represents the disappearance of passion and the latter its transformation into a more reasonable form. The personal point of reference develops into the transpersonal; the spiritual evolution transcends the biological.

D. T. Suzuki[6] explained how the Zen masters were able to communicate in the Collective Unconscious through the conjuring up of what appear to the uninitiated to be simple verses. The following haiku by Basho (1643–1694) would be interpreted by the casual observer merely as a peaceful scene:

The old pond, ah!

A frog jumps in:

The water's sound.

But Suzuki takes the reader through a subtle labyrinth of understanding until the haiku reveals the master's participation in the world beyond time. Basho was not speaking of the surface consciousness. He was living in the deepest recesses of the unthinkable, even beyond the Unconscious of the Occidental psychologist. "Basho's old pond lies on the other side of eternity, where timeless time is. It is so 'old,' indeed, that there is nothing more ancient. No scale of consciousness can measure it. It is whence all things come, it is the source of this world of particulars, yet in itself it shows no particularization. We come to it when we go beyond the 'rainfall' and the 'moss growing greener.'"

This state cannot be grasped intellectually, for it then becomes an idea, which separates itself from this world of particulars. The timelessness of the Unconscious can be conceived only through intuition in which the "two worlds, sensual and supersensual, are not separate but one. Therefore, the poet sees into his Unconsciousness not through the stillness of the old pond but through the sound stirred up by the jumping frog. Without the sound there is no seeing on the part of Basho into the Unconscious, in which lies the source of creative activities and upon which all true artists draw for inspiration."

Following the neo-Taoist view of things, I directed attention in an earlier book[7] to the all-embracing no-knowledge. "With rational knowledge, one is in tune with the scientific man; with intuitive knowledge added, one is in tune with the total man; with no-knowledge added, one is in tune with nature." No-knowledge does not mean the absence of knowledge. It is called no-knowledge in that it is a state which is not that of knowledge; it is not a piece carved out of the total realm. It is a sharedness of the uncarved totality. "Having-no knowledge is sheer ignorance but having no-knowledge is ultimate enlightenment and universal sensibilities."

The Taoist Master had said[8] that "The Tao is eternal, nameless, the uncarved block. . . . Once the block is carved, there are names." Since the ineffable Tao is the beginning of everything, it never ceases to be. "A name that never ceases to be is an abiding name, and such a name is in reality not a name at all. Thus it has been said that 'The name that can be named is not the abiding name.'"

Analogously, we may say that the knowledge that can be carved, the knowledge that can be named, is not the abiding knowledge. Only the unnameable can be the abiding. This we call no-knowledge. No-knowledge does not emanate from the yourself of the conventional description. It can be regarded as coming from yourself only if yourself is defined as the sum of all of your impacts on others in the universe. Then there will be no difference between you and the not-you. This is the state of the uncarved block.

Actually, this view is not a peculiarly Eastern one. It is clearly implied in *Genesis*. But our worship of abstracted knowledge has led the Western mind to forget one of the Bible's most fundamental points and inferences on salvation. This is: Knowledge is the direct result of the Fall of Man. The first time the word "knowledge" is mentioned in the Bible is in relation to "the tree of knowledge of good and evil." Here we see a differentiation of good from evil, a carving out from the undifferentiated uncarved block. Then there comes the commandment of God: "But of the tree of the knowledge, thou shalt not eat of it." Again more carving, separating things you may do from things you may not and separating the one who orders from the one who is ordered. Then, after Adam and Eve have eaten of the forbidden fruit: "And the eyes of them both were opened, and they knew that they *were* naked." More carving out of things to be ashamed of from things not to be ashamed of. Before the first sin, "they were both naked, the man and his wife, and were not ashamed." The Fall led to even more disjunctions—enmities, death.

Before the sin, Adam and Eve dwelled in the realm of largely no-knowledge, where distinctions are minimal. Redemption for today's man, then, comes with casting aside the bondage of Original Sin, which is knowledge, and regaining the harmony of no-knowledge, the togetherness in the Garden of Eden. This is what the neo-Taoist gathers from reading *Genesis*.

But to touch the realm of no-knowledge is to touch Basho's other side of eternity—before the separation of Night from Day, the firmament from the waters, before God said: "Let there be light!"

49. Longevity
LI

Although lifespans vary considerably among groups of organisms, the spans within each given species of animals follow the same mathematical distribution. For most human populations, the probability of death increases logarithmically as the age rises linearly.

With the endowed range of longevity for the species, the length of life to be enjoyed by a specific individual is influenced by many factors. Typical ones are discussed below.

Cell division. There is a belief that protozoa and other animals that reproduce by asexual division are immortal.[1] Strictly speaking, this is not a case of immortality of the cell but rather one of the indeterminateness of cell lineages. The question arises whether or not some nuclear reconstitution is required from time to time to reinvigorate the line.[2] Some workers are of the opinion that unless there is some such rejuvenation, the lineage will undergo the normal cycle of growth, maturity, decay, and death. Others are of the opposite opinion, that vegetative division alone would suffice. The second alternative had been generally accepted for a number of years, since it was believed that the experimental support for the former was based on faulty technique. It now seems, however, that a nuclear rehabilitation of some kind does take place and may be required.[3]

When the cell undergoes asexual fission, the organism is divided into exactly equal parts. Daughter organisms receiving bad genes soon die off or fail to reproduce, while the others, usually a minority, carry on.[4]

Heredity. Although some birds live longer than some mammals, generally speaking, lifespans vary inversely with the phylogenetic order among the smaller vertebrates. The fish, amphibia, and reptiles have the longest lives, when compared against the other vertebrates of the same size and activity.[5]

Careful human population studies have all confirmed the commonly held knowledge that longer-lived parents by and large produce longer-lived offspring. The statistical picture is particularly impressive when presented in terms of the "total immediate ancestral longevity," which is the sum of the two parental and four grandparental lifespans.[6]

Highly reproducible results have been obtained in the laboratory with rotifers.[7] In *Philodrina citrina,* adolescence is reached on the second day of life, maturity on the third, and decline on the fifth. To develop an orthoclone of actively growing mothers, eggs laid on the second day of each successive generation are set aside. An old orthoclone can be developed similarly by isolating eggs laid on the fifth or sixth day of the life of the parental stock, then the fifth or sixth of each of the following generations. It has been found that the average lifespan of the adolescent line slowly increases over seven generations. In contrast, the old line dies out in several generations.

Sex. On the average, the female of the species lives longer than the male. The respective male and female lifespans for the fruit fly are 31 and 33 days, for the beetle 60 and 111 days, for the spider 100 and 271 days, and for the rat 750 and 900 days. Women live six years longer than men.

Consensus is lacking on the reason for the sex differences. The sociological explanation based on the greater leisure and the more sheltered life of the female of the species is unconvincing. Other biological explanations, which have been offered with even weaker support, include the male's andric components, androgenically conditioned higher metabolism, susceptibility to degenerative diseases, and lack of appropriate genes.

Metabolic rate. Within a given group there seems to be an inverse relation between the heart rate and longevity. The total number of heartbeats over the life of the mouse is comparable to that of the elephant. The former with a rate of 520 to 780 beats per minute and a lifespan of 3.25 years experience 1110 million heartbeats over a lifetime. The latter with a rate of 25 to 28 beats per minute and a lifespan of 70 years experience a total of 1012 million. The similarity has led some authors to speculate on the existence of biological clock springs, the final winding down of which brings about the cessation of life.

Experiments have been conducted, however, which show that lifespan can be varied considerably by changing such simple factors as nutrition. Keeping rats in a state of immaturity for periods of about 800 days by restricting the caloric intake, before allowing them to resume normal diet and growth, extends their lives 200 days.[8]

50.
Aging
LII

The central question on aging is: Why does an individual die *when* he does?

Most of the aging studies explain later events on the basis of earlier ones. In some cases the link is immediate, as with biochemical factors. In other cases, it is remote and indirect, through the intermediary of a chain of events, as with social factors. The variables differ in character, as well as the statistical requirements for validity. The more remote factors are generally more statistically oriented. The variables also vary in temporal and physical proximity to the end event under consideration. Thus, one should not expect to compare the relative effects of a biochemical factor, say, with that of a psychological factor with any degree of confidence.

A. Comfort[1] considers efforts to discover the "cause" of aging as much of an intellectual gymnastic as those to discover the "cause" of development. He has proposed that the increasing probability of death with age is due to the progressive loss of the "power to remain in stable function" toward the end of the programme of development and function provided by evolutionary pressure. The operational meaning of this explanation, however, remains unclear. What is required for experiments on aging is a statement that would hold for a general group of individuals under a range of circumstances. "Thus we may ask of Comfort as well as ourselves," said J. E. Birren,[2] "an example of a mechanism of senescence which is invariant to a set of transformations."

The most obvious thing about aging is that the different changes proceed at different rates and follow different kinds of curves.[3] But sooner or later everything takes a turn for the worse. In the case of man, secretions come less profusely. Muscle is replaced increasingly by connective and adipose tissues. The collagen becomes more crystalline. Within the cells, aberrations appear in the cytoplasm and nucleus. The erythrocytes in the blood become more fragile to heat. The walls of the blood vessels are less elastic. Pigmentation of body cells rises. The amount of brain tissues is lessened and the number of viable cells in some areas decreases. Loss occurs in efficiency in most of the physiological functions, including breathing capacity, oxygen uptake, skin glycolysis, cerebral blood flow, renal plasma flow, sweating, and cardiac output. A decline sets in in the auditory threshold, vibration sensitivity, speed of voluntary responses, and the integration of complex mental skills. Simple psychosis, hypochondriasis, insomnia, and nocturnal wandering become more probable.

In 1961 Zh. A. Medvedev[4] identified over a hundred hypotheses in the literature attempting to explain the process of aging.

Some suggest somatic mutations giving rise to inferior cells.[5] This theory appeals to those who believe that somatic mutations by ionizing radiations would explain the similarity between radiation syndrome and aging.[6]

Many authors favor the view that aging is due to incomplete metabolism by the cell, leaving deleterious by-products.[7]

The idea that the protoplasm wears out in a fashion analogous to an engine has attracted some attention. Related to it is the thought of cumulative damage.[8] The analogy is only approximate, of course. Protoplasm has the ability to regenerate itself. The real question is: Why did it stop or slow down in its self-synthesis? And why did cell division stop imparting renewed vitality?

The diminishing capacity of cells for biochemical regeneration is a quite important factor in aging.[9] It is especially significant in the case of nerve cells, which are not able to multiply. Once destroyed, these cells are not replaced. It is estimated that a seventeen-year-old dog has only a third of the number of cells in the brain as a young one.

A slow immobilization of proteins has been looked upon as a cause. This may take the form of thermal denaturation[10] or cross-linking reactions.[11]

Yet another explanation is based on cell economy, which reflects the interplay of complex sets of multiple genes, modifiers, suppressors, and the like.[12] Geneticists have postulated that genes determine the enzymes responsible for the biochemical capabilities of the cells. The autosynthetic function requires the integrated smooth working together of many processes, which are interdependent to varying degrees. Aging is considered in terms of the proper equilibrium among the waxing and waning of the various enzyme systems. At times several or more systems may reach their minima at the same time. This leads to a progressive decline in vigor. Death ensues when these quasi-periodic fluctuations become excessive.

Aging has also been associated with the differentiation of cells.[13] Fibroblasts, which are undifferentiated and proceed from one division to the next, do not age. Muscle cells, which begin with differentiation and are not capable of multiplying, do age.

System hypotheses have been offered. P. R. J. Burch[14] believed that aging results from changes in the control system ordering the growth of different tissues of the body. Each tissue is independently regulated. The mitosis-controlled proteins home in on the appropriate target tissue. As a feedback from the local site, tissue coding factors provide incoming signals. A hundred million such codings are estimated for man. The protein components of both types for a given tissue are the same and are induced by the same gene. This identity relationship is their means for mutual recognition. Diseases and aging arise from spontaneous gene change or somatic mutation in the central growth control stem cells operating as the comparator. In turn, the autoaggressive disorders adversely affect the vigor of the tissues, which subsequently become diseased. Invading microorganisms exacerbate the situation.

In surveying the attempts at theorizing, N. W. Shock[15] listed the following ten criteria which should be met by a satisfactory theory:

1. Mortality probability increases logarithmically with age but the functional capacities decrease linearly.
2. Genetic factors influence longevity.
3. Females live longer than males.
4. Diet affects longevity.
5. Higher temperature shortens the lifespan of poikilothermal animals, while lower temperature extends it.
6. Nonlethal doses of radiation shorten lifespan.
7. Changes with age occur at different rates for different aging systems.
8. Capacity to withstand stress declines with age.
9. Age changes in total organ or animal performance are greater than in intracellular biochemical processes.
10. Age changes of more complex tasks increase more rapidly than those of less complex tasks.

None of the current hypotheses comes close to satisfying Shock's conditions.

In the meantime, the possible discovery of a youth nostrum keeps intriguing people. A belief persisted for many centuries concerning the rejuvenation of an old body by young blood. Pope Innocent VIII had blood transfused from three youths.[16]

Another wishful concoction was sex preparations. S. Voronoff[17] grafted the testicles of chimpanzees to old men and claimed to have improved their well-being and sexual function for a short time.

Other recipes included vaccines of reticulo cells,[9] embyronic extracts,[18] royal jelly,[19] procaine,[20] sodium rhodanate,[21] and yogurt.[22]

Many cases have been recorded of unexplained sudden death. Apparently healthy persons have been known to die within a day under the influence of voodoo.[1] Frequent deaths occur among zoo animals after transference to unaccustomed cages.[2]

C. P. Richter[3] called attention to Oscar Riddle's experience with Peruvian wild pigeons dying while being put on the scales and the Baltimore coroner R. S. Fischer's report of men dying after barely scratching their skins or after taking a few aspirins in suicide attempts. He also mentioned his own observations on the sudden mysterious deaths of wild rats. Richter concluded that men and animals may well die from a reaction of hopelessness.

Such strange manifestations of death have driven men to seek beyond the conventions of science for a comforting explanation.

It appears that the idea of death as the cessation of time began to attract fear unto itself with the progression of culture along certain lines.[4] With primitive men, the thought of survival after death did not carry with it the living obligations of modern Western thinking. The living were only required to provide the departing soul with appropriate provisions of conciliatory sacrifices. As civilization advanced, the fear of being absolutely removed from the present environment and human association gradually took hold. The idea of various realms and modes in the Hereafter of the soul developed to assure personal survival. Finally, the conditions requisite for the period on earth in order to insure survival in the Hereafter were continually refined by the emerging religions.

Death itself would be meaningless without the experience of time. The clock is a symbol of death.[5] It is in reply to the question as to what happens when time stands still that an explicit content is given to death. In this regard, K. R. Eissler[6] believed that death enables a person to fill out his future. The present and the future become one. There is no present as such; neither is there any past. The memory-forming apparatus has been abolished. The personality ceases to grow.

In the acute terror of death the ego experiences itself as having reached the point when time comes to a standstill and the whole future has been reduced to the pinpoint of the last moment of life. . . . It is possible that in the terror of death, when death becomes an inescapable immediate reality, the ego comes close to the experience of pure future. It is very remarkable that, when suddenly and under circumstances quite unforeseen by a person external circumstances enforce the certainty of impending death, mechanisms of denial automatically set in and a regression into the past is enforced. . . . Strangely enough, this temporary solution so very pleasing and so really useful for the ego in terms of the pleasure-unpleasure economy, is usually not accessible when death by internal reasons is threatening or when the danger has covered a longer period of time.

H. Plessner[7] analyzed the relation between time and death from a mythological and an anthropological viewpoint. "In a culture where the chain does not break off, or more precisely, where transience is subject to the law of recurrence, the significance of individual death remains limited and veiled, so to speak. It is only with the transformation of mythical consciousness of time from its cyclical to its eschatological form that a vision opens on the 'nevermore' and a separation between past, present, and future." The primordial time does not admit of a beginning time and an ending time. With the advent of the idea of linear time, however, there arises the conception of unique and unrepeatable events.

World and man become worthy of being remembered in tradition, monuments, and documents. Past, present, and future become distinct. The more deeply this temporal consciousness takes hold of a living community, the more it will be drawn into the individualization of its members and feel death as a threat, whose gravity depends on the mode and measure of the individual's delimitation against the world and chain of generations. Thus the growth of ego-consciousness, the development of death as a problem, and the actualization of the linear time that unfolds in past, present, and future belong together.

Three stages can be seen in the development of a child's attitude toward death.[8] In the first, between three and five years of age, death is usually seen as a departure to an existence elsewhere. It is regarded as a temporary event. It is not considered as a regular process. The child begins to recognize the eventuality of death during the period of five to nine years. However, he tries to keep the thought away from himself. The people who actually die are those "whom the death-man carries off." Finally, at age nine or ten, the child recognizes the reality of death occurring in every man's life, accompanied by a dissolution of the body.

The concepts of good, real, life, bright, and myself appear to be structured within a single framework by the adolescent.[9] The concept of death, however, is isolated as a self-contained organization, differing completely from the other group. The adolescent lives in the immediate now. All of the important things of life exist in the present or near future. More explicit structuring is accorded the past than the future. Remote time fields both of the past and the future are regarded as risky and unpleasant by fifteen- to seventeen-year-olds. They exhibit a low acceptance of death-connoting experience. Being alone or in a dark room for any length of time is uncomfortable. They want to put as much time as they can between themselves and the remote future field. Only the actively religious adolescents, who comprise about 15 percent of the population, react differently.

Faced with the certainty of death, men have devised various techniques of accommodation. Various euphemisms have been formulated, such as "Papa is all" and "Father made old." C. W. Wahl[10] noted the recourse to magic and irrationality in the alleviation of this anxiety. He pointed out that the child's feeling of omnipotence, in that his wishes bring about needed satisfaction, persists throughout the adult's life in varying degrees. In the statement of the psalmist David, "A thousand shall fall at thy right hand and ten thousand at thy left, but it shall not come nigh to thee." Such repeated assurances contribute some stability in the face of threatening facts. Yet even so, the realization that death is neither causal nor reversible forces itself through the veneer and the attendant dread often gives rise to neurotic symptoms.

W. E. Hocking[11] inquired into "the actual conditions under which alone the idea of immortality could be legitimate."

He considered death as not a necessity but only a possibility of destiny. "The quality of the human self . . . is not immortality, but immortability, the conditional possibility of survival." It is neither substance nor energy that enters into a man when he dies. "For death is not the erasure of life by an entity called Death, nor by an entity called Nature. Death is an encounter of the real with the Real: and the Real, whatever it is, is conscious and living, not inanimate."

We need a continuance of the human self; otherwise we would be weighed down by the failures of God. The issue of immortality is not met full face by resorting to an "absorption in universals or in The One." Instead it involves a personal issue of "continuous identity of self-awareness, with elements of memory, questioning, and purpose. . . . And clearly, it is this concrete concern that creates our most radical impasse, our most spontaneous reading of the facts as implying extinction." The physical aspects do not perish; the chemical matter remains; the energy content follows the same equations. What is lost is "the livingness of structure and function, the organic and personal integration of the persisting elements." Hocking wondered about this perishing—"whether it is absolute, cutting through every strand of personal being —most vulnerable through its very marvel of unified complexity; or whether it, too, may be relative, leaving a germinal strand of selfhood intact." He wanted to show how such a relativity of death can occur.

The line of reasoning finally led to the concept of an "organic unity with feeling." Creativity is tied to a subjective factor, with feeling, "that there is a *total élan* of our being toward an undefined goal, that the various impulses welling up in us through the subconscious tend to merge in a single self-sublimating Eros. And this central and pervasive longing presents to us images of total fulfillment, as it has to the race through all reflective history." The fulfillment is symbolized by the time-transcending Beatific Vision of The Good and "the continued working of love through time." In love, the loved one is regarded "as worthy of permanence," "forever above the accidents of time and death—as if one could!" Vision is united with time. The experience, which comes to us in the midst of desperate gropings, "Now, for the first time, I see!" is not only the conclusion of a chain of activities but a beginning as well.

"So if, in death," Hocking had hoped,

some fragment of the beatific vision should be our lot, arresting and beckoning the passing spirit—one who had already known love in its truthfulness—it would be indeed a glimpse of eternity, and a oneness with the One: but not a terminus of time in eternal changelessness. For the first time which can be untimed, *at a time,* is not ended. It would be at once self-recovery, remembrance, and the continued lure to create through love in ongoing time. Our oneness with the One is participation, not in fixity, but in partnership with him that continually labors and creates, world without end.

Continuum

A classical point of departure for discussions on continuity is the Arguments of Zeno.

Aristotle[1] tried to refute them. The First Argument says that a moving thing must first reach the midpoint before arriving at the goal. It must then reach the midpoint of the half-distance, then the midpoint of the remaining distance, *ad infinitum*. Each of these midpoint traversals, of which there is an infinite number, requires a finite time. The sum of an infinite number of finite periods is an infinite length of time. The net result is that the goal will never be reached. There can be no motion.

Aristotle noted in reply that magnitude as well as time is continuous and length as well as time is infinite in extremities and in diversity:

Hence Zeno's argument makes a false assumption in asserting that it is impossible for a thing to pass over or severally to come in contact with infinite things in a finite time. For there are two senses in which length and time and generally anything continuous are called "infinite": they are called so either in respect of divisibility or in respect of their extremities. So while a thing in a finite time cannot come in contact with things quantitatively infinite, it can come in contact with things infinite in respect of divisibility: for in this sense the time itself is also infinite: and so we find that the time occupied by the passage over the infinite is not a finite but an infinite time, and the contact with the infinities is made by means of moments not finite but infinite in number.

The Second Argument states that, in a race between Achilles and a tortoise, in which the tortoise is given a head start, Achilles is unable to overtake the tortoise because he must first reach the point where the tortoise was and hence the latter will always maintain a lead in the interim. This is the same in principle as the First Argument and the same response holds.

With respect to the Third Argument, claiming that a flying arrow is at rest, Zeno assumed that time is composed of moments. Aristotle disagreed in that "if this assumption is not granted, the conclusion will not follow." In other words, while the tip of the flying arrow is occupying one of the infinite contiguous points in space, it must be at rest at one of the infinite contiguous moments. The problem remains: How can a flying arrow be motionless? The Third Argument rests on the false assumption that "a body occupies an equal time in passing with equal velocity a body that is in motion and a body of equal size that is at rest."

In effect, Zeno's arguments state that motion is impossible. There is the inference that because of the lack of change in an instant or in the now, everything is in the same position at one moment as at another. It may be that Zeno actually wanted to point out the contradictions in our concepts of space, time, and continuity through apparently attacking the accepted reality of motion.

Bertrand Russell[2] located Zeno's motion "*merely* in the occupation of different places at different times," which means rejecting "the notion of a *state* of motion." This raises the issue of the dissimilarity between motion as perceived by our senses and motion as conceived in mathematics. In mathematical motion, there is a functional relation between position and time. We can easily imagine a moving arrow occupying a particular position at a particular moment. But it would be difficult to conceive of an actual physical procedure of ascertaining the situation without destroying the motion itself. Mathematicians, especially since d'Alembert in the eighteenth century, regard motion as a contiguous succession of states of rest.

There is a general feeling that Zeno's proofs conceal a subtle mistake, although consensus is lacking as to *the* mistake. Morris Lazerowitz[3] analyzed the language involved and showed why no error in reasoning can be found in Zeno's line of argument. In effect, it is of the form: "*p* implies that *q* implies *r*." Since motion implies a change in position in an instant of time and since no change can take place in an instant, therefore (so the argument runs), motion is impossible. Actually, the validating proposition that no change can take place in an instant is not based on sense-observations. No one can see what happens in an instant. The proposition only appears empirical in character. In reality, it represents a special kind of language. In similar manner, the statement that "motion consists merely in the occupation of different places at different times" does not allow for the transition of a moving body from one place to the next. The person seems to be saying that "A particle in motion looks to be in a state of transition in the path along which it is moving, but its motion nevertheless consists of a succession of static states of rest. It does not get from one place to another; it simply *is* in one place at one time and in another place at another time."

This kind of talk is artificial in nature and not useful for practical purposes. The sentence "Motion is impossible" expressses not a proposition in the ordinary language but one in "a special language of *metaphysical wish-fulfillment.*" It constitutes

a *linguistic grievance,* which is used to justify the artificial realization of a linguistic wish. It is a source of dissatisfaction to some people that the word "instant," or the term "the *now,*" should be one thing and masquerade as another thing, that it should wear the outer cloak of a time-interval-denoting substantive and not be one in fact. . . . the philosopher vents his grievance and soothes his feelings by composing a language which has no place for them. . . . It is no wonder, then, that no error of reasoning has been found in the proof, for there is none.

53.
The logic
of infinity
LIV

The Dedekind cut. The notion of the infinitesimal was developed by the Greeks. It was considered to be the difference between the circle and the corresponding polygon with a large number of equal sides. When Newton and Leibnitz invented calculus, the infinitesimal assumed a fundamental importance in higher mathematics. But the intellectually curious could not resolve the dilemma of the infinitesimal being smaller than any fraction that can be mentioned, yet being neither zero nor finite. This deadlock lasted until the later nineteenth century when Karl Weierstrass showed that the infinitesimal was not needed after all.

But, as Bertrand Russell[1] has noted,

the banishment of the infinitesimal has all sorts of odd consequences, to which one has to become gradually accustomed. For example, there is no such thing as the next moment. The interval between one moment and the next would have to be infinitesimal, since if we take two moments with a finite interval between them, there are always other moments in the interval. Thus if there are to be no infinitesimals, no two moments are quite consecutive, but there are always other moments between any two. Hence there must be an infinite number of moments between any two, because if there were a finite number one would be nearest the first of these two moments, and therefore next to it. This might be thought to be a difficulty; but, as a matter of fact, it is here that the philosophy of the infinite comes in and makes all straight.

The polemic over the reality swung back and forth for two thousand years until the arrival of Dedekind and Cantor. Rigorous mathematical treatment of the continuous independent variable began with Richard Dedekind's essay of 1872.

Dedekind felt that there are infinitely more point-individuals in the straight line than there are number-individuals in the domain of rational numbers. This is due to the presence of continuity in the former and discontinuity in the latter. He arrived at continuity in the following manner.

Attention was directed to the fact that every point of the straight line separates the line into two portions with every point of one portion lying to the left of every point of the other. The essence of continuity lies in the converse:

If all points on a straight line falling into two classes, so that every point of the first class lies to the left of every point of the second class, then there exists one and only one point which produces this division of all points into two classes, this severing of the straight line into two portions. . . . I think I shall not err in assuming that everyone will at once grant the truth of this statement; moreover, the majority of my readers will be very much disappointed to learn that by this commonplace remark the secret of continuity is to be revealed.[2]

This principle is known as the Dedekind Cut. He began by showing that every real number can be used to divide all rational numbers into two nonoverlapping groups. We may employ the process of rational partition or irrational partition. In the former case, as in the number 2, the lower class includes all rational numbers less than or equal to 2; the upper class includes all rational numbers greater than 2. In the case of irrational partition, as in $\sqrt{2}$, neither of the two classes includes the $\sqrt{2}$ as member.

Although the Dedekind principle does not use the word "infinite" explicitly, nevertheless the infinite is implied. There is a close analogy to our everyday intuition of time. We divide time into the past and the future by the present. Together these parts of time comprise all of time. We conceive of no gaps in this totality of time. We can think of a continuous flow. In terms of the Dedekind analogy, the present can be regarded as an irrational partition. It belongs neither to the past nor future. This is an important aspect to note.

Dedekind's contributions gained full appreciation with the appearance of the 1895 essay of Georg Cantor.[3] Following the foundations laid by Dedekind, Cantor finally solved the problem of infinity, at least to the satisfaction of most mathematicians, by means of the theory of sets.

Sequence and series. Before going into the theory of sets, a few words on the concepts of sequence, series, and correspondence may be of some help.

Each of the terms of an infinite sequence has a successor. One of the most important sequences is the geometrical sequence, which is derived from multiplying successive terms by the same factor. Successive multiplication by 1/2 gives the following decreasing geometrical sequence:

$$\frac{1}{2}, \frac{1}{4}, \frac{1}{8}, \frac{1}{16}, \frac{1}{32}, \dots \quad \left(\frac{1}{2}\right)^n$$

Using the serial process, whereby the new term is successively added to the previous total of all the prior terms, the following geometrical series is generated:

$$\frac{1}{2}, \frac{3}{4}, \frac{7}{8}, \frac{15}{16}, \frac{31}{32}, \dots$$

This particular series converges to the limit 1. Despite the First Argument of Zeno that an infinite number of terms are involved, the limit is still finite. The Second Argument of Zeno, involving Achilles and the tortoise, also relates to the geometrical series. Actually, if Achilles traveled at the rate of 100 feet per minute and the tortoise at the rate of one foot per minute, the handicap of say 990 feet would have been reduced in accordance with the following geometrical series:

$$990, 9.9, .099, .00099, \dots$$

The sum of the terms is 1000 feet, which can be determined according to the equation: The sum of the terms of a geometrical series equals the original term of the series divided by the difference between one and the multiplying ratio. Zeno notwithstanding, Achilles would cover 1000 feet in ten minutes and overtake the tortoise.

Correspondence. The character of various infinite series can be distinguished by matching the members of a series against those of another in a one-to-one process.

A one-to-one correspondence is established between two sets when, according to an accepted rule, one and only one element of one set is paired with one and only one element of the other set and vice versa. The set of men can be put into a one-to-one correspondence with the set of shirts they wear.

Two sets are equivalent if a one-to-one correspondence can be established. If the matching process results in one set being exhausted before the other, then the set with residual unmatched elements is considered to be of a higher power. In finite arithmetic the concept of power can be identified with that of cardinal number. If we assume an analogous situation in the case of infinite sets, a new type of arithmetic can be developed. The powers of infinite sets will then be considered to belong to the numbers of a higher order. Cantor named them transfinite cardinal numbers, and the arithmetic of the infinite he called transfinite arithmetic. Let us examine a few examples involving sets of numbers.

Sets that are equivalent to the set of all natural numbers are called denumerably infinite sets. As defined, all of these sets have the same transfinite number. This particular number is called aleph-null. By means of the matching process, it can be shown that the set of all even numbers is also denumerably infinite. Its transfinite cardinal number is also aleph-null. The matching procedure is depicted as follows:

$$1 \quad 2 \quad 3 \quad 4 \quad 5 \quad 6 \quad \ldots$$
$$2 \quad 4 \quad 6 \quad 8 \quad 10 \quad 12 \quad \ldots$$

That the set of all pairs of natural numbers is denumerably infinite can be demonstrated in a similar way. The elements are first arranged in a diagrammatic array as follows:

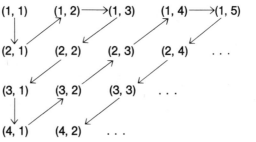

A one-to-one correspondence can then be made between the set of natural numbers and the above set of number pairs as follows:

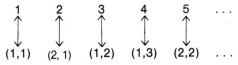

If, instead of arranging the pairs of numbers in the manner shown, they are actually the quotients or rational fractions, such as 1/2, 2/3, and so on, a similar conclusion is drawn regarding the denumerably infinite power of the set of all rational fractions. This may appear surprising in view of the normal tendency to believe that there are far more fractions than natural numbers.

The same approach is used in showing that an infinite aggregate can be put into a one-to-one correspondence with a part of itself in geometrical situations, as in the case of a line.

Thinning and filling infinite sets. Removing elements from an infinite set will still leave it infinite. Let A be the original infinite set, E the element to be excluded and B the remaining subset. As in previous discussion there is a part A_1 of the original set A, which can be matched against the whole of A on a one-to-one basis, and therefore is infinite. If the element E is not present in A_1, E will be in subset B and the contention is upheld. On the other hand, if the element E is present in A_1, there will be at least one element F which belongs to B and not to A_1. By replacing E by F, we will have another part, A_2, of A_1. The A_2 will again be an infinite set and part of B. Thus, the infinity of an infinite set is not changed by any attempt at thinning out.

The same retention of infinity holds after filling in. This too would be contrary to our normal expectations. We would suspect that the power of a rational series, which is everywhere dense, would be greater than that of a natural discrete sequence. But Cantor proved his case by showing that the rational set is also denumerable. He was able to arrange the rational numbers in sequence and to assign each rational number a definite rank. In the sequence, each rational number is succeeded by another. At the same time they are discrete. There is succession without continuity. This is in contrast to the common notion of compactness, whereby an infinite number of terms can be sandwiched between any two rational numbers.

There are thus two types of equivalences. One is a one-to-one correspondence between two sets. The other is complete equivalence or similarity. In the latter, in addition to the matching process, the order of arrangement is preserved: If element *a* precedes *a'* in set *A,* and if these are matched with elements *b* and *b',* respectively, in a set *B,* then *b* will precede *b'* in set *B.* The set of rational numbers in increasing magnitude is equivalent to the set of natural numbers in the first sense of matching equivalence but not from the standpoint of order. In other words, they are characterized by the same cardinal number but by different ordinal types. This happens only in the arithmetic of the infinite, which is quite different from the situation in the arithmetic of the finite. In the latter realm, sets with the same cardinal numbers have the same ordinal number.

Power of the continuum. Not all infinite sets are denumerable or equivalent. Although the set of all rational fractions and other infinite sets can be put into a one-to-one correspondence with the natural numbers, the set of all real numbers can not. There are always some real numbers unmatched. The two types, therefore, have different cardinal numbers. Cantor called the cardinal number of the set of real numbers the power of the continuum.

He demonstrated the thesis by demonstrating that the set of all real numbers between 0 and 1 are denumerably infinite real numbers, which can be placed in a one-to-one correspondence with the natural numbers, in the following way:

The set of natural numbers is first placed on a one-to-one correspondence against an arbitrary set of decimal-fraction real numbers, such as

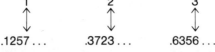

Without much difficulty, one can think of a real number which is not present in the assumed set of denumerably infinite natural numbers. Such a number would have as its first decimal digit one that differs from the first digit of the first decimal real number, as the second digit one

that differs from the second digit of the second decimal real number in the assumed sequence, and so on. In this way it can be demonstrated that there is at least one decimal real number between 0 and 1 unaccounted for.

The set of all real numbers can also be paired off on a one-to-one correspondence basis with the set of all points of a straight line. Furthermore the set of points on a given line can be paired off, element for element, against the set of points on a longer or shorter line, on a plane, in a three-dimensional volume, and in a space of any number of dimensions. They are all equivalent, with the same power of the continuum. Cantor's approach is illustrated by the case involving the set of all points on the plane. A one-to-one correspondence is established between a line of unit 1 and a square with sides of unit 1. A point P on the plane is represented by the coordinates (x, y). These coordinates are decimal fractions, less than 1, which can be given in the form:

$$x = .A_1 / A_2 / A_3 / A_4 / A_5 / A_6 / \ldots$$
$$y = .B_1 / B_2 / B_3 / B_4 / B_5 / B_6 / \ldots$$

A third decimal fraction is formed by alternating the digits of x and y as follows:

$$z = .A_1 / B_1 / A_2 / B_2 / A_3 / B_3 / A_4 / B_4 / \ldots$$

The decimal fraction z, represented as a point on the line, is also a real number. By means of such a sequence of steps, the point on the line can be matched always with a point P on the plane and vice versa. The set of all points on the line is therefore equivalent to the set of all points on the plane.

Higher transfinite numbers. So far, we have discussed two transfinite numbers, the cardinal number for the set of all natural numbers and the power of the continuum. Although it is theoretically possible, no transfinite numbers have been found between the two. There are certain transfinite numbers, however, which are higher. One is that of the correspondences between two continua. This is called a functional manifold. Here again, there appears to be no set with power between the power of the continuum and the functional manifold.

Sets with successively higher cardinal numbers can be formulated without termination. According to the Cantor theory, there can be no last transfinite number, just as there can be no last finite number.

Infinity consummated. Through deliberations of this kind, Cantor was led to ascribe a definite mathematical entity to infinity. He spent much time on the rigorous examination of pairs of contradictory, yet each apparently provable, propositions. He found that the propositions against infinity, even though logical on the surface, actually turned out incompatible with the fundamentals of mathematics. This was not the case with propositions accepting the concept of infinity. In 1883, he was able to state with confidence:[4]

It is traditional to regard the infinite as the indefinitely growing or in the closely related form of a convergent sequence, which it acquired during the seventeenth century. As against this I conceive the infinite in the definite form of something consummated, something capable not only of mathematical formulations, but of definition by number. This conception of the infinite is opposed to traditions which have grown dear to me, and it is much against my own will that I have been forced to accept this view. But many years of scientific speculation and trial point to these conclusions as to a logical necessity, and for this reason I am confident that no valid objection could be raised which I would not be in a position to meet.

54.
Order, direction, and irreversibility
LV

There is an order, a direction, an irreversibility about time.[1] Yet there seems to be no consensus among the leading thermodynamicists as to the origin of irreversibility and time asymmetries. Benjamin Gal-Or[2] identified four main schools of thought: (1) Traditional axiomatic thermodynamics with some modifications. (2) The belief that time asymmetries are generated from a combination of initial conditions, probability theory, and the local behavior of the universe. (3) The belief that the origin of irreversibility and electromagnetic and thermodynamic time asymmetries lies in the large-scale nonequilibrium dynamics of the expanding universe. (4) The belief that primary emphasis must be placed on quantum principle and relativity to tie the world of the very large with that of the very small. After a review of these and other schools, he concluded that "the problem of the origin of irreversibility in nature, which is intimately coupled to the very concept of time and initial conditions incorporates in it issues that are as far beyond our reach now as they were in the early days of thermodynamics." He emphasized that statistics itself does not produce irreversibility. It is not the mathematical formulations but the *a priori* choice on the part of the physicist that gives rise to irreversibility, time symmetry, and the law of increasing entropy noted in statistical mechanical theorems.

This can be related to the empirical fact that blind statistical prediction is "physical," whereas blind statistical retrodiction is not. Thus one can calculate the probability that something physical will happen, but not the probability that something physical did happen. This should be recognized as an imposed direction of time or an imposed initial condition on symmetric probability theory. It is a selection which is usually undeclared but which is essentially equivalent to an *a priori* introduction of the essence of irreversibility (and the so-called second law) into what is widely (and wrongly) believed to be a deduced statistical time asymmetry, statistical law of the increase of entropy or mixing, and so forth. Consequently, I stress that statistical (classical or quantum) mechanics fails to deduce the origin of irreversibility and time anisotropies in nature.[3]

He preferred the replacement of the term "flow of time" by such terms as "anisotropy of time."

Scientific time invariance. Substitution of plus t by minus t in the Newtonian laws of physics does not invalidate the equations. Reversing the t in Maxwell's differential equations would be accompanied by a reversal in the electrical current and magnetic field strength, again leaving the net rules unaltered. Physical time appears to be symmetrical or isotropic in gravitational and electromagnetic forces.

The same time-reversal invariance had been assumed also to hold in the interactions between nuclear particles. J. H. Christiansen and coworkers,[4] however, obtained laboratory results not permitted by the *CPT* theorem, a respected deduction from Special Relativity. This theorem states that the combination of *CP* is interdependent with *T*, where *C* is charge reversal (replacement of an elementary particle by its antiparticle), *P* is parity reversal (replacement of a situation with its mirror image), and *T* is time reversal. Their experiments showed that two out of every thousand decays of a neutrally charged K_2 meson produce a positively charged and a negatively charged pi-meson, which violates the *CP* invariance. This means that the situation is not invariant with time reversal.

The actual effects for measurement have been rather small. R. G. Sachs[5] suggested a more direct measure of

T-invariance, such as one associated with angular correlation between the spin and velocity vectors of decay
products. Measurements of this kind have been made
before, however, and have been found to be consistent
with *T*-invariance. It appears that new kinds of observations on time-reversal symmetry will be possible within
several years with the completion of particle accelera-
tors at the 100 or more billion electron-volt level.

If the *CPT* theorem holds then, as G. J. Whitrow[6] has
put it, "not all the fundamental non-statistical laws of
physics have been found to be invariant under time reversal." But it is too early to say for certain.

Time order. Time order should not be confused with
time direction. The points *A, B, C* on a line can be arranged in a certain order. *A* is to the left of *B, B* left of
C. The relation is asymmetrical and transitive in a serial
order. It does not possess a direction. By this we mean
that there is no structural difference between the relation "to the left of" and "to the right of." We can tell
them apart by pointing to the line and arbitrarily desig-
nating the situation involved.

The condition is quite different in the directional order
of a series of increasing numbers, such as 1, 2, 3, . . .
on a line. Two is less than 3, 3 less than 4. The numeri-
cal case of "less than" is asymmetrical, connected, and
transitive. But unlike the relation "to the left of," the
relation of "less than" has a direction. "Less than" is
structurally different from "greater than." In the set of
real numbers we may define "greater than" as follows:
Any number which is the square of another number is
greater than any number which is not. Thus the relation
"greater than" is defined without need to point at a diagram of the line.

Relation in time is more like a "greater than" relation
than a "to the left of" relation. "Earlier than" differs
structurally from "later than." Time possesses not only
an order but also a direction.

A distinction should also be made between the repara-
bility of actions and the irreversibility of time. Picking
up a book that has been dropped repairs the original
positioning of the book. But it does not alter the fact
that the book has been dropped. The physicist may do
his experiment again by restarting the pendulum, but
this does not erase his previous attempt. We can never
repair the date of the event. Since the date is an essen-

tial property of an event, it seems obvious that we can never actually reverse an event. The real time, not an empty time, is irreversible.

Causal order. Causal propositions of the type "x causes y" may have any one of three meanings.[7] The first is the conventionally understood one which, strictly speaking, is the only proper sense. In this case, a conscious and deliberate agent is involved. Causing someone to do something means inducing, making, or otherwise providing him a motive for doing it. Two elements are implicated in the relationship. One is the efficient cause, which is the condition required to make the act possible. The other is the final cause, which is the purpose or intention.

The second meaning of the causal proposition can be found in what Aristotle called "practical science." It resembles the first in that human action is entailed. However, this action is directed not toward another human being but toward things in nature. In this sense, then, a cause is a state of things which we can bring about or prevent and, in so doing, produce or prevent that whose cause our action is said to be. Overloading a boat is the cause of its sinking.

The third meaning refers to the "causal relations" in theoretical science. Actually, the first meaning is presupposed in the other two. The second and the third meanings are somewhat misleading, in that what we say in the word "cause" and what we mean are not necessarily the same. There is the danger of thinking that certain relations actually exist when we are only talking of them *as if* they exist. In fact, the ambiguity of the notion of the law of causation is such that many thinkers consider it of little value. Because of this, scientific propositions about causes are being replaced by those about laws.

Prediction is no criterion of causality. The rising of the sun can be predicted by the crowing of the cock. Similarly, the plane's arrival can be predicted by the timetable. The law of the timetable is deterministic, capable of prediction. But it is not causal. The connection between two successive events makes causal sense only if there is a timeless causal feature in its regularity.[8] The Great Irish Famine was caused by crop failure. In this case, a particular event was caused by another at a specific time and place. The cause-and-effect relation makes sense because there is the timeless relation between famine and crop failure behind it.

Causal definition of time order. We normally think of an effect as immediately following its cause in time. But as Bertrand Russell[9] reflected, it appears strange that the cause which has persisted for some time should, for some unknown reason, turn into an effect at some particular moment. Why not at an earlier instant? Or a later one? Or why did not something else come up in the interim to prevent the effect from materializing? No matter how small the interval between cause and effect, it is still sufficiently long for something else to intervene. "I put my penny in the slot, but before I can draw out my ticket there is an earthquake which upsets the machine and my calculations."

There are further complications.[10] The assumption that the cause precedes the effect in time implies that the conditions or even the totality of the environment is not sufficient to constitute the cause which can bring about the effect. Somehow the time interval seems to have something to do with it. If this is not granted, then it would be difficult to reconcile the cause being separated from the effect, since how can one act on the other? If there is no time interval between cause and effect, the two would be simultaneous. Morris Kline[11] ascribed the notion of causality to the limitations of human sense perceptions: "Cause is nothing but reason." Given the axioms of Euclidean geometry, the properties of geometrical bodies are already determined as necessarily logical consequences. The theorems are implied in the axioms.

Russell recognized that the dilemmà can be partly alleviated if time is not explicitly introduced in our formulas. Mechanical laws can describe acceleration as a function of configuration, not of configuration and time together. This "principle of the irrelevance of the time may be extended to all scientific laws. In fact we might interpret the 'uniformity of nature' as meaning just this, that no scientific law involves the time as an argument, unless, of course, it is given in an integrated form, in which *lapse* of time, though not absolute time, may appear in our formulae." D. J. B. Hawkins,[12] however, claimed that Russell and others had overlooked the possibility of continuous change. Their difficulty in reconciling the so-called time interval between cause and effect was due to their thinking in terms of successive instantaneous events. Hawkins insisted that there is no paradox in continuous time permitting continuous change in which cause and effect are simultaneous. It is only when the continuous change has reached a certain threshold that a discrete event appears to our senses or measuring apparatus.

Hans Reichenbach[13] stated that Einstein's criticism of simultaneity constituted the decisive argument for defining time order in terms of causal order. According to the Special Theory of Relativity, the time order is invariant if two events are connected causally. By causal relation is meant that they can be connected by signals. If two events cannot be connected by signals, then there is no way of telling which of the two is prior in time. This means that invariant time order exists only in the case of causal order. Otherwise the Lorentz equations and Einstein's Special Theory cannot be accepted. These considerations led Reichenbach to propose that temporal order is reducible to the primitive relation of cause and effect. We should not adopt the layman's description of cause as that which precedes what is to be known as the effect in time. This would produce a circularity, which cannot cast any light on the attempt to reduce time order to causal order. The cause-and-effect relationship should be characterized without reference to time order or duration.

Causality and retribution. When causality is not restricted to the context of the physical sciences but considered in the widest expanse of human thought, many intriguing ramifications emerge. We shall discuss just one example —the gradual separation of the notion of causality from that of retribution in the evolution of Occidental thinking, so well elucidated by Hans Kelsen.[14]

Primitive man did not consider nature to be governed by cause-and-effect laws as distinct from social categories. The legal framework of his community was assumed·to apply also to the community of nature herself. The basic rule governing the social sphere was that of retribution. A person expected to be punished for an evil act and rewarded for a good one. This reciprocity held not only between him and his fellow men, but also between him and animals, plants, or inanimate objects. All nature followed the same pattern.

It was the Greeks who gradually separated the comprehensive principle governing both nature and society into two independent ones. The law of nature became that of causality. The law of the state became the social norm. Thales (640–546 B.C.), the original Greek philosopher, was still thinking in terms of a government or monarchy-like rule when he sought to understand the functioning of the cosmos. His notion of cause was still endowed with a personalistic quality. A magnet, for example, is considered to contain a soul which intentionally attracts iron. Things that affect each other must have originally come from the same source, otherwise their natures would not be so similar as to be mutually reactive. Just as a wrong social act attracts retribution, so does the cause attract the effect. Just as the wrong act attracts a coordinate magnitude of retribution, so does the cause result in an equal effect. "Greater deaths," wrote Heraclitus (ca. 500 B.C.), "receive greater rewards."[15]

Anaximander (611–544 B.C.) proposed an eternal, unlimited substance as the ultimate source which gives rise to opposites of hot and cold, wet and dry, and so on. Excessive heat in the summer is unjust, just as is excessive cold in the winter. These opposites must return to the eternal source in order to regain the just equilibrium. "Into that from which things take their rise they pass away once more, according to necessity. For they make reparation and satisfaction to one another for the injustice according to the order of time."[16] This statement may be regarded as the first explicit formulation of the law of causality. Yet, as Kelsen emphasized, it remains essentially the law of retribution:

Just as necessity is the compulsion of the legal rule of retribution, so is the chronological order, the earlier and the later, the sequence of wrong and punishment. In this dynamism of retribution the scientific thought for the first time realizes the time category. The reason that modern science still characterizes the relationship of cause and effect as asymmetrical and still maintains that the cause must precede the effect in time, is that the cause was originally the wrong, and the effect the retribution.

As time went on, Leukippos, Demokritos, and the other atomist-founders of natural science eliminated all animistic and theological inferences in the interpretation of nature and presented the principle of causality in its pure form. Their contemporary Protagoras propounded the belief that punishment of a wrongdoer by the state is not for the purpose of retribution but prevention of future crimes. "No one punishes a wrongdoer with regard to and because he has committed an offense, unless one takes unreasoning vengeance like a wild beast. But he who undertakes to punish with reason does not avenge himself for the past offense, since what has been done cannot be undone. He looks rather to the future, and aims at preventing that particular person and others who see him punished from doing wrong again. Whoever thinks in this way . . . punishes to deter."[17] Thus the law of the state became detached from the principle of retribution.

55.
Varieties of
nothingness
LV

Absences themselves may be of different kinds and the absence of something may even be its own effect.

An illustration of this state was provided by the playwright Harold Pinter[1] in his perceptive explanation of the difference between pause and silence in a play:

The pause is a pause because of what has just happened in the minds and guts of the characters. They spring out of the text. They're not formal conveniences or stresses but part of the body of the action. I'm simply suggesting that if they play it properly they will find that a pause —or whatever the hell it is—is inevitable. And a silence equally means that something has happened to create the impossibility of anyone speaking for a certain amount of time—until they can recover from whatever happened before the silence.

Nothingness is not the end, therefore, into which all has disappeared and out of which nothing will appear. It may be looked upon as a stage of transformation. The traditional account of Buddha's entrance into Nirvana[2] mentioned this facet in passing:

The blessed One addressed the priests:
"And now, O priests, I take my leave of you; all the constituents of being are transitory; work out your salvation with diligence."
And thus was the last word of The Tathāgata.
Thereupon The Blessed One entered the first trance; and rising from the first trance, he entered the second trance; and rising from the second trance, he entered the third trance; and rising from the third trance, he entered the fourth trance; and rising from the fourth trance, he entered the realm of the infinity of space; and rising from the realm of the infinity of space, he entered the realm of the infinity of consciousness, and

rising from the realm of the infinity of consciousness, he entered the realm of nothingness; and rising from the realm of nothingness, he entered the realm of neither perception nor yet non-perception; and rising from the realm of neither perception nor yet non-perception, he arrived at the cessation of perception and sensation.

Thereupon the venerable Ānanda spoke to the venerable Anuruddha as follows:

"Reverend Anuruddha, The Blessed One has passed into Nirvana."

"Nay, brother Ānanda, The Blessed One has not passed into Nirvana; he has arrived at the cessation of perception and sensation."

Thereupon The Blessed One rising from the cessation of his perception and sensation, entered the realm of neither perception nor yet non-perception; and rising from the realm of neither perception nor yet non-perception, he entered the realm of nothingness; and rising from the realm of nothingness, he entered the realm of the infinity of consciousness; and rising from the realm of the infinity of consciousness, he entered the realm of the infinity of space; and rising from the realm of the infinity of space, he entered the fourth trance; and rising from the fourth trance, he entered the third trance; and rising from the third trance, he entered the second trance; and rising from the second trance, he entered the first trance; and rising from the first trance, he entered the second trance; and rising from the second trance, he entered the third trance; and rising from the third trance, he entered the fourth trance; and rising from the fourth trance, immediately The Blessed One passed into Nirvana.

It was awareness of this kind that might have led the poet Lu Chi[3] to compose the following couplet in 303 A.D.:

We poets struggle with Nonbeing to force it to yield Being;

We knock upon silence for an answering music.

**Speculations
on the Time-
Light-Life
Continuum**

56.
Time-binding
LVI

Alfred Korzybski[1] regarded plants as the chemistry-
binding class of life, animals as space-binding, and man
as time-binding. Plants convert solar energy into organic
chemical energy. Animals move in space. Men mobilize
the past.

He elaborated on his concept as follows:[2]

In the human class of life, we find a new factor, nonexistent in other forms of life; namely, that we have a
capacity to collect all known experiments of different
individuals. Such a capacity increases enormously the
number of observations a single individual can handle,
and so our acquaintance with the world around, and in,
us becomes much more refined and exact. This capacity,
which I call the time-binding capacity, is only possible
because, in distinction from the animals, we have evolved,
or perfected, extraneural means by which, without altering our nervous system, we can refine its operation and
expand its scope. Our scientific instruments record what
ordinarily we cannot see, hear, etc. Our neural verbal
centers allow us to exchange and accumulate experiences, although no one could live through all of them;
and they would be soon forgotten if we had no neural
and extraneural means to record them.

The principle can be seen operating in the evolution
of art. Charles Beidermann[3] asserted that "The future
artist will not be judged primarily on how 'different' he
is from anyone else, but on the degree to which his work
expresses his capacity to absorb the best that is present
in art as a whole, and integrate it into his 'individual'
achievement in the general art effort. What we are ad-
vocating is the very form of behavior which enabled all
the great creative men of history to make their contributions to the evolution of human beings." Goethe[4] had
said: "What am I myself? What have I done? All that I
have seen, heard, notes I have collected and used. My
works are reverenced by a thousand different individuals.
. . . Often I have reaped the harvest that others have
sown. My work is that of a collective being and it bears
Goethe's name."

Human beings excel over animals particularly in the
communication of time-binding symbols.[5] Animals are
capable of limited, essentially one-valued abstracting,
while human beings are at least potentially capable of
infinite valued abstracting. In addition, human beings
have the capacity to record the resulting abstracts or
symbols for subsequent use or subsequent generations.

Man's unique ability to create virtual presences, which has been introduced in Commentary 6, is a natural accompaniment of speech and language. Like other animals, man learns from examples. The young bird is taught to fly by its parents. The young rabbit is taught to pick up danger signals by its mother. The child is taught to wave goodbye. The onset of speech made possible the connection of certain sounds with certain objects. Once this was achieved, the relating of a given sound to movements, ideas, actions, and other abstractions became possible. Man was no longer restricted to direct concrete examples for learning. The savage was able to substitute a verbal lion for a real one in his instruction to the boy on the savanna plains. As speech became richer and as language became recorded in written form, the range and duration of man's influence expanded rapidly. When viewed against this unique ability to conjure up virtual presences, the evolution of man may be divided into four major stages: (1) the invention of speech as a rudimentary vehicle of virtual presences, (2) the widespread acceptance of the virtual presences as a medium of mutual influence, (3) the invention of writing as the first stored form of virtual presences, and (4) the displacement of real presence by the virtual as the dominant means of human control. The first stage began before the last Ice Age. The second occurred during that Ice Age, about 700,000 years ago. The third started about 6000 years ago. The fourth got into full swing about a century ago, with the invention of photography, movies, radio, TV, modern electronics, and mass media.

It was the increasing longevity of virtual presences that made history possible. In this way, history can be related to thought and time. As pointed out by R. G. Collingwood,[6] the ancients had no historians in the modern sense of the term. The memoirs and legends by Thucydides and Tacitus were not historical criticisms. Critical history began in the nineteenth century with such individuals as Vico, Gibbon, and Herder. The historical view pervaded all fields of human thought. "Biologists like Darwin and Huxley, philosophers like Hegel, theologians like Baur and Newman, and economists like Marx explicitly resolved the problem of their special sciences into historical problems. . . . [People] talk of Evolution, of Progress, of the metaphysical reality of

Time, as if these were notions of the first importance and grand discoveries of modern science. But they are only half-understood and mythological expressions of the concept of history." History is not just a succession of events. Each phase of history is a new art perpetually summing up the whole of previous history and consists in demonstrating "in detail the necessity of every individual to the whole."

People's minds are united by "the concrete universal of history." The process involved is not one of mechanics but of thought. It is not in time but above time. Whereas sensation is temporal, thought is extratemporal:

Sensation apprehends the here and now, thought apprehends the everywhere and the always. . . . To describe the life of man as temporal or finite and the life of God as eternal or infinite is only a way of saying that time is not real in abstraction, but real only in relation to its opposite. In the absolute process of thought the past lives in the present, not as mere "trace" or effect of itself in the physical or psychical organism, but as the object of the mind's historical knowledge of itself in an eternal present.

Historiographers have attempted to divide man's history into definite periods. The concept of the great year, for example, was advanced by the Etruscans as the period for a given race to succeed in its ascendancy. W. M. F. Petrie[7] quoted the following from Plutarch's *Life of Sulla,* concerning the last days of the Etruscan's period of 1100 years in 87 B.C.:

One day, when the sky was serene and clear, there was heard in it the sounds of a trumpet, so shrill and mournful that it frightened and astonished the whole city. The Tuscan sages said that it portended a new race of men, and a renovation of the world, for they observed that there were eight several kinds of men, all different in life and manners, that Heaven had allotted to each its time; and that when each race came to a period, and another was rising, it was announced by some wonderful sign from either earth or heaven. So that it was evident at once to those who attended to these things and were versed in them, that a different sort of man was come into the world, with other manners and customs, and more or less in the care of the gods than those who had preceded them. . . . Such was the mythology of the most learned and respectable of the Tuscan soothsayers.

Petrie himself believed that there were eight separate periods of civilization in Egypt. Each was in turn longer than the preceding one and began with "an onrush of barbarian races and an interlude of destruction and admixture of blood." The sculpture of every period goes through a comparable cycle of growth and decay. The old form first begins to be marked by boldness and vigor. The archaic influence is decreased and the effect becomes more free. Details are sacrificed for the harmony of the entirety. Soon thereafter the high point is reached. The archaic influence is gone, creativity and inspiration is high with workmanship of quality. Before long, degeneration sets in, marked by over-elaboration, repetitious copying, and uninspired efforts.

Not all of the people living at any given time, of course, are operating at the same cultural level. There is marked staggering. As shown by René Grousset,[8] contemporary people

are actually separated by tremendous chronological gaps. The Islamic calendar has today reached the fourteenth century after the Hegira, and in fact a good many of its faithful are still living in the equivalent of our *Trecento*. The least we can say of Hitler's invasions is that they belong to the age of Alaric and Genseric. . . . Most of our misfortunes spring from the fact that, not living in the same era culturally, people do obeisance neither to the same logic nor the same ethics.

Nevertheless the practice of dividing men into distinct groups for general historical treatment has been useful. The most convenient historical unit has been the nation.[9]

The nation may be defined in ways other than a geographical political entity. For Vico, it was the synthesis of time and idea.[10] He considered that the perfection of the positive structures of society appears in temporal succession. Idea is not a timeless essence. It unfolds into the time-forms of the human spirit, as finite man aspires to the infinite. The Vichian unit of historical life is involved in a contrapuntal fashion within the time-structure of history. It reacts autonomously in its internal life and also participates in the universality of humanity. This dualism enables the nation to evolve and contribute to the historical pageant.

Other authors have dealt with historical-cultural units. Danilevsky portrayed twelve chronological types.

Spengler traced the birth, growth, decay, and death of hundreds of civilizations. He tried to draw from his study a set of general principles governing the practices of art, science, religion, politics, economics, and other manifestations of organized society.

Toynbee did not think highly of the contemporary deterministic theories of the decay of civilization. Instead he adopted the principle of a progressive rhythm wherein a society is faced with repeated challenges which it either responds effectively to or is destroyed by.

In any case, the continuity of time lies at the foundation of historical order, relation, and quality. "It is upon this historical reality," wrote E. Jordan,[11]

that the act previsions its end. The details of order are the capacities for action of an organized body, anticipations of changes in the body organization; and they have been implanted in the organism not by the durational aspects of time, or by the fact that time in its "lapsation" enters into the structure of life as a permanent character in the fixed psychological tendencies to act in given or characteristic ways; but by time solidified into history, which provides not fixed tendencies but ordered impulses of spontaneity established hard in the nature of things. It is in this way that a capacity to act may be objectively, even physically real.

Heredity is not to be looked upon as the connection of "the capacities of an individual with empirical characters of individual forebears in their succession, which is subjective nonsense." Instead, Jordan emphasized the substantial reality of the species itself. The hereditary force is considered to be what gives rise to the possible forms of action which the species provides to the individual as motive. There is no necessary connection to the individual mind. This constitutes the basis for Jordan's concept of moral judgment, in which an individual is presented with a choice within the general objective scheme. The spontaneity of will in choice is not simply a matter for the individual's exercise of freedom. It is a much more complex issue, which depends upon the presentation of the circumstances for decision by the corporate structure of the culture. It is

the generic scheme within which the individual agent's capacities and his opportunities are all bodied forth. Every moral judgment, that is, asserts that an act is *characteristic* of an agent, is such as faithfully to represent and express the inner constitution and structure of the agent as the constitution and structure are made by his act permanent details within the system of reality. The relational system by and in which acts and agents are characterized, or woven into the structure of reality, is what we mean by heredity. The motive of an act is thus outside the act and not a psychological fact in the agent's nature. It is a fact within the objective structure of things. . . . It is through this concept of objective history that morality, as the account of actions of men, is given its metaphysical ground without which no judgment about action could be true or false.

As an element of history, therefore, time has an aspect of uniqueness.[12] There is a progressive transition in the evolution of historical event-quality, novelty, and creativity.[13] There is no repetition of exact replicas. Acceptance of the concept of historical ascent, however, does not necessarily imply that each moment is imperfect, awaiting evolution in the next. As M. Maisels[14] presented it:

Each moment of creativity in the world of human association is borne and willed in the present *as it is*, and it is thus absolutized for all time. Even when conceived from within the present, each moment of the past is seen as complete and perfect from within itself, as a moment of eternity in human time, wherein the individual, personal Being of man was utterly and exhaustively expressed, and as such, the moment is *willed* in the present. It is the very ascent-value of the present moment that, as seen above, affirms the time-order, hence absolutizes the past moment for its time—from the present.

Each present exerts a will to the future. Its thought and world-view have "always been laden with a mission, the mission to the future. . . . the historical value and reality of the past, as of the present, lies in its charge for the future. From this is derived the accepted and approved criterion for the measurement of the 'historicity' of a past event: To what extent is it laden with consequences for the future?"

Much of Eastern philosophy rests on the complete acceptance of the notion of the ineffability of life.[1] Its literature is accordingly filled with richly nebulous phrases toward holistic evocation.

One of the most important terms in the Taoist lore is *ch'i*. The word has been variously translated as "passion nature,"[2] "material principle,"[3] "constitutive ethers,"[4] "force, energy, breath, power,"[5] "ether or force,"[6] "the great breath of the universe,"[7] *et cetera*.[8]

The essence was originally given prominence by Lao

Tzu (604–511 B.C.). Various nuances were emphasized by different subsequent authors. Chang Tsai (1020–1077)[9] regarded it as a vital force, which is forever changing, like Chuang Tzu's (399–295 B.C.) "wandering air." It pervades the Great Void and is perpetually ceaseless. Its changes follow the *yin-yang* principles in the emergence of constantly new forms. "When the *ch'i* condenses, its visibility becomes apparent so that there are then the shapes (of individual things). When it disperses, its visibility is no longer apparent and there are no shapes. At the time of its condensation, can one say otherwise than that this is but temporary? But at the time of its dispersing, can one hastily say that it is nonexistent?"[10]

Chu Hsi (1130–1200) expanded upon Chang Tsai's thesis of the condensation of *ch'i*. The universe is formed by the *ch'i*, as activating essence, putting the *li*, as ultimate reason or purpose, into concrete form.[11]

In the universe, there are *Li* and *Ch'i*. The *Li* is the *Tao* that pertains to "what is above shapes," and is the source from which all things are produced. The *Ch'i* is the material (literally, instrument) that pertains to "what is within shapes," and is the means whereby things are produced. Hence men or things, at the moment of their production, must receive this *Li* in order that they may have a nature of their own. They must receive this *Ch'i* in order that they may have their bodily form.[12]

Thus, the *ch'i* can condense in different ways, thereby giving rise to the distinct characteristics of a flower or a leaf.

The *li* is the same for all men. The *ch'i*, however, provides the uniqueness of concrete existence. Chu Hsi added: "Whenever there is *Li*, then there is *Ch'i*. Whenever there is *Ch'i*, there must be *Li*. Those who receive a *Ch'i* that is clear, are the sages in whom the nature is like a pearl lying in clear cold water. But those who receive a *Ch'i* that is turbid, are the foolish and degenerate in whom the nature is like a pearl lying in muddy water." This represented his concept of good and evil. On the other hand, Wang Shou-jen (1472–1529) interpreted *li* as moral truth and *ch'i* as moral existence, but as one and the same. Moral knowledge cannot be separated from moral action.[13]

The concept of *ch'i* has also guided specific activities,

such as personal conduct, acupuncture, swordsmanship, and painting.

In swordsmanship, Tagyu Tajima no kami Munemori (1571–1646) stressed going beyond the mere mastery of technique to achievement of the inner strength of the ch'i. D. T. Suzuki[14] explained the workings of the ch'i by means of Chuang Tzu's "mind-fasting." The old sage suggested that

in hearing do not use the ear, but the mind; do not use the mind but ch'i. When you use the ear, the hearing stops there, and the mind cannot go further than the symbol; ch'i is something empty and waiting. Tao abides in the emptiness, and the emptiness is mind-fasting. . . . When Chuang-tzu defines "mind-fasting" as seeing and hearing with ch'i, the idea is to transcend the centripetence of the ego-consciousness. . . . This sword (of mystery) stands as a symbol of the invisible spirit keeping the mind, body, and limbs in full activity. But we can never locate it in any part of the body. It is like the spirit of a tree. If it had no spirit, there would be no splitting buds, no blooming flowers.

The Six Canons of Chinese Painting formulated about 500 A.D. placed primary importance on ch'i. As the first of the canons, the artist must give expression to ch'i to reflect the vitality of life. In the words of Mai-Mai Sze,[15]

The first Canon . . . is a terse statement of the idea that Ch'i . . . stirs all of nature to life and sustains the eternal processes of movement and change; and that if a work has Ch'i it inevitably reflects a vitality of spirit that is the essence of life itself. Man's spiritual resources are regarded as a direct manifestation of this creative power of Heaven. Through developing them, a painter not only nourishes that part of Heaven in himself but, possessing it, is capable of revealing it in his conduct and activity. In his painting he can draw on these spiritual resources to express the same force in every other natural thing that he depicts; for the subjects of his compositions have always been predominantly from nature.

Though expressed by the brush and the ink, the ch'i is beyond them. It was this that inspired the eighteenth-century painter Chang Keng[16] to say: "Ch'i may be expressed by ink, by brush-work, by an idea, or by absence of idea. . . . It is something beyond the feeling of the brush and the effect of ink, because it is the moving power of Heaven, which is suddenly disclosed. But only those who are quiet can understand it."

The conventional theories of physics and chemistry have not been successful in clarifying the intrinsicalness of life and the specificity of biological responses. We may mention a few examples.

The first involves the use of chemical formulas to represent compounds. These formulas have been very useful in explaining physical and chemical properties as well as reactions in test tubes. Pharmacologists, however, have had little satisfaction in the use of these representations in predicting physiological and medicinal properties. A case in point is quinine and dihydroquinine, whose formulas are shown below. They resemble each

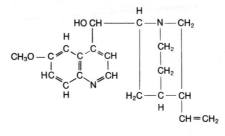

Quinine

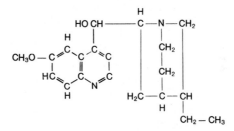

Dihydroquinine

other very closely. There is a difference of only two tiny hydrogen atoms (H) in the lower right-hand corner in an assemblage of carbon (C), oxygen (O), nitrogen (N), and other hydrogen atoms. Physically and chemically, the two compounds are quite similar. Pharmacologically, however, they are as different from each other as night is from day. Quinine is an effective drug against malaria; the other is inactive.

A second example is cane sugar and saccharin. Sweetness is exhibited by both compounds. Yet their chemical formulas are entirely dissimilar, as shown below.

A third example of the inadequacy of physics and chemistry in explaining living processes lies in the field of nutrition and metabolism. The unit of the calorie has been the primary measure of nutritional value. It has

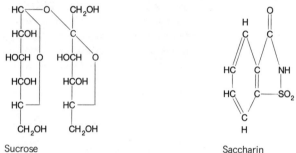

Sucrose   Saccharin

been used with great rigor in determining the energy relations in an operating engine. A given process can be described in terms of the number of calories absorbed or liberated. Calories can be employed in quantifying chemical reactions occurring in a living organism as it grows and in a dead organism as it decays. Exactly the same equations hold in both cases. Clearly then the term "calorie" does not describe the essence of living.

The intriguing manifestations of living organisms in complex timings, temporal creations, and other time-linked activities encourage us to probe further. The complicated interlocking temporal sequences in the lives of the oak, slime mold, earthworm, and dragonfly have been described in Commentaries 2 to 5. The question of temporality becomes even more fascinating as we observe the interplay between two or more individuals. Each responds to the other, as exemplified by the Pederson cleaning shrimp and its fish client. When the fish wants to be cleaned, it swims about in the neighborhood of the hole in which the shrimp lives in the waters of the Bahamas. At times the fish waits at the station for quite a while before the shrimp opens office. When the latter is ready, it moves to the opening of the hole, whips out the long antennae, and sways its body back and forth. If the fish wants to have its head attended to first, it swims toward the hole head first. If the tail, then it backs toward it. The shrimp climbs aboard, makes a quick inspection, and goes to work. Parasitic growths and accretions are scraped off and pulled away. Remaining perfectly still, the fish opens its gills and mouth as necessary to permit a thorough job. The shrimp finally crawls off and the customer swims away.

Bees incorporate tempo as language. The location of nectar is communicated to an associate through a series of patterned dances. The more bountiful the store of nectar, the livelier the dance. With the Australian honey bee, a distance of 1000 feet is conveyed by completing the pattern fifteen times in thirty seconds. When the crop is 2000 feet away, a slower dance of eleven completions in the same length of time is performed.

The sense of rhythm in the arctic tern is transmitted genetically from one generation to the next. The chicks are fed by their parents for about a month after hatching. At the end of this period, the young terns take to the air without any prodding. Those in Northern Europe cross the continent over the coast of Africa to spend some time in the Antarctic regions. They return to their ancestral breeding grounds the following May.

Man is the most versatile in terms of the diversification and depth of temporal ramifications. In an inanimate system, such as a tuning fork, the same equation of motion describes the vibrations, regardless of the kinds and manner of succession of sounds. In the case of man, however, something new is created upon the rendition of certain combinations and sequences of sound. This he has called music. Man has transformed something related to time into a heretofore nonexistent entity—a poem, a song, a symphony. We identify this time-related X as *ch'i*.

We suggest that living systems possess some unique capability of marshaling *ch'i*, which is not present in inanimate systems. The living organism processes *ch'i* in conjunction with the energy transformations which are characteristic of inanimate reactions. Death sets in when the capacity to process *ch'i* is disrupted and the corpse reverts to the inanimate world of energy exchanges, pure and simple.

Energy is the essential stuff for structural integrity and mechanical and chemical processes, while *ch'i* is the essential stuff for pattern perpetuity and thinking and feeling. While energy-metabolism accounts for the

vigor of health in the physical sense, *ch'i*-metabolism
accounts for the well-being of the person in the psychic
sense. A smoothly operating cross-feed exists between
energy and *ch'i* in the normal and serene human being.
Thermodynamic and tempodynamic forces join in harmony.

Since plants serve as food for animals, directly or a
few steps removed, we can trace the principal source of
metabolic raw materials back to light. In addition to the
calorie, *ch'i* must also ultimately come from light utilized
in the process of photosynthesis.

There are many ways in which the metabolism of time-
related substances can be represented. For pedagogic
simplicity *pro tempore,* we may follow conventional
expressions of energy transfers depicted in chemistry
and physics, pending further clarification of the metabolic picture in the light of the *ch'i* concept.

In photosynthesis energy from light is stored in the
dextrose molecule as follows:

$$\underset{\text{dioxide}}{\overset{\text{carbon}}{}} + \text{water} \xrightarrow[\text{energy}]{\text{light}} \underset{\text{(with energy)}}{\overset{\text{dextrose}}{}} + \text{oxygen}$$

When the dextrose molecule is assimilated, the captured
energy is released for work or dissipated as heat, as
follows:

$$\underset{\text{(with energy)}}{\overset{\text{dextrose}}{}} + \text{oxygen} \xrightarrow{} \underset{\text{dioxide}}{\overset{\text{carbon}}{}} + \text{water} + \text{energy}$$

In our musings on the metabolism of *ch'i*, light would
be looked upon as containing both energy and a time-
substance. A given quantity of light would consist of
certain units of energy and stretches of time-substance.
The energy component would be fixed in the dextrose
molecule in photosynthesis, the time-substance in a
temporal matrix, as follows:

$$\text{light} + \underset{\text{dioxide}}{\overset{\text{carbon}}{}} + \text{water} \xrightarrow{} \underset{\text{(with energy)}}{\overset{\text{dextrose}}{}} + \text{oxygen} + \underset{\text{(with ch'i)}}{\overset{\text{temporal matrix}}{}}$$

Just as the dextrose molecule can be assimilated so
that the energy fixed therein can be processed in varying bits and pieces to be utilized for inanimate work,
so can the temporal matrix be assimilated so that the
ch'i fixed therein can be transformed in varying stretches
and compositions to be utilized for animate purposes.

The important aspect of photosynthesis is not the activity of the chlorophyll molecule *per se* in the plant mechanism. It is entirely possible that one day some chemist will be able to synthesize dextrose in a test tube from carbon dioxide and water in the presence of light. But by itself this would not be considered photosynthesis in our conjecture. We envision the concomitant fixing of the time-substance. The latter can only be achieved by a preexisting temporal score. The nature of the score determines the way in which the time-substance from light is to be fixed and subsequently metabolized as *ch'i*. Other characteristic scores guide the metabolic transformations in different creatures. These compositional complexes should not be regarded necessarily as structures in the sense of discrete, recognizable, histological features, but as arrays of temporal templates for the formation of new scores, guiding the myriad metabolic changes in the metamorphosis, growth, and behavior of the new-born organism.

Herein—so our speculations continue—may lie the intrinsicalness of the species.

Actually, the metaphysical bush around which we have been beating is not new. Illustrative quotations are given below, which have not appeared earlier in this book, to show a long-standing and widespread subconscious feeling for some kind of Time-Light-Life continuum. The individual statements are admittedly taken out of context. But as a reverberating assembly, they tend to suggest that our musing on the metabolism of *ch'i* is only an echo of their collective unconscious.

ibn-Arabi:[1] "The Divine Light pervades the beings of the elect and radiates from them, reflected as if by mirrors, on everything around them."

Erwin Biser:[2] *"Events do not occur in time,* if by the latter is meant an absolute continuum of instants existing apart from actual throbs and pulsations, and somehow releasing portions of its being to be miraculously wedded to the happenings of nature in order to date them for convenience. . . . Time is within nature and not conversely."

John Boodin:[3] "The only possible solution . . . is to regard time as nonserial or prior to series and to regard series as a derivative construction. Time must, somehow, be involved as a property or substance of the real, conditioning the whole world of subjective construction. . . . We must introduce a nonspatial negative dimension of being, a pure dynamic principle, which shall necessitate incompatible judgments with regard to reality. By incompatible judgments we mean such judgments as that the rose is red and not-red with regard to the same spatial point."

Gai Eaton:[4] "The nucleus of a living being . . . is the point at which a ray of the Supernal Sun strikes the surface of the Ocean; a kind of crystallization of certain of these vital possibilities is said to take place at this point, and this crystallization is the psycho-physical individual; for the rest, other elements of the environment are drawn in and assimilated and, in this little patch of light, a cycle of experience runs its course. When the light is extinguished, the nucleus breaks up and the various elements go back into circulation."

Jiddu Krishnamurti:[5] "Thought is the product of time and without the thinking process time is not. The mind is the Maker of time, it *is* time."

Osip Mandelstam:[6] "Light of the beam threshed from rapidities . . ."

Friedrich Nietzsche:[7] "Every great man has a power which operates backwards; all history is again placed on the scales on his account, and a thousand secrets of the past crawl out of their lurking-places—into *his* sunlight. There is absolutely no knowing what history may be some day. The past is still perhaps undiscovered in its essence! There is yet so much reinterpreting ability needed!"

M. Pradines:[8] "For matter time is an 'environment'; for life it is a form of being."

Igor Stravinsky:[9] "Music is the best means we have of digesting time."

T'ai I Chin Hua:[10] "There correspond in the corporeal-personal man the following bipolar tensions. The body is activated by the interplay of two psychic structures: first, *hun,* . . . [namely] animus, and secondly, *p'o,* . . . [namely] anima. Both ideas come from observation of what takes place at death. . . . The anima was thought of as especially linked with the bodily processes; at death it sinks to the earth and decays. The animus, on the other hand, is the higher soul; after death it rises in the air, where at first it is still active for a time and then evaporates in ethereal space, or flows back into the common reservoir of life. In living men, the two correspond in a certain degree to the cerebral system and the system of the solar plexus respectively. The animus dwells in the eyes, the anima in the abdomen. The animus is bright and active, the anima is dark and earthbound."

Tsi I:[11] "Tsai Ngo said: 'I have heard the words *kwei* and *shen,* but I do not know their meaning.' Confucius thereupon said to him: 'The *khi,* or breath is the full manifestation of the *shen,* and the *p'oh* is the full manifestation of the *kwei;* the union of the *kwei* with the *shen* is the highest of all doctrines. Living beings must all die, and the soul which must then return to earth is that which is called *kwei.* But while the bones and the flesh moulder in the fields, the *khi* or breath departs to move on high as a shining light."

<table>
<tr><td>

59.
The *ch'i*-energy
duplexity of light
LVIII

</td><td>

At first reading, the proposition that light possesses both energy and temporal features may appear strange. Yet the speculation may not be inconsistent with accepted theories about its nature.

In the first place, physicists agree that light may be considered as particles in certain situations and as waves in others. "Particles" connotes mass and energy; "waves" connotes frequency and time.

In the second place, the particles of light, called photons, are supposed to have zero mass. This means a packet of something without mass. Why not an array of massless time-related elements cohabiting the same entity with mass-energy elements in varying proportions?

In the third place, it is to be noted that the frequency of vibration of atoms is described in Maxwell-Einstein equations as "time" but in quantum theory as "energy."

In the fourth place, measurements of the velocity of light, relativity theory, and conventional scientific thinking all point to the constant velocity of light as the reference maximum for a moving body. If one wishes to express this in another way, one might say that light serves as a universal reference for unprocessed time-substance.

It is interesting to note J. T. Fraser[1] surmising:

That time somehow relates to the coexistence of the electromagnetic and the gravitational worlds may be inferred from the proper-time concept of Relativity Theory. If proper-time is identified with the coordinate time of a clock, the curious condition arises that what we perceive as time as requested by this clock is recognized by observers in relative translation as something

</td></tr>
</table>

of a lag-time behind a light signal. For objects of zero rest-mass, such as photons, this lag-time, and with it time itself, vanishes. It follows that a meaningful relativistic definition of time for a world made up exclusively of radiant energy would be very difficult. One may elect to believe that before time began there was light, "and the light shone in the darkness, and the darkness did not comprehend it" for, it could not, until well after energy in form of ponderable mass had appeared in the universe.

It is not surprising, then, that, according to Roland Fischer,[2] "the Sanskrit root of the word 'time' meant 'to light' or 'to burn,' a meaning which is etymologically contained in the words *tempo* (Ital.), *tempus* (Lat.), *temperature,* and *temperament;* their common element being the frequency of vibrational periods. Does this all point, then, to the biological origin of time? Is time the fire of life?"

Think as we may wish about light, we have not been able to shake it loose from the shadows of time.

60.
Harmonious
complementarity
LIX

Life cannot be explained on the basis of protoplasmic mass alone. Otherwise the whale would have more life than the mayfly.

We may say that life is a function of *ch'i,* which has no mass. But it needs a carrier which has mass as well.

Thus it was that Lao Tzu said:

Thirty spokes unite in one nave and on that which is nonexistent [the hole in the nave] depends the wheel's utility. By cutting out doors and windows we build a house and on that which is nonexistent [the empty space within] depends the house's utility. Therefore, existence renders actual but nonexistence renders useful.

In this connection, a quotation from R. D. Laing[1] may be of interest. Referring to the "divided self," the embodied and the unembodied self, of the schizophrenic, he wrote:

In many schizophrenics, the self-body split remains the basic one. However, when the "centre" fails to hold, neither self-experience nor body-experience can retain identity, integrity, cohesiveness, or vitality, and the individual becomes precipitated into a condition the end result of which we suggested could best be described as a state of "chaotic nonentity." In its final form, such complete disintegration is a hypothetical state which has no verbal equivalents. We feel justified, however, in postulating such a hypothetical condition. In its most extreme form it is perhaps not compatible with life. The thoroughly dilapidated, chronic catatonic-hebephrenic is presumably the person in whom this process has gone on to the most extreme degree in one who remains biologically viable.

Organisms have been traditionally divided into plant and animal kingdoms. Following the scheme put forth by Carl Linnaeus (1707–1778), the photosynthesizing, rooted higher plants represent one kingdom and the food-ingesting, motile animals the other. The diffusion of these typical characteristics among unicellular organisms, such as *Euglena,* introduced some difficulty. Whereupon, Ernst Haeckel (1834–1919) introduced a third kingdom, called *Protista.*

A four-kingdom division was suggested by H. F. Copeland[1] in 1956. With modification by later workers,[2] the four kingdoms are: Monera (bacteria and blue-green algae), Protoctista (algae other than blue-green, protozoans, slime molds, and fungi), Metaphyta or Embryophyta (land plants and derivative aquatic plants), and Metazoa (multicellular animals). There is some problem regarding the position of the fungi in this grouping and the category of Protoctista does not appear well knit.

In recent years, R. H. Whittaker[3] has proposed a five-kingdom arrangement to overcome the difficulty. The fungi are separated as an independent kingdom, with a regrouping of some of the others, into Kingdoms Monera, Protista, Plantae, Fungi, and Animalia. The basis for classification includes level of organization and principal means of nutrition, namely photosynthesis, absorption, or ingestion.

If we tentatively accept the metabolism of *ch'i* as the characteristic of the living, then our phylogenetic sequence would follow the progressive advancement of this capacity. In general, this should parallel other schemes based on increasing morphological and physiological complexity. But there should be expected differences of separation within organisms of the same order of physical complexity. The determining rationale, however, would be different. The governing criterion would be the increasing capacity in the metabolism of *ch'i*. More advanced organisms are more able to sustain a wider range of activities, provide more intricate scores, and compose more elaborate pathways for the expression of life. Physical form is a result and not the initial evolutionary response.

In its quasi-equilibrium with the ecological complex, the species undergoes concurrent adaptations in the capacity to process *ch'i,* which modifies the protocol of processing energy and gives rise to the attendant physical structure and physiological functions. When the conditions are such that the evolving capacity to process *ch'i* requires a physical structure or physiological function not permitted by the constraints of the ecological entity of which it is a member, an evolutionary frustration sets in with stabilization of the species. When the differential becomes excessive, the species passes off the biological stage.

It is possible that J. V. McConnell and his associates[1] have observed the transmission of *ch'i* through the digestive route. They conditioned planaria worms to respond to light. The trained and the untrained worms were respectively chopped into little pieces and fed to other untrained worms. Those fed trained worms exhibited a higher score on conditioned responses than those fed untrained worms.

Their results were confirmed by A. L. Harty and her coworkers.[2] They also found that untrained planaria-fed worms exposed to photic stimuli only, without the conditioning shock, or to handling alone, likewise performed significantly better in the light-shock learning than the controls. The data may be taken to indicate that "experience-fed" or "enriched-*ch'i*-fed" planaria were somewhat more "intelligent" than the controls.

J. B. Best,[3] however, was hesitant about endorsing such an inference. "Does this perhaps mean that human cannibals were right in believing they would acquire the personality traits of some respected person if they ate him? Probably not." Because of the incomplete digestion process of planaria, he suggested that large units of the engulfed food particles remain undegraded. "It is therefore not improbable that many cells of the eaten planarian, escaping detection because of their similarity to the cannibal's cells, infiltrate the cannibal and migrate to appropriate sites in its tissues."

Observations have been made by others that suggest that ribonucleic acid is implicated in memory storage.[4] These include changes in the ratio of basic to nuclear ribonucleic acid of vestibular neurons in rats after they have experienced a wire-climbing task.[5] The neural ribonucleic acids formed during the early part of the training even seem to be different from those of the latter stages.

Preliminary experiments showed that injecting ribonucleic acid from a trained planarian into naive animals imparted a more efficient learning capability.[6] Similar experiments were conducted with rats.[7] Ribonucleic acid was extracted from the brain of rats trained to approach a food cup at the sound of a click. Untrained rats which received an injection of this material tended to approach the food cup upon the click, much more so than the controls.

The mouth is not the only, nor even the principal channel necessarily, of the transmission of *ch'i*. There are many others, especially for the more advanced forms of *ch'i*. These are far more subtle in attunement than even those less familiar internal sensors, such as the stretch receptors of the muscles and joints, which convey the feeling of movement.

A creation, for example, may be inspired or a feeling may be stimulated by the sense of sight, touch, hearing, or any other contact with one's environment or within oneself. All fuse into one sensation, as in the enjoyment of a Kuan Yao vase of the Sung Dynasty. In this case, there is a subtle interplay among the seeing of the appealing colors and glazes; the touching of surface shapes, textures, pits, and undulations; and the evoking of charm and dignity to the mind.

To quote François Fourcade[8] on Chinese ceramic art:

A piece should *speak* to the fingers that touch or fondle it. Some objects . . . are unctuous to the touch, recalling the flesh of pretty women who use makeup. Particularly prized are the ever-so-lightly uneven glazes, dotted with tiny holes . . . also glazes with a faintly wavy surface, comparable to the skin of an orange. . . . Timbre plays a very important part in the appreciation of hard-paste stoneware and porcelain; the piece should give off a ringing tone, frequently compared to that of the jade "sounding stones" in ancient Chinese orchestras. . . . Lastly . . . a ceramic work is expected to speak a poetic language addressed to the whole of our sensibility, culture and education. . . . a vase for Chrysanthemum will through the use of half tones in the glazes or painted enamel decorations be in tune with the nostalgic charm of summer's last warm days and the first falling leaves of autumn.

Finally, there is a host of as yet mysterious ways in the movements of the *ch'i*. The only thing we feel somewhat certain about is that it has probably been transmitted. But as to how or precisely when, we do not know at all. Typical occasions of this kind occur in psychotherapy. E. D. Hoedemaker's account of one of his schizophrenic patients is illustrative:[9]

The technical problem posed by the pathological intro- jects leads directly to the question, namely, can func- tioning introjects be effectively provided for the schizo- phrenic early in treatment which will stay with him and provide a psychologic graft to his embattled ego and allow him to work in an analytic partnership with his therapist? I am satisfied that they can be provided and must be provided or treatment will fail. For illustrative material I have turned to my sickest patient, who, only after six years of work, is able to perceive (and I too!) the distorted, regressed, fragmented, cliché-packed prim- itive identifications from the past with which she has literally been stuffed. This deluded, hallucinating woman whose schizophrenic father committed suicide when she was fifteen, and whose cold impersonal mother had from the start been unable to tolerate her crying as an infant, has, as an outpatient, never missed an appointment, has lain on the couch most of her hours and talked through- out almost every hour, has computed her bill each month, paid it promptly, and has not acted out since the third month of treatment when a specific and definite limit- setting crisis was successfully passed. . . . The early introjection of one of my traits appears to have served as an ego graft upon which a progressive and accretive process has continued.

63.
Eternal actuations
LIV

The concepts of a past, present, and future *ch'i* are as unnecessary for the appreciation of a living organism, as those of a past, present, and future energy for the explanation of an operating engine.

As there is only an existent energy, so is there only an existent time-related X or *ch'i*. One can no more pre- vent the state of becoming of *ch'i* than one can prevent the state of becoming of energy. Schizophrenic patients and compulsive neurotics, interestingly enough, are positively oriented toward the past.[1] In effect, they try to suppress the natural becoming of *ch'i* and drive them- selves crazy doing it. Repressing the past, as if it were past, is refusing the present. Both attempts are forms of self-truncations.

If one wishes he may carry the analogy further. He may

postulate such laws as the conservation of *ch'i,* which would read: The totality of *ch'i* is a constant; it is neither created nor destroyed; it is only transformed. Comparable psychological formulations come readily to mind, such as: *ch'i* gradients, as a basis of explaining dominance, power, and influence, which would be analogous to thermodynamic gradients; matching *ch'i* impedance, as a basis of explaining harmonious social operations, which would be analogous to electrical requirements in circuit designs; signal-to-noise ratios; resonance; complementarity; and so on. He may proceed to classify the qualitative types of *ch'i* forms, just as energy has been categorized into potential and kinetic, or into mechanical, electrical, and so on varieties. He may even postulate a quantitative unit for *ch'i.* Just as the quantitative unit for energy has been adopted as the calorie, after the Latin *calor,* meaning heat, so the quantitative unit for *ch'i* may be the menosie, after the Greek *menos,* meaning intent, spirit, passion, force, and disposition.[2]

Of course, one should guard against being carried away by such mental gymnastics. But they may be stimulating to those who wish to put psychology on a "scientific basis" and amusing to those who do not believe it can be.

The present then is the active existent, as exemplified by its retroactive power.[3] With the rise of new ideas and values, earlier works of art, for example, are seen in different lights and with different interrelationships.[4] Arnold Hauser[5] informs us that mannerism was finally given "historical existence" as a definite feature of the past only with the rise of modern expressionism and surrealism. A rhyme and reason is now seen to connect previously unrelated episodes. Similarly,

Franz Hals, Rubens, and Chardin now appear to have anticipated the painterly attitude of Manet, Delacroix, and Cezanne; the former grow in stature with the emergence of these new masters. On the other hand, Perugino loses value directly as one thinks of Raphael; alongside with Michelangelo, Signorelli seems pedantic and monotonous; they are suddenly reduced to the rank of mere "precursors." From the standpoint of impressionism, the late style of Titian, Rubens, and Velasquez takes on a new dimension; on the other hand, set beside the works of Rembrandt, the whole of the seventeenth-century Chiaroscuro painting looks to us like mannerism.

Perhaps this line of reasoning was in Hermann Weyl's mind when he wrote:[6] "The objective world simply *is*, it does not happen." In any case, as Bertrand Russell[7] reminded us, it is impossible to prove that we have not been created all this very second with the mental state of believing that there has been a long past, evolving to this point in time. There "is no *logical* reason why any memories should be vericidal; so far as logic can show, all my present memories might be just what they are if there had never been any historical past. Our knowledge of the past therefore depends upon some postulate which is not to be discovered by mere analysis of our present rememberings."

This discussion recalls the cosmology of Ismailism.[8] For the Ismaili, eternity is not synonymous with immutability. On the contrary, the primordial Archangel is eternally actuating himself at the origin of the Pleroma. As far as he is concerned, there is no past, which recedes into time. Nor is he surpassed in the sense of being left behind. Through the process of hypostasis, all events are eternally present. Harmony prevails through a perfect hierarchy.

Beginning in the sixteenth century, many individuals began to look upon art as the projection of an inner image. An unfinished block by Michelangelo had been said to be of greater art than a finished one because it is closer to the state of conception. Ernst Kris[1] evaluated the greatness of a piece of art by its approximation to the psychic life of the artist.

In a psychoanalytic discussion of art, A. Ehrenzweig[2] suggested that a piece of creative art requires "a temporary, cyclical paralysis of the surface attention." A state of diffused attention merging figure and background and an absent-minded watchfulness are necessary conditions to grasp the creative vision. However, these visions are not those that are convertible to definitive imagery in the surface consciousness, as mystics have long realized. The mystic returns from the depth mind to surface consciousness with the imprint of significant visions but avoids their destruction by forced communication with consciousness.

Marion Milner[3] concluded that

the discovery of the nature of this capacity . . . is illustrated by Blake in the Job series beginning with the appearance of Elihu; also that Blake means to show that it is a very new development, as compared with the millions of years of blind living, when he puts in the margin of the Elihu picture the text: "I am young and ye are old wherefore I was afraid." And I think Blake is also implying the same idea when he brings the figure of Christ into his study of creative sterility. In fact, I think he implies, although he does not actually say so, that he believes that it is the creative contact with the un-split "depth" mind that Christ was talking about, in poetic terms, in such phrases as "Take no thought for the morrow . . . ," and "Consider the lilies of the field, they toil not, neither do they spin . . ." the measure of genius in the arts is linked up with the extent to which the artist does succeed in cooperating with his unconscious mind by means of his medium.

In this regard, Erich Neumann[4] stressed the influence of the Zeitgeist upon creative minds. This is a conceptual transpersonal and unconscious force which seems to move the thinking and the activities of men at a given period along the same general direction. It is an expression of the Collective Unconscious, the common psychic substratum, which sets its imprint on the times—in literature, painting, philosophy, politics, and a wide array of human endeavors. The reaction of the individual artist to the influence of this Collective Unconscious lies at the base of the transcendance of art. "The need of his times works inside the artist without his wanting it, seeing it, or understanding its true significance. In this sense, he is close to the seer, the prophet, the mystic. And it is precisely when he does not represent the existing canon but transforms and overturns it that his function rises to the level of the sacral, for he then gives utterance to the authentic and direct revelation of the numinosum."[5]

Regardless how one defines creativity, Arthur Koestler[6] felt that the "actualization of surplus potentials" is discernible at all levels of evolution and that "certain basic principles operate throughout the whole organic hierarchy—from the fertilized egg to the fertile brain of the creative individual; and that phenomena analogous to creative originality can be found on all levels."

65.
Well-being
LXV

Freud divided the total human personality into the *id, ego,* and *superego.* The id is something that acts upon a person as from the outside. It consists of congenital instincts, such as love and aggression. It drives him to do certain things, for which he is really not responsible. It is given to man's existence before he is free and conscious.

Ego is the real "I." This is a difficult notion and Freud frequently was not consistent in its treatment. He partly resolves the uncertainty by suggesting that the id and the ego interact by some internal arrangement. The ego is considered the essence or nature of the individual. It is the conscious and deliberate aspect of man. In cooperation with the superego, the ego restrains the id from inducing particular behavior on the part of the individual. Acts recognized by the ego as destructive are screened out by the normal individual.

The superego of the human psyche, like the id, belongs to the unconscious. The superego internalizes such influences as social precepts.

For Freud, the unconscious impulse is the major determinant of human behavior. Other schools, especially the existentialists, disagree. The latter feel that the only factor which counts really is free and conscious choice. Sartre pointed to the common experience that psychiatric patients often reach an impasse in therapy just as the exercise is on the verge of uncovering the cause of the neurosis. This would not happen, so he said, if the unconscious were the determinant. He explained:[1] "The censor in order to apply its activity with discernment must know what it is repressing. . . . The resistance of the patient implies on the level of the censor an awareness of the thing repressed as such, a comprehension of the end toward which the questions of the psychoanalyst are leading, and an act . . . by which it compares the truth of the repressed complex to the psychoanalytic hypothesis which aims at it. These various operations . . . imply that the censor is conscious."

Furthermore, Sartre did not believe that man can be free sometimes and not at other times; "he is wholly and forever free, or he is not free at all."

The *ch'i* may be intellectually fitted into this discussion in the following way: It comes to the individual in varied forms, such as food, the sound of a song, the sight of a fight, and so on. Each of these serves as raw material for further metabolism by the person. The raw material belongs to the realm of what Freud called the id. It may not necessarily be the id. But like the id, it operates as an external source. It influences man's behavior by furnishing the raw material for life's transformations.

The next step is the metabolism of ch'i by man at the same level as other animals. This includes the same drives of aggression, sex urge, and impulse actions. The raw material below this level can be converted into forms compatible with it. This corresponds to the action of the ego. There is freedom in the sense that the ego can transform the ch'i in various directions, depending upon its metabolic capacity. However, there is no freedom in the sense that the raw material is given. The range of metabolic products from a starting ch'i is delimited.

The third level is characteristic of human nature, as distinguished from the basic animal nature. Herein is the capacity of producing virtual presences. Perhaps, manifestations of this activity led Freud to postulate the superego.

Well-being rests on the harmonious interpervasiveness of these infusions in the individual.

66.
Image-makers
LXVI

In Genesis, we read: "And God said, Let us make man in our image, after our likeness; and let him have dominion over the fish of the sea, and over the fowl of the air, and over the cattle, and over all the earth, and over every creeping thing that creepeth upon the earth.

"So God created man in his own image, in the image of God created he him . . ."

Image. Through that word, the chroniclers sang of the desire of God Himself as the Creator of virtual presences par excellence in Heaven. And man himself became the facsimile, creator of virtual presences par excellence on earth, who then proceeded in turn to create a god in his own image.

67.
Virtual crises
LXVII

Virtual presences have greatly increased in power in recent times because of the efficient communications media and the profitable news and public relations enterprises.

The art of public relations is being continually refined, honed, and passed from master to apprentice in an annual multibillion dollar business. The controllers keep reaching out for that ever-receding next increment, until they are enmeshed in a fixation on that virtual ultimate of Nature plus one. In rallying support for their drive to power, they spur the communications media to even higher efficiencies.

But quite apart from these cunning distortions of information, there is a natural tendency of large information-dispensing systems to distort in substance and in effect. This holds regardless of the good intentions of the purveyors. Since a person's opinion is primarily shaped by what he sees and hears, the frequency of appearance of a report is taken by him to be the index of significance of the event, as well as a reconfirmation of the accuracy of the original statement. Repetition, of course, is the trademark of our continuous radio and television broadcasts. What is trivial and unreliable becomes important and gospel truth after the fifth airing.

Then there is the inevitable distortion. The normal shape of the curve of occurrence is initially distorted somewhat by rumor and the attraction of man for the bizarre and the unusual. This is aggravated by the craze of technological society for the new, the creative, and the spectacular. At each stage of transmission, the mass of reports has to be culled down in volume. Persistently, the process fractionates out the more normal aspects and passes on the more newsworthy. After ten or so stages of fractionation, the original report becomes drastically reshaped. The final news items are always bimodal, with emphasis on the extremes. The stabilizing centers are given scant attention.

The noised-about extremes become psychological bogeymen, threats to moderate and timid souls, and the basis of fashionable styles for the adventurous. The publicized minority acts as if it will soon take over but never really does. Their antics, each in its own turn, become ignored as soon as they lose their newsworthiness. A new dire danger splashes over the front pages. Meanwhile the majority remains under continuous anxiety in the concatenation of threats. The public media keeps churning out the virtual disasters, which paralyze the spirit and envenom the mind.

One needs to keep a discriminating filter against the virtual presences if one is to retain his peace of mind with the real in these times of technological paraphernalia.

Public policy seldom emerges in a fully deliberately planned form. Instead it is launched in a general orientation with, admittedly, much fanfare of specific objectives and assurances, but it is always the result of a compromise with a multitudinous array of as yet unknown influences. Each of these shifts the trend, molds the substance, and gives rise to higher-order effects. As a rule neither officials nor citizens are wise enough to anticipate these higher-order effects. Nor would they believe accurate prophecies, had they been made at the time. But they are there nevertheless for good or ill.

The homogenizing of ends and means has been described very well by Harold Nicolson.[1] He observed that:

> Nobody who has not watched "policy" expressing itself in day-to-day action can realize how seldom is the course of events determined by deliberately planned purpose, or how often what in retrospect appears to have been a fully conscious intention was at the time governed and directed by that most potent of all factors—"the chain of circumstance." Few indeed are the occasions on which any statesman sees his objective clearly before him and marches towards it with undeviating strides; numerous indeed are the occasions when a decision or event, which at the same time seemed wholly unimportant, leads almost fortuitously to another decision which is no less incidental, until, little link by link, the chain of circumstances is forged.

The point can be illustrated by looking at the contemporary case of the higher-order effects of the United States Government's generous support of academic research beginning in the 1940s. Impressed by the contributions of research and development to the economic and military strength of the country in World War II, the government embarked upon a policy of technological supremacy. Two important implementing actions were the subsidy of higher education and the advancement of science. Huge sums were poured into the universities for this purpose. By 1965, three fourths of the academic research was paid for by the government at a cost of two billion dollars a year. In some schools, as much as 60 percent of the total operating costs came from this source.

Not bargained for in the process, however, was the drastic change in the character of the American universities, as well as a host of ancillary social disruptions, stimulated in considerable degree by this support.

Prior to the forties, nearly all of the research on the campuses, except for agricultural investigations in land grant colleges, was carried out by individuals or small groups within the academic departments. Financial resources came principally from the university endowments or private foundations. With increasingly major participation in research supported by the the government and industry, various transformations took place, imperceptibly at first, but welcomed as a breath of exhilarating air to the action-oriented members of the community.

More full-time research staff was added. This was accompanied by cohesive groupings of outside-sponsored research activities in the form of institutes. Heavy capital investments were committed. Universities competed for the management of large nonacademic off-campus installations. Joint ventures with nonprofit organizations became accepted practice.

The former loose administration of research in universities could not cope with these far-flung operations. A more formal organizational structure appeared, involving vice-presidents in charge of research, government contracting offices, negotiating attorneys, public relations experts, and administrative hierarchies. Nonteaching oriented managerial competence assumed increasing importance. This is the cadre of personnel who can manage complex multimillion dollar combines, weld diverse talents into directional programs, and beat the political and financial bushes for the required resources, recruits, and recognitions. They soon replaced the scholars in national and international influence and status. The tone of the campus shifted considerably from the scholarly to the executive and from student teaching to program research.

After two decades of large-scale research, engineering, and even production activity and the return to the campus of professors who had whetted their appetites in the action whirl of World War II, the universities became a reservoir of technical and managerial talent for nonacademic purposes. There was the call for technical coordinators to organize huge international cooperative programs, for administrators of affiliated research institutions, for innumerable industrial consultants, and confidential advisors to governments. In an effort to bring more money onto the campus, efforts were intensified to facilitate such relationships with the outside world of practical affairs and power.

A concomitant drifting resulted, away from the personal problems of young students and toward the competitive designs of big-time enterprises. The university community paid the concomitant price of ecological ills for its urban sophistications.

In the sponsorship of research, the Federal agencies have attempted to be above suspicion in the awarding of grants and contracts. Nongovernmental advisory panels were set up for the purpose. These were usually dominated by university professors. As a result, the research being undertaken by a group of professors on Campus A was dependent for support, to a considerable extent, upon the opinions of a group of professors on Campus B, C, D, E, etc., and vice versa. By the late fifties, the more successful professors became financially independent of their respective deans, presidents, and trustees on many campuses. As a matter of aggravating fact, employment of the academic staff was sometimes contingent upon their potential for being financially independent of the university and their ability to bring income into the organization. The character of the school was no longer shaped by the directives of the administrative leaders or the inspiration of the instructional leaders. These began to be regarded by many of the income-bringers as overhead burdens upon the monies being brought into the academic coffers for free-wheeling research. The social order of power became inverted from the supposedly scholarly president and supposedly venerable deans to a loose federation of self-sufficient professorial barons.

Such was the happy equilibrium for about a decade, so the prosperous professors thought to themselves. But the highest-order process was not to be halted. The inversion of power from the president and deans to the professors went on to its extension to the students. Kicked off by the Berkeley Free Speech Movement, the struggle for power erupted into the campus riots beginning in the sixties. The symbol of the transformation finally splashed over the front pages of the newspapers—the picture of students occupying the president's suite in prestigious Columbia University, with one of the most unkempt of the lot sitting at the president's desk, leaning back in the soft swivel chair, plopping his dirty shoes on the writing pad, and puffing away on one of the president's choice cigars.

A typical observation of the influence of animals upon one another's behavior is that of the Harlows.[1] Monkeys kept apart from other infants during the first six months are incapable of normal relations with other monkeys later in life. They behave quite differently from those reared in the wild. Many of them develop strikingly abnormal behavior "including sitting and staring fixedly into space, repetitive circling movements about the cage clasping the head in the hands and arms while engaging in rocking autistic-type movements, and intrapunitive responses of grasping a foot, hand, arm, or leg and chewing or tearing it with the teeth to the point of injury."

Another example of the modification of the social behavior of animals is the antagonism of fish.[2] Green sunfish were conditioned for five days by being placed in the company of other fish either larger and more dominant or smaller and more submissive than themselves. Upon regrouping, the attack behavior and/or dominance reversal was influenced largely by the experience of the previously dominant fish during the conditioning period.

Comparable experience has been repeatedly reported for human beings. Herman Lantz[3] asked a thousand patients at random referred to a United States Army mental hygiene clinic as to the number of friends they had at any typical moment between the times when they were four and ten years of age. All of the normal individuals had friends; 47.5 percent of those who had no friends during their childhood were severe psychoneurotics, while 37.5 percent were psychotic. Of those adults with five or more friends, 39.5 percent were neurotic and only .8 percent psychotic.

During recent years, there has been renewed discussion of the so-called born criminal. In 1876, Caesare Lombroso[4] presented the thesis of a physical criminal type, who is born that way. His conclusion was refuted by Charles Goring,[5] who studied 3000 English prisoners and a like number of normal people. After much work, David Abrahamsen[6] showed that the criminal is a resultant of his own personality and the environment in which he lives. A multiplicity of causative factors is involved. His antisocial tendencies need to be exposed to criminal influences and a precipitating event. Past experiences must develop his guilt feelings, which emerge as a strong unconscious desire for punishment.

The worsening state of affairs resulting from the interactions between available *ch'i* from the surroundings and the capacity of the developing internal *chi*-metabolizing apparatus is illustrated further by the finding that intrafamilial interactions,[7] especially the mother-child relationship, are most important factors in the development of schizophrenia.[8]

Actually, we need not resort to such scientific analogies to suggest the altering of the internal metabolizing capabilities by externally proffered *ch'i*. We need only recall our own personal experience of how we have come to enjoy something we disliked on initial contact—Picasso's cubism, Wagner's *Meistersinger,* Chinese bitter melon, etc. And, of course, Alexander Pope had repeated it to us during our high school days again and again, as we attempted to commit his verse to memory:

Vice is a monster of so frightful mien,
As, to be hated, needs but be seen;
Yet seen too oft, familiar with her face,
We first endure, then pity, then embrace.

70.
Social equity
LXXIII

Democracy takes on a different connotation for those who subscribe to the concept of *ch'i*.

The basis of positive morality and social justice is the provision of qualitatively more than the minimum energy necessary to sustain the inanimate workings of the human body. It calls for the granting of opportunities for the person to mature to the level of *ch'i* metabolism representing the upper reaches of the range characteristic of the species.

The issue of public discussion takes on a different aspect when viewed in this light. Words like Lewis Mumford's on conservation[1] gain added perspective: The "purpose which we must cling to when we consider the improvement of habitat, is to become more conscious through thought and action and all the works of human art of the possibilities for further development. It's not just to save the grasslands or the primeval forest, or to save the whooping crane."

71.
The critical
packing density
LXXIV

Konrad Lorenz's observation[1] of two turtle doves placed in a cage is instructive. After two days

a horrible sight met my eyes. The (male) turtle dove lay on the floor of the cage; the top of his head and neck, as also the whole length of his back, were not only plucked bare of feathers, but so flayed as to form a single wound dripping with blood. In the middle of his gory surface, like an eagle on his prey, stood the second harbinger of peace. Wearing that dreamy facial expression that so appeals to our sentimental observer, this charming lady pecked mercilessly with her silver bill in the wounds of her prostrated male.

In those cramped quarters, the weaker bird could not flee into safety. Nor could the stronger vent its feelings elsewhere. The saving spatial and temporal generosity of nature had been upset.

72.
Repression
LXXV

The basic approach of many religions in contests of conscience is that of repression. Often, however, this approach reduces to an attempt at simply refusing to look and hoping that whatever it is that is giving offense will go away. But this does not always work.
    "Dynamic psychology proves that if the evil is driven out of the light of consciousness, it merely goes underground," Joshua Liebman[1] reminded us.

The reality of childish shame or rage is not exterminated by disavowal; it is merely locked up—potential dynamite in a hidden stockroom of our psyche. Outraged by tyrannical repression, our unconventional or unacceptable impulses outwit us by disguising themselves in new forms. They become our worst inner enemies, assaulting our nerves, laying siege to our peace of mind, tormenting us with a sense of failure, making us feel depressed and inferior, driving us from excess against our will. We develop high blood pressure or stomach ulcers. . . . Men and women who, influenced by traditional religion, try to uproot every vagrant desire from their minds sometimes transform themselves into self-torturing masochists or intolerant fanatics. Many so-called "good" people are moral hypocrites who compensate for the enormous "inner lie" of their lives by displaying subtle cruelties to their mates, children, or society.

In most instances, reality is not such a terrible thing to face squarely. People who refuse to look at reality clearly but insist on keeping themselves in the dark often find themselves in the ridiculous position of Sancho Panza in Cervantes' Don Quixote. The poor fellow was clinging desperately one night to a window ledge. He sweated, squirmed, and prayed for dear life all through the night. When day broke, he noted that his feet had been only an inch from the ground.

73.
Privacy
LXXV

As men have found it necessary to live together in groups, they have developed standards of social characteristics that are considered acceptable within the community in the resolution of quarrels, conceptions of God and the afterlife, values, and attitudes.[1] In some cultures, there is a premium placed on the spreading of these beliefs and ways.

There are suggestions that this missionizing propensity is now being coupled with advanced communications technology by our modern commercial interests. In this profiteering of the aggressive spirit, the mass media are able to maximize returns on investments by spreading a relatively few messages of mummified simplicity to a large number of recipients, rather than a rich variety of complete stories to a small number. The inner personality of modern man is being simplified and regimented under the guise of enlightenment. It is this insidious penetration of his inner personality by molding its development through the limitation of *ch'i,* rather than the public display of his statistics, that is obliterating his privacy. He has progressively limited opportunities for fashioning that uniqueness which is the basis of personal privacy. His soul has already been made public because he has been made predictable and conformably transparent. He is given the guarantee of the virtual sanctity of his privacy. But it is of little real value. The real sanctity of his real privacy has already been de-existed.

74.
Needless anguish
LXXVI

From the prelude to life for the individual to its very end, uncertainty hangs over every miniscule event along the way. Will the trigger mechanism function properly or not in the fertilization of the egg? Every reaction between chemicals is probabilistic, as is every interaction between human beings. There is uncertainty over the reliability of one's observations, the truth of public statements, the feasibility of proposals, and the prudence of actions. There is uncertainty over pass-fail in examinations, over promotion-demotion at work, over war-peace in international relations. And so it goes, on and on.

Many institutions exercise domination over people through the transformation of selected uncertainties into personal anxieties. This is achieved by encouraging the individuals to internalize what had previously been a purely external objective uncertainty. By further manipulating the situation such that the only avenues for relief from the personal stress is within the control of the institutions themselves, the authorities are able to become operating tyrants while appearing in the role of noble benefactors.

The concept of synchronicity was introduced by Carl Jung[1] to account for otherwise unexplained acausal relations.

A mass of facts on unexplained coincidences had been collected by Edmund Gurney and his associates.[2] Paul Kammerer[3] recorded medical examples of what he called a law of series, in which a trebling or even more of the same case occurs. Wilhelm Stekel[4] spoke of the compulsion of names, as exemplified by illusions of grandeur on the part of Herr Gross and inferiority complex on the part of Herr Kleiner. Arthur Schopenhauer[5] wrote of the "simultaneity of the causally unconnected."

C. Flammarion[6] calculated a probability of 1 in 804,-622,222 in some of his "phantasms of the living." As an example of triple coincidences, he related the story of M. de Fortgibu and the plum pudding. When M. Deschamps was a boy in Orleans he was given a delicious piece of plum pudding by a M. de Fortgibu. After the incident he never had any occasion to meet M. de Fortgibu again, and he promptly forgot all about him. A decade later, while strolling past a restaurant window in Paris, M. Deschamps noticed what appeared to be the same type of plum pudding which he had enjoyed so much as a boy. Whereupon he went into the shop to buy a piece, only to be told that it had been ordered by M. de Fortgibu. Years later, while M. Deschamps was at a friend's party, the same kind of plum pudding was served. He could not help remarking that the only thing missing to complete the occasion was M. de Fortgibu. Just at that moment a knock was heard on the door. In walked a disheveled old man, who had gotten into the wrong house. It was M. de Fortgibu.

Jung did not feel these incidents to be the results of mere chance.[7] He preferred to call them meaningful coincidences without a causal link, or instances of synchronicity. "Synchronistic events rest on the simultaneous occurrence of two different psychic states. One of them is the normal probable state (i. e., the one that is causally explicable), and the other, the critical experience, is the one that cannot be derived causally from the first." He even considered biological morphogenesis and radioactive decay as synchronistic phenomena.

In this connection, A. M. Dalcq[8] stated that the biological form is a "continuity that is superordinate to the living organism." James Jeans[9] said that "Radioactive break-up appeared to be an effect without a cause." He suggested that "the ultimate laws of nature are not even causal."

Herbert Read[10] depicted the essence of Jung's concepts by means of Richard Wilhelm's story of the rainmaker from Shantung who was asked to break the terrible drought in Kiou Chou. On arrival at the scene he asked that a hut be built on the outskirts of town. Leaving word that he was not to be disturbed, he entered the hut and remained for three days and three nights. On the fourth day, a snow storm broke out which was the heaviest for the time of year in the memory of the inhabitants.

When Wilhelm inquired of the man as to how he did it, he replied that he did not.

It was simply that he came from Shantung where everything was right. Here in Kiou Chou heaven and earth were separated, everything was wrong and it took him three days to become right again himself. But as soon as he was right rain or snow would naturally fall. . . . Like most Chinese stories, at first it seems too simple and pointless, but the meaning grows as we meditate upon it. The inactivity it seems to advocate is merely external. The invisible spheres revolve, and at a certain point in time they coincide, and at that moment we find ourselves in harmony with nature. At such times things happen as we wish them to happen: we are instruments of the divine power, vessels filled with grace. This is the full meaning of *integration* in Jung's psychology, and he believes that the world would be saved, if it is saved at all, by integrated personalities.

76.
Uncertainty
LXXVII

The fragility of events, the stopping of light by the thinnest of foils, the paralysis of decisions by conflicts of interests, and the onset of death by the flimsiest of circumstances invite an analysis of the question of certainty.

We would surmise that life would be impossible were everything fixed. In place of the metabolism of *ch'i*, there would be only a set of inanimate coordinates. Yet we have learned that even in the field of the inanimate, certainty is unattainable. We may mention Heisenberg's Uncertainty Principle in physics and Gödel's proof in mathematics.

Centuries ago, scientists were much surer of themselves than are their successors today. Pierre Laplace[1] wrote in the eighteenth century that the state of the universe can be regarded

as the effect of its anterior state and as the cause of the one which is to follow. Given for one instant an intelligence which could comprehend all the forces by which nature is animated and the respective situation of the beings who compose it—an intelligence sufficiently vast to submit these data to analysis—it would embrace in the same formula the movements of the greatest bodies of the universe and those of the lightest atom; for it, nothing would be uncertain and the future, as well as the past, would be present to its eyes.

There seemed to be no theoretical barrier prohibiting man's attainment of this herculean analysis.

In contrast, the twentieth century has witnessed a multitude of postulates of impotence, which assert "the impossibility of achieving something, even though there may be an infinite number of ways of trying to achieve it."[2] These range from the impossibility of recognizing absolute velocity and identifying a given electron with one observed earlier to that of telling where one is in the universe. The most celebrated of these is Werner Heisenberg's *Uncertainty Principle.* This principle states that the more accurately one determines the position of a particle, the less accurately can its momentum be measured, and vice-versa. The product of the errors always exceed $h/2\pi$, where h is Planck's constant.

In 1931, Kurt Gödel[3] published a mathematical proof of a limitation of formal deduction. He showed, in the words of Ernest Nagel and James Newman,[4]

that the axiomatic method which has served mathematics so long and so well has limitations; in particular, that it is impossible within the framework of even a relatively simple mathematical system—ordinary whole-number arithmetic, for example—to demonstrate the internal consistency (noncontradictoriness) of the system without using principles of inference whose own consistency is as much open to question as that of the principles of the system being tested.

Formal deduction proves it cannot make formal deductions with certainty beyond certain boundaries. It seems to have refuted itself in places. Gödel's conclusions

show that there is an endless number of true arithmetical statements which cannot be formally deduced from any specified act of axioms in accordance with a closed set of rules of inference. It follows, therefore, that an axiomatic approach to number theory, for example, cannot exhaust the domain of arithmetic truth and that mathematical proof does not coincide with the exploitation of a formalized axiomatic method.

77.
Occam's razor
LXXVII

Theoretical science has flourished under "Occam's razor," which directs: Given a set of alternatives, adopt that theory which is the simplest to explain the specific facts at hand.

For dealings with our fellow men, however, we may wish to depart from the narrow confines of Occam when we are devising actual courses of action. We should be satisfied with alternatives which *generally* but not *specifically* explain all the facts at hand, yet at the same time appear to be the most socially useful as an extension of man's virtues. We should not succumb to the intellectual temptation of theoretical simplicity. Beneficence is to be the determinant; cold scholarship can wait.

The pursuit of general laws is the bugaboo of conventional scholarship—not the pursuit of general laws *per se,* but the hedge-clipping of the particular instances at hand to conform to the pattern hypothesized. This leads to brushing aside the unusual, minimizing the significance of misfits, and ignoring the standard deviations, to which categories all of us belong in one respect or another at one time or another. But life is variety. Variety is departure from the mean. The mean is a figment.

There needs to be an openness in scholarship, a maturity in the perception of reality in flux. It is not to be hemmed in by a procedure or framework that constrains to fixedness. Even in a fixed activity the number of combinations and permutations is immense. In the game of chess, for example, at the end of the tenth move, the player is faced with the order of 10^{29} alternative choices.

In this regard Allan Nivens[1] explored what seems to be bothering modern poets, novelists, and historians so that they write on such weak themes and in such unacceptable moods. He concluded that

the central disability for most writers of history, as of poetry, drama, and fiction, is probably bewilderment and anxiety in the loss of old landmarks, and the overturn of long-accepted truths. They are stunned by the rapidity, multiplicity, and immensity of the revolutions of our age, and baffled by the enormous enlargement of knowledge. The historians have suffered particularly because the value of all good history depends upon a clear sense of perspective and a strong grasp of the tools of research and interpretation. And how can these be kept available when perspective whirls incessantly and new tools constantly replace old?

Besides the vast changes in technology and revolutions in social thinking, it is frequently the little unnoticed annoyances, the mundane frailties of man, or sheer wisps of luck that constitute the decisive trigger. It was such a petty thing, for example, which led to the resignation of the president of the Central State University of Ohio in 1967. As he stated to reporters: "In this hour of genuine institutional crisis, brought about by elements determined to destroy the university, I find many students, parents, alumni and faculty members not discussing improvements in developments of the university, or even the really basic issues threatening the life of the institution, but calling upon me to defend an allegation that I changed the route of march for graduate ceremonies and such equally inane charges. . . . I was prepared for the larger battles. I am disgusted by the trivia."

It was another of the minor things that led to a disruption of secret and delicate negotiations between the two sides during the latter part of 1966 in the American Vietnam war.[2] A senior government official in Washington was reported to have sat down for breakfast during the culmination of five months of painstaking efforts on December 3rd. He opened the newspapers and saw the headlines: U.S. Bombs Site 5 Miles from Hanoi. "Oh, my God!" he exclaimed. "We lost control." He later learned that the President and his chief lieutenants had forgotten that they had authorized the strike a while back!

In the light of such complex interrelationships in human

affairs, what in reality constitutes the facts at hand? How can the wise then follow Occam, when the welfare of his neighbors is at stake?

In dealing with human affairs, it is preferable to react to the reality rather than be guided by theoretical models. But most of us in the West are so used to the idea of models, that we are often lost without one. Since this is the practical state of our operational approaches, an extended *yin-yang* model is offered.

The traditional *yin-yang* model of the universe depicts it as consisting of *yin* and *yang* forces. The former stands for darkness, female, negative, and so on, while the latter stands for light, male, positive, and so on. There cannot be a reality with a *yin* and no *yang*, nor one with a *yang* and no *yin*.

We would extend the concept to say that there are no singularities in nature, only in abstractions. Everything is a resultant of many concurrent vectors.

We may illustrate the model using numbers. The hypothetical *yin* numbers are separated from the hypothetical *yang* numbers as follows:

Hypothetical *yin:* −1, −2, −3, −4, . . .
Hypothetical divider: 0
Hypothetical *yang:* +1, +2, +3, +4, . . .

In reality, as we have just stated, *yin* does not exist without *yang*, nor *yang* without *yin*. A truer model, then, would be one in which each of the actual *yin* and actual *yang* numbers is a resultant of many vectors, rather than being a singularity of its own. Thus, −1 may be the resultant of (+7, −8), (+8, −2, +15, −22), and so on.

One should not be surprised, therefore, to find contradictions within the same person or event. These are intrinsic to being. *A* is both *A* and not-*A*.

It is difficult to imagine that the vectors pertaining to any given trait would balance themselves exactly so that the resultant is zero. Even if such an infinitesimal possibility exists for a fleeting moment, the other sets of vectors pertaining to the rest of the infinite traits would not come to zero at the same instant. For this reason, zeroes can be regarded as nonexistent in reality, although they do exist to good purpose in virtual presences.

Following such an extended model, you are never faced with the choice between good and evil, the moral analogies of + and −. There is never a perfectly good man or perfectly good event; neither is there an absolutely bad man or absolutely bad event. The resultants are always integrated contributions of both *yin* and *yang* vectors.

It is interesting to note that the fourth-century Manichees tried to resolve the dilemma of evil by claiming that evil had no origin because it had always been there. God was said to rule with absolute authority over half the world and the devil over the other half. This explanation has a kind of *yin-yang* tang to it. To be consistent with the extended *yin-yang* model, however, there should be no separation between good and evil. Both vectors should be present in the same being. God Himself would be looked upon as not absolutely all-good; He may be infinitely good and only infinitesimally bad, but not absolutely good. The devil would be looked upon as not absolutely bad, but infinitesimally good. This, of course, would constitute one possible explanation of the problem of Job. But the Manichean doctrine was officially "proven" by ecclesiastical authorities to be heretical. Besides, any hypothesis impugning God's power, goodness, or wisdom in the slightest is *a priori* unacceptable in the West. For these reasons, and following pragmatic Chinese tradition, we limit our metaphysical musing to earthly applications.

Man thus is a nexus of vectored instants. One cannot hope to modify the resultant behavior by one thrust because the resultant singularity is only a virtual presence and not directly opposable. One can only work on the vectors which are real and many. This requires an indirection and patience in dealing with the social context in which the individual is immersed. One becomes appreciative of the complexities involved in bringing about social progress and reasonable in his expectations.

79.
Kairos
LXXVIII

"If a special moment of time is good for the fulfillment of something," wrote Paul Tillich,[1] "this moment is its *kairos.*"

80.
The artist
LXXIX

The true artist is at one with the leisurely exchanges of Nature. To quote John Chapman:[1]

What makes us happy in art and letters is the power in them that has been unconsciously absorbed by the artist, and is unconsciously conveyed to us by his work. For want of a better word, I have been using the idea of "leisure" to express the mystery. Leisure is a laic and secular word which points toward the gateway of spiritual truth, much as the word "contemplation," tinged as it is with religion, points in the same direction; and both of them imply receptivity, a reliance on some solution which shall swim into our minds without aid from us, a half-consciousness that our own faculties are part of the operation of Nature. This knack of a loose and dreamy attention seems to be lost to the world for the time being, and the loss prevents our seeing life in the enormous perspectives in which it really looms.

Chuang Tzu[2] spoke of the great artistry of the famous woodworker Ch'ing, who knew how to maintain this enormous perspective by relaxing all rigid focusing on irrelevancies.

When the Duke of Lu saw a beautiful carved wooden bell stand, he asked how such an unusual technique can be developed. Ch'ing replied:

I am a mere mechanic and do not know of any special art. But I have one thing to say. When I am about to work on a bell stand, I try not to waste my (ch'i). I fast in order to preserve serenity of mind. After three days I cease to cherish any desire for prize, emolument, or official glory. After five days the ideas of praise or no praise and the question of workmanship depart therefrom. After seven days I attain to a state of absolute serenity, forgetting that I have a body and four limbs. At that moment I forget that I am working for the court. My sole concern is about my work, and nothing of external interest disturbs me. I now enter the woods and select the most suitable tree whose natural frame harmonizes with my inner nature. I know then that I can work out my bell stand. I then apply my hands to the work. When all these conditions are not fulfilled I do not work. For I perceive that it is heaven (in Nature) that unites with heaven (in Man). It is probably due to this fact that my finished product is suspected to be supernatural.

81.
A vignette
LXXXI

My father, Siu Yan, and my mother, Kau Shee, came to Hawaii from Kwangtung, China. Neither had any schooling in the poor villages from which they came. They struggled through the life of the illiterate immigrant in a foreign land. But they were good people and brought up a modest family.

Father died at the age of seventy-two, when mother was forty-three, leaving her with six children. Mother raised chickens and pigs, sewed clothes, made rice flour, cured skin disorders, and prayed at temples to keep the family in school and in reasonable health. With whatever energies were left over from her weary labors, she tried to inculcate her children with the traditions of old China. But it was a losing proposition. We were rapidly being assimilated into the ways of the West. The first thing to go was the Chinese religion. Our Occidental teachers told us it was idolatry.

Nevertheless, mother kept up the Chinese rituals as best she could. One of the most important was the commemoration of the anniversaries of father's birth. On that day without failure, prayers, incense, and appropriate observances with a liturgical meal would be offered at father's little shrine at home. Filial devotion called for its continuation up to father's hundredth birthday.

On that hundredth anniversary in December 1965, the entire family gathered together in Honolulu. My brothers, sisters, and I, with our families, traveled from Illinois, Pennsylvania, Massachusetts, and Washington, D.C., to join mother in this final celebration. Following age-old customs, we made pilgrimages to father's grave and to the principal Chinese temples. At each place, roast pig, chicken, wine, tea, and other delicacies were spread on the altar; punks and candles lit; prayers offered; paper symbols burnt. The prophecies were auspicious.

The climax took place at home. Mother conducted it herself. As the eldest son, I knelt by her side in the yard. We lit the last of the candles and punks and stuck them into the ground. She bowed low, touched her head to the earth several times, and chanted. Somehow I sensed that something special was going on. Finally, she lit the last of the paper symbols and watched them burned to the end. She then bowed three times and turned to me with a smile. But she said nothing. We both got up and walked back into the house as the sun sank behind the grove of pandanus and palms.

Later that evening she passed on an important message to me, as the future head of the family group. She said that in her prayers she had explained to our ancestors that the coming generations of Sius will be living in an Occidental country, that the Chinese tradition will no longer survive among them, that this is through no fault of theirs, and that therefore it would be unreasonable to expect the same diligence in religious devotion in the future as had been exhibited in the past. Would the venerable, wise, and loving ancestors be agreeable to accept this final offering as meeting all future requirements of traditional ancestral observances and would they continue to rain blessings upon their descendants for all time to come? Mother then asked for a favorable sign. They had understood, agreed, and given the propitious sign.

Mother then assured me that my brothers, sisters, and I need no longer keep up the traditional religious observances after she has joined them in the Hereafter.

"And that includes your future religious obligations to me as well," mother added, with an endearing look in her expression. "With the permission of our ancestors, I have included myself among them in my supplication."

References

Commentary Number

1
1. R. G. H. Siu, *The Man of Many Qualities,* Cambridge: MIT, 1968, introduction.
2. R. G. H. Siu, *The Tao of Science,* Cambridge: MIT, 1958, chap. 9.

7
1. H. Frankfort, H. A. Frankfort, J. A. Wilson, and T. Jacobsen, *Before Philosophy,* Harmondsworth: Penguin, 1949, p. 32.
2. M. P. Nillson, *Acta Soc. Humaniorum Littarum Lundensis* 1:270. 1920.

8
3. A. J. Wensinck, *Acta Orientalis* 1:158. 1923.
4. W. Wili, translated by R. Manheim, in *The Mysteries* (Eranos Yearbooks), New York: Pantheon, 1955, pp. 64–92.
5. M. Eliade, *The Myth of the Eternal Return,* translated by W. R. Trask, New York: Pantheon, 1954, pp. 85–92.
6. S. G. F. Brandon, *Time and Mankind,* London: Hutchinson, 1951, chap. 2.
7. M. Eliade, *Traité d'Histoire des Religions,* Paris: Payot, 1949, p. 336.
8. A. G. van Hamal, in *Saga Book of the Viking Society,* Coventry, 1928–1936, p. 209.

1. S. Radhakrishnan, *The Philosophy of Sarvepalli Radhakrishnan,* edited by P. A. Schilpp, Evanston: Library of Living Philosophers, 1952, pp. 45–46.
2. H. Zimmer, *Philosophies of India,* edited by J. Campbell, New York: Pantheon, 1951, p. 62.
3. M. Eliade, *J. Psychol. Norm. Path.* 45:430. 1952.
4. M. Sadhu, *Concentration: A Guide to Mental Mastery,* New York: Harper, 1959.
5. M. Eliade, *The Myth of the Eternal Return,* translated by W. R. Trask, New York: Pantheon, 1954, pp. 85–92.
6. M. Müller, *The Six Systems of Indian Philosophy,* London: Longmans, Green, 1916, p. 393.

9
1. F. S. C. Northrop, *The Meeting of East and West,* New York: Macmillan, 1950, p. 342.
2. W. S. Haas, *The Destiny of the Mind, East and West,* New York: Macmillan, 1956, pp. 44–54.
3. R. Wilhelm, *The I Ching,* translated by C. F. Baynes, New York: Pantheon, 1950.

4. R. G. H. Siu, *The Man of Many Qualities,* Cambridge: MIT, 1968.
5. H. Wilhelm, in *Man and Time* (Eranos Yearbooks), New York: Pantheon, 1957, pp. 212–232.

10

1. H. S. Nyberg, *J. Asiatique,* 214:210. 1929.
2. H. Corbin, in *Man and Time* (Eranos Yearbooks), New York: Pantheon, 1957.

11

1. H. Lietzmann, *A History of the Early Church,* translated by B. L. Woolf, London: Nicolson and Watson, 1953, vol. II, p. 196.
2. G. van der Leeuw, in *Man and Time* (Eranos Yearbooks), New York: Pantheon, 1957, p. 349.
3. R. Otto, *Kingdom of God and the Son of Man,* translated by F. V. Filson and B. L. Woolf, Boston: King, 1957, p. 105.
4. O. Cullman, *Christ and Time—The Primitive Christian Conception of Time and History,* translated by F. V. Filson, Philadelphia: Westminster, 1950.
5. *Romans* 6:10.
6. *Mark* 1:15.
7. G. Quispel, in *Man and Time* (Eranos Yearbooks), New York: Pantheon, 1957, pp. 85–107.
8. *Matthew* 11:5.

12

1. Plato, *Timaeus,* in *Dialogues of Plato,* translated by B. Jowett, Oxford: Clarendon, 1953, vol. III, pp. 715–724.
2. Plato, *Phaedo,* in *Dialogues of Plato,* translated by B. Jowett, Oxford: Clarendon, 1953, vol. II, p. 246.
3. F. H. Brabant, *Time and Eternity in Christian Thought,* London: Longmans, Green, 1937.
4. Aristotle, *Physics,* in *Basic Writings of Aristotle,* edited by R. McKeon, New York: Random House, 1941.
5. P. F. Conen, *New Scholast.* 26:441. 1952.
Oxford University, 1948, pp. 106–108.

13

1. W. R. Inge, *The Philosophy of Plotinus,* New York: Longmans, Green, 1929.
2. G. H. Turnbull, *The Essence of Plotinus,* New York: Oxford University, 1948, pp. 106–108.
3. J. F. Callahan, *Four Views of Time in Ancient Philosophy,* Cambridge: Harvard University, 1948.
4. Plotinus, *Tractate on Eternity and Time,* in *Works,* translated by K. S. Guthrie, London: Bell, 1918.

5. G. H. Clark, *Philos. Rev.* 53:337. 1944.

6. C. Rau, *Philos. Rev.* 62:514. 1953.

7. Augustine, *Confessions,* translated by J. G. Pilkington, Edinburgh: Clark, 1876.

8. Augustine, *City of God,* translated by M. Dods, Edinburgh: Clark, 1934.

9. D. B. Macdonald, *Isis* 9:326. 1927.

10. L. Massignon, in *Man and Time* (Eranos Yearbooks), New York: Pantheon, 1957, pp. 108–114.

11. S. Alexander, *Spinoza and Time,* London: Allen and Unwin, 1921, pp. 26–27.

12. S. Hampshire, *Spinoza,* Harmondsworth: Penguin, 1951, pp. 171–172.

13. B. Spinoza, *Cogitata Metaphysica,* translated by F. Hayes, Indianapolis: Bobbs-Merrill, 1963.

14. H. A. Wolfson, *The Philosophy of Spinoza,* Cambridge: Harvard University, 1948.

15. B. Spinoza, *Ethics,* translated by D. D. S., New York: Van Nostrand, 1876.

14

1. I. Kant, *Critique of Pure Reason,* translated by M. Müller, New York: Macmillan, 1900, pp. 24–25.

2. M. F. Cleugh, *Time,* London: Methuen, 1937.

3. I. Kant, *Critique of Aesthetic Judgment,* translated by J. C. Meredith, London: Clarendon, 1911.

4. J. A. Gunn, *The Problem of Time,* London: Allen and Unwin, 1929.

5. A. C. Ewing, *The Fundamental Questions of Philosophy,* New York: Collier, 1962, pp. 164–165.

6. W. James, *Principles of Psychology,* New York: Dover, 1950, vol. I, p. 201.

7. H. Nichols, *Am. J. Psychol.* 3:453. 1891.

8. F. H. Bradley, *Appearance and Reality,* New York: Macmillan, 1902.

9. F. H. Bradley, *The Principles of Logic,* London: Oxford University, 1922, vol. I.

10. J. H. Cotton, *Royce on the Human Self,* Cambridge: Harvard University, 1954, pp. 19–22.

11. J. Royce, *The World and the Individual,* New York: Macmillan, 1901, vol. II.

12. J. Royce, *William James and Other Essays on the Philosophy of Life,* New York: Macmillan, 1911, p. 268.

13. J. Royce, *The Spirit of Modern Philosophy,* New York: Houghton Mifflin, 1897, p. 387.

14. G. Marcel, *Royce's Metaphysics,* translated by V. and G. Ringer, Chicago: Regnery, 1956, p. 79.
15. B. Bosanquet, *Principles of Individuality and Value,* London: Macmillan, 1912, pp. 397 *et seq.*
16. A. P. Stiernotte, *God and Space-Time. Deity in the Philosophy of Samuel Alexander,* New York: Philosophical Library, 1954.
17. S. Alexander, *Space, Time and Deity,* London: Macmillan, 1920.
18. C. H. Hinton, *The Fourth Dimension,* London: Allen and Unwin, 1934.
19. J. W. Dunne, *Experiment with Time,* New York: Macmillan, 1938.
20. J. W. Dunne, *Serial Universe,* London: Faber and Faber, 1942.
21. L. J. Lafleur, *J. Philos.* 37:169. 1940.
22. C. D. Broad, *Religion, Philosophy, and Psychical Research,* New York: Harcourt, Brace, 1953.
23. P. D. Ouspensky, *Tertium Organum,* translated by N. Bessaraboff and C. Bragdon, New York: Knopf, 1947.
24. P. D. Ouspensky, *A New Model of the Universe,* New York: Knopf, 1949.
25. G. E. Moore, *Some Main Problems of Philosophy,* London: Allen and Unwin, 1953.
26. M. Lazerowitz, *The Structure of Metaphysics,* New York: Humanities, 1955.

15

1. C. Hartshorne, in *Whitehead and the Modern World,* edited by V. Lowe, Boston: Beacon, 1950, pp. 25–41.
2. A. N. Whitehead, *Process and Reality,* New York: Macmillan, 1929.
3. I. Leclerc, *Whitehead's Metaphysics,* New York: Humanities, 1955.
4. A. N. Whitehead, in *Sixth International Congress on Philosophy,* edited by E. B. Sheffield, New York: Longmans, Green, 1927, pp. 59–64.
5. W. W. Hammerschmidt, *Whitehead's Philosophy of Time,* New York: Crown, 1947, pp. 31–32.
6. N. Lawrence, *Whitehead's Philosophical Development,* Berkeley: University of California, 1956.

16

1. H. Bergson, *Time and Free Will,* translated by F. L. Pogson, London: Allen and Unwin, 1910.
2. H. Bergson, *Creative Evolution,* translated by A. Mitchell, New York: Holt, 1913.

3. H. Bergson, *Matter and Memory,* translated by N. M. Paul and W. S. Palmer, New York: Macmillan, 1911, p. 275.

4. J. M. Stewart, *A Critical Exposition of Bergson's Philosophy,* London: Macmillan, 1913, pp. 207–235.

5. E. B. McGilvary, *Philos. Rev.* 23:121. 1914.

6. J. C. Smuts, *Holism and Evolution,* New York: Macmillan, 1926; pp. 93–94.

17

1. M. Heidegger, *Being and Time,* translated by J. Macquarrie and E. Robinson, London: S. C. M., 1962.

2. J. Wild, *The Challenge of Existentialism,* Bloomington: Indiana University, 1955, pp. 100–101.

3. T. Langan, *The Meaning of Heidegger,* New York: Columbia University, 1959, pp. 44–45.

4. W. Brock, *Martin Heidegger,* Chicago: Regnery, 1949, pp. 64–65.

5. M. Heidegger, *Einführung in die Metaphysik,* Tübingen: Niemeyer, 1966.

6. D. E. Roberts, *Existentialism and Religious Belief,* New York: Oxford University, 1957, pp. 159–160.

7. J.-P. Sartre, *Being and Nothingness,* translated by H. E. Barnes, New York: Philosophical Library, 1956.

18

1. N. A. Berdyaev, *The Meaning of History,* translated by G. Reavy, London: Bles, 1936, pp. 63–75.

2. P. W. Bridgman, *Nature of Physical Theory,* New York: Dover, 1936, pp. 29–32.

3. M. Buber, *Between Man and Man,* London: Routledge and Kegan Paul, 1947, pp. 140–141.

4. E. Cassirer, *The Philosophy of Symbolic Forms,* translated by R. Manheim, New Haven: Yale University, 1951, vol. I, pp. 95–96.

5. H. Corbin, in *Man and Time* (Eranos Yearbooks), New York: Pantheon, 1957, pp. xvi–xviii.

6. A. Ghose, *The Life Divine,* New York: Greystone, 1949, p. 179.

7. C. Hartshorne, in *Philosophical Essays for Alfred North Whitehead,* New York: Longmans, Green, 1936, pp. 207–210.

8. J. MacMurray, *The Self as Agent,* London: Faber and Faber, 1957, pp. 138–139.

9. M. Maisels, *Thought and Truth,* translated by A. Regelson, New York: Bookman, 1956.

10. G. H. Mead, *The Philosophy of the Present,* edited by

A. E. Murray, Chicago: Open Court, 1932, pp. 146–147.
11. A. Portman, in *Man and Time* (Eranos Yearbooks), New York: Pantheon, 1957, pp. 303–323.
12. W. C. Sheldon, *God and Polarity,* London: Oxford University, 1954, p. 587.

19

1. N. Wiener and A. Winter, *Nature* 181:561. 1958.
2. R. B. Way and N. D. Green, *Time and Its Reckoning,* Redhill: Wells, Gardner, Darton, 1951, pp. 165–166.
3. H. Weyl, *Space-Time-Matter,* translated by H. L. Brose, New York: Dover, 1952.
4. M. K. Munitz, *Space, Time and Creation,* Glencoe: Free, 1957.
5. H. Salecker and E. P. Wigner, *Phys. Rev.* 109:571. 1958.
6. H. T. Flint, *Phys. Rev.* 74:209. 1948.

20

1. H. Jensen, *Arch. Ges. Psychol.* 101:289. 1938.
2. A. R. Brown, *The Adaman Islanders,* London: Cambridge University, 1922, p. 311.
3. A. W. Howitt, *The Native Tribes of Southeast Australia,* New York: Macmillan, 1904, p. 432.
4. C. von Strehlow, *Das Soziale Leben der Aranda und Loritza Völkermus,* Frankfurt, 1913, vol. II, p. 44.
5. L. Cape, *University of California Publ. Am. Archeol. Ethnol.* 16:4. 1919.
6. American Council of Education, *Telling Time Throughout the Centuries,* Washington, 1933.
7. H. J. Cowan, *Time and Its Measurement,* Cleveland: World, 1958, pp. 18–19.
8. E. Achalis, *Of Time and the Calendar,* London: Hermitage, 1955, p. 38.
9. F. Kingdon-Ward, *Footsteps in Civilization,* London: Cape, 1950, pp. 215–216.
10. J. M. Richardson, *Intern. Sci. Technol.* June, 1962.
11. H. Lyons, *Scientific Am.* 196(2):71. 1957.
12. R. H. Dicke, *Science* 129:621. 1959.

22

1. I. Barrow, *Mathematical Works,* edited by W. Whewell, Cambridge: University, 1860, vol. II, pp. 160 *et seq.*
2. I. Newton, *Principia Mathematica,* London: Innys, 1726.

23

1. G. W. Leibnitz, *The Leibnis-Clark Correspondence,*

edited by H. G. Alexander, Manchester: Manchester University, 1956.

2. C. R. Morris, in *Philosophical Writings of Leibniz,* translated by M. Morris, London: Dent, 1934, pp. xxiii–xxiv.

3. G. W. Leibnitz, *Philosophical Papers and Letters,* edited by L. E. Loemker, Chicago: University of Chicago, 1956, p. 87.

4. K. S. Ballard, *J. History Ideas* 21:49. 1960.

5. A. A. Michelson and E. W. Morley, *Am. J. Sci.* 134: 333. 1887.

6. H. A. Lorentz, *Proc. Amsterdam Acad.* 6:809. 1903.

24

1. A. Einstein, *Relativity,* translated by R. W. Lawsen, New York: Hartsdale, 1947, p. 44.

2. A. Einstein, in *Albert Einstein: Philosopher-Scientist,* edited by P. A. Schilpp, Evanston: Library of Living Philosophers, 1949, pp. 1–96.

3. A. Einstein and L. Infeld, *The Evolution of Physics,* New York: Simon and Schuster, 1938, p. 186.

25

1. G. Gamow, *Matter, Earth and Sky,* Englewood Cliffs: Prentice-Hall, 1958.

2. I. Asimov, *The Universe,* London: Penguin, 1967.

3. G. Lemaître, *Ann. Mtg. Soc. Helvetique Sci. Naturelles,* Freibourg, September, 1945.

4. W. H. McCrea, *The Times Science Review* Autumn, 1960.

5. E. A. Milne, *Kinematic Relativity,* Oxford: Clarendon, 1948.

6. E. A. Milne, Foreword to *Time, Knowledge and the Nebulae* by M. Johnson, New York: Dover, 1947.

7. E. A. Milne, in *Albert Einstein: Philosopher-Scientist,* edited by P. A. Schilpp, Evanston: Library of Living Philosophers, 1946, pp. 409–435.

8. J. B. S. Haldane, *Nature* 155:133. 1945.

9. E. Whittaker, *From Euclid to Eddington,* Cambridge: University, 1949.

10. F. Hoyle, *The Nature of the Universe,* New York: Harper, 1960.

11. F. L. Arnot, *Time and the Universe,* Sydney: Australian Medical, 1941.

12. W. H. McCrea, *Science* 160:1295. 1968.

13. G. C. McVittie, *Science* 133:1231. 1961.

14. A. C. B. Lowell, *The Individual and the Universe,* London: Oxford University, 1959.

30

1. E. Schrödinger, *What is Life?*, New York: Macmillan, 1945.
2. V. M. Garshin, translated by B. G. Guerney, in *A Treasury of Russian Literature,* New York: Vanguard, 1943, p. 709.

31

1. D. Thompson, *On Growth and Form,* Cambridge: University, 1917.
2. J. L. Kavanau, *Am. Naturalist* 81:161. 1947.
3. F. H. C. Crick, *Scientific Am.* 215(4):55. 1966.
4. A. Kornberg, *Science* 131:1503.1960.
5. R. D. Allen, *Scientific Am.* 201:124. 1959.
6. J. Runnstrom, B. E. Hagstrom, and P. Pearlmann, in *The Cell,* edited by J. Brachet and A. E. Mirsky, New York: Academic, 1959, vol. I, pp. 327–398.
7. B. I. H. Scott and D. W. Martin, *Aust. J. Biol. Sci.* 15:83. 1962.
8. F. J. Mandriota, R. L. Thompson, and M. V. L. Bennett, *Animal Behavior* 16:448. 1968.
9. L. Langman and H. S. Burr, *Am. J. Obstet. Gynecol.* 57:274. 1949.
10. R. G. Grenell and H. S. Burr, *Yale J. Biol. Med.* 18:517. 1946.
11. A. Nodon, *Rev. Sci.* 65:609. 1927.
12. E. S. Russell, *The Interpretation of Development and Heredity,* Oxford: Clarendon, 1930, pp. 169–171.
13. E. B. Wilson, *The Cell in Development and Heredity,* New York: Macmillan, 1925, p. 1005.

32

1. W. Wolf, editor, *Ann. New York Acad. Sci.* 98:753–1326. 1962.
2. H. Kalmus, *Nature* 180:1100. 1957.
3. W. Schleidt, *J. Comp. Physiol. Psychol.* 66:743. 1968.
4. E. Bünning, *Ann. New York Acad. Sci.* 98(4):901. 1962.
5. W. S. Glock, *Principles and Methods of Tree Ring Analysis,* Washington: Carnegie, 1937.
6. W. Spector, editor, *Handbook of Biological Data,* Philadelphia: Saunders, 1956, pp. 277 *et seq.*
7. O. P. Pearson, in *First Book of Animals,* New York: Simon and Schuster, 1955, pp. 93–99.
8. E. Era, *Endem. Dis. Bull. Nagasaki Univ.* 1:252, 1959.
9. F. W. Flattery, *Rhythm in Nature,* Washington: Smithsonian, 1920, pp. 389–397.
10. F. Keeble, *Plant Animals,* Cambridge: University, 1910.

11. G. Bohn, *Attractions et Oscillations des Animaux Marins sous l'Influence de la Lumière,* Paris: Institut Psychologique, 1905.
12. F. A. Brown, Jr., *Am. J. Physiol.* 178:510. 1954.
13. A. Wetmore, *The Migration of Birds,* Cambridge: Harvard University, 1926.
14. J. P. Chapin and L. W. Wing, *Auk* 76:153. 1959.
15. W. B. Grange, *The Way to Game Abundance,* New York: Scribner's, 1949.
16. F. E. Clements and V. E. Shelford, *Bio-ecology,* New York: Wiley, 1939, p. 192.
17. T. J. Headlee, *New Jersey Exp. Sta. Bull.* no. 579. 1934.
18. E. B. Phelps and D. L. Belding, *A Statistical Study of the Records of Salmon Fishing on the Restigouche River,* Riverside: Foundation for Study of Cycles, 1947.
19. C. S. Elton and M. Nicolson, *J. Animal Ecol.* 11:215. 1942.
20. J. L. Kennedy, R. M. Gottsdanker, J. C. Armington, and F. Gray, *Science* 108:527, 1948.
21. E. M. Dewan, *Intern. Sci. Technol.* January, 1949.
22. H. Gastaut, in *Brain Mechanisms and Consciousness,* edited by J. F. Delafresnaye, Springfield: Thomas, 1954, pp. 249–283.
23. L. G. Augenstine, in *Information Theory in Psychology,* edited by H. Quastler, Glencoe: Free, 1955, pp. 208–226.
24. B. Duell, *Wetter und Gesundheit,* Dresden: Steinkopff, 1941.
25. J. Malek, J. Gleich, and V. Maly, *Ann. New York Acad. Sci.* 98:1042. 1962.
26. R. A. Reimann, *J. Am. Med. Assoc.* 183:879. 1963.
27. W. F. Peterson, *The Patient and the Weather,* Ann Arbor: Edwards, 1934.
28. H. Eufinger and I. Weikersheimer, *Archiv Gynäkologie* 154:15. 1933.
29. C. P. Richter, *Proc. Natl. Acad. Sci. U. S.* 46:1506. 1960.
30. J. Tinbergen and J. J. Polak, *The Dynamics of Business Cycles,* Chicago: University of Chicago, 1950.
31. E. R. Dewey, *Putting Cycles to Work in Science and Industry,* New York: Foundation for the Study of Cycles, 1940.

32. H. L. Moore, *Generating Economic Cycles,* New York: Macmillan, 1923.
33. J. A. Estey, *Business Cycle,* Englewood Cliffs: Prentice-Hall, 1956, pp. 15–17.
34. W. C. Mitchell, *Business Cycles, the Problems and Its Setting,* New York: Natl. Bur. Econ. Res., 1927, p. 411.

33

1. J. A. M. Meerlo, *The Two Faces of Man,* New York: International Universities, 1954.
2. C. E. Osgood, *Method and Theory in Experimental Psychology,* New York: Oxford University, 1953.
3. G. A. Brecher, *Z. Vergl. Physiol.* 18:204. 1932.
4. N. Oka, *Jap. J. Psychol.* 11:543. 1936.
5. M. Beniuc, *Z. Vergl. Physiol.* 19:724. 1933.
6. L. Dobkiewicz, *Biol. Zentralb.* 23:664. 1912.
7. I. Beling, *Z. Physiol.* 9:259. 1929.
8. O. Wahl, *Z. Vergl. Physiol.* 16:529. 1932.
9. M. Metfessel and J. M. Babbitt, *Psychol. Bull.* 31:602. 1934.
10. C. F. Sams and E. C. Tolman, *J. Comp. Psychol.* 5:255. 1925.
11. T. J. Hudson, *The Law of Psychic Phenomena,* Chicago: McClure, 1905, p. 70.
12. H. Woodrow, *J. Comp. Psychol.* 8:395. 1928.

34

1. E. G. Boring, *Sensation and Perception in the History of Experimental Psychology,* New York: Appleton-Century-Crofts, 1942, p. 576.
2. G. Iacono, *Contr. Lab. Psicol. Univ. Sacro Cuore (Milano)* 15:99. 1952.
3. A. C. Moulyn, *Philos. Sci.* 19:33. 1952.
4. J. Cohen, *Humanistic Psychology,* London: Allen and Unwin, 1958.
5. A. S. Eddington, *The Mathematical Theory of Relativity,* Cambridge: University, 1957, pp. 23–25.
6. D. Krech and R. S. Crutchfield, *Elements of Psychology,* New York: Knopf, 1958, pp. 24–25.
7. J. D. Mabbott, *Mind* 60:153. 1951.
8. A. Charpentier, *Compt. Rend. Soc. Biol.* 39:360. 1887.
9. C. Durup and A. Fessard, *Année Psychol.* 31:52. 1931.
10. H. Piéron, *The Sensations,* translated by M. H. Pirenne and B. C. Abbott, New Haven: Yale University, 1952.
11. G. Schaltenbrand, *Ann. New York Acad. Sci.* 138:632. 1967.

12. G. J. Whitrow, *Intern. Sci. Technol.* June, 1965.
13. P. H. Hock and J. Zubin, editors, *Psychopathology of Childhood,* New York: Grune and Stratton, 1925.
14. L. B. Ames, *J. Genet. Psychol.* 68:97. 1946.
15. P. Fraise and F. Orsini, *Année Psychol.* 58:1. 1958.
16. A. J. Carlson, *Science* 98:407. 1943.
17. R. MacDougall, *Science N. S.* 19:707. 1904.
18. W. Stern, *Acta Psychol. (Hague)* 1:220. 1935.
19. E. Jaensch and A. Kretz, *Z. Psychol.* 126:312. 1932.
20. Y. Usizima, *Jap. J. Appl. Psychol.* 3:165. 1935.
21. S. Fischer and R. L. Fischer, *J. Pers.* 21:496. 1953.
22. L. Leshan, *J. Abn. Soc. Psychol.* 47:589. 1952.
23. D. C. McClelland, J. W. Atkinson, R. A. Clarke, and E. Lowell, *The Achievement Motive,* New York: Appleton-Century-Crofts, 1953.
24. R. H. Knapp, in *The Assessment of Human Motive,* edited by J. W. Atkinson, New York: Van Nostrand, 1957.
25. K. Lewin, *A Dynamic Theory of Personality,* New York: McGraw-Hill, 1935, p. 286.
26. A. Berman, *J. Exp. Psychol.* 25:281. 1939.
27. E. Fredericson, *Psychol. Rev.* 58:41. 1951.
28. R. J. Filer, *J. Exp. Psychol.* 39:327. 1949.
29. M. François, *Compt. Rend. Soc. Biol.* 98:201. 1928.
30. S. H. Bartley, *J. Exp. Psychol.* 22:388. 1938.
31. J. Siegel, quoted in H. Piéron, *The Sensations,* translated by M. H. Pirenne and B. C. Abbott, New Haven: Yale University, 1952.
32. J. Cohen, C. E. M. Hansel, and J. D. Sylvester, *Nature* 172:901. 1953; 174:642. 1954.
33. M. Abbe, *Jap. J. Psychol.* 3:1. 1936; 4:1. 1937.
34. R. B. MacLeod and M. F. Roff, *Acta Psychol.* 1:388. 1936.
35. J. F. Brown, *Psychol. Forsch.* 14:233. 1931.
36. G. C. Myers, *J. Exp. Psychol.* 1:339. 1916.
37. H. Munsterberg, *On the Witness Stand,* New York: Doubleday, Page, 1913.
38. G. Oléron, *Année Physiol.* 52:543. 1936.
39. E. Meumann, *Phil. Stud.* 10:393. 1894.
40. H. Woodrow, *Arch. Psychol.* 11:1. 1909.
41. A. Guttman, *Arch. Ges. Psychol.* 85:331. 1932.
42. P. Ram, *Indian J. Psychol.* 19:129. 1944.
43. C. O. Weber, *Am. J. Psychol.* 38:597. 1927.
44. F. Etienne and W. Kutschbach, *Sammlung* 4:120. 1949.

45. H. Gulliksen, *J. Exp. Psychol.* 10:52. 1927.
46. P. M. Symonds, *The Dynamics of Human Adjustment,* New York: Appleton-Century-Crofts, 1946, p. 492.
47. W. T. Lhamon and S. Goldstone, *Arch. Neurol. Psychiat.* 76:625. 1956.
48. J. Coheen, *J. Nerv. Ment. Dis.* 112:121. 1950.
49. G. M. Davidson, *J. Nerv. Ment. Dis.* 94:336. 1941.
50. W. van Woerkom, *Monatschr. Psychiat. Neurol.* 57:59. 1925.
51. O. Fenichel, *The Psychoanalytic Theory of Neuroses,* New York: Norton, 1945, p. 204.
52. W. R. Brain, *Diseases of the Nervous System,* London: Oxford University, 1951.
53. W. R. Dobson, *J. Gen. Physiol.* 50:277. 1954.
54. F. Fischer, *Z. Neurol. Psychiat.* 121:544. 1929.
55. E. Minkowski, *La Schizophrénie,* Paris: Payot, 1927.
56. N. Israeli, *Abnormal Personality and Time,* New York: Social Science Research Council, 1936, p. 59.
57. P. Schilder, *Mind,* New York: Columbia University, 1942.
58. H. Hartmann, *Monatschr. Psychiat. Neurol.* 56:1. 1924.
59. O. Sterzinger, *Z. Psychol.* 134:100. 1935; 143:391. 1938.
60. M. Frankenhauser, *Estimation of Time,* Stockholm: Almquist and Wiksell, 1959.
61. T. de Quincey, *Confessions of an Opium Eater,* London: Oxford University, 1934.
62. W. Mayer-Gross, E. Slater, and M. Roth, *Clinical Psychiatry,* London: Cassell, 1954, p. 363.
63. W. Bromberg, *Am. J. Psychiat.* 41:301. 1934.
64. P. Delaye, *et al., Arch. Mus. Nat. d'Histoire,* Nat. Ser. 7, Tome VI. 1958–1959.
65. L. F. Cooper and M. H. Erickson, *Time Distortion in Hypnosis,* Baltimore: Williams and Wilkins, 1959.
66. F. Podmore, *Studies in Psychical Research,* London: Paul, Trench, and Trübner, 1897, p. 394.
67. W. R. Wells, *J. Psychol.* 9:137. 1940.

35

1. S. K. Langer, *Feeling and Form,* New York: Scribner's, 1953, pp. 109–129.
2. B. de Selincourt, *Music and Letters* 1(4):286. 1920.
3. G. Brelet, translated by S. K. Langer, in *Reflections on Art,* edited by S. K. Langer, Baltimore: Johns Hopkins, 1958, pp. 103–121.

4. A. Copland, *Music and Imagination,* Cambridge: Harvard University, 1953, p. 2.
5. J. T. Howard and J. Lyons, *Modern Music,* New York: New American Library, 1958, chap. 2.
6. L. Jones, *Blues People,* New York: Morrow, 1963.
7. I. A. Richards, *Principles of Literary Criticism,* London: Paul, 1924.
8. H. Simons, *The Sewanee Rev.* 53(4):566. Autumn, 1945.
9. W. Stevens, *The Necessary Angel,* New York: Knopf, 1951, pp. 71–82.

36

1. J. Dewey, *Art as Experience,* New York: Minton, Balch, 1934, pp. 166, 171.
2. R. Bayer, translated by S. K. Langer, in *Reflections on Art,* edited by S. K. Langer, Baltimore: Johns Hopkins, 1958, pp. 186–201.
3. M. Sauvage, translated by S. K. Langer, in *Reflections on Art,* edited by S. K. Langer, Baltimore: Johns Hopkins, 1958, pp. 161–173.
4. É. Souriau, translated by S. K. Langer, in *Reflections on Art,* edited by S. K. Langer, Baltimore: Johns Hopkins, 1958, pp. 122–141.
5. W. Grohmann, *Paul Klee,* London: Humphries, 1954.
6. P. Klee, *The Inward Vision,* New York: Abrams, 1958.

37

1. L. K. Frank, *J. Soc. Phil.* 4:589. 1952.
2. L. R. Heath, *The Concept of Time,* Chicago: University of Chicago, 1936.
3. P. A. Sorokin and R. K. Merton, *Am. J. Sociol.* 42:615. 1937.
4. S. C. Laha, *Samīksā* 6:12. 1952.
5. R. J. Pumphrey, *The Origin of Language,* Liverpool: University, 1951.
6. B. L. Whorf, *The Technology Rev.* 42:229. 1940.
7. B. L. Whorf, *Int. J. Am. Linguistics* 16:67. 1950.
8. L. Levy-Bruhl, *How Natives Think,* translated by L. A. Clare, London: Allen and Unwin, 1926, p. 254.
9. D. Lee, *J. Philos.* 46:401. 1944.
10. A. H. Gardiner, *Egyptian Grammar,* Oxford: Clarendon, 1927, p. 219.
11. A. Dorner, *The Way Beyond Art,* New York: Wittenborn, Schulz, 1947, pp. 51–52.
12. E. Pinchon, *Rech. Phil.* 5:197. 1935–1936.
13. J. A. Gunn, *The Problem of Time,* London: Allen and Unwin, 1929.

14. A. W. Green, *Sociology,* New York: McGraw-Hill, 1960, pp. 105 *et seq.*
15. G. Soule, *Time for Living,* New York: Viking, 1955, chap. 6.
16. P. A. Sorokin, *Sociocultural Causality, Space, Time,* Durham: Duke University, 1943, pp. 158–225.
17. D. Cartwright, *Am. J. Psychol.* 54:175. 1941.
18. A. W. Levi, *Philosophy and the Modern World,* Bloomington: Indiana University, 1959.
19. E. Bergler and G. Róheim, *Psychoanal. Quart.* 15:190. 1946.

38

1. W. Lewis, *Time and the Western Man,* London: Chatto and Windus, 1927.
2. A. A. Mendilow, *Time and the Novel,* London: Nevill, 1952.
3. H. Meyerhoff, *Time and Literature,* Berkeley: University of California, 1955.
4. G. Poulet, *Studies in Human Time,* translated by E. Coleman, New York: Harper, 1956.
5. R. M. Fox, *Dante Lights the Way,* Milwaukee: Bruce, 1958.
6. M. de Montaigne, *Complete Works,* translated by D. M. Frame, Palo Alto: Stanford University, 1957.
7. B. Pascal, *Pensées et Opuscules,* Paris: Brunschwicq, 1904–1914.
8. M. Wilson, *The Life of William Blake,* London: Hart-Davis, 1948.
9. J. Wicksteed, *William Blake's Jerusalem,* London: Trianon, 1953.
10. W. Blake, "Auguries of Innocence," in *Poetry and Prose of William Blake,* edited by G. Keynes, London: Nonesuch, 1927.
11. N. Frye, *Fearful Symmetry,* Princeton: Princeton University, 1947, p. 47.
12. W. Blake, *The Marriage of Heaven and Hell,* New York: Dutton, 1927.
13. W. Blake, *Jerusalem,* London: Blake, 1804.
14. G. Brée, *Marcel Proust and Deliverance from Time,* translated by C. J. Richards and A. D. Truitt, New Brunswick: Rutgers University, 1950.
15. M. Hindus, *The Proustian Vision,* New York: Columbia University, 1954.
16. G. Pirone, *Proust's Way,* translated by G. Hopkins, London: Heineman, 1957.

17. M. Proust, *Remembrance of Things Past,* translated by C. K. S. Moncrieff, New York: Random House, 1934.
18. M. Proust, *The Past Recaptured,* translated by F. A. Blossom, New York: Boni, 1932, pp. 166–167.
19. M. Proust, *On Art and Literature,* translated by S. T. Warner, New York: Meridian, 1958.
20. M. Proust, *Chroniques,* Paris: Nouvelles Revue Français, 1927.
21. M. Proust, *Les Plaisirs et les Jours,* Paris: Nouvelles Revue Français, 1924.
22. V. Woolf, *Orlando,* New York: Harcourt, Brace, 1928, p. 28.
23. V. Woolf, *To the Lighthouse,* New York: Random House, 1937, p. 158.
24. V. Woolf, *The Moment and Other Essays,* New York: Harcourt, Brace, 1948, pp. 3–4.
25. H. Levin, *James Joyce,* Norfolk: New Directions, 1941, pp. 87–88.
26. J. Joyce, *Ulysses,* London: Egoist, 1922.
27. W. Y. Tindall, *James Joyce, His Way of Interpreting the Modern World,* New York: Scribner's, 1950, p. 93.
28. W. T. Noon, *Joyce and Aquinas,* New Haven: Yale University, 1957, pp. 132–133.
29. G. S. Fraser, *The Modern Writer and His World,* New York: Criterion, 1957, pp. 305–306.
30. G. Wagner, *Wyndham Lewis,* New Haven: Yale University, 1957, pp. 184–188.
31. W. Lewis, *Art of Being Ruled,* London: Chatto and Windus, 1926, p. 398.
32. W. Lewis, *The Artist,* London: Laidlaw and Laidlaw, 1939.
33. L. Frankenberg, *Pleasure Dome,* Boston: Houghton Mifflin, 1949.
34. D. E. S. Maxwell, *The Poetry of T. S. Eliot,* London: Routledge and Kegan Paul, 1952.
35. T. S. Eliot, *The Family Reunion,* London: Faber and Faber, 1939.
36. T. S. Eliot, *The Sacred Wood,* London: Methuen, 1964.
37. T. S. Eliot, *Selected Essays,* New York: Harcourt, Brace, 1934.
38. T. S. Eliot, "Burnt Norton," in *Complete Poems and Plays,* New York: Harcourt, Brace, 1952.
39. T. S. Eliot, "The Dry Salvages," in *Complete Poems and Plays,* New York: Harcourt, Brace, 1952.

40. S. O'Faolain, *The Vanishing Hero,* Boston: Little, Brown, 1957, pp. 72–111.

41. J.-P. Sartre, *Literary and Philosophical Essays,* translated by A. Michelson, New York: Criterion, 1955.

42. O. W. Vickery, *The Novels of William Faulkner,* Baton Rouge: Louisiana State University, 1959, chap. 14.

43. W. Faulkner, *The Sound and the Fury,* New York: Modern Library, 1946, p. 104.

44. W. Faulkner, *Mosquitoes,* New York: Liveright, 1927, p. 37.

45. W. Faulkner, *Requiem for a Nun,* New York: Random House, 1951.

46. W. Faulkner, *Sartoris,* New York: Harcourt, Brace, 1929, p. 203.

47. W. Faulkner, *Intruder in the Dust,* New York: Random House, 1948.

48. A. Camus, *The Myth of Sisyphus,* translated by J. O'Brien, New York: Vintage, 1960, p. 10.

49. P. Claudel, *Poetic Art,* translated by R. Spodheim, New York: Philosophical Library, 1948, p. 3.

50. J. Cocteau, *Journals,* New York: Criterion, 1956, p. 67.

51. B. Constant, *Adolphe,* Paris: Charpentier, 1839, chap. 3.

52. R. W. Emerson, *Prose Works,* Boston: Riverside, 1879, vol. III, p. 104.

53. A. Gide, *Les Nourritures Terrestres,* Paris: Nouvelles Revue Français, 1918.

54. N. Hawthorne, *The House of the Seven Gables,* Boston: Houghton Mifflin, 1883.

55. E. Hemingway, *Death in the Afternoon,* New York: Scribner's, 1932.

56. A. Huxley, *After Many a Summer Dies the Swan,* New York: Harper, 1939.

57. T. Mann, *The Magic Mountain,* translated by H. T. Lowe-Porter, New York: Knopf, 1951, p. 102.

58. P. Valéry, *Variété,* in G. Poulet, *Studies in Human Time,* translated by E. Coleman, Baltimore: Johns Hopkins, 1956, p. 284.

59. A. de Vigny, *Correspondence,* Paris: Conard, 1953, vol. I, p. 286.

39

1. W. G. Walter, *The Living Brain,* New York: Norton, 1963.

2. J. A. V. Bates, *J. Physiol. Lond.* 113:240. 1951.

3. A. E. Fessard, in *Brain Mechanism and Conscious-*

ness, edited by J. F. Delafresnaye, Springfield: Thomas, 1954, pp. 200–236.

4. K. S. Lashley, *Cerebral Mechanisms in Behavior,* New York: Wiley, 1951, pp. 112–146.

5. E. von Hartmann, *Philosophy of the Unconscious,* translated by W. C. Coupland, London: Routledge and Kegan Paul, 1931, vol. II, pp. 222–223.

6. H. Nunberg, *Principles of Psychoanalysis,* translated by M. and S. Kahr, New York: International Universities, 1953, pp. 34–41.

7. E. Bergler and G. Róheim, *Psychoanal. Quart.* 15: 190. 1946.

8. M. Bonaparte, *Intern. J. Psychoanal.* 21:427. 1940.

9. L. F. A. Maury, quoted in S. Freud, *The Interpretation of Dreams,* translated by J. Strachey, New York: Basic Books, 1930, pp. 26–27.

10. S. Freud, *The Interpretation of Dreams,* translated by J. Strachey, New York: Basic Books, 1930.

40

1. G. Birenbaum, *Psychol. Forsch.* 13:218. 1930.

2. K. Lewin, *Psychol. Forsch.* 7:330. 1926.

3. F. H. Bradley, *Essays in Truth and Reality,* Oxford: Clarendon, 1914, pp. 356–357.

4. T. V. Moore, *Cognitive Psychology,* New York: Lippincott, 1939.

5. D. Bovet, F. Bovet-Nitti, and A. Oliverio, *Science* 163:139. 1969.

6. D. A. Norman, *Psychol. Rev.* 75:522. 1968.

7. N. C. Waugh and D. A. Norman, *Psychol. Rev.* 72:89. 1965.

8. H. Kay, in *Handbook of Aging and the Individual,* edited by J. E. Birren, Chicago: University of Chicago, 1954, pp. 614–654.

9. W. Penfield, *Science* 129:1719. 1959.

10. W. Penfield and H. Jasper, *Epilepsy and the Functional Anatomy of the Human Brain,* Boston: Little, Brown, 1954.

11. N. Wiener, *Ann. New York Acad. Sci.* 50:197. 1948.

12. H. E. Jones, in *Handbook of Aging and the Individual,* edited by J. E. Birren, Chicago: University of Chicago, 1959, pp. 700–738.

13. D. Rapaport, *Emotions and Memory,* New York: International Universities, 1950.

14. M. Abeles and P. Schilder, *Arch. Neurol. Psychiat.* 34:587. 1935.

15. J. M. Charcot, *Rev. Med.* 12:81. 1892.
16. E. B. Sullivan, *Psychol. Monogr.* 36:1. 1927.
17. M. R. Benon, *J. Practiciens* 47:515. 1933.
18. P. Haushalter, *Rev. Neurol.* 25:118. 1918.
19. S. S. Korsakow, *Arch. Psychiat.* 21:702. 1890.
20. L. Stanojevic, *Arch. Psychiat.* 79:171. 1927.
21. C. Dana, *Psychol. Rev.* 1:570. 1894.
22. G. E. Störring, *Arch. Ges. Psychol.* 95:436. 1936.
23. G. Zimmerman, *Monatschr. Kinderh.* 66:4. 1936.
24. P. Goodhart, *J. Am. Med. Assoc.* 61:2297. 1913.
25. P. Schilder, *Studien zur Psychologie und Symptomatologie der progressiv Paralyze,* Berlin: Karger, 1930.
26. A. Gregor, *Experimentelle Leitfaden der Psychopathologie,* Berlin: Karger, 1910.
27. H. Hartmann, *Monatschr. Psychiat. Neurol.* 56:1. 1924.
28. J. G. Gilbert, *J. Abn. Soc. Psychol.* 36:73. 1941.
29. D. Rapaport, M. Gill, and R. Schafer, *Diagnostic Psychological Testing,* Chicago: Year Book, 1945–1946, vol. I, p. 79.
30. M. Scheerer, E. Rothman, and K. Golstein, *Am. Psychol. Assoc. Psychol. Monogr.* no. 4, 1945.
31. E. Jaensch, *Eidetic Imagery,* London: Paul, Trench and Trübner, 1930.
32. H. Werner, *Comparative Psychology of Mental Development,* New York: International, 1957, pp. 143–152.
33. F. Galton, *Inquiries into Human Faculty and Its Development,* London: Dent, 1908.
34. W. E. Roth, *Ethnological Studies among the N. W. Central Queensland Aborigines,* Brisbane: Gregory, 1897, no. 19. p. 199.
35. S. Toksvig, *Emanuel Swedenborg,* New Haven: Yale University, 1948, pp. 254–258.
36. E. Swedenborg, *The Spiritual Diary,* translated by H. Smithson, London: Newberry, Hodson, 1846.
37. T. Reid, *Essays on the Intellectual Powers of Man,* edited by A. D. Woozley, London: Macmillan, 1941.
38. J. Mill, *Analysis of the Phenomena of the Human Mind,* London: Longmans, Green, 1869.
39. P. Rieff, *Freud,* New York: Viking, 1959, p. 38.
40. S. Freud, *A General Introduction to Psychoanalysis,* New York: Garden City, 1943, pp. 250–251.
41. S. Freud, *The Interpretation of Dreams,* translated by J. Strachey, New York: Basic Books, 1930.

42. S. Freud, *Moses and Monotheism,* translated by K. Jones, New York: Knopf, 1939.
43. J. C. Flugel, *A Hundred Years of Psychology,* London: Duckworth, 1951, pp. 34–35.
44. E. Hering, *Über des Gedächtnis als Eine Allgemeine Funktion der Organisierte Materie,* Leipzig: Englemann, 1921.
45. E. Rignono, *Biological Memory,* translated by E. W. MacBride, London: Paul, Trench and Trübner, 1926.
46. R. Semon, *Mnemic Psychology,* London: Allen and Unwin, 1923.
47. M. Verworn, *Z. Allg. Physiol.* 14:277. 1913.
48. M. Verworn, *Z. Allg. Physiol.* 6:118. 1907.
49. D. E. Broadbent, *Perception and Communication,* New York: Pergamon, 1958.
50. W. Kohler, *Gestalt Psychology,* New York: Liveright, 1947.
51. J. A. McGeoh, *Psychol. Rev.* 39:352. 1932.
52. G. Katona, *Organizing and Memorizing,* New York: Columbia University, 1940, chap. 8.
53. F. C. Bartlett, *Remembering,* Cambridge: University, 1932.
54. D. Gabor, *Science* 177:299. 1972.
55. P. Pietsch, *Harpers Mag.* May, 1972.
56. P. Schilder, *Mind,* New York: Columbia University, 1942.

41

1. J. D. Spikes, R. Lumry, H. Eyring, and R. Wayrynen, *Proc. Natl. Acad. Sci. U. S.* 36:455. 1950.
2. H. I. Virgin, *Proc. Sixth Intern. Congr. Exp. Cytology,* Stockholm, 1947.
3. O. Schmidt, *Z. Botan.* 30:289. 1936.
4. H. P. Bottelier, *Rev. Trav. Botan. Neerl.* 31:474. 1934.
5. K. C. Smith and P. C. Hanawalt, *Molecular Photobiology,* New York: Academic, 1969.
6. H. J. Müller, in *Radiation Biology,* edited by A. Hollaender, New York: McGraw-Hill, 1954, vol. I, pp. 351–474.
7. S. Pomper and K. C. Atwood, in *Radiation Biology,* edited by A. Hollaender, New York: McGraw-Hill, 1954, vol. II, pp. 431–453.
8. E. Altenburg, *Am. Naturalist* 68:491. 1934.
9. R. Geigy, *Rev. Suisse Zool.* 38:187. 1931.
10. K. Mackenzie, *Proc. Roy. Soc. Edinburgh* 61:67. 1941.

11. L. J. Stadler and G. F. Sprague, *Proc. Natl. Acad. Sci. U. S.* 22:579. 1936.
12. D. Shugar, *Experientia* 7:26. 1951
13. R. Dulbecco, *J. Bact.* 59:329. 1950.
14. A. Kellner, *Bull. New York Acad. Med.* 26:189. 1950.
15. S. H. Goodgal, *Genetics* 35:667. 1950.
16. R. F. Kimball and N. T. Gaither, *Genetics* 35:118. 1950.
17. P. H. Wells and A. C. Giese, *Biol. Bull.* 99:163. 1950.
18. H. F. Blum and M. Matthews, *J. Cellular Comp. Physiol.* 39:57. 1952.
19. F. C. Bawden and A. Kleczkowski, *Nature* 169:90. 1952.
20. H. Schildmacher, *Biol. Zentralb.* 59:653. 1939.
21. R. D. Lisk and L. R. Kranswischer, *Science* 146:272. 1964.
22. R. R. Kinkaid, *Florida Agr. Exp. Sta. Bull.* no. 277. 1935.
23. L. H. Flint and E. D. McAlister, *Smithsonian Inst. Misc. Coll.* 96:1. 1937.
24. M. W. Parker, S. B. Hendricks, H. A. Borthwick, and F. W. Went, *Am. J. Botany* 36:194. 1949.
25. A. W. Galston, *Botan. Rev.* 16:361. 1950.
26. J. H. C. Smith, *Arch. Biochem.* 19:449. 1948.
27. S. Granick, *Ann. Rev. Plant Physiol.* 2:115. 1951.
28. W. M. Laetsch, *Am. J. Botany* 55:875. 1968.
29. H. G. du Buy and E. Nuernbergk, *Ergeb. Biol.* 9:358. 1932.
30. H. G. van der Wey, *Proc. Koninkl. Ned. Akad. Weten.* 32:65. 1929.
31. W. W. Garner and H. A. Allard, *J. Agr. Res.* 18:553. 1920.
32. K. C. Hamner and J. Bonner, *Botan. Gaz.* 100:388. 1938.
33. R. Harder, *Symp. Soc. Exp. Biol.* 2:117. 1948.
34. G. L. Funke, *Lotsya* 1:79. 1948.
35. S. D. Beck, *Scientific Am.* 202:108. 1960.
36. S. Marcovitch, *J. Agr. Res.* 27:513. 1924.
37. T. H. Bissonnette, *Physiol. Zool.* 14:379. 1941.
38. J. W. Burger, *Wilson Bull.* 61:211. 1949.
39. J. Benoit and L. Ott, *Yale J. Biol. Med.* 17:27. 1944.
40. L. J. Milne, in *Radiation Biology,* edited by A. Hollaender, New York: McGraw-Hill, 1956, vol. III, pp. 621–692.
41. A. A. Schaeffer, *Biol. Bull.* 32:45. 1917.

42. H. P. Langeloh, *Zool. Jahrb., Abt. Allg. Zool. Physiol.* 57:235. 1937.
43. J. E. Smith, *Phil. Trans. Roy. Soc. Lond.* B227:11. 1937.
44. R. P. Cowles, *Johns Hopkins Univ. Circ.* 30(2):55. 1911.
45. N. Millot, *Biol. Bull.* 99:329. 1950.
46. R. Dubois, *Proc. Intern. Zool. Congr.* 1:148. 1913.

42

1. C. G. Jung, *Symbols of Transformation,* translated by R. F. C. Hull. New York: Pantheon, 1956.
2. A. Erman, *Life in Ancient Egypt,* translated by H. M. Tirard, London: Macmillan, 1894, pp. 261–267.
3. A. Dieterich, *Eine Mithrasliturgie,* Leipzig: Teubner, 1910.
4. Philo Judaeus, *De Sommis,* in *Works,* translated by F. H. Colson and G. H. Whitaker, New York: Putnam, 1929–1962, vol. V, pp. 285 *et seq.*
5. M. Abeghian, *Der Armenische Volksglaube.* Leipzig: Drugulin, 1899, p. 43.
6. J. B. F. Lajard, *Nouv. Ann. Inst. Archeologique (Rome).* 1873.
7. L. Frobenius, *Das Zeitalter des Sonnengottes,* Berlin: Reimer, 1904.

43

1. F. Mainx, in *International Encyclopedia of Unified Science,* edited by O. Neurath, R. Carnap, and C. Morris, Chicago: University of Chicago, 1955, vol. I, pp. 567–654.
2. M. Hartmann, *Die Philosophischen Grundlagen der Naturwissenschaften,* Jena: Fischer, 1948.
3. L. V. Bertalanffy, *Problems of Life,* London: Watts, 1952.
4. H. F. Blum, *Time's Arrow and Evolution,* Princeton: Princeton University, 1955.
5. P. W. Bridgman, *The Nature of Thermodynamics,* Cambridge: Harvard University, 1943, pp. 208–216.
6. P. Laslett, editor, *The Physical Basis of Mind,* Oxford: Blackwell, 1950.
7. G. Ryle, *The Concept of Mind,* New York: Hutchinson's University Library, 1949.
8. H. H. Price, quoted in F. S. Edsall, *The World of Psychic Phenomena,* New York: Mackay, 1958, p. 206.
9. C. J. Herrick, *The Evolution of Human Nature,* Austin: University of Texas, 1956, pp. 453–454.

10. L. L. White, *The Unitary Principle in Physics and Biology*, New York: Holt, 1949.
11. E. Jacobsen, *Am. J. Physiol.* 91:567. 1930; 94:22. 1930; 97:200. 1931.
12. J. C. Powys, *The Meaning of Culture*, New York: Norton, 1929, p. 180.

44

1. A. I. Oparin, editor, *International Symposium on Origin of Life on Earth*, Moscow: USSR Acad. Sci., 1957.
2. J. D. Bernal, *The Physical Basis of Life*, London: Routledge and Kegan Paul, 1951.
3. S. W. Fox, *Science* 132:200. 1960.
4. S. L. Miller and H. C. Urey, *Science* 130:245. 1959.
5. B. Goodwin, *Temporal Organization in Cells*, New York: Academic, 1963.
6. A. S. Iberall, in *Advances in Bioengineering*, edited by R. G. Buckles, New York: American Institute of Chemical Engineers, 1971, pp. 190–194.
7. A. Zarkin and A. Zhabotinsky, *Nature* 225:535. 1970.
8. A. Katchalsky, *Second Intl. Conf. on Theoret. Physics and Biology (Versailles).* July, 1969.

45

1. J. Needham, *Biol. Rev.* 13:225. 1938.
2. L. Dollo, *Bull. Soc. Belge Géol. Pal. Hydr.* 7:164. 1893.
3. H. Gaussen, *Rev. Gen. Sci. Pur. Appl.* 52:4. 1942.
4. O. Abel, *Grundzüge der Paleo-biologie des Wirbeltiere*, Stuttgart: Schweizerbart, 1912.
5. V. Haecher, *Schaxel's Abhandlungen* no. 15. 1922.
6. D. Keilin, *Parasitol.* 18:370. 1926.
7. O. H. Schindewolf, *Jenaische Z. Med. Naturw.* 75:324. 1942.
8. G. G. Simpson, *Life of the Past*, New Haven: Yale University, 1953, pp. 111–117.
9. T. Dobzhansky, *Evolution, Genetics and Man*, New York: Wiley, 1955, p. 296.
10. F. E. Zeuner, *Dating the Past*, London: Methuen, 1950, p. 385.
11. N. J. Berrill, *You and the Universe*, New York: Dodd, Mead, 1958, p. 195.
12. J. G. Kemeny, *A Philosopher Looks at Science*, New York: Van Nostrand, 1959. pp. 199–202.
13. B. Hocking, *Scientific Month.* 85:237. 1957.

46

1. N. Tinbergen, *Scientific Am.* 203(6):118. 1960.

2. H. Harlow, in *Behavior and Evolution,* edited by A. Roe and G. G. Simpson, New Haven: Yale University, 1958, pp. 269–290.
3. W. J. Thorpe, *Learning and Instinct in Animals,* London: Methuen, 1956, p. 133.
4. N. Tinbergen, *The Study of Instinct,* Oxford: Clarendon, 1951, p. 9.
5. R. C. Tryon, in *Comparative Psychology,* edited by F. A. Moss, New York: Prentice-Hall, 1934, pp. 409–448.
6. D. Bovet, F. Bovet-Nitti, and A. Oliverio, *Science* 163:139. 1969.
7. G. E. McLearen and W. Meredith, *Ann. Rev. Psychol.* 17:515. 1966.
8. L. Lejeune, M. Gautier, and R. Turpin, *Compt. Rend.* 248:1721. 1959.
9. J. Shields, *Monozygotic Twins,* London: Oxford University, 1962.
10. L. L. Heston, *Science* 167:249. 1970.
11. R. B. Cattrell, *Proc. Intern. Congr. Hum. Genet.* 3: 1712. 1963.

47

1. E. Gurney, F. W. H. Myers, and F. Podmore, *Phantasms of the Living,* London: Trübner, 1896.
2. L. F. Nicoll, in the Ciba Foundation, *Symposium on Extrasensory Perception,* Boston: Little, Brown, 1956, pp. 24–38.
3. H. F. Saltmarsh, *Foreknowledge,* London: Bell, 1938.
4. F. S. Edsall, *The World of Psychic Phenomena,* New York: McKay, 1958, p. 202.
5. J. G. Pratt, J. B. Rhine, B. M. Smith, C. E. Stuart, and J. A. Greenwood, *Extrasensory Perception after Sixty Years,* New York: Holt, 1940.
6. S. G. Soal and F. Bateman, *Modern Experiments in Telepathy,* London: Faber and Faber, 1954.
7. J. B. Rhine, *Extra-Sensory Perception,* Boston: Boston Soc. Psych. Res., 1934.
8. M. Guthrie, *Proc. Soc. Psychol. Res. Lond.* 3:424. 1885.
9. T. D. Duane and T. Behrendt, *Science* 150:367. 1965.
10. D. J. West, *Psychical Research Today,* London: Duckworth, 1954, p. 81.
11. S. G. Soal, *Proc. Soc. Psych. Res. Lond.* 46:152. 1940.
12. S. G. Soal and K. M. Goldney, *Proc. Soc. Psych. Res. Lond.* 47:21. 1943.

13. C. D. Broad, *Aristotelian Soc. Bull.* Suppl. 16:225. 1937.

48

1. C. G. Jung, *St. Bartholomew's Hosp. J.* 44(3):46. 1936.
2. H. Read, *The Tenth Muse,* London: Routledge and Kegan Paul, 1957.
3. G. Adler, *Studies in Analytical Psychology,* New York: Norton, 1948, pp. 130–131.
4. H. G. Baynes, *Mythology of the Soul,* London: Methuen, 1940.
5. P. Reps, editor, *Zen Flesh, Zen Bones,* Rutland: Tuttle, 1957, pp. 163–187.
6. D. T. Suzuki, *Zen and Japanese Culture,* New York: Pantheon, 1959.
7. R. G. H. Siu, *The Tao of Science,* Cambridge: MIT, 1958, chap. 9.
8. Lao Tzu, *Tao Teh King,* chap. 32.

49

1. P. B. Medawar, *The Uniqueness of the Individual,* New York: Basic Books, 1957, pp. 26–28.
2. H. S. Jennings, in *Problems of Aging,* edited by E. V. Cowdry, Baltimore: Williams and Wilkins, 1942, pp. 24–46.
3. H. S. Jennings, *J. Exp. Zool.* 99:15. 1945.
4. T. M. Sonenborn, *Biol. Bull.* 74:76. 1938.
5. A. Comfort, in *Methodology of the Study of Aging,* edited by E. E. W. Wolstenholme and C. M. O'Conner, London: Churchill, 1957, vol. II, pp. 2–19.
6. R. Pearl, *Human Biology* 3:245. 1931.
7. A. I. Lansing, *J. Gerontol.* 2:228. 1942.
8. C. M. McCoy, in *Cowdry's Problems of Aging,* edited by A. I. Lansing, Baltimore: Williams and Wilkins, 1952, pp. 139–220.

50

1. A. Comfort, *The Biology of Senescence,* London: Routledge and Kegan Paul, 1956.
2. J. E. Birren, editor, *Handbook of Aging and the Individual,* Chicago: University of Chicago, 1959.
3. A. L. Vischer, *Old Age,* London: Allen and Unwin, 1947.
4. Zh. A. Medvedev, *Uspekhi Sovremennoy Biologii* 51:299. 1961.
5. S. Zamenhof, *The Chemistry of Heredity,* Springfield: Thomas, 1959.
6. B. L. Strehler, *Quart. Rev. Biol.* 34:117. 1959.

7. C. M. Child, *Senescence and Rejuvenescence,* Chicago: University of Chicago, 1915.
8. H. Simms, *J. Gerontol.* 1:13. 1946.
9. A. A. Bergomolets, *The Prolongation of Life,* translated by P. A. Karpovich and S. Bleeker, New York: Duell, Sloan and Pearce, 1946.
10. F. M. Sinex, *J. Gerontol.* 12:190. 1957.
11. J. Bjorksten and F. Andrews, *J. Am. Geriatrics Soc.* 8:632. 1960.
12. C. Hinshelwood, *J. Chem. Soc. Lond.* 1953:1947.
13. H. S. Jennings and R. S. Lynch, *J. Exp. Zool.* 50:345. 1928.
14. P. R. J. Burch, *An Inquiry Concerning Growth, Disease and Ageing,* London: Oliver and Boyd, 1968.
15. N. W. Shock, in *Aging, Some Social and Biological Aspects,* Washington: Am. Assoc. Adv. Sci., 1960, pp. 250–251.
16. A. Carrell, *Man the Unknown,* New York: Harper, 1935, p. 182.
17. S. Voronoff, *Testicular Grafting from Apes to Man,* London: Brentano, 1929.
18. P. Niehans, *Die Zellular Therapie,* Berlin: Urban and Schwarzenberg, 1954.
19. R. Egger, *Proc. Intern. Congr. Biogenetics (Rome).* April, 1955.
20. A. Aslan, A. L. Vrabescu, and H. Zimel, *Rumania Med. Rev.* 3:95. 1959.
21. W. D. Bancroft, E. C. Farnham, and J. E. Rutzler, Jr., *Science* 80:539. 1934.
22. I. I. Metchnikoff, *The Nature of Man,* New York: Putnam's, 1903.

51

1. W. B. Cannon, *Am. Anthropologist* 44:169. 1942.
2. J. L. Christian and H. L. Ratcliffe, *Am. J. Pathol.* 28:725. 1952.
3. C. P. Richter, in *The Meaning of Death,* edited by H. Feifel, New York: McGraw-Hill, 1959, pp. 302–313.
4. M. Maisels, *Thought and Truth,* translated by A. Regelson, New York: Bookman, 1956.
5. C. Gottlieb, in *The Meaning of Death,* edited by H. Feifel, New York: McGraw-Hill, 1959, pp. 157–188.
6. K. R. Eissler, *The Psychiatrist and the Dying Patient,* New York: International Universities, 1955, pp. 282–283.

7. H. Plessner, in *Man and Time* (Eranos Yearbooks), New York: Pantheon, 1957, pp. 233–263.
8. M. H. Nagy, *J. Genet. Psychol.* 73:3. 1948.
9. R. Kestenbaum, in *The Meaning of Death*, edited by H. Feifel, New York: McGraw-Hill, 1959, pp. 99–113.
10. C. W. Wahl, *Bull. Menninger Clinic* 22:214. 1958.
11. W. E. Hocking, *The Meaning of Immortality in Human Experience*, New York: Harper, 1957.

52

1. Aristotle, *Physics*, in *Basic Works of Aristotle*, edited by R. McKeon, New York: Random House, 1941.
2. B. Russell, *Principles of Mathematics*, New York: Norton, 1938, p. 473.
3. M. Lazerowitz, *The Structure of Metaphysics*, New York: Humanities, 1955.

53

1. B. Russell, *Intern. Month.* 4:83. 1901.
2. R. Dedekind, quoted in T. Dantzig, *Number*, Garden City: Doubleday, 1954, pp. 172–173.
3. G. Cantor, *Math. Ann.* 46:481. 1895.
4. G. Cantor, quoted in E. V. Huntington, *The Continuum*, Cambridge: Harvard University, 1929.

54

1. G. J. Whitrow, *The Natural Philosophy of Time*, London: Nelson, 1961.
2. B. Gal-Or, *Science* 176:11. 1972.
3. B. Gal-Or, *Science* 178:1119. 1972.
4. J. H. Christiansen, J. W. Cronin, V. L. Fitch, and R. Turlay, *Phys. Rev. Lett.* 13:138. 1964.
5. R. G. Sachs, *Science* 176:587. 1972.
6. G. J. Whitrow, *Ann. New York Acad. Sci.* 138:422. 1967.
7. R. G. Collingwood, *Proc. Aristotelian Soc.* 38:85. 1938.
8. M. Born, *Natural Philosophy of Cause and Change*, Oxford: Clarendon, 1949.
9. B. Russell, *Mysticism and Logic*, London: Allen and Unwin, 1932, pp. 184–205.
10. N. K. Brahma, *Causality and Science*, London: Allen and Unwin, 1939.
11. M. Kline, *Mathematics in Western Culture*, Oxford: Oxford University, 1953, p. 107.
12. D. J. B. Hawkins, *Being and Becoming*, New York: Sheed and Ward, 1954, pp. 156–157.

13. H. Reichenbach, *The Direction of Time,* edited by M. Reichenbach, Berkeley: University of California, 1956.
14. H. Kelsen, *Philos. Sci.* October, 1941.
15. Heraclitus, in H. Diels, *Die Fragmente der Vorsokatiker,* Berlin: Weidermann, 1934, fifth edition, fragment 25.
16. Anaximander, in J. Burnet, *Early Greek Philosophy,* London: Black, 1920, third edition, p. 52.
17. Plato, *Protagoras,* in *Works,* translated by H. Cary, *et al.,* London: Bell, 1880–1885, vol. I.

55
1. H. Pinter, *New York Times Mag.* December 5, 1971.
2. *Maha-Parinibbana-Sutta, Digha-Nikāya,* translated by H. C. Warren, in *Buddhism in Translations,* Cambridge: Harvard University, 1896, vol. III, pp. 109–110.
3. Lu Chi, translated by A. Fong, in A. MacLeish, *Poetry and Experience,* Baltimore: Penguin, 1964, p. 18.

56
1. A. Korzybski, *Manhood of Humanity; the Art and Science of Human Engineering,* New York: Dutton, 1923.
2. A. Korzybski, *Science and Sanity,* Lancaster: Science, 1933, p. 376.
3. C. J. Beidermann, *Art as the Evolution of Visual Knowledge,* Red Wing, Minn.: Art History. 1948, pp. 15–33.
4. J. W. von Goethe, quoted in O. Rank, *Art and the Artist,* New York: Knopf, 1932.
5. W. Johnson, *People in Quandaries,* New York: Harper, 1946, pp. 162–166.
6. R. G. Collingwood, *Speculum Mentis,* Oxford: Clarendon, 1924.
7. W. M. F. Petrie, *The Revolution of Civilization,* London: Harper, 1912.
8. R. Grousset, *The Sum of History,* translated by A. and H. T. Peterson, Hadleigh: Tower Bridge, 1951, p. 85.
9. J. Marias, *Reason and Life,* translated by K. S. Reid and E. Sarmiento, New Haven: Yale University, 1956, pp. 41–46.
10. A. R. Capanigri, *Time and Idea,* Chicago: Regnery, 1953, pp. 71–72.
11. E. Jordan, *The Good Life,* Chicago: University of Chicago, 1949, pp. 126–128.

12. J. E. Salomaa, *Theoria* 15:276. 1949.
13. H. G. Alexander, *Time as Dimension and History*, Albuquerque: University of New Mexico, 1945.
14. M. Maisels, *Thought and Truth*, translated by A. Regelson, New York: Bookman, 1956.

57

1. R. G. H. Siu, *The Tao of Science*, Cambridge: MIT, 1958.
2. J. Legge, quoted in R. H. Mathews, *A Chinese English Dictionary*, Cambridge: Harvard University, 1943, p. 73.
3. Y. M. Pei, in *The Chinese Mind*, edited by C. A. Moore, Honolulu: University of Hawaii, 1967, p. 162.
4. E. R. Hughes, in *The Chinese Mind*, edited by C. A. Moore, Honolulu: University of Hawaii, 1967, p. 92.
5. W.-t. Chan, in *The Chinese Mind*, edited by C. A. Moore, Honolulu: University of Hawaii, 1967, p. 137.
6. K. S. Latourette, *The Chinese. Their History and Culture*, New York: Macmillan, 1946, p. 248.
7. M. Knoll, in *Man and Time* (Eranos Yearbooks), New York: Pantheon, 1957, p. 304.
8. Y. Lin, *My Country and My People*, New York: Day, 1937, p. 122.
9. S.-c. Huang, *Philos. East and West* 18:247. 1968.
10. Chang Tsai, quoted in Y.-l. Fung, *A Short History of Chinese Philosophy*, New York: Macmillan, 1948, p. 279.
11. G.-H. Wang, *The Chinese Mind*, New York: Day, 1946, p. 136.
12. Chu Hsi, quoted in Y.-l. Fung, *A Short History of Chinese Philosophy*, New York: Macmillan, 1948, pp. 299–301.
13. D. S. Nivison, *The Life and Thought of Chang Hueh-ch'eng*, Palo Alto: Stanford University, 1966, p. 13.
14. D. T. Suzuki, *Zen and Japanese Culture*, New York: Pantheon, 1959, p. 149.
15. M.-m. Sze, *The Tao of Painting*, Princeton: Princeton University, 1956, chap. 2.
16. Chang Keng, quoted in O. Sirén, *The Chinese on the Art of Painting*, Peking, 1936, p. 215.

58

1. ibn-Arabi, quoted in M. A. Pallacio, *Islam and the Divine Comedy*, London: Murray, 1926.
2. E. Biser, *Philos. Sci.* 19:50. 1952.

3. J. E. Boodin, *Time and Reality,* New York: Macmillan, 1904.
4. G. Eaton, *The Richest Vein,* London: Faber and Faber, 1949.
5. J. Krishnamurti, *Commentaries on Living,* edited by D. Rajagopal, New York: Harper, 1958, p. 108.
6. O. E. Mandelstam, "Poems about an Unknown Soldier," 1937.
7. F. Nietzsche, *The Joyful Wisdom,* New York: Russell and Russell, 1964, pp. 73–74.
8. M. Pradines, *Traité de Psychologie Générale,* Paris: University of France, 1946, vol. I, p. 122.
9. I. Stravinsky, quoted in Robert Craft, *Stravinsky,* New York: Knopf, 1972.
10. *T'ai I Chin Hua,* explained in the words of R. Wilhelm in *The Secret of the Golden Flower,* translated and explained by R. Wilhelm, New York: Harcourt, Brace and World, 1962, revised edition, pp. 13–14.
11. Tsi I, translated by J. J. M. de Groot, in *Religion in China,* New York: Putnam's, 1912, pp. 6–20.

59
1. J. T. Fraser, *Ann. New York Acad. Sci.* 138:837. 1967.
2. R. Fischer, *Ann. New York Acad. Sci.* 138:371. 1967.

60
1. R. D. Laing, *The Divided Self,* New York: Pantheon, 1960, p. 175.

61
1. H. F. Copeland, *The Classification of Lower Organisms,* Palo Alto: Pacific, 1956.
2. P. B. Weisz, *The Science of Biology,* New York: McGraw-Hill, 1967.
3. R. H. Whittaker, *Science* 163:150. 1969.

62
1. J. V. McConnell, *J. Neuropsychiat.* 3(1):342. 1962.
2. A. L. Harty, P. Keith-Lee, and W. D. Morton, *Science* 146:274. 1964.
3. J. B. Best, *Scientific Am.* 208(2):55. 1963.
4. J. Gaito and Z. Zavala, *Psychol. Bull.* 61:45. 1964.
5. H. Hyden and E. Egyhazi, *Proc. Natl. Acad. Sci. U. S.* 48:1366. 1962.
6. C. Fried and S. Horowitz, *Worm Runner's Digest* 6:3. 1964.
7. F. R. Babich, A. L. Jacobson, S. Babash, and A. Jacobson, *Science* 149:656. 1965.

8. F. Fourcade, *Art Treasures of the Peking Museum,*
New York: Abrams, 1965, pp. 119–120.
9. E. D. Hoedemaker, in L. B. Boyer and P. L. Giovac-
chini *Psychoanalytic Treatment of Schizophrenic and
Characterological Disorders,* New York: Science
House, 1967, pp. 191–192.

63

1. J. Finke, *Confin. Psychiat.* 7:47. 1964.
2. R. G. H. Siu, *Bioscience* 14(9):34–39. 1964.
3. F. Nietzsche, *Die Fröhliche Wissenschaft,* in *Werke,*
Leipzig: Naumann, 1899–1904, vol. V.
4. T. S. Eliot, *Selected Essays,* New York: Harcourt,
Brace, 1934.
5. A. Hauser, *The Philosophy of Art History,* New York:
Knopf, 1959, pp. 241–253.
6. H. Weyl, *Philosophy of Mathematics and Natural
Science,* Princeton: Princeton University, 1949.
7. B. Russell, *Human Knowledge,* New York: Simon and
Schuster, 1948, p. 216.
8. H. Corbin, in *Man and Time* (Eranos Yearbooks), New
York: Pantheon, 1957.

64

1. E. Kris, *Psychoanalytic Exploration in Art,* London:
Allen and Unwin, 1953.
2. A. Ehrenzweig, *The Psychoanalysis of Artistic Vision
and Hearing,* London: Routledge and Kegan Paul, 1953.
3. M. Milner, in *Psycho-analysis and Contemporary
Thought,* edited by J. Sutherland, London: Hogarth,
1958, pp. 77–102.
4. E. Neumann, in *Man and Time* (Eranos Yearbooks),
New York: Pantheon, 1957. pp. 3–37.
5. E. Neumann, *Art and the Creative Unconscious,* translated by R. Manheim, New York: Pantheon, 1959,
pp. 81–134.
6. A. Koestler, *The Act of Creation,* New York: Dell, 1967.

65

1. J.-P. Sartre, *Being and Nothingness,* translated by
H. E. Barnes, New York: Philosophical Library, 1956.

68

1. H. Nicolson, *The Congress of Vienna,* New York: Harcourt, 1946.

69

1. H. F. Harlow and M. K. Harlow, *Bull. Menninger Clinic*
26:213. 1962.

2. A. L. McDonald, N. H. Heimstra, and D. K. Damkob, *Animal Behavior* 16:437. 1968.
3. H. Lantz, *Marriage and Family Living* May, 1965.
4. C. Lombroso, *The Criminal in Relation to Anthropological Jurisprudence and Psychiatry,* Paris: Alcan, 1887.
5. C. Goring, *The English Convict,* London: H. M. Stationery, 1913.
6. D. Abrahamsen, *The Psychology of Crime,* New York: Columbia University, 1960.
7. R. D. Laing and A. Esterson, *Sanity, Madness, and the Family,* New York: Basic Books, 1971, second edition.
8. T. Lidz, S. Fleck, and A. Cornelison, *Schizophrenia and the Family,* New York: International Universities, 1965.

70
1. L. Mumford, in a speech at the conference of the *Conservation Foundation,* Warrenton, Virginia, 1965.

71
1. K. Lorenz, *King Solomon's Ring,* New York: Crowell, 1952, p. 184.

72
1. J. L. Liebman, *Peace of Mind,* New York: Simon and Schuster, 1946, pp. 27–28.

73
1. D. Martindale, editor, *National Character in the Perspective of the Social Sciences,* Philadelphia: Am. Acad. Pol. Soc. Sci., 1967.

75
1. C. G. Jung, in C. G. Jung and W. Pauli, *The Interpretation of Nature and the Psyche,* New York: Pantheon, 1955, pp. 14–21.
2. E. Gurney, F. W. H. Myers, and F. Podmore, *Phantasms of the Living,* London: Trübner, 1886.
3. P. Kammerer, *Das Gesetz der Series,* Stuttgart, 1919.
4. W. Stekel, *Z. Psychotherapie Med. Psychol.* 3:110. 1910.
5. A. Schopenhauer, *Essays from Parerga and Paralipomena,* translated by T. B. Saunders, London: Allen and Unwin, 1951.
6. C. Flammarion, *The Unknown,* London: Harper, 1900, pp. 191 *et seq.*
7. C. G. Jung, in *Man and Time* (Eranos Yearbooks), New York: Pantheon, 1957, p. 202.

8. A. M. Dalcq, *Verhandl. Schweiz. Naturforsch. Gesell. Ann. Meeting (Lausanne),* 1949, pp. 37–72.
9. J. Jeans, *Physics and Philosophy,* Cambridge: University, 1942, pp. 127, 151.
10. H. Read, *The Tenth Muse,* London: Routledge and Kegan Paul, 1957.

76

1. P. S. Laplace, *A Philosophical Essay on Probabilities,* translated by F. W. Truscott and F. L. Emory, New York: Wiley, 1902, p. 4.
2. E. Whittaker, *From Euclid to Eddington,* Cambridge: University, 1949.
3. K. Gödel, *On Formally Undecidable Propositions of Principia Mathematica and Related Systems,* translated by B. Meltzler, New York: Basic Books, 1962.
4. E. Nagel and J. R. Newman, in *The World of Mathematics,* edited by J. R. Newman, New York: Simon and Schuster, 1956, pp. 1668–1695.

77

1. A. Nivens, *Horizon* September, 1963.
2. D. Kraslow and S. H. Loory, *The Secret Search for Peace in Vietnam.* New York: Random House, 1968.

79

1. P. Tillich, *Kairos,* reprinted in *The Protestant Era,* translated by J. L. Adams, Chicago: University of Chicago, 1948.

80

1. J. J. Chapman, *Letters and Religion,* Boston: Atlantic, 1924.
2. Chuang Tzu, translated by D. T. Suzuki, in D. T. Suzuki, *Zen and Japanese Culture,* New York: Pantheon, 1959, p. 438.

Index

Aborigines, 192, 193
Abrahamsen, David, 280
Abramenko, R., 123
Achilles and the tortoise, 233, 237
Action, 22, 180–181, 187, 219, 255–257
Actualization, 75, 84–85
Acupuncture, 258
Adam, 19
and Eve, 222
Adaman Islanders, 109–110
Adaptability, 29, 33, 39, 143
Adenine, 144
Adler, Gerhard, 219
Adolescents, 154, 230
Advertising, 44
Aesthetics, 164
Age, 11, 13, 154, 190
Ages of the world, 50–51
Aging, 15, 224–228
Ahriman, 7, 56
Ahuvar, 56
Alacrity, 164
Alcohol, 176
Alexander, Samuel, 8, 76–80
Algonquin, 167
Allah, 8, 65–66
Allergy, 150
Alpha rhythm, 149, 184, 218
Ambrose, Saint, 206
Ames, Louise, 154
Amino acids, 29–30
Amnesia, 190–191, 195
Amoeba, 203
Amphetamine, 160
Amphibian, 145, 223
Amusements, 44
Anaximander, 248
Anguish, 8, 100–101, 175, 283–284
Anima, 264–265
Animals,
behavior of, 280
effect of light on, 200–203
ideas in, 188
metabolism in, 146
radioactivity in, 145
rate of evolution in, 211–212
sense of time by, 11, 150–151, 171, 187–188
space-binding by, 251
Animus, 264–265
Annelids, 204
Annoyances, 288
Anticipation, 163
Antinomies, 51
Anxiety, 21, 169, 276, 284
Aphasia, 159
Apophis, 49
Appearance, 70, 73–74, 118–119
Aranda, 110
Archetypes, 219
Aristotle, 7, 59–61, 233
Arnot, F. L., 128
Arpeggios, 164
Art,
in bullfighting, 183
and creative vision, 272
eternity in, 179
evolution of, 251
as future's history, 12, 180
greatness in, 164
and the moment, 180
phases of, 165
rhythm in, 164–165
and virtual presence, 44
Arthropods, 204, 213
Artist, 180–181
inspiration of, 221
and Nature, 290–291
psychic life of, 272
and the unconscious, 273
Atom, primeval, 10, 125
Attitude,
American, toward Nature, 169
American, toward Time, 169
and temporal perception, 11, 155
Augustine, Saint, 8, 63–65
Autarchic fiction, 185
Autistic behavior, 280
Axiomatic method, 286–287

Bach, Johann Sebastian, 162
Bacteria. *See* Microorganisms.

Ballard, Keith, 116
Barnabas, epistle of, 56
Barrow, Isaac, 9, 113
Bartlett, F. C., 197
Basho, 220–221
Baudelaire, Pierre, 183
Baur, Ferdinand, 252
Bayer, Raymond, 164
Beatific Vision, 231
Becoming,
  in actual entities, 92
  and being, 57–58, 99
  and ch'i, 270
  and duration, 93
  emphasis on, 179
  in music, 75
  and Nature, 58
  and Time, 100
  Trobriander's concern
    over, 167
Bees, 11, 150, 261
Beethoven, Ludwig van,
  162
Before-and-after,
  as basic relation, 107
  as higher dimension, 84
  and motion, 60
  and Space, 77
  and Time, 72–73, 100
Beginning,
  absence of, in real Time,
    181
  coincidence with end, 51
  eternal, 55
  and the Fable, 184
  return to the, 55
  in Time, 85
Beidermann, Charles, 251
Being, 97
  and becoming, 57–58, 99
  dimension of, 263–264
  discontinuity of, 173
  dynamic principle of, 264
  and form, 105, 174, 264
  modes of, 55, 99, 164
  and Nature, 58
  and nonbeing, 99, 250
  and nothingness, 98–99
  and the Scholastic, 170
  search for, 95
  totality of, 98
  Trobriander's concern
    over, 167–168
Beneficence, 287

Beneke, Friedrich, 196
Benon, M. R., 191
Berdyaev, Nicolai, 101
Bergler, Edmund, 169, 185
Bergson, Henri, 8, 92–95,
  179
Bertalanffy, L. V., 209
Best, J. B., 268
B-fields, 218
Bigamul, 109
Birds,
  anticipation of future in,
    146
  effect of light on, 203
  longevity of, 15, 223
  memory in, 151
  migration of, 11, 148
  sense of pitch in, 151
  sense of time in, 11
Birenbaum, G., 187
Birren, J. E., 225
Births, rhythm in, 150
Biser, Erwin, 263
Blake, William, 12, 173–
  175, 272–273
Blood pressure, rhythm in,
  148
Bohr, Niels, 139
Boltzmann, Ludwig, 136
Bondi, Hermann, 128
Boodin, John, 263
Books, 44
Boring, E. G., 151–152
Bosanquet, Bernard, 76
Brabant, Frank, 59
Bradley, F. H., 8, 72–74, 87
Brahmaloka, 51
Brain,
  diseases of, 158–159, 190
  electrical stimulation of,
    189
  and memory, 189, 194,
    198
  waves, 11, 149
Brelet, Gisele, 161
Bridgman, Percy, 102
British Journal for the
  Philosophy of Science,
  122
Broad, C. D., 82
Brock, Werner, 97
Brown, F. A., 148
Buber, Martin, 102–103
Buddha, 52, 249–250

Buddhist, 48
Bullfighting, 183
Burch, P. R. J., 227

Caffeine, 160
Calculus, 235
Calendar, 108, 110–111,
  169
Callahan, John F., 62
Calorie, 13, 21, 260, 282
Camus, Albert, 182
Cannabis, 160
Cannibals, 268
Cantor, Georg, 237–242
Carbon dioxide poisoning,
  191
Care, 96–97
Carlson, A. J., 154
Cassirer, Ernst, 103
Cat, 150
Cattrell, R. B., 215
Causality,
  Algonquin's concept of,
    167
  executive, 208
  and existence, 67
  historical, 103
  and memory, 92
  and the moment, 246
  order in, 245–246
  and precognition, 218–219
  and prediction, 245–246
  and psychological mani-
    festation, 219
  and retribution, 247–249
  and synchronicity, 284–
    285
  and Time order, 69
  Trobriander's concept
    of, 168
Cell, 11, 29, 31, 143, 146,
  200, 223
Ceramic art, 269
Certainty. *See* Uncertainties
Cervantes, Miguel de, 282
Chain of circumstances,
  276
Chaldeans, 110
Challenge-and-response,
  255
Chapman, John, 290
Change, 74, 92, 103–104,
  167, 169, 172, 179, 182
Changelessness, 232

Chang Keng, 258
Chang Tsai, 257
Charcot, J. M., 190
Charisma, 45
Charpentier, A., 153
Chemistry, 259–260
Ch'en Tu-hsiu, 45
Ch'i,
  and action, 22
  in acupuncture, 258
  adorning, 22
  and calorie, 21, 282
  channels of, 19, 268–270
  complementarity of, 271
  and conduct, 258
  conservation of, 271
  and creativity, 18
  and death, 17, 18, 261
  definition of, 256–257
  and ego, 19, 275
  and ethics, 20–21, 281
  and evolution, 17, 18,
    267–268
  and existence, 257
  and experience, 18
  future of, 19, 270
  and good and evil, 20, 281
  gradient of, 271
  hysteresis of, 19
  and id, 19, 274
  and idea, 258
  and *li,* 257
  and Light, 16–18
  limitation of, 283
  and living, 18, 21, 281
  and maturity, 18
  and means and ends, 20
  in mental illness, 18
  metabolism of, 17–18,
    20, 261–263, 267–268, 281
  and mind, 258
  in music, 261
  in musing, 6
  and origin of Life, 18
  in painting, 258
  past of, 19, 270
  and personality, 18
  in photosynthesis, 262–263
  in poetry, 261
  potentiality of, 19
  present of, 270–272
  properties of, 18, 266
  in psychic development,
    18

Ch'i (continued)
  as raw material, 18, 261
  and responsibility, 20
  resonance of, 271
  satisfaction, 21
  and serenity, 18, 22, 291
  and species, 18, 267–268
  and superego, 19, 275
  in swordsmanship, 258
  as Time-related *X*, 16, 261
  transactor of, 22
  unit of, 271
  variety of, 18
  and virtual presence, 17
Child, 154, 229–230
Chimpanzee, 150
Chinese, 7, 52–54
Chinese baseball, 25, 27
Chlorophyll, 30, 201
Chloroplast, 30, 201
Christians, 7, 56–57
Christiansen, J. H., 243
Chromosomes, 200, 215
Chronology, 55, 63, 66, 159
Chuang Tzu, 257–258, 291
Chu Hsi, 257
Churches, 44
Civilization, 20, 48
Clark, Gordon, 62
Classification of organisms, 267
Claudel, Paul, 183
Claustrophobia in Time, 159
Clocks, 159
  and age of universe, 123–124
  atomic, 111–112
  calibration of, 118, 126–127
  congruence among, 108–109, 118, 127
  effect of gravity on, 121
  electronic, 111
  ideal, 108–109
  and Life, 181
  and man's alienation, 169
  mechanical, 111
  moving, 120
  and relativity, 118–120
  sundial, 110
  as symbol of death, 228
  and Time, 265–266
  water, 111

Cocaine, 160
Cocteau, Jean, 183
Cognition, 103
Coheen, J., 158
Cohen, J., 152
Collective Unconscious, 14, 219–220, 273
Collingwood, R. G., 252
Comfort, A., 224
Command post, 5
Common sense, 8, 84–88, 152, 180
Communication, 251
Competition, 169
Complementarity, 266–267, 271
Compton Effect, 131
Compulsion, 170
Computer, 189–190
Confucius, 265
Conscience, 282
Conscious, 12, 184–185, 219–220
Consciousness,
  and cerebral activity, 184
  continuity of, 70–71
  and death, 15
  and duration, 170
  and imagination, 174
  and memory, 13, 194–195
  of musical measure, 103
  and the mystic, 272
  as nothingness, 98
  of oak, 174
  omniscient, 76
  and sense of space, 82–85
  symbol of, 13, 207–208
  of temporal form of motion, 103
  and Time, 74, 152–153
  and wisdom, 219
Conservation, 281
Constant, Benjamin, 183
Contemplation, 291
Continuance, 15, 231
Continuity, 172, 182
Continuum, 15–16, 233–250
  four-dimensional, 119–120
  and mind, 78
  of nows, 73
  power of the, 240–241
  as source of manifestations, 7, 52–53
  space-time, 119–120

Continuum *(continued)*
  as Time, 77
  undifferentiated, 7, 52–53
Contradictions, 28, 185
Coordinates, 107, 117–120,
  152–153
Coordination in oak, 5
Copeland, H. F., 267
Copland, Aaron, 161
Corbin, Henry, 55, 103
Correspondence, 237–241
Cosmogenesis, 7, 54–55
Cosmological Principle,
  125, 127
Cosmologic constant, 124–
  125
Cosmology, 10, 50–51,
  122–129, 272
Cosmos. *See* Universe
Courage, 19
CPT theorem, 243–244
Craving, 183
Creativity, 272–273
  and archaic influence, 254
  and *ch'i*, 18
  and evolution, 273
  and feeling, 231
  and the present, 91
  and Time, 88–89
  and totality, 89
  and virtual presence, 19
  and Zeitgeist, 273
Credo (Klee), 166
Criminal, 21, 280–281
Crises, personal, 49
Critical fusion frequency,
  156
Culture, 12, 43, 92, 166–
  169, 255
Cytoplasm, 144
Cytosine, 144

Dalcq, A. M., 285
d'Alembert, Jean, 234
Danilevsky, Nicolai, 254
Dante Alighieri, 12, 169–
  170
Dasein, 96–98
Davidson, G. M., 159
Darwin, Charles, 212–213,
  252
Death, 228–232
  and anima, 264
  and animus, 264

apprehensiveness of, 175,
  228–229
and autosynthetic function,
  226
and *ch'i*, 17–18, 21, 261
and consciousness, 15
and continuance, 15, 231
and *Dasein*, 98
definition of, 11
as encouragement, 8
and For-itself, 98–99, 101
freedom toward, 98
and hopelessness, 228
and In-itself, 98–99
and the instant, 183
and memory, 193
and relativity of, 231
and retribution, 15
and return to origin, 55
suddenness of, 15, 228·
and Time, 12, 183, 228–
  229
as ultimate reference, 170
and the unknown, 15
and voodoo, 228
de Broglie, Louis, 137–138
Decision, 169, 255
Dedekind, Richard, 235–
  236
Dedekind cut, 235–237
Deduction, 286–287
Delacroix, Ferdinand, 183,
  271
Democracy, 281
Demokritos, 248
Descartes, René, 112
Desire, 158, 170
de Sitter, Willem, 10, 124–
  125
Density, 170
Devil, 57, 290
Dewan, E. M., 149
Dewey, John, 164
Diaphototropism, 202
Dihydroquinine, 259
Dionysius, 49
Diptheria, 191
Dirac, Paul, 139–140
Disappointments, 163, 169
Disavowals, 282
Diseases, 13, 150, 191
Dogs, 11, 151
Dollo's Law, 211
Dominance reversal, 280

Don Quixote (Cervantes), 282
Doom, 182
Doppler Effect, 130
Doubt, 20
Doves, 282
Dragonfly, 5–6, 38–41
Dreams, 185–187, 196
Driesh, Hans, 208
Drugs, 13, 160
Dualism, 209
Dunne, J. W., 8, 80–82, 218
Duration,
and becoming, 193
and clocks, 108
and completion, 54
as creative, 8, 94–95
divisions of, 94
estimation of, 151–161
features of, 67
irreversibility of, 94–95
as isolated moments, 177
and mind, 172
as momentary conscious-ness, 170
in music, 161
in physics, 118
and quality of movement, 183
rhythm of, 93–94
and Time, 8, 67, 69, 71, 93–95
units of, 92–93
See also Eternity, and duration

Earth, 124
Earthworm, 5, 34–37
Eaton, Gai, 264
Ecclesiastes, 164
Echinoderms, 204
Eclampsias, 150
Economy, 44
Eddington, A. S., 128, 152
Eel, 146
Eggs, 38, 44
Ego, 19, 93, 184, 229, 274–275
Egyptians, 110–111, 205
Ehrenzweig, A., 272
Eidetic image, 192–193
Eigenfunctions, 139
Eigenvalues, 139

Einstein, Albert, 10, 118–122, 124, 126, 134, 247
Eissler, K. R., 228
Élan, 93
Elections, 44
Electricity, 10, 131, 135, 140, 144–145, 149
Electrodynamics, 140
Electromagnetic fields, 140
Electromagnetic rays, 141
Electronic devices, 44
Electrons, 134, 138–141
Elephants, 224
Eliot, T. S., 12, 180–181
Embryo, human, 145
Emerson, Ralph Waldo, 183
Emotions, 13, 74, 155, 190–191
E., Mrs., 217
End, 51, 181, 232
Endocrine secretions, 15
Endurance, 88–89
Enemy, 21
Energy, 18, 31, 121, 133, 142, 144, 261
Engram, 196
Entelechy, 208
Entropy, 209
Environment, 14, 29, 33, 143, 213, 215
Enzymes, 29, 142
Ephapax, 57
Equity, social, 281
Equivalence, 120–121, 176, 240
Erman, Adolf, 205
Eros, 231
Eschatology, 57
Eskimos, 110, 193
Eternity, 174
concept of, and culture, 169
and duration, 67, 116
glimpse of, 232
and history, 101
and immutability, 272
intentio toward, 65
and mental patients, 160
of the mind, 67
still point of, 181
temporal implications of, 68
and Time, 51, 55, 62, 64, 75–76, 101

Ether, 10, 117–118, 132, 209
Ethics, 20–21, 254, 281
Etruscans, 253
Events, 53, 168, 263, 285
Evil, 183, 282
  See also Good
Evolution, 14, 211–214
  of art, 251
  and ch'i, 17–18, 267–268
  and creativity, 273
  and environment, 14, 213
  and force of reason, 14
  irreversibility of, 14, 211
  of languages, 166
  of learning, 214
  of man, 252
  of mind, 14, 214–215
  and mutation, 14, 212
  rate of, 14, 211–212
  of self, 92
  sequence of, 267–268
  and virtual presences, 19
Ewing, A. C., 70
Excitement, 19
Existence,
  authentic, 96–98
  and Care, 96
  and ch'i, 257
  co-, 29
  and experience, 70
  higher levels of, 80
  as linkage to duration, 67
  losing one's present, 176
  nature of, 88–89
  order of, 115
  sense of, 175
  and Time, 69, 77, 85–86, 95, 113
  unauthentic, 96–98
  by virtue of cause, 67
Existentialists, 8–9, 95–101
Expectancy, 161, 163
Experience,
  change of, 104
  and ch'i, 18
  cycle of, 264
  and dreams, 187
  and existence, 70
  integrated, 184
  as living transplant, 47
  momentary, 158
  musical, 161–162
  pastness as, 79

Externality, 93, 95
Extrasensory perception, 14, 216–219
Extroverts, 155

Fable, 184
Facts, 74, 103–104, 289
Failure, 181, 190
Fairy fly, 38
Family, 53
Fantasy, 158–159
Faraday, Michael, 135
Faulkner, William, 12, 181–182
Fear, 170
Fechner-Weber Law, 157
Feeling, 172, 261
Fenichel, O., 159
Fermat, Pierre de, 137
Fertilization, 31, 144
Fibroblasts, 226
Filer, R. J., 155
Finnegan's Wake (Joyce), 179
Fischer, F., 159
Fischer, Roland, 266
Fischer, R. S., 228
Fish,
  antagonism of, 280
  electrical output of, 144–145
  evolution of, 211–212
  interplay with cleaning shrimp, 260–261
  longevity in, 15, 223
  population cycle in, 11, 148
  sense of Time in, 11, 150
Flame, 143
Flammarion, C., 284
Flatworms, 11, 147
Flowers, 31, 146
Flux, 88
Folly, 53
Food, 3, 19, 268
Forces, 10, 115, 124–125
Forgetting, 159, 187–188
For-itself, 98–101
Forms, 103–105, 143, 167
Fourcade, François, 269
Four Zoas (Blake), 175
Fraser, J. T., 265
Freedom, 22, 100, 181, 274
Freud, Sigmund, 13, 186–187, 195–196, 273–274

Friedman, Alexander, 10, 125
Friend, 21, 280
Frog, 146
Fruit flies, 18, 200, 224
Frustration, 158
Fungi. See Microorganisms
Funke, G. L., 202
Future, 152
  and anguish, 100–101
  in animal life, 187
  anthropological, 102
  anticipation of, 170, 173
  and Care, 96
  and ch'i, 270
  as construct, 73
  and death, 228–229
  and desire, 170
  and determinacy, 104
  as ecstasy of Time, 8
  and emotion, 155
  as expectation, 65
  and fear, 170
  and For-itself, 99–100
  as given, 219
  history of the, 180
  and hope, 170
  Hopi concept of, 167
  as law, 104
  living on the, 182
  and mental patients, 160
  and morphogenesis, 145
  in music, 161
  and Possibility, 100
  predictability of, 286
  pure, 229
  reality of, 66
  remembering the, 184
  and responsibility, 96
  responsiveness to, 4, 145–146
  as sign, 103
  and speech, 166
  uncertainty of, 103
  and wish-fulfilling, 158

Gabor, Dennis, 198
Galaxies, 124–126
Galilean transformation, 117–118
Galileo Galilei, 9, 112, 142
Gal-Or, Benjamin, 242–243
Game cycles, 148

Gardiner, A. H., 168
Garshin, V. M., 142
Gastaut, H., 149
Genes, 144
Genesis, 4, 63, 222, 275
Geometry, 112, 119, 122, 125
Germination, 32–33, 200–201
Gestalt, 184, 208
Gētīk, 55
Ghose, Aurobindo, 103–104
Ghurrat al-hilāl, 66
Gibbon, Edward, 252
Gide, André, 183
Gioconda, 165
Goals, 75
God,
  and Creation, 169–170
  creation of, 19, 275
  as creator of Time, 63–64
  as emergent highest Quality, 81
  eternity of, 66, 116
  and goodness, 163, 290
  independence of, 116
  Light from, 170
  love from, 170
  reasons of, 114
  symbols of, 13, 205–206
  temporal priority of, 63
  union with, 67
  virtual, 44
Gödel, Kurt, 286–287
Goethe, Johann von, 251
Gold, Thomas, 128
Good, 20, 106, 281, 289–290
Goring, Charles, 280
Grace, 171, 173, 285
Gravitational fields, 120–122, 126–127
Greatness in art, 164
Greeks, 7, 57–61
Grievance, linguistic, 235
Grousset, René, 254
Guanine, 144
Gulliksen, H., 158
Gulls, 214
Gunn, John, 69
Gurney, Edmund, 284
Guttman, A., 157
Gwyne-Bettany, Jeanie, 216

Haas, William, 53
Haeckel, Ernst, 267
Haldane, J. B. S., 128
Hamilton, William, 137
Hampshire, Stuart, 66
Happenings, 89
Harlow, H. F., 280
Harmony, 163
Hartshorne, Charles, 104
Harty, A. L., 268
Hashish, 160
Hathayoga-pradipikā, 52
Hauser, Arnold, 271
Haushalter, P., 191
Hawkins, D. J. B., 246
Hawthorne, Nathaniel, 183
Hearing, 19, 269
Haydn, Joseph, 162
Heart,
  beats, 11, 146, 148
  of man, 167
  of Nature, 167
Heaven, 54, 58, 258
Heidegger, Martin, 8, 95–98
Heisenberg, Werner, 139–
  140, 286
Helios, 205
Hemingway, Ernest, 183
Heraclitus, 248
Herder, Johann von, 252
Hering, Ewald, 196
Hero, 136
Hertz, Heinrich, 136
Higher-order effects, 277–
  280
Hindus, 7, 48, 50–52, 161
Hinton, C. H., 80–81
Historians, 253–255, 288
History,
  as *Dasein,* 98
  determinism of, 179
  and eternity, 101
  and ontogeny, 145
  as perpetual summing,
    253
  refusal of, 50
  reinterpreting, 264
  unfolding of, 57
Hitler, Adolf, 254
Hocking, W. E., 230
Hoedemaker, E. D., 270
Hölderlin, Friedrich, 207
Holography, 198
Homeostasis, 211

Hope, 54, 66, 106, 170
Hopelessness, 228
Hopis, 166–167
Hormonal activity, 200
Hoyle, Fred, 128
Hubble, E. P., 124–125
Hudson, T. J., 151
Human condition, 170
Humanity, 182
Hummingbird, 147
Hun, 264
Huxley, Aldous, 183
Huxley, Julian, 252
Huygens, Christian, 135
Hymns on Epiphany (Sy-
  rus), 49
Hypnosis, 11, 160, 191
Hypocrisies, 46, 282

Iacono, G., 152
Iambus, 157
ibn-Arabi, 263
ibn-Hazm, 8, 65–66
I Ching, 53–54
Id, 19, 274
Ideas, 58–59, 74–75, 171–
  172, 188, 194
Identity, 53, 182, 195
Identity of discernibles,
  principle of, 114–115
Idiots, 150, 188, 192
Ignorance, 59
Illness, 145, 158
Image, 161, 275
Imagery, 13, 192–193
Imagination, 87, 115, 158,
  161–163, 174, 194
Immortability, 230–231
Immortality,
  argument for, 81
  and becoming, 174
  and being, 174
  and causation, 91
  of the cell, 223
  and death, 68
  and eternal change of
    form, 103–104
  feeling of, 183
  idea of, 230
  and imagination, 174
  and irreversibility of Time,
    91–92
  and memory, 91
  of soul, 59

Impotence, postulates of, 286
Impression, authentic, 176
Impressionism, 271
Incompleteness, 89, 91
Indeterminacy, 128
Indians, 7, 50–52
Individuality, 143, 164
Infants, 154
Infinite regress, 81–82
Infinitesimal, 15, 235
Infinity, 174
  mathematics of, 15–16, 235–242
  of mind, 104
  retention of, 239
  temporal implications of, 68, 86–87
  and Zeno's paradox, 15
Influence, 47, 254, 271
Information, 149, 275–276
Inheritance,
  of behavior, 214–215
  of biological defects, 14, 215
  conformal, 88–89
  cultural, 255–256
  of remembrances, 14
  of schizophrenia, 215
  of sense of rhythm, 261
In-itself, 99
Innocent VIII, 227
Insects, 145, 148, 151, 200, 203, 214
Instants. See Moments
Institutions, 284
Intellect, 62, 175
Intelligence, 13, 191–192, 214–215
Intention, 165, 187
Interval, 11, 156–157
Intrinsicalness of organisms, 13, 259, 263
Introverts, 155
Irreversibility, 16, 74, 91–92, 94–95, 242
Irritability, 143
Ismailism, 272

Jaensch, E., 155, 192
James, William, 8, 70–72, 218
Janet, Paul, 154
Janet's Law, 154

Jeans, James, 285
Jerusalem (Blake), 173, 175
Jesus, 7, 56–57, 184
Job, problem of, 290
Jordan, E., 255
Joy, 3
Joyce, James, 12, 178–179
Judgment, 71, 171, 184, 255–256, 264
Jung, Carl, 204, 206–207, 219, 284–285

Kairos, 57, 290
Kammerer, Paul, 284
Kant, Immanuel, 8, 68–70, 82, 85–86
Kappa effect, 156
Katona, George, 197
Kelsen, Hans, 247
Kierkegaard, Sören A., 96
Klee, Paul, 166
Kline, Morris, 246
Knowledge,
  and action, 257
  baffling enlargement of, 288
  carving up, 221–222
  clouded, 59
  as dead inventory, 47
  and education, 48
  and facts, 74
  and Fall of Man, 222
  genuine, 67
  highest level of, 66
  intuitive, 221
  no-, 14, 220–223
  moral, 257
  preconceived, 171
  rational, 221
  through subsuming and resonating, 26–27
  and temporal concepts, 168
Koestler, Arthur, 273
Koran, 65
Korsakow syndrome, 191
Korzybski, Alfred, 250
Kris, Ernst, 272
Krishnamurti, Jiddu, 264
Kwei, 265

Laborer, 21
Lafleur, L. J., 81
Laing, R. D., 266

Lamarck, Jean de, 213
Langer, Susanne, 161
Language, 88, 166–168,
    234–235, 252
Lantz, Herman, 280
Lao Tzu, 48, 256–257, 266
Laplace, Pierre, 286
Lasers, 130–131
Lashley, Karl, 198
Last Judgment, 7, 66
Law, 104, 248–249
Lazerowitz, Morris, 88, 234
Learning, 152, 171, 197,
    199, 252
Least Action, Principle of, 137
Least Time, Principle of, 137
Lee, Dorothy, 167
Leeuw, G. van der, 57
Leibnitz, Gottfried Wilhelm,
    9, 114–116, 208, 235
Leisure, 180, 290–291
Lemaître, Georges, 10,
    125–126
Leukippos, 248
Levi, Albert, 169
Lewin, Kurt, 155, 187
Lewis, Wyndham, 12, 179–
    180
Li, 257
Libido, 13, 166, 206, 220
Liebman, Joshua, 282
Life, 10–15, 142–232
  beginning of, 13, 15, 18,
    210–211
  and ch'i, 18, 256–258
  and the clock, 181
  and conative élan, 93
  and continuum, 15
  differentiation in, 61–62
  ending of, 15
  as Grand Illusion, 19
  as image of eternal Time, 55
  individual, 208–209
  ineffability of, 256
  as Light's awakening, 6
  and predetermined goal, 13
  psychical, 93
  scheme of, 17
  and temporal perception,
    183–184
  and temporal sequences,
    260
  unity of, with Time and
    Light, 4

Life of Sulla (Plutarch), 253
Light,
  beginning of, 15
  biological effects of, 13,
    149, 199–204
  and ch'i, 16–18, 262–263
  components of, 16–18
  and continuum, 15
  corpuscular theory of, 10,
    132–134, 136–141
  as dimension of eternal
    Time, 7, 54–56
  duplexity of, 265–266
  ending of, 15
  and experience, 264
  living, 170
  and mass, 265
  optical paths of, 137
  and origin of Life, 18
  primordial, 54
  properties of, 10, 116–118,
    129–140
  and psyche, 13, 204–207
  as root for Time, 18
  symbolisms of, 13, 204–
    207
  and temporal perception,
    11, 156
  theoretical reconciliation,
    136–141
  and Time, 264–265
  velocity of, 116–118, 126,
    129, 132, 140, 265
  unity of, with Time and
    Life, 4
  wave theory of, 134–136
L'Imaginaire (Sartre), 162
Linnaeus, Carl, 267
Literature and Time, 169–
    184
Liturgy, 7, 56
Living, 20–23, 277–293
Logic, 254
Lombroso, Caesare, 280
Loneliness, 14
Longevity, 14–15, 222–224,
    227
Longfellow, Henry Wads-
    worth, 207
Lorentz, Hendrik Antoon,
    9–10, 116–118, 247
Lorentz transformation,
    117–118
Lorenz, Konrad, 282

Louis XIV, 162
Lowell, A. C. B., 128
Love, 170, 172, 183, 231
Lu Chi, 250
Lucifer, 19

McConnell, J. V., 268
McCrea, W. H., 126, 128
McGilvary, E. B., 95
MacLeod, R. B., 157
MacMurray, John, 104
Magnetic field, 131, 135,
  140
Mainx, F., 208
Maisels, Misha, 104–105,
  256
Malaria, 191
Mammals, 15, 145, 223
Man,
  alienation of, 169
  ambitious, 22
  as amplifier, 41
  attitude of, toward Time,
    12, 168–169
  as ch'i-processor, 17
  as creator of virtual pres-
    ences, 6, 42
  defying God, 19
  development of, 281
  dignity of, 169
  evolution of, 213
  insatiability of, for change,
    41
  insufficiency of, 173
  inventiveness of, 42
  Neanderthal, 166
  and nothingness, 98
  Paleolithic, 166
  possessed, 46
  regimentation of, 283
  sense of time in, 11, 151–
    161
  simplification of, 283
  as Time-binder, 25
  uniqueness of, 6, 11, 41
  voltage patterns in, 145
  yearning of, for longer
    life, 15
Management, 45–46, 278
Mandelstam, Osip, 264
Manic-depressive attacks,
  150
Manichees, 290
Mann, Thomas, 183

Mannerism, 271
Marcel, Gabriel, 75
Marihuana, 160
Marx, Karl, 252
Mass, 121, 265
Massignon, Louis, 65
Mass media, 275–276, 283
Materiality, 89
Mathematics, 9, 107, 112,
  126–128, 286–287
Mating, 5, 14, 37, 41
Matter, 121
Maturity, 18
Maupertuis, Pierre de, 137
Maury, L. F. A., 186
Maxwell, James Clerk, 135
Mazdaism. See Persians
Mead, George, 105
Meaning, 98
Meaningfulness, 188
Means and ends, 20, 277
Mechanism, 208
Medvedev, Zh. A., 225
Meistersinger (Wagner),
  281
Melody, 159
Memory,
  and action, 195
  and age, 13, 190
  of animals, 187–188
  in bees, 151
  and brain amputation, 198
  and brain centers, 189
  and causation, 91
  common factors of, 198–
    199
  components of, 195
  as computer analogy, 189–
    190
  and consciousness, 13
  and death, 193
  development of, 188
  and diseases, 13, 191
  and drugs, 13
  and emotions, 13, 190–
    191
  as entwined with person-
    ality, 13
  as entwined with Time, 13
  and fear of failure, 190
  as God-given faculty, 13,
    194
  holographic theory of, 198
  and idea, 194

Memory (continued)
and identity, 195
and imagery, 13, 192–193
and imagination, 194
and imbeciles, 188, 192
and immortality, 91
and incompleteness, 91
and injuries, 13, 191
intellectual, 188
and intelligence, 13, 191–192
and intuition of duration, 71
kinds of, 187–188
as levels of the Conscious, 13, 193
and life-giving principles, 172
and logic, 272
and meaningfulness, 188
and mental illness, 190
in music, 161
as neural traces, 13, 194, 196–197
and poisons, 191
and present moment, 79
of primitive people, 193
and repetition, 199
and repression, 195
and resemblance, 198
retention of, 190–191, 198
and ribonucleic acid, 268–269
sensory, 188
and soul, 193
and Time, 12–13, 175–177
and unity of self, 94
Menōk, 55–56
Menosie, 271
Mental illness, 18, 160, 191, 195–196
Mescal, 160
Mesopotamians, 169
Metabolism, 11, 20, 143, 146–147, 224, 281
Metamorphosis, 5, 11, 39–40, 144
Metaphor, 163
Metre, 163
Meumann, E., 157
M-fields, 218
Michelangelo Buonarroti, 272
Michelson, A. A., 116–117

Microfilaria worms, 11, 147
Microorganisms, 143–144, 200
Mill, James, 13, 194–195
Milne, E. A., 10, 126–128
Milner, Marion, 272
Mind, 184–185
and ch'i, 19, 258, 269–270
evolution of, 14, 214–215
as experienced continuum, 78
function of, 176
instability of, 171
Spinoza's concept of, 66–67
and Time, 264
and virtual presences, 44
Mind-fasting, 258
Mind-matter problem, 13, 209
Minkowski, E., 160
Minkowski, Hermann, 76, 119
Mithras, 205
Modeling, scientific, 22
Mollusks, 204, 211
Moment, 152–153, 175
and art, 180
and celestial archetype, 56
and continuity, 172
and death, 183
discontinuous, 177
of enlightenment, 7, 52
expanding the, 84
and feeling, 172
fragmented, 96
and the infinitesimal, 235
and kairos, 290
of Kierkegaard, 96
musical, 161
and mutual externality, 93, 95
and Nature, 263
in painting, 166
passage of, 172
perfect, 66
of personality, 104–105
present, 171–172, 178
seizing the, 52, 172
in Time, 180–181
in Time galaxy, 8, 65–66
vectored, 290
witnesses of the, 66
and Zeno's paradox, 233

Monads, 116
Mona Lisa, 164
Monism, 209
Monkeys, 11, 150–151,
 280
Montaigne, Michel de, 12,
 170–171
Moore, George E., 8, 84–88
Moore, T. V., 188
Morality, 256–257, 281
More, Henry, 113
Morley, E. W., 116–117
Morris, C. R., 115
Mortality curve, 227
Motion, 58, 60–61, 121,
 233–234
Motivation, 155
Moulyn, A. C., 152
Mouse, 224
Mover, Prime, 61, 170
Mozart, Wolfgang Ama-
 deus, 162
Multidisciplinary approach,
 26
Mumford, Lewis, 281
Muscle cells, 226
Music,
 acid rock, 162
 blues, 162
 and ch'i, 261
 duration in, 161
 as embodiment of Time,
  161
 evocation by, 163
 existence of, 162
 flow of, 162
 as idea through Time, 75
 jazz, 162
 madrigal, 162
 plenitude of, 177
 from silence, 250
 tempo in, 157–158
 Time of, 103
 Time-digesting by, 264
Musical composition, 161
Musical conductors, 157–
 158
Musical performance, 157
Musing, 3–4, 6, 20, 25–28
Mutation, 14, 199–200,
 212–213, 226
Mysteries, 19
Mysticism, 68, 272
Myth, 19, 21, 204

Nagel, Ernest, 286
Nations, 44
Nativity, 7
Nature, 210
 American attitude toward,
  159
 and the artist, 290–291
 and ch'i, 258
 downgrading, 19
 encompassed yet focused,
  28
 generative force of, 205
 interaction with, 182
 links to, 21
 order of, 66
 original, 48
 Time within, 263
 uniformity of, 246
 union with, 67
 virtual, 275
Neighbor, 21
Neumann, Erich, 273
Neuroses, 6, 46–48, 159,
 230, 280
Neurotics, 185, 196
Newman, Francis, 252
Newman, James, 286
News, 44, 275–276
Newton, Isaac, 9, 112–114,
 132, 235
New Year, 49
Nichols, Herbert, 72
Nicolson, Harold, 277
Nietzsche, Friedrich, 264
Night VII (Blake), 175
Nirvana, 249–250
Nivens, Allan, 288
Nodon, Albert, 145
No Exit (Sartre), 101
No-knowledge, 14, 220–
 223
Norman, D. A., 188
Northrop, F. S. C., 52–53
Not-knowing, realm of, 3
Noon, William, 179
Nothingness, 98, 100, 173,
 249–250
Now, 59–60, 73, 83–84, 88,
 105
 See also Present
Nucleic acid, 144
Nucleotides, 144
Numbers, 58, 61–62, 107,
 241

Numinosum, 273
Nunberg, Herman, 185

Oak, 4
  command and coordina-
    tion in, 5
  consciousness of, 174
  life cycle of, 29–32
Observers, equivalence of,
  120–121, 125, 127
Occam's razor, 287, 289
Occasions, 88–92, 171
Odin, 50
Ōhrmazd, 7, 56
Oikonomia, 57
One, The, 22, 62–63, 232
Oneness, 210
Ontogeny, 145
Ontological principle, 88–
  89
Opium, 160
Optical activity, 10
Optics, 140
Organism, 10–11, 17–18,
  142–146, 266
Origin. See Beginning
Osiris, 50
Ouspensky, P. D., 8, 82–85
Oysters, 11, 148

Painting, 166, 258, 271
Parabiological speculations,
  13, 207–209
Parental dominance, 155
Pascal, Blaise, 12, 171–173
Passion, 220
Past, 152
  in animal life, 187
  apprehension of, 79
  as burden on present, 183
  and ch'i, 270
  concept of, and culture,
    168–169
  as cosmological Time, 102
  as datum of experience,
    79
  discovering the, 264
  echo of, in music, 161
  as ecstasy of Time, 8
  embodiment of, 175–176
  without future, 104
  and the intellect, 175
  as memory, 65

and mental illness, 160,
  196, 270
as organized mass, 197
reality of, 66
repressing the, 270
resemblance of, 175
responsiveness to, 145–
  146
as sign, 103
and wish-fulfilling, 158
Patterns, 261
Patriotism, 5
Pauli, Wolfgang, 140
Pause, 249
Payday, 169
Peace, 178
Pendulum, 108
Penfield, W., 189
People,
  degeneration of, 254
  See also Primitive people
Perception,
  confused, 116
  and contemplation, 179
  and leisure, 179
  in the present, 73
  temporal, factors affecting,
    11, 154–160, 183–184
  of Time, 151–153
Periodicity. See Rhythm
Periods of history, 253–
  255
Periwinkles, 11, 147
Persians, 7, 54–56
Personality,
  ceaseless change in, 94–
    95
  and ch'i, 18, 268
  and environment, 280–281
  integrated, 21, 285
  and memory, 13
  of modern man, 283
  regions of, 187
  and Time, 11, 13, 104–
    105, 155
Perspective, 77–78, 168,
  288
Petrie, W. M. F., 253
Phaedo (Plato), 59
Phanes, 49
Phase-locking, 218
Philo Judaeus, 205
Photochemical reactions,
  131

Photoelectric effect, 134, 140
Photon, 3, 13, 134, 138, 140–141, 265–266
Photoperiodism, 202–203
Photoreactivation, 200
Photoreceptors, 203–204
Photosensitivity, 203–204
Photosynthesis, 4, 19, 30–31, 146, 201–202, 262–263
Phototropism, 201–202
Phylogenetic position, 150, 214, 223, 267–268
Phylogeny, 145
Physics, 9, 152, 259–260
Picasso, Pablo, 281
Pietsch, Paul, 198
Pinter, Harold, 249
Planarians, 268
Planck, Max, 133–134
Planck's constant, 109, 133–134, 286
Planck's Law, 133, 140
Planning, 277
Plants, 3, 142, 144–146, 199–204, 211, 251, 262
Plasmodium, 33–34
Plato, 7, 57–59
Pleasure, 164, 199
Plessner, H., 229
Plotinus, 8, 61–63
Plutarch, 253
P'o, 264
Podmore, F., 160
Poet, 173, 288
Poetry, 163, 261
Point-instants, 77, 81
Pope, Alexander, 281
Population cycles, 11, 148
Portman, Adolf, 105–106
Positron, 140
Poussin, Nicolas, 165
Powys, J. C., 210
Pradines, M., 264
Prānāyāma, 52
Precognition, 14, 80–81, 216–217, 219
Prehensions, 89–91
Presence, virtual,
 and Adam, 19
 and advertising, 44
 and amusements, 44
and anxiety, 21
and arts, 44
and books, 44
characteristics of, 42–43
and charisma, 45
as ch'i forms, 17
and churches, 44
and civilization, 20, 43, 48
conflict of, with real presence, 19–20, 48
and courage, 19
and culture, 43
definition of, 6
destruction of, 43, 47
and doubt, 20
and economy, 44
and elections, 44
and electronic devices, 44
and excitement, 19
and the executive, 45–46
exploitation of, 44–46
and evolution, 19, 252
and God, 19, 275
and innovation, 19
and language, 252
and learning, 252
longevity of, 252
and Lucifer, 19
and mysteries, 19
and myths, 19
and nations, 44
of neighbors, 21
and neuroses, 6, 46–47
and newspapers, 44
power of, 20, 275–276
proclivity toward, 21
production of, 43–45
and psychotherapy, 47–48
and reputation, 44
and schools, 44
and society, 46
and soul, 19
and speech, 252
substrate for, 43
and success, 45
and superego, 19
and Superman, 19
and thrills, 19
and values, 20
and wars, 44
and writing, 44

Present,
  as Agent, 104
  in animal life, 187–188
  and Art, 180
  consciousness of, 194–195
  creativity of, 91
  an ecstasy of Time, 8
  elasticity of, 71–72
  escape from, 175
  existence in, 183
  and fact, 104
  fleeting, 180
  impure, 180
  interaction with future by,
    101
  interaction with past by,
    101
  and memory, 79
  and mind, 76
  reality of, 64–66
  retroactive power of, 271
  as revelation of lack, 101
  seizing the, 170–171, 173
  specious, 71, 152
  turning into past, 73
  and the Vortex, 180
  See also Now
President, 21
Price cycles, 150
Primitive people,
  attitude of, toward death,
    228
  and causality, 247
  concept of Time among,
    6, 49–50
  thinking and doing by,
    196
  Time-reckoning by, 109–
    110
Prison life, 158
Privacy, 283
Process, 88
Production cycles, 150
Professions, 11, 158
Progress, 172
Protagoras, 248
Proteins, 15, 29–30, 142,
  226
Protoplasm, 10, 13, 142–
  143, 199
Protozoa, 145, 203
Proust, Marcel, 12, 175–
  177, 179, 183
Psyche, 13, 187, 204–207

Psychopathology, 158
Psychotherapy, 47–48, 270
Psylocybin, 160
Public policy, 277
Public relations, 275
Purgatorio (Dante), 170
Purgatory, 170
Purpose, 146, 155
Pythagoras, 7, 59
Pythagorean theorem, 119

Qualities, 80, 167
Quantum, 133–134
Quantum mechanics, 109,
  140
Quantum theory, 128, 133–
  134, 137–138, 265
Quinine, 259
Quispel, Gilles, 57

Ra, 49, 205
Radhakrishnan, Sarvepalli,
  51
Radiation, 133, 140
Radioactivity, 10, 145, 285
Raman Effect, 140
Rats, 150–151, 224, 269
Rayleigh-Jeans Law, 133
Read, Herbert, 285
Real estate cycles, 150
Reality,
  and appearance, 70, 73
  and experience, 70
  looking at, 282
  nature of, 115
  perception of, 287
  and Time, 53–54, 67, 75,
    87, 115
Reason, 172
Reasonableness, 22
Redemption, 222
Refractive index, 130
Reichenbach, Hans, 247
Reid, Thomas, 13, 194
Relationships, 115, 164
Relativity,
  in Time measurement,
    106–107
  Special Theory of, 119–
    120, 243, 247, 265
  General Theory of, 120–
    122
Religion, 282

Remembrances, transmission of, 14
Repetition, 276
Reptiles, 15, 145, 200, 211, 223
Repression, 195, 282
Reproduction, 5, 11, 37–38, 143–144
Reputation, 44
Resemblances, 163–164, 198
Resonating, 25–28
Respiration, 31–32, 146
Responsibility, 20, 96
Resultants, 289
Retribution, 247–249
Revolt of the flesh, 183
Rhine, J. B., 218
Rhythm,
  and aesthetics, 164
  of alacrity, 164
  appreciation of, and brain disease, 159
  archetype of, 164
  in art, 164
  in bird migration, 148
  in civilization, 255
  cloying, 163
  of collective life, 166
  cryptogrammatic stage of, 165
  and duration, 93–94
  in game populations, 148
  in human activities, 149–150
  in metabolism, 146–149
  mimetic stage of, 164
  in organisms, 11, 33, 146–150
  in painting, 12, 164–166
  in parasite activity, 147
  pictorial, 164
  in plant growth, 146
  in poetry, 163
  and recurrence, 164
  in sculpture, 12, 165
  in shore animals, 147–148
  in slime mold, 33
  symbolic stage of, 165
  and tension, 164
Ribonucleic acid, 268–269
Richards, I. A., 163
Richet, Charles, 217
Richter, C. P., 228

Riddle, Oscar, 228
Rieff, Philip, 195
Rig-Veda, 206
Ring of the Nibelungs (Wagner), 162
Rituals, 49
Roff, M. F., 157
Róheim, Géza, 169, 185
Rotifers, 223–224
Royce, Josiah, 8, 74–76
Rueckle, 191
Russell, Bertrand, 234–235, 246, 272
Russell, E. S., 145

Sabbath, 56
Sabianus, 110
Saccharin, 258–259
Sachs, R. G., 243
Saint, 21, 181
St. Matthew Passion (Bach), 162–163
Sakti, 51
Sales cycles, 150
Saltmarsh, H. F., 216
Salvation, 57
Sartre, Jean-Paul, 8–9, 98–101, 162, 274
Satisfaction, 155, 163
Sauvage, Micheline, 165
Schedules, 169
Schilder, P., 160, 198
Schizophrenia, 159–160, 215–216, 266–267, 270, 281
Schlegel, R., 123
Scholarship, 287
Scholastic, 170
Schools, 44
Schopenhauer, Arthur, 284
Schrödinger, Erwin, 138–139
Science and rational Time, 172
Scriven, M., 123
Sculpture, 12, 165
Sea urchin, 143, 204
Self,
  -body split, 266–267
  continuance of, 231
  departing, 170
  and diversity of faces, 171
  essential, 177

Self (continued)
evolving, 171
and memory, 94
psychic, 164
regaining the, 175
-replication, 144
sentient, 195
that truly is, 22
uniqueness of, 283
virtual, 21, 46
Selincourt, Basil de, 161
Sensations, 74, 179–180, 253
Senses, 11, 59, 152–154
Sequences, 237
Serenity, 18, 22, 291
Series, 237, 263
Sets, 238–241
Seventh Symphony (Beethoven), 162
Sex, 11, 154, 224
Shackleton, Basil, 217–218
Shakti, 14, 220
Sharing, 4, 28
Sheldon, William, 106
Shen, 265
Shepherds in Arcadia (Poussin), 165
Shiva, 220
Shock, N. W., 227
Sight, 19, 269
Silence, 161, 249–250
Simultaneity, 68–69
and causality, 247, 284
Hopi concept of, 166
and painting, 166
primitive concept of, 168
in Special Relativity, 119–120
verification of, 120
Sinceness, 152, 156
Singularity, 74
Siu Kau Shee, 291
Siu Yan, 291
Skin, 148
Sleep, 12, 160
Slime mold, 5, 32–34
Smuts, J. C., 95
Snails, 11, 150
Snell's Law, 130
Soal, S. G., 218
Social class, 155
Solitude, 175
Somnambulism, 71

Soul,
and the animus, 264
as counter of Time, 61
creation of, 19
fantasies by, 193
and kwei, 265
mummifying the, 21
rebeginnings of the, 179
remembering by, 193
thinking by, 193
and Time, 61–63
Sound, 156–157, 161, 261
Souriau, Étienne, 165
Space,
as construct, 126
and brain disease, 158–159
choice of, 127
coordinates of, 116–120
divisions of, 94
and earlier-and-later, 77
empty, 115
and events, 115–116
as fixed frame, 9, 112
and imagination, 115
and monads, 116
as noncontinuous externality, 95
and perception, 116
physical, 78
psychological, 78
and temporal perception, 11, 156
and things, 115–116, 122
with variable radius, 125
Space-time,
as construct, 126
as coordinates, 76, 119
creativity of, 80
curvature of, 122
interval of, 120
as system of motions, 76–80
Species, 5, 18, 143, 255, 267–268
Speech, 97, 166, 252
Spengler, Oswald, 254
Sperm, 144
Spinoza, Benedict, 8, 66–68
Spores, 32–34
Spontaneity, 172
Stark Effect, 131
Stekel, Wilhelm, 284
Stevens, Wallace, 163

Stimulus in music, 161
Stoic, 170
Stonehenge, 110–111
Strangeness, 165
Stravinsky, Igor, 264
Subsidy of research, 277–278
Subsuming, 25–28
Succession,
 without externality, 93
 mental, 194
 modes of, 103
 primitive concept of, 168
 and sense impressions, 152
 in Time, 69, 74, 76–77, 92
Sufficient reason, principle of, 114–115
Sugars, 29–30, 259–260, 262
Sumerians, 111
Sun, 13, 49, 107, 129, 205
Sunrise, 49
Superego, 19, 166, 275
Superman, 19
Supersession, 89–91
Suppression, 21
Surprisals, 163
Survival, 4, 32, 39, 143
Susumnā, 52
Suzuki, D. T., 220, 258
Swedenborg, Emmanuel, 13, 193
Swordsmanship, 258
Symbols, 164, 169, 251
Symonds, P. M., 158
Synchronicity, 284–285
Syrus, Ephraem, 49
Sze, Mai-Mai, 258

Taboo, 49
Tacitus, 252
Tagyu Tajima no kami Munemori, 258
T'ai I Chin Hua, 264
Taking into oneself, 171
Tao, 53, 221, 258
Taste, 155
Teacher, admonition to, 171
Technology, 169
Telepathy, 14, 217
Temperature, 11, 155–156
Tempo, 261

Tempodynamic forces, 262
Temporality, 9, 89, 97–98, 100–101, 165
Temporal relations, 11, 145–146
Ten Bulls, The, 220
Tenses, 166, 168
Tension, 22, 164
Terns, 11, 148, 261
Thales, 248
Thermodynamics, 209, 242, 262
Thinking, 158, 253, 264
 and ch'i, 261
 and crying, 25
 in dragonfly, 39
 in earthworm, 5, 36–37
 in sea urchin, 204
 and Time, 264
Thorpe, W. J., 214
Thrills, 19
Thucydides, 252
Thymine, 144
Thyroxine, 160
Tibetans, 161
Tillich, Paul, 290
Timbre, 269
Time, 6–10, 49–128
 abolishment of, 183
 absolute, 9, 112–115, 123, 246
 and the Absolute, 8, 74–76
 abstract, 103
 as action of God, 57
 Alexander's concept of, 8, 76–80
 allegory on, 174–175
 and anguish, 8, 100–101
 anisotropy of, 243
 as anxiety of death, 9
 as appearance, 8, 72–74
 Aristotle's concept of, 7, 59–61
 attributes of, 54
 Augustine's concept of, 8, 63–66
 as background, 153
 Barrow's concept of, 113
 and becoming, 51, 57–58
 and before-and-after, 60, 72
 beginning in, 85
 beginning of, 15, 55, 266
 beyond, 220–221

Time (continued)
broadness in, 159
and change, 182
Bergson's concept of, 8,
92–95
in Blake's writings, 12,
173–175
Bradley's concept of, 8,
72–74
and *brahmaloka,* 51
and Care, 96
and causality, 69
and the Changeless, 12,
170
Chinese concept of, 7,
52–54
Christian concept of, 7,
56–57
and chronology, 55, 181
claustrophobia in, 159
as cognition, 9, 103
and common sense, 8, 84–
88
and consciousness, 12, 74,
82, 184
as continuum, 15, 77, 93,
95
coordinates of, 116–120
and craving, 183
and Creation, 4, 63–64,
113
and creativity, 8, 80, 88,
94–95
and culture, 12, 92, 166–
169
cyclical, 6, 49–50, 181
in Dante's writings, 12,
169–170
and death, 12, 183, 228–
229
derivation of, 62
dilatation of, 10, 118
dimensions of, 84
direction of, 102, 242,
244
domination by, 12, 169,
177
and doom, 182
Dunne's concept of, 8,
80–82
dynamic, 127
earthbound, 173
economy of, 169
ecstasies of, 8, 96

as elasticity of present, 8,
70–72
in Eliot's writings, 12,
180–181
embodiment of, 55
and emotions, 74
ending of, 15, 51
and environment, 264
escape from, 51–52
eternal, 173
and eternal origin, 55
and events, 53, 115–116
and evil, 106, 183
and existence, 77, 85–86,
95
existentialist concept of,
8, 95–101
experienced, 53, 152, 161
of fallen soul, 173
and family, 53
in Faulkner's writings,
12, 181–182
features of, 74–75
as figure, 153
final, 56–57
as fire of Life, 266
as fixed frame, 9, 112
flow of, 113, 176
as form of being, 264
as galaxy of instants, 8,
65–66
Galileo's concept of, 112
in geometry, 112
and goals, 75
and God, 8
and good, 106
of grace, 12, 171–173
and gravity, 121
Greek concept of, 7, 57–
61
harmony with, 12, 53–54
as heard, 12, 161–164
and heaven, 54, 58
as heavenly Person, 54–56
as heavenly weapon, 56
Heidegger's concept of, 8,
95–98
and higher space, 8, 82–
85
and history, 50, 78
homogeneous, 115
and hope, 54, 106
Hopi classification of,
167

Time (continued)
  human, 182
  ibn-Hazm's concept of, 8,
    65–66
  in the I Ching, 53–54
  and ideas, 74–75
  and identity, 53, 105
  illusions of, 183
  and imagination, 12, 115,
    174–175
  implied, 165
  importance of, 170
  and incompleteness, 89,
    91
  independence of, 57, 61
  Indian concept of, 7, 50–
    52
  and infantile disappoint-
    ments, 169
  and infinite regress, 81–82
  inner cohesion of, 54
  intersection of, 12, 180–
    181
  interval of, 152–153, 246
  as intuition, 8, 68–70
  as invalid, 123
  invariance of, 11, 243–244
  as invention, 153
  and irrelevancies, 182
  irreversibility of, 7, 57, 74,
    242–243
  James' concept of, 8, 70–
    72
  in Joyce's writings, 12,
    178–179
  and kairos, 57
  Kant's concept of, 8, 68–
    70, 85–86
  kinematic, 127–128
  and knowledge, 168
  lapse of, 246
  Leibnitz's concept of, 9,
    114–116
  in Lewis' writings, 12,
    179–180
  and libido, 166
  and Life, 8, 61–63, 93
  and Light, 7, 54–56, 264
  linear, 7, 56–57, 181–182,
    229
  linking of, 184
  and literature, 169–184
  living, 76–78, 92–93, 102,
    104–105, 169
  as local property, 123
  and love, 183
  and materiality, 88
  mathematics of, 10, 127–
    128
  and matter, 84
  measurement of, 9, 92,
    106–113, 119–120
  and memory, 12–13, 102,
    175–177
  Mesopotamian attitude
    toward, 169
  metabolism of, 261–264
  and metamorphosis, 55
  and mind, 12, 177–178,
    264
  and monads, 116
  in Montaigne's writings,
    12, 169–170
  Moore's concept of, 8,
    84–88
  and motion, 7, 57–61, 67,
    103, 114, 170
  and motivation, 155
  as moving field, 8, 80–82
  and music, 75, 103
  mutability of, 10
  natural, 182
  and Nature, 49
  and neurotics, 159
  Newton's concept of, 112–
    114
  and nows, 59, 73
  and number, 61
  and occasions, 8, 88–92
  as operational criterion,
    9, 102
  order of, 242, 245–247
  as organic unity, 100
  Ouspensky's concept of,
    8, 82–85
  overcoming, 182
  in painting, 165–166
  in Pascal's writings, 12,
    171–173
  as passage, 12, 170
  as patterned quality, 9,
    105
  perceived, 153
  and perception, 116,
    152
  Persian concept of, 7,
    54–56
  and personality, 13

Time (continued)
and phenomena, 68
physical, 76–78, 92–93, 102, 104–105
Plato's concept of, 7, 57–59
Plotinus' concept of, 8, 61–63
poetic, 173
as pool, 7, 52
and precognition, 80–81
and prehension, 89–91
and Prime Mover, 61
and the primeval, 12, 182
primitive peoples' concept of, 6, 49–50
primordial, 50, 229
and prison life, 158
production of, 58, 174
proper, 27
in Proust's writings, 12, 175–177
psychological, 78, 181–182
psychological aspects of, 70–71
Pythagoras' concept of, 7, 59
as purity of sensibility, 9
as purveyor of value, 9, 106
rational, 171–172
as raw material, 12, 161, 260–263
as relational, 9, 114–118
and rendering present, 97
represented, 165
as resource, 169
root of, 266
Royce's concept of, 8, 74–76
and Salvation, 57
Sartre's concept of, 8–9, 98–101
and schizophrenia, 160
as seen, 12, 164
and sensations, 74
sense of, 11, 72, 150–161
as shining present, 9, 104–105
simultaneity of, 68–69
and soul, 12, 61, 179
source of, 89

as specious present, 8, 70–72
as Sphere, 7, 59
Spinoza's concept of, 8, 66–68
as substance, 8, 61–63, 76–80, 263
succession in, 68–69, 74, 76–77
and superego, 166
and supersession, 89–91
and susumnā, 52
symbol of, 160
and Tao, 53
and taste, 155
and technology, 169
and tenses, 166
and things, 9, 113–116, 122
and thought, 264
as trait of Life, 106
transcending, 51, 53, 177
trinity of, 173
as ultimate, 123
and unconscious, 12, 184–186
union with cosmic, 7, 51–52
unit of, 109
unity of, 62
as unity of consciousness, 9, 102
unity with Light and Life, 4
universal, 60–61
variation in, 74
virtual, 43, 161
Whitehead's concept of, 8, 88–92
and will, 174–175
in Woolf's writings, 12, 177–178
and yin-yang, 54
and yoga, 158
and youthful folly, 53
and Zeno's paradox, 86
and Zervān, 56
See also Duration; Eternity; Existence; Moments; Perception, temporal; Reality, and Time
Time-binding, 250–256
Timeliness, 169, 175, 185, 245–246

Time-Light-Life Continuum, 16–20, 251–276
Time-related X, 16, 261, 270
Time-scale, 127–128
Timetable, 169
Tinbergen, N., 215
Tobacco, 191
Toksvig, Signe, 193
Tomorrow, 182–183
Tosca (Verdi), 42
Touch, 269
Toynbee, Arnold, 255
Tradition, 196
Transitoriness, 175
Tree rings, 11, 29–30, 146
Trees, 4, 15, 142
Trobrianders, 167–168
Trochee, 157
Tryon, R. C., 215
Tsi I, 265
Tuning fork, 261
Turkeys, 146
Twain, Mark, 216–217

Ultraviolet catastrophe, 133–134
Ulysses (Joyce), 179
Uncertainties, 283–287
Uncertainty Principle, 286
Unconscious, 12, 176, 184–186, 273
United States Government, 277
Universe, 51–52, 128
age of, 122–124
cosmic force in, 10, 124
creation of, 49, 63–64, 113, 169
cyclic expansion and contraction of, 10, 125
empty, 124
evolutionary history of, 126
expansion of, 10, 124–126
filled, 124
models of, 124–126
origin of, 10, 122–124, 128–129
as space with constant curvature, 10, 124
Universities, American, 277–279
Usizima, Y., 155

Vacuum, 115
Valéry, Paul, 184
Values, 9, 20, 101
van Woerkom, W., 159
Vectors, 289
Verdi, Giuseppe, 42
Verworn, Max, 197
Vice, 59, 281
Vico, Giovanni, 252, 254
Vietnam War, 288
Vigny, Alfred de, 184
Vitality, 145
Virtual presence. See Presence, virtual
Vitalism, 208, 213
Voodoo, 228
Voronoff, S., 227

Wagner, Richard, 162, 281
Wahl, C. W., 230
Wang Shou-jen, 257
Wars, 44
Waves, 135–136, 138–140
Wave equation, 139
Wave mechanics, 138–141
Wave packets, 138–139
Weierstrass, Karl, 235
Well-being, 19, 273–275
Wells, W. R., 161
Werner, Heinz, 192
West, D. J., 218
Weyl, Hermann, 106, 272
Whitehead, Alfred North, 8, 88–92
Whitrow, G. J., 123, 244
Whittaker, R. H., 267
Whole, the, 27–28, 75, 142
Whorf, Benjamin, 167
Wiener, Norbert, 189
Wilhelm, Helmut, 53–54
Wilhelm, Richard, 285
Will, 103, 174–175, 255
Wisdom, 170, 219
Wish-fulfilling, 158
Woodrow, H., 151, 157
Woolf, Virginia, 12, 177–178
Work performance, 149–150
Workers, 169
Writers, 288
Writing, 44
Words, 87–88

X rays, 141

Yin-yang,
  and hope, 54
  model, 289–290
  and propitiousness, 20,
    290
  and understanding, 27
Yoga, 51–52, 158, 220
Youth nostrums, 227–228
Yuga, 50–51

Zeeman Effect, 131, 140
Zeitgeist, 273
Zen, 14, 220–221
Zeno's paradox, 15, 86,
    233–235, 237
Zero, 16, 289
Zervanism. *See* Persians
Zeus, 50
Zimmer, Heinrich, 51
Zoroastrian. *See* Persians